Willful Defiance

Willful Defiance

*The Movement to Dismantle the
School-to-Prison Pipeline*

MARK R. WARREN

OXFORD
UNIVERSITY PRESS

OXFORD
UNIVERSITY PRESS

Oxford University Press is a department of the University of Oxford. It furthers
the University's objective of excellence in research, scholarship, and education
by publishing worldwide. Oxford is a registered trade mark of Oxford University
Press in the UK and certain other countries.

Published in the United States of America by Oxford University Press
198 Madison Avenue, New York, NY 10016, United States of America.

CIP data is on file at the Library of Congress
ISBN 978-0-19-761151-7 (pbk.)
ISBN 978-0-19-761150-0 (hbk.)

DOI: 10.1093/oso/9780197611500.001.0001

1 3 5 7 9 8 6 4 2

Paperback printed by LSC Communications, United States of America
Hardback printed by Bridgeport National Bindery, Inc., United States of America

Cover graphic: The graphic of the backpack with a raised fist was designed by
19 the Agency and commissioned and adopted by the Dignity in Schools
Campaign for its Week of Action against School Pushout.

Cover photograph: The background photograph was taken by the Labor Community
Strategy Center at it march and rally at the Los Angeles Board of Education in 2016 demanding
an end to the federal program that provided military-grade weapons to LA's school police

With deep respect to all the young people and parents who willfully defy a system designed to discipline and punish them and who organize for education and liberation

Contents

Willful Defiance

Disrupting school activities or otherwise willfully defying the authority of
supervisors, teachers, administrators, school officials, or other school per-
sonnel engaged in the performance of their duties.
—California Education Code, Section 48900

Every year, public schools suspend hundreds of thousands of students,
mostly Black and Brown students and those with disabilities, for behavior
that is sometimes called "willful defiance." Starting in the 1990s, state after
state passed laws granting local school districts the authority to punish
students for this kind of reason. Mississippi schools suspend students for
"disruptive behavior" and Louisiana for "willful disobedience." In South
Carolina, it is called "disturbing school" and for many years was cause not just
for suspension but criminal penalty; so was "acting in an obnoxious manner."
In a widely publicized case in the state, Niya Kenny was charged with criminal "disrupting school" when she used her cell phone to capture a police officer violently dragging another Black girl from her desk and throwing her
to the floor. Meanwhile, South Dakota bans "boisterous" behavior, while
Arkansas prohibits "annoying conduct." Maine makes interrupting a teacher
by speaking loudly a civil offense, punishable by up to a $500 fine.[1]

Suspensions for willful defiance or disruption make up a sizable proportion of all suspensions, and in many school districts students are suspended
for this reason more than any other. For example, in 2012, schools suspended
over a quarter of a million students in California for disruption or defiance,
representing well over half of all suspensions. As a broad and vague category,
willful defiance and disruption relies on a subjective assessment by a teacher
or school official and is particularly subject to racial bias. Schools suspend
students of color for "willful defiance" for a wide range of infractions, including talking back to teachers, refusing to take off a hoodie, or using a cell
phone in class.[2]

Using "willful defiance" as the title of this book flips the script. It signifies defiance of school authority that serves to discipline and punish students and to
push them out of school and into the juvenile and criminal justice systems—the

school-to-prison pipeline. When students and parents stand up to this kind of authority, they are consciously and intentionally challenging this system. As we will see in this book, when students rebel, they are often punished, while parents who stand up for their children are silenced, excluded, and sometimes even arrested. Community organizing groups bring parents and students together to move from individual acts of defiance to a collective movement to build the power to dismantle the school-to-prison pipeline.

Glorya Wornum, a Black girl (now woman) in Boston tells this story that I believe perfectly captures the spirit of the title and of the movement. Wornum was disciplined and suspended for challenging the type of history taught in her school's curriculum.

> I asked a lot of questions in school. For example, our history textbooks came from Texas. "Is this really history?" I would ask. Teachers would tell me, "You're being disruptive; please go take a walk." I would get into fights and arguments and I was suspended about twelve times. Once you're suspended for a fight, then you're suspended for asking questions.
>
> I realized I was fighting the wrong way when I met a nonprofit organization that supports youth organizing. They allowed me to be angry and to feel what I was feeling. I started positively struggling instead of negatively struggling. A lot of things need to be changed, and you're allowed to change it.
>
> Before, everyone told me, "No, don't do that!" or "Be quiet!" or "Put your hand down!" Then I went into an environment where people said, "Raise your hand. Say something. Reach out to somebody. Be a part of something. Do something!"[3]

As a result of the organizing documented in this book, the movement to dismantle the school-to-prison pipeline has begun to roll back exclusionary discipline policies across the country. A coalition of organizing groups and their allies, for example, got the Los Angeles Unified School District (LAUSD) to ban suspensions for willful defiance in 2013. The next year, the state of California banned suspensions for willful defiance for grades K–3 and extended it to grade eight in 2019. As a result of these and other changes, the number of out-of-school suspensions dropped 46% in California from the 2011–2012 to the 2016–2017 school year while Los Angeles suspensions fell dramatically. In the 2007–2008 school year, LAUSD students lost 74,765 days due to out-of-school suspensions. By the 2016–2017 school year, that number had dropped to fewer than 5,600 days.[4]

Despite these gains in ending zero-tolerance approaches to discipline and more recent success in reducing police presence in schools, the school-to-prison pipeline remains deeply entrenched in our public education system. This book reveals the experiences of students and parents of color enmeshed in the school-to-prison pipeline and tells the story of the movement they have built to "willfully defy" and dismantle it.[5]

Introduction

Confronting the School-to-Prison Pipeline: Journeys to Racial Justice Organizing

When Zakiya Sankara-Jabar's three-year-old African American son was suspended from his pre–K program in Dayton, Ohio, she was shocked at first. The preschool kept calling to say Amir was in trouble for biting other students or having difficulty transitioning from one activity to another. In Sankara-Jabar's view, "They made normal three-year-old behavior sound very pathologized and abnormal." The school wanted to have her son evaluated. On the advice of her pediatrician, Sankara-Jabar refused. She worried that Amir would be unfairly labeled and that the label would stick with him throughout his schooling years. Eventually, under pressure from the school administration, she decided to withdraw her son from the school, but he was subsequently suspended and expelled from several other preschools.

Sankara-Jabar had to drop out of college to care for her son. Before she did, however, she used the college's library services to search for articles on the experiences of Black boys in public education. She quickly learned that her son's experiences were not unusual.

> I suddenly realized that I wasn't a bad parent, and my son wasn't abnormal. This was something larger, more societal that was happening to African American parents. That's when I began organizing.

Sankara-Jabar started talking to other Black parents and many shared similar stories.

> I found out from the other parents who had Black boys with the same behavior or personality as my son—kids who are energetic, who know what they want, who have strong personality traits—that they had the same experience. I was coming to the realization that schools are not working for Black children, regardless of whether they are urban, rural, or suburban.

Willful Defiance. Mark R. Warren, Oxford University Press. © Mark R. Warren 2022.
DOI: 10.1093/oso/9780197611500.003.0001

Sankara-Jabar reached out to Vernellia Randall, an African American law professor at the University of Dayton. Together they founded Racial Justice NOW! (RJN) in Randall's living room in the fall of 2011 with a mission to address racially targeted punitive discipline and address the larger crisis in education for Black children. Randall gathered data on school discipline in public schools while Sankara-Jabar organized parents. The fledgling group joined the Dignity in Schools Campaign (DSC), the national coalition of organizing and advocacy groups working to dismantle the school-to-prison pipeline. DSC provided the new group with crucial support and resources— like a model alternative code of student conduct to replace zero-tolerance policies and training opportunities for parents to learn how to advocate for policy change. In a few short years, with assistance from DSC and the powerful voice and leadership of Black parents on the ground, RJN won a moratorium on pre–K suspensions in Dayton schools—the first district in the state to do so—and changed the district's code of student conduct to end zero-tolerance policies. The group also won restorative justice programs in eight schools, which featured an alternative approach that helps schools get at the root causes of behavioral issues rather than punish and suspend students. Continuing its work to support the education of Black boys, RJN got the district to establish an Office for Males of Color, modeled on the successful program pioneered in Oakland, California, only the third in the country at the time. RJN also issued school discipline report cards for 1,100 school districts across Ohio and became a key force behind passage of a state law in 2018 banning suspensions and expulsions for students who commit minor infractions in pre–K through third grade.[1]

Speaking proudly, Sankara-Jabar notes, "A little volunteer group, Racial Justice NOW!, did all that." Nevertheless, in her view, this is just the beginning of what needs to be done to tackle a system where "the abnormal has been normalized." Too many schools today will routinely suspend Black children, especially boys, label them failures, and send them down the road that eventually leads to prison and a life struggling with poverty.

> The Black community is in a state of crisis when it comes to education. I feel angry sometimes that there is not more outrage. We keep seeing these reports and this data, but nobody is up in arms. We need to make some drastic changes right now. I want to jolt the consciousness of the parents in our community to not accept the abnormal as normal.

Sankara-Jabar soon joined DSC's national leadership body, its coordinating committee, and took advantage of a variety of leadership development opportunities. Within a year she became the coalition's national field organizer, helping parent- and youth-led organizing groups work to dismantle the school-to-prison pipeline in their localities. Nevertheless, when I interviewed her, Sankara-Jabar was still struggling with the school system and its impact on her son. Amir was coming home saying, "Mom, I'm bad."

> Amir is in fourth grade now and this school year has been one of the most difficult. No matter what I do, I can't make the teacher see us differently. I can't make her see him as a little energetic 9-year-old boy who has some leadership qualities that, if she could see it, she could cultivate instead of viewing him as a menace or a nuisance.
>
> I have tried to show my son's teachers that we are human. He has parents who love him and support him. He is not abnormal. He is not somebody you should be afraid of.
>
> But I can't make a teacher love my son.

By the time of this writing, however, Amir was in middle school and had begun joining his mother at organizing events to speak for himself about his experiences as a Black boy and the need for schools to radically change.

* * *

One day Chicago high school sophomore Carlil Pittman stayed in the cafeteria past the end of lunch period. A security guard confronted him and, a few hours later, he found himself expelled from the school. According to Pittman:

> I found out my girlfriend was pregnant during that lunch period. Being fifteen years old, I didn't know how to act; so I sat in the lunchroom. I just sat there thinking about it and thinking about it and security was like, "You were here last period, why are you still here?" And I said, "I don't feel like being in class." And he said, "Well, you need to go to the office." They asked to see my grades. They said, "Just kick him out." So that was it.

Although Pittman had never even been suspended before, the school expelled him on the spot.

I feel like there is no way I should have been kicked out of school for cutting a class. No one even asked me, "Well, why were you cutting class? What's the problem? Do you need someone to talk to?" There should be something in place rather than just kicking me out of school.

With the support of his mother who didn't want her son to become "just another statistic," Pittman, an African American male, searched for a good high school to attend. He had difficulty finding another high school that would accept him.

I was home for about two and a half months because I couldn't find another high school that would let me in. I tried to go to a high school out in the suburbs with my aunt, but no one would let me. They saw me as a problem child because I had been kicked out of school.

Pittman eventually entered Gage Park High School, the local neighborhood school required to admit him. The delay, however, meant he had to go to summer school and Saturday school from sophomore year until senior year so that he could graduate on time.

While a senior at Gage Park, Pittman got involved as a student leader with the Southwest Organizing Project (SWOP), a community organizing group that was a part of VOYCE, a coalition of youth organizing groups in Chicago. When Pittman graduated from high school, he continued to participate as a VOYCE leader. Several years later, he became a paid organizer working with other students in VOYCE to write and advocate for SB100, state legislation designed to end the kind of zero-tolerance practice that pushed him out of high school in the first place. When the Illinois legislature passed SB100, it was the strongest state law in the country at the time to dismantle the school-to-prison pipeline.[2]

Like other VOYCE leaders, Pittman believes zero tolerance is a racist practice that is part of a larger system that pushes out Black and Latinx students. Speaking of Gage Park, he says:

There's nothing in the school. Nothing draws you to the school. The college career center is gone, the librarian, the books. There's no money getting pulled into the schools of students of color. They keep putting money into placing police officers and police stations inside of schools, making students feel like they're being criminalized and like they're going to prison every day.

As a youth leader in VOYCE, Pittman traveled to national meetings with other young people organizing for educational and racial justice. These meetings opened a world to Pittman and helped him feel part of a national movement. Speaking of a youth convening in Philadelphia, Pittman says:

> For three days, I was surrounded with young men of color from all over the United States. We come together, we go to different workshops, and we see what common problems we have. I've never been surrounded by so many powerful, intelligent young men of color. I was like, "Wow, this is really amazing."

Pittman credits the SWOP community organizer Joel Rodriguez and the opportunities he's had through VOYCE for helping him find a new path.

> Joel's my mentor. I blame Joel for being the man that I am today. He's played a big role in my life. He's always been there to support me, to push me to speak, to teach me skills. . . . I've been able to speak with legislators and lobby at the state capitol.

In the photos and selfies taken the day the Illinois House of Representatives passed SB100, one can see Pittman smiling broadly with student leaders just a few years younger than him.

> I'm really grateful for being able to share my journey from where I started off as a teenage African American boy who had a baby in high school and was kicked out of the school to a youth organizer. It's really powerful to share that with people who feel like giving up, that they've messed up and it's too late. I help them realize it's not too late.

He also spoke warmly about being the proud father of his then seven-year-old son.

* * *

The experiences of Zakiya Sankara-Jabar and Carlil Pittman with the school-to-prison pipeline are unfortunately all too common. I heard story after story like these about school pushout as I conducted the research for this book. Stories of pain and trauma but also stories of transformation through organizing and movement building. I wanted the voices of those most impacted by racial injustice to center this book just as they ground the movement to end the school-to-prison pipeline.

The personal stories I gathered and the experiences I witnessed serve to document systemic policies and practices that routinely pushed thousands of students of color out of school and onto the road to prison. While in Chicago interviewing Carlil Pittman, I learned that Chicago police had substations located in high schools where they arrested and booked children right in the school, sometimes leading them away in handcuffs. In Los Angeles, I met a Latino student who told me that the police would stop him at least once a week for riding his bicycle to and from school. Apparently, they assumed that a Latino teenager must be fleeing a crime or about to commit one. I learned that the Los Angeles school police owned semi-automatic weapons and other military grade hardware including a tank.[3]

I discovered that many students, including young children, were literally brutalized by these racist practices. In Mississippi, for example, I met two sisters who had been incarcerated repeatedly in a juvenile detention facility where they were both physically abused. The so-called training school was really a notorious jail, where children who misbehaved were hog-tied and, like one of the sisters, were confined to a windowless, stifling cinder-block cell, with nothing but the concrete floor to sleep on and a hole in the floor for a toilet.[4]

When I traveled to the suburbs of Richmond, Virginia, I had one of the most disturbing experiences of my research in the field. I discovered that while schools brutalized students, they also often bullied parents who stood up for their children. I had come to visit Advocates for Equity in Schools and I Vote for Me, local organizing and advocacy groups fighting racially discriminatory school discipline policies, with a special focus on students with special needs. The morning after I arrived, I was scheduled to interview leaders Kandise Lucas and Lorraine Wright. But I received a call from them at 11 p.m. that night. They had to cancel our morning meeting because a distraught mother had just contacted them about a school security officer who had accosted her son outside his middle school that day. Lucas and Wright invited me to join them as they accompanied the mother to a meeting at the school the next morning.

I sat there in shock and anger as the mother recounted what had happened. Her African American son had an IEP (Individualized Education Plan) that specified he could take a break from class and get some fresh air out on the school grounds if he needed to. When he took a break that day, however, a security officer followed him outside, handcuffed him, and dragged him along the ground. The school sent him home, where he arrived with his clothes full of mud from the assault all the way down into his underwear. The mom said that the vice principal called and told her to keep him home for a few days. He wasn't suspended, an action that would have created a written record, but she was told to keep him home, nonetheless.

The mom faced an array of impassive school and district officials at the meeting. They had just watched a video taken of the incident but refused to show it to the mother. Although they agreed that handcuffing was wrong, none of the staff seemed to care that a child had been abused. No one apologized or offered to do anything to help. At one point, the district administrator got up from her seat and said she had to leave because "some of us actually have to work." The mother had, in fact, taken time off from her job to attend the meeting. In the end, the mother felt she had to accept the three hundred dollars the district offered to replace the young man's damaged clothing in exchange for her agreement not to pursue any further claims.

To be honest, I was traumatized by hearing these stories and witnessing this kind of brutality toward Black and Brown young people and their families again and again over the three-year period of my research. I was deeply disturbed and emotionally wounded, even as I was able to return to my relatively privileged life after these travels. I hope that through this book, readers will gain an appreciation for the deep trauma experienced by families who are directly impacted by violence and injustice and its lasting impact on their lives.

I spend time in Chapter 1 to demonstrate that these stories are not exceptional. Rather, they are common. In that chapter I systematically describe the operations of the school-to-prison pipeline as part of a larger system of mass criminalization of people of color, especially African Americans. I provide the data that demonstrate its racist nature and harmful impacts. I believe the personal stories, however, are critically important for people to hear. Poor Black people and people of color have been silenced in this country, so one purpose of the book is to provide at least one place where people most impacted by racial injustice can speak their truth.

The school-to-prison pipeline embodies the deep-seated and systemic racism in our public school system and in our broader society. Fifty years after the end of the civil rights movement, we have constructed a society in which nearly half of all Black children grow up poor, many desperately poor and even homeless. They often reside in neighborhoods that suffer from environmental degradation, violence, and police brutality. Rather than providing opportunities for a better future for these children, public education has become part of the system perpetuating racial oppression.[5]

When I speak about my research, I find that most white and affluent Americans have no idea that this kind of oppression is happening in American schools. The Movement for Black Lives and the mass protests of 2020 have exposed police brutality and killings on the streets, but Black and Brown children are being brutalized in schools every day and their families disrespected and bullied. There are simply two worlds of American public education. What many white people fail to realize, however, is that the unacknowledged phenomenon of the school-to-prison pipeline buttresses the system of white supremacy upon which their own world rests and that provides the privileged education their children receive.

Stories and analysis of racial oppression and educational injustice lay the foundation for the focus of this book: how parents, young people, and communities of color with their allies have built a powerful movement to challenge the school-to-prison pipeline. In other words, we need to understand the depth, violence, and systematic nature of the racial oppression that communities are facing to appreciate the movement Black people and people of color have built. Recounting the stories I have heard about experiences with the school-to-prison pipeline plays a key role in raising consciousness and setting the stage for movement building.

People like Zakiya Sankara-Jabar and Carlil Pittman are not simply victims of injustice. Through participation in organizing, they have become change agents in their lives and the lives of their communities. African American parents in rural Mississippi started speaking out about brutality at juvenile facilities and school policies that put children on the school-to-jail track as far back as the late 1990s. By the 2000s, students in schools in low-income communities of color started to cry out that their schools "feel like jails." Yet few were listening. The larger world of community organizers, school reformers, civil rights activists, and the scholars who studied educational equity had focused their attention elsewhere—on low graduation rates and so-called "dropout factories," on access to college, on the harms of high-stakes standardized testing, and on school privatization, to name some important issues. Many—including me—would later start to address the school-to-prison pipeline, but only after parents and young people in low-income communities of color began to tell their stories about the depth and extent of racialized violence and oppression in their schools.

Black and Brown parents and students did more than speak up. They organized in their districts and connected across localities and with civil rights and educational advocacy organizations and other allies to build a powerful movement that has shifted educational systems away from zero-tolerance school discipline and challenged school policing practices. Despite organizing in small and underfunded community groups, they have changed discipline policies and practices and won alternative approaches like restorative justice at local and state levels across the country. In 2014, the movement realized a major national victory when the federal government under the Obama administration issued new guidelines warning against zero tolerance and promoting restorative alternatives. Despite the rise of white nationalist movements and civil rights rollbacks by the Trump administration, the movement continued to grow. Suspensions and expulsions have begun to fall significantly in places like Los Angeles and California where the movement has won major policy changes to reduce exclusionary discipline. After many years of organizing to reduce and remove the presence of police in schools, parents, young people, and community members in Black communities and communities of color won the defunding of school police in a series of districts as part of the mass protests against racism in 2020.[6]

This book tells the story of the movement. It begins in rural Mississippi where Black parents, young people, and community organizers were some of the first to speak out against harsh and racist discipline and juvenile justice policies and name what they called the schoolhouse-to-jailhouse track. It then traces the development of a national movement with deep local roots, showing how local organizing grounded the national movement which, in turn, helped strengthen and spread campaigns to end zero tolerance and challenge discriminatory policing and police brutality in schools across the country. The book draws out lessons from the movement to end the school-to-prison pipeline for how to combine local organizing and national movement building to transform deep-seated systems of racial injustice in education and beyond.

From Local Organizing for Education Reform to National Movements for Racial Equity and Educational Justice

In the late 2000s I was finishing a major research project with Karen Mapp and fifteen doctoral students at the Harvard Graduate School of Education. We studied six community organizing groups across the country and produced a book called *A Match on Dry Grass* documenting the critical contributions that parent, youth, and community organizing groups in low-income communities of color were making to education reform efforts in public schools. We described these groups almost entirely as local phenomenon, operating in isolation from groups in other localities. At the time we started the project in 2006, our local approach was a fairly accurate representation of the education organizing field.[7]

By the time the book came out in 2011, however, the world of education organizing had started to change. Groups were finding ways to connect across localities and a range of national alliances began to emerge, including the Dignity in Schools Campaign and the Alliance for Educational Justice, which focused on ending the school-to-prison pipeline. Soon after, the Journey for Justice Alliance formed to challenge large-scale school closings in Black and Brown communities and the Alliance to Reclaim Our Schools brought teachers unions and community groups together to advocate for sustainable community schools.

Soon after our book was published, I decided to shift my attention to examine how organizers were combining local organizing with national movement building. I focused on the movement to end the school-to-prison pipeline for several reasons. First, this movement had emerged as the largest among the national movement efforts, involving scores of local organizing groups across the country. I also wanted to study what appeared to be the most successful effort at the time, to offer models for scholars and movement builders to learn from. By 2012 the school-to-prison pipeline movement was having demonstrable success in beginning to change zero-tolerance discipline policy.

Meanwhile, during this time I had learned enough to be convinced that the school-to-prison pipeline was perhaps the critical issue facing low-income students of color and their families. Children were not likely to graduate high school or go to college if they had been repeatedly suspended and expelled. It seemed to me that local organizers, parents, and young people had identified this issue and I needed to follow their lead.

I also had a personal reason to care about the school-to-prison pipeline. I am married to a Black British woman—Roberta Udoh—and we have two Black, biracial daughters who were attending public schools that were racially diverse at the time. As our oldest daughter entered her middle school years, we started witnessing a dramatic change in the treatment of Black students at her school. Teachers and school administrators adopted zero tolerance for students of color—not the white students—and were harshly disciplining and suspending them. The students of color became increasingly alienated from school and our daughter increasingly distressed. I was deeply disturbed to see that, as a child who loved learning, she stopped wanting to go to school.

My wife and I became increasingly angry about the treatment of Black children at the school and its impact on our daughter. When we complained about the racism students were experiencing and the growing apartheid conditions at the school, we were ostracized by the school leaders. Infuriated by the intransigence of teachers and school officials, we eventually had to leave the school district. I have more resources and options than the people who are featured in this book. Nevertheless, I am part of a family and community directly impacted by racist school discipline and that experience was a powerful motivator for me to begin this project.

Meanwhile, as I started this project, my wife Roberta became a pre–K teacher in Boston Public Schools. She entered teaching committed to holistically supporting Black and Brown children and partnering with their families to encourage the joy of learning in young children. Yet she entered an under-resourced and dysfunctional school system that signaled very clearly to poor children of color that they didn't matter. She came home night after night with stories of the stereotyping and labeling of children of color, the lack of respect and support for their families, and a relentless focus on standardized test-based teaching that drove out the joy of learning and alienated children from school. It was through Roberta that I saw how the school-to-prison pipeline started in preschool and became deeply entrenched in the racist policies, practices, and the very psyche of urban schools. I also saw how some educators like Roberta, who were deeply connected to the families and communities of their students, could become key allies and activists for creating humane and empowering forms of education. In this way, through my own family experiences, I began to appreciate the educational justice movement as a racial justice movement, best exemplified by the movement to end the school-to-prison pipeline.

At the same time as the movement began to emerge in the early 2000s, another important shift was taking place in the world of community organizing and education reform. Formerly, organizing groups centered in low-income communities of color had often been led by white organizers. In the early 2000s more and more groups either shifted their leadership to people of color or were founded as new groups led by people of color. The groups that had been at the forefront of education organizing tended to work from the Alinsky organizing tradition. At the time, these groups did not name racism as the problem and usually offered their demands without featuring racial equity in explicit terms. Of course, many participants knew full well that racism was implicated in the failures of the educational system, but the groups chose to organize nonracially. They framed their objective as education reform not racial equity and educational justice.[8]

By contrast, the groups in the emerging school-to-prison pipeline movement had an explicit anti-racist analysis and highlighted racial disparities, calling for educational justice. They tended to draw from the African American civil rights and sometimes the Chicano/a organizing traditions and spoke of their struggle as part of historic racial liberation movements. The subtitle of *A Match on Dry Grass* was "Community organizing as a catalyst for *school reform*." I was now interested in community organizing as the foundation for a newly emergent movement focused on *racial equity and educational justice*.

Around the time I began this study, the Black Lives Matter movement emerged and pushed issues of anti-Black racism and police violence onto national consciousness. In some ways, the movement to dismantle the school-to-prison pipeline with its explicit anti-racist perspective, emphasis on the voices of the most impacted, and focus on policing and criminalization predated this movement and helped lay the foundation for it. At the same time, the Black Lives Matter movement also strengthened the police-free schools campaigns of the school-to-prison pipeline movement and, more broadly, helped create a more receptive climate for its demands. My community engaged research seemed more urgent than ever, and I hoped that the new racial justice movements that excelled at mass mobilizations and consciousness-changing could also learn from the successes of the movement to dismantle the school-to-prison pipeline, including its ability to win policy changes.

I soon found that previous scholarship would be limited in what it could offer to help me with this study. As explained in Chapter 2, the scholarship on community organizing, including my own, was relentlessly local and rarely addressed how local organizing connected to national movements. Meanwhile, contemporary scholarship on social movements had surprisingly little to say about the world of local community organizing. It treated movements as nationally focused, professionalized, and dominated by advocacy groups based in Washington, DC. I believed that the organizers of color in the school-to-prison pipeline movement were creating new models for connecting organizing across localities and creating national movements that served to strengthen, spread, and "nationalize" local struggles. I was excited at the prospect of setting out to study these efforts and identify new, emerging models to analyze and share with scholars, organizers, educators, and the broader public who care about racial equity and educational justice.

Studying Movement Building through Community Engaged Scholarship

As a community engaged scholar, I conducted the research for this book in partnership with community organizers, parents, and youth leaders who are building the movement to dismantle the school-to-prison pipeline. Early on in my academic career, I rejected the notion that scholars should study communities "from above," believing that this hierarchical structure was one of the forces that kept low-income communities of color subjugated. In fact, there was a long tradition of white male sociologists like me studying poor, Black communities and reinforcing racial stereotypes about them. For my part, I value the knowledge and analysis that organizers, parents, young people, and community members hold. I want to learn with them, not just about them. In my view, this approach makes research more rigorous as it must be accountable to multiple audiences, including scholars but also people on the front lines in communities. I also believe it makes the findings of my research more relevant to building the understanding and action necessary to address systemic injustice. If anything, the mass protests against systemic racism in 2020 have challenged white scholars and all researchers to consider the role their research plays in supporting or confronting the structures of systemic racism.[9]

I have long practiced this kind of co-production of knowledge. As a white college professor studying organizing efforts in low-income communities of color, I try to pay careful attention to building relationships and trust with community participants. I know that I have many privileges connected to what scholars call my positionality, that is, my race, gender, and professional position. I want to make sure that I have open and ongoing conversations with my partners about the power dynamics in our relationship and who benefits from it. I start by listening carefully to the views of the people I study and remain constantly in dialog with them, trying to be responsive to their concerns. As we work together over time, we grow a stronger partnership based upon shared values, commitments. and goals. At the same time, we each have different roles, and, in the end, I am responsible for what I write about the movement. I take that as a deep responsibility to be as fair and accurate as I can be.[10]

When I began this study in 2014, however, I faced new challenges. The Movement for Black Lives had shed a spotlight on American racism and its violent core and had led activists and organizers of color to challenge white allies to demonstrate their commitment more fully to Black and Brown communities. It was a new era for community engaged scholars, particularly white scholars like me. Even though I had built a reputation as a collaborator with many organizing groups across the country, my newer partners in this project, like those in the Dignity in Schools Campaign (DSC), wanted extended time to get to know me and agree on the terms of our partnership. I found myself listening to a new set of concerns by community participants—for example, the need to compensate groups financially for their participation with stipends, even if they were modest in size. I was also challenged to think and act in some new ways. Why, some organizers wanted to know, did I— particularly as a white man—always do the writing? Why couldn't they have the opportunity to tell their own stories and offer their own analysis in their own words? This led me to produce the book *Lift us up! Don't push us out!* in which I helped organizers and movement builders write essays of their own. That book grew out of this study and is a companion volume to this one, offering complementary documentation and analysis of movement building for educational justice.[11]

Partnering with the groups I wanted to study proved newly challenging also because I wanted to research both local organizing and national movement building, so there were a lot of groups and many moving parts. I created a formal partnership with DSC, as the largest national coalition focused on ending the school-to-prison pipeline. DSC set up a subcommittee and we met monthly for over a year, building relationships and discussing research plans. Although I was primarily responsible, we worked together to design the research project. We agreed on procedures for working with local members, including offering stipends to host community groups and gift cards to parents and young people as important forms of appreciation for the value of their participation. As part of the project, I raised funds that supported the creation of a toolkit of resources for community groups working to end the school-to-prison pipeline. I partnered with DSC to create this toolkit as a concrete manifestation of making research relevant to change efforts, and DSC housed it on their website as a freely available resource. I continued to consult with DSC, sharing findings and drafts with the subcommittee and receiving feedback from DSC members at its annual meetings. I also built a relationship with the Alliance for Educational Justice, consisting of over two dozen youth organizing groups, consulting with its national director on a regular basis about research plans and progress. Finally, I built relationships with the local groups in the study, including similar kinds of consultations with these groups, and shared drafts of my writings with them.[12]

Working in this engaged way, I conducted research at the national level, interviewing participants, allies, and observers in national formations including DSC, AEJ, the Advancement Project, and other organizations. I wanted to chart the history of the development of the national movement and analyze the processes that connected it to local organizing. I also focused on work to influence the federal government and interviewed current and former federal officials. I attended a wide variety of national meetings and actions or events sponsored by national alliances.

I also conducted extensive research in three local areas, Chicago, Los Angeles, and the Mississippi Delta, spending weeks interviewing participants, allies, observers, educators, and public officials and observing meetings, actions, and events. I chose these locations to reveal the dynamics of organizing in different social and geographic contexts as well as for their significance to the national movement. I also conducted shorter fieldwork trips to five other locations—Denver, Dayton, Ohio, New Orleans, and the suburbs of Atlanta and Richmond, Virginia—to get a more comprehensive perspective on the development of the movement across the country. In all localities, I wanted to understand how local organizing influenced the national movement and was influenced by it.

In the course of three years of research, I interviewed a total of 140 people and conducted an additional thirteen focus groups including an additional fifty parents and youth leaders. I observed over fifty events, including internal organizational meetings, public sessions, multi-day conferences, rallies, marches, and training sessions. I also reviewed an array of relevant documents, including leaflets, organizational reports, school district data, and news accounts. Further details on research design and methods can be found in the Appendix. I note here, though, that I refer to the position of people quoted or mentioned in the text held at the time of the interview or the incident in question; their roles and positions may have changed since that time. Unless otherwise noted, all quotations come from the interviews I conducted.

I believe my extensive and sustained engagement with the movement and the large number and diverse perspectives of interview participants provide a comprehensive account of the development of the movement to dismantle the school-to-prison pipeline. Although I listened carefully and responded to the feedback I received from participants through the project, in the end I am responsible for the analysis presented in this book.

The Plan of the Book

Chapter 1 offers an analysis of the school-to-prison pipeline as the modern incarnation of a system of white supremacy based upon the mass criminalization of Black and Brown communities. I document the rise of the school-to-prison pipeline in zero-tolerance school discipline policies and the increasing presence of police and security measures in public schools. I argue that the school-to-prison pipeline is more than a set of well-intentioned but misguided school discipline policies that require reform, as many educators believe. Rather, I show that the school-to-prison pipeline represents an interlocking system of racial domination and control that keeps communities of color poor and lacking in power. It signifies the current version of the historic effort to maintain white supremacy by denying education to African Americans and criminalizing generations of young people of color and their families. The larger analytical framework of systemic racism I construct is important because it establishes the need for a racial and educational justice movement to dismantle it.

Chapter 2 offers a new model for understanding the dynamic relationship between local community organizing and national movement building. I highlight the critical contributions of local organizing to building the participation and leadership of those most impacted by injustice and to create organizational forms capable of sustaining campaigns to win policy changes. At the same time, I reveal the fundamental limitations of local organizing to dismantle a system of racial inequity deeply embedded in national structures, policies, and consciousness. I consider the particular contributions of national movements, like influencing federal policy and challenging racist stereotypes and narratives. But, I argue, they are typically too narrowly focused on federal policy and dominated by Washington-based professional advocacy groups. I suggest, instead, that movements can be stronger when they seek to strengthen and spread local organizing, "nationalizing local struggles," and when groups grounded in communities most impacted by injustice share power with professional advocates.

Chapter 3 charts the development of the movement to dismantle the school-to-prison pipeline as a national movement with deep local roots. I document the beginnings of the movement in places like Holmes County, Mississippi, where African American parents and community organizers first raised the alarm about what they called the schoolhouse-to-jailhouse track. I show how national actors and institutions emerged to play important roles in lifting up and spreading breakthrough local victories, while both strengthening local organizing and working to influence federal policy. In this chapter and throughout the book, I show how local organizing efforts shaped the national movement and were, in turn, supported by it.

I discuss the struggle between community organizers and professional advocates in the emerging Dignity in Schools Campaign to create a coalition in which community groups would have a majority say and keep the national coalition focused on supporting local organizing rather than inside-the-beltway Washington politics. Nevertheless, the movement had important national victories, like shifting the national discourse away from zero tolerance and getting the federal government to issue new guidelines warning school districts against racially inequitable zero-tolerance discipline practices. These victories became resources to groups as they expanded local and state level campaigns, creating a rolling series of policy wins across the country.

Chapter 4 documents the development of the Mississippi Delta Catalyst Roundtable to reform a deeply racist and abusive juvenile justice system and to build power in Black communities. I stress the importance of grounding the national movement in African American communities in the South. I show how these groups created models to combine community organizing with legal strategies and advocacy work in ways that centered the leadership of groups rooted in communities of those most impacted. Nevertheless, I demonstrate the critical importance of statewide and national networks to support local organizing carried out by small groups facing entrenched systems of oppression. I show how people most impacted by injustice facing powerful white resistance spoke out and used intergenerational community organizing to confront systemic racism. Combining deep local organizing and national support, they made important breakthroughs and helped inspire a new racial justice movement.

Chapter 5 turns to Los Angeles where I discuss the variety of ways that organizing groups have sought to confront a vast school district and militarized system of police control. I feature the role of Black and Brown parents in CADRE as key leaders in the struggle. These parents won the first districtwide breakthrough against harsh discipline approaches in the country when they got the LA Unified School District to adopt schoolwide positive behavioral supports in 2006. The movement "nationalized" this local victory, inspiring groups across the country to launch campaigns against zero tolerance. I also highlight the youth organizing work of the Labor Community Strategy Center to end police ticketing of students, one of the pioneering efforts to address policing in the school-to-prison pipeline movement. Finally, I examine the Youth Justice Coalition and its Free LA High School, which supports young people returning from the juvenile justice system and attempts to create a model for police-free schools based upon transformative justice. Through a variety of organizing campaigns, Los Angeles has experienced a dramatic decline in school suspensions, even as groups like CADRE remain persistently focused on holding the system accountable for deep and sustained change in its treatment of students and their parents.

Chapter 6 closely examines the campaign by Voices of Youth in Chicago Education (VOYCE) to pass SB100, mentioned earlier as the strongest state law at the time designed to combat the school-to-prison pipeline. I highlight the role of high school students in leading a struggle for their own liberation. I identify key elements of VOYCE's organizing strategy—elements that I found groups used across the country: personal storytelling to bring a human face and moral force to policy campaigns; participatory action research to demonstrate the systemic nature of racial inequities; and alliance building to provide greater resources to organizing efforts led by those most impacted. I also show how the SB100 campaign emerged through an interaction between authentic, bottom-up concerns of VOYCE youth of color and national-level learning from the experiences of organizing groups across the country.

Chapter 7 discusses the spread of the movement across the country. I show how small, under-resourced groups. like Racial Justice NOW! in Dayton, Ohio, proved able to win significant victories in a conservative area by combining strong parent organizing with critical support from the national Dignity in Schools Campaign. In New Orleans, I chart the efforts of Families and Friends of Louisiana's Incarcerated Children to combat the school-to-prison pipeline in a privatized district dominated by charter schools. Moving to suburbs with newer populations of students of color, I examine the work of the Gwinnett Parent Coalition to Dismantle the School-to-Prison Pipeline (SToPP) outside of Atlanta. I show how students of color face sharply inequitable discipline despite attending higher-performing schools and the challenges of confronting the school-to-prison pipeline in white-dominated districts used to serving majority white populations. The chapter ends in the suburbs surrounding Richmond, Virginia, seat of the Confederacy, where local organizers confront a system that has systematically denied educational opportunities to students of color with special needs.

Chapter 8 examines the expansion of the movement to new issues and newly forceful constituents. I chart the rise of the police-free schools movement and discuss the influence of the Movement for Black Lives. I document the assertion of voice and leadership by Black girls, girls of color, and gender nonconforming students in the movement, highlighting the intersectional ways that they experience the school-to-prison pipeline. Finally, I examine the role of teachers as allies to the movement and highlight efforts to implement restorative justice as an alternative to zero tolerance. I emphasize the need to connect restorative justice to school-site organizing that connects teachers with students and parents in ways that transform relationships and create liberatory education.

The concluding chapter begins by discussing the impact of the school-to-prison pipeline movement on reducing suspensions and challenging policing practices in schools. I then highlight the features documented in this book, which help explain the growth and success of the movement and its emerging intersectional nature. I draw lessons from this study for reconceptualizing social justice movements as ones that "nationalize local struggles." I consider the enduring challenges facing the movement to dismantle the school-to-prison pipeline, including the persistence of racial disparities in exclusionary discipline, tensions between local and national organizing, and the difficulties of implementing restorative alternatives that serve to transform deep-seated racialized processes. I end with a discussion of the challenges and opportunities to building racial and educational justice movements powerful enough to fully transform entrenched systems of racial inequity and educational injustice, particularly in an era that has witnessed the rise of white nationalism.

I have several goals in writing this book. I want to publicize the stories I heard from parents and students of color about racist treatment at the hands of school systems as well as their journeys to racial justice organizing. I want to document and offer an analysis of how, with few resources, these parents and students and their allies working in community organizing groups built a movement that has begun to dismantle an entrenched school-to-prison pipeline. In doing so, I want to provide readers of this book with a deep appreciation for the role of people most impacted in building movements for racial and social justice. I want to encourage educators and policymakers to join as allies with parents, young people, and communities of color to move beyond piecemeal reform to systemic transformation of racist systems. Drawing from the creative achievements of movement organizers, I offer scholars and the broader public a different way to think about social justice movements, appreciating them as connected local struggles that are "nationalized." Finally, I hope to supply organizers and movement builders with new models for connecting deep local organizing to national movements that can build the power necessary to transform deep-seated systems of racial injustice.

1

The School-to-Prison Pipeline

Criminalization as Racial Domination and Control

The school-to-prison pipeline refers to an interlocking system of policies and practices that push students of color from low-income communities out of school and into the juvenile and criminal justice system. These policies and practices include exclusionary discipline (suspensions and expulsions) and increased policing and security practices, including metal detectors, searches, ticketing, and arrests of students in school. Many educators and observers understand the school-to-prison pipeline as a set of wrong-headed policies requiring reform. If we set these policies and practices, however, in a larger historical and systemic framework, we can see that the school-to-prison pipeline represents a system of control and repression that reproduces racial inequity in our society, keeping low-income students of color and their communities poor and powerless. In fact, the school-to-prison pipeline forms a key part of a larger system of criminalization and mass incarceration that buttresses the system of white supremacy, the latest phase of racialized oppression in the United States. Some scholars prefer the term school-to-prison "nexus" to "pipeline" to highlight the interlocking nature of systems of oppression and the commonalities across schools and jails as systems of racial discipline and control. In any case, if we recognize the school-to-prison pipeline not simply as a set of misguided policies, but as a deep-seated form of systemic racism, then we can appreciate the vital importance of a social justice movement to dismantle it.[1]

The Early Origins of the School-to-Prison Pipeline

The seeds of the school-to-prison pipeline were sown just as the civil rights movement reached its peak in the early to mid-sixties. As the historian Elizabeth Hinton has revealed, President Lyndon Johnson's War on Poverty

Willful Defiance. Mark R. Warren, Oxford University Press. © Mark R. Warren 2022.
DOI: 10.1093/oso/9780197611500.003.0002

was fueled as much by fear of urban disorder and particularly of young African Americans as any desire to uplift communities. Johnson may well have been responding to immense pressure from the movement and its supporters to address racial inequality and poverty, as well as having his own moral and political motivations to take action. Nevertheless, in March of 1965, in addition to the Housing and Urban Development and Voting Rights Acts, Johnson also submitted the Law Enforcement Assistance Act, signed into law a month after the Watts uprising, which gave the federal government a direct role in local police, courts, and prisons for the first time. In 1968, the Safe Streets Act created the Law Enforcement Assistance Administration, which began delivering federal funds to local police departments—strengthening law enforcement and surveillance particularly in cities with large African American populations. Law enforcement agencies increasingly began to administer programs meant for health, housing, education, recreation, and job training. President Nixon increased punitive policing practices while the Ford administration expanded juvenile detention facilities and the Carter administration expanded policing in public housing. By the eighties, police had become a ubiquitous and controlling force in urban communities of color.[2]

The school-to-prison pipeline intensified, though, as a response to the gains of the civil rights movement. As schools started to desegregate, and Black and Latinx students began to gain access to better education through the sixties and seventies, educational outcomes improved. By the mid-seventies, urban schools spent about as much as suburban schools, while childhood poverty rates fell dramatically—to below the levels of today. As Linda Darling-Hammond has shown, test scores rose in response to more equitable educational access as well as anti-poverty investments. The differences in reading scores between Black and white students was cut in half and was also reduced substantially in math; for a short time, Black college attendance rates were comparable to white rates. Through educational access and affirmative action programs, important segments of Black and Latinx communities began to gain access to the middle class.[3]

Just as Black and Latinx communities were making substantial progress, racial retrenchment intensified, and the tide turned. Social programs and affirmative action were restricted in the 1980s, while criminalization of people of color intensified. Progress in educational improvement for Black and Latinx children largely stalled. The so-called achievement gap, that is, the difference in educational attainment between white students and students of color, began to grow again in the 1980s.[4]

Mass Incarceration and White Supremacy

The story of the rise of mass incarceration during this time has been more extensively told and is better understood than the rise of the school-to-prison pipeline, yet the two are intimately connected as part of one larger phenomenon. Michelle Alexander has aptly named mass incarceration "the new Jim Crow," that is, the new system of racial control put in place after the success of the civil rights movement in ending legal segregation. Alexander documents the development of mass incarceration as a bipartisan phenomenon. President Reagan significantly escalated the War on Drugs even though use of most illicit drugs had been falling since 1979. Federal legislation in 1986 and 1988 enacted new mandatory sentencing for many drugs, including a minimum sentence of five years without parole for first-time possession of five grams of crack cocaine. President Clinton's 1994 crime bill provided for 100,000 new police officers and $9.7 billion in funding for prisons. It also featured the "three strikes and you're out" requirement that increased the use of mandatory sentencing, often for nonviolent drug offenses. Clinton may have been responding to the peak in crime rates in the early nineties as well as trying to position the Democratic Party as hard rather than soft on crime to attract white voters. Nevertheless, because of this bipartisan escalation, the number of people incarcerated for drug crimes increased from about 41,000 in 1980 to over 488,000 in 2014—a 1,000% increase.[5]

Defenders of get-tough criminal justice policies point to the rise of the crack cocaine epidemic in inner city communities in the eighties that followed a rise in crime rates in the sixties and seventies. Crime rates peaked in the early nineties, however, and were falling at the time that zero tolerance took hold. We also know that perceptions of drug use were highly racialized, as cocaine use was just as prevalent in whiter suburbs as the inner city, yet drug criminalization policies targeted Black and Latinx communities.[6]

Racist myths of the "super-predator" justified and fueled the rise of mass incarceration, which targeted Black and Brown boys and young men as violent, amoral, and out of control. John DiIulio popularized the term in the 1996 book *Body Count*, where he and his coauthors said:

America is now home to thickening ranks of juvenile "super-predators"—
radically impulsive, brutally remorseless youngsters, including ever more
preteenage boys, who murder, assault, rape, rob, burglarize, deal deadly
drugs, join gun-toting gangs and create serious communal disorders.

This myth of the Black criminal has deep historical roots and had been used
to justify lynching of Black people during the Jim Crow period of racial control. In its contemporary form, the myth had devastating consequences for
many completely innocent youth of color. It underlay the railroading of the
Central Park Five, for example, a group of four Black and one Latino boy
aged fourteen to sixteen years, falsely accused of attacking and raping a white
woman in Central Park in 1989. The media sensationalized the incident with
the *New York Times* calling it a "wilding" attack by a "wolfpack," described
as "a loosely organized gang of 32 schoolboys whose random, motiveless
assaults terrorized at least eight other people over nearly two hours." The
boys served six to thirteen years in prison before their sentences were vacated
when the real attacker confessed in 2002. The racist fear of youth of color as
"super-predators" came into wide circulation in the nineties, forming an important part of the foundation for exclusionary discipline and increased police measures in schools.[7]

The rise of mass incarceration also occurred at the same time as deindustrialization eliminated many good-paying blue-collar jobs that African
Americans, especially men, were able to attain despite discrimination.
As William Wilson has shown, deindustrialization in the 1970s and 1980s
concentrated poverty in urban Black communities and drastically reduced
employment opportunities. In other words, it made many young people dis-
posable from a capitalist point of view. As neoliberal economic trends continued to take hold in the 1990s, mass incarceration served as a system of
social control for an increasingly poor population subject to precarious and
unstable employment in the new economy that was widening the gap between the wealthy and the poor. Many observers began to argue that if, in an
earlier period, public schools tracked young African Americans to factories,
schools now served to track them to jail.[8]

By the early 2000s, the United States was incarcerating two million people,
more than six times the three hundred thousand people serving sentences in
the early 1980s and more than any other country in the world by sheer numbers and proportion of the population. In addition to the two million incarcerated, many more were on probation or had criminal records. In 2007, fully

seven million people were in prison or on probation or parole. The large majority of those serving sentences or with criminal records had been convicted for nonviolent, often drug-related, offenses.

As is now well-known, Black and Latinx people made up the majority of those incarcerated in the mid-2000s. African Americans were fully seven times more likely to be in prison than white Americans. Incarceration became particularly targeted on Black men in urban communities. According to Alexander, 75% of young Black men in Washington, DC, and nearly all the men from poor neighborhoods, could expect to serve time. Fifty-five percent of Black men in Chicago had a felony conviction. Disproportionate incarceration came as the result of racial discrimination all through the law enforcement process. People of color were more likely to be stopped by police than white people, a phenomenon that came to be known as racial profiling. If stopped, they were more likely to be arrested; if arrested, they were more likely to be convicted, and, if convicted, they were likely to serve longer sentences.[9]

Mass incarceration constituted a new system of social control and domination because it served to keep Black and Brown communities poor and without political power. Once people received a felony conviction, they were subject to legalized discrimination and the loss of many of their civil rights. Clinton's 1996 Welfare Reform Act banned people convicted of felony drug offenses from receiving food stamps or welfare benefits. Employers could legally discriminate against felons; public housing authorities could deny them a place to live; schools often banned them from activities with their children; and in many states, felons lost the right to vote, sometimes for life. In Florida, one in four African Americans could not vote because of a felony conviction. In some Chicago neighborhoods, 80% of Black men had criminal records and were typically unable to get a decent job, live in adequate housing, or fully participate in democratic life. Many ended up back in prison.[10]

Meanwhile, mass incarceration fueled a boom in private prison construction and management, often in rural or outlying exurban areas. These prisons typically hired white Americans as guards, providing jobs and economic resources to areas suffering from deindustrialization. Meanwhile, public and private prisons employed prisoners at low wages, making increasing profits. Consequently, many have argued that mass incarceration serves to buttress racial capitalism, profiting from the labor of people of color as well as public funds to incarcerate them. Meanwhile, the system strengthens the economic base and political power of regions with majority white populations as it drains resources from urban communities of color.[11]

Mass Incarceration Begins in School

One striking association was sometimes overlooked in the discussions of mass incarceration: people in prison are among the least educated in society, and lack of education is a stronger predictor of future incarceration even than race. Many Black and Brown people who end up in prison have their first contact with police in school. One study found that in North Carolina, school-based referrals make up about 40% of the referrals to the juvenile justice system and most of these referrals are for minor, nonviolent offenses.[12]

Two striking statistics demonstrate the school-to-prison pipeline, that is, how school pushout places youth of color on the road to prison: fully two-thirds of Black men without a high school degree will end up in prison at some point in their lives; one-third of Black men without a degree are in prison at any one time. By the mid-2000s, the main routes to upward mobility for African American men in the past—military service and college degrees—had become less common than a prison record.[13]

In other words, mass incarceration starts in school. In fact, just as the criminal justice system was adopting a deeply racialized zero-tolerance approach to crime, public schools began adopting a deeply racialized zero-tolerance approach to student conduct. Schools radically expanded the presence of police and associated practices like metal detectors and searches and drastically increased the use of exclusionary discipline like suspensions and expulsions. No one has traced the historical development of the school-to-prison pipeline in as much detail as the system of mass incarceration, but the essential elements remain clear.

As public institutions and public discourse turned to "law and order" approaches to urban communities of color, public schools turned to discipline and control. Early efforts to deploy police and discipline students of color in schools began in the 1960s along with the rise of policing and criminalization in response to Black and Latinx protest. The concept and practice of zero tolerance itself had its origins in the War on Drugs in the 1980s and it quickly migrated to schools. School systems accelerated zero-tolerance approaches to discipline in the late 1980s and early 1990s. Public schools began practicing exclusionary school discipline, that is, out-of-school suspensions and expulsions, on a widespread basis. The 1994 federal Gun-Free Schools Act, signed by then-President Bill Clinton, who was preparing the crime bill mentioned earlier at the time, accelerated the spread of zero tolerance in schools. The act mandated states that received federal funds pass a law requiring local educational agencies to expel, for at least one year, any student who brought a weapon to school and to refer the student to juvenile or criminal justice officials. Prior to this point, states did not typically have extensive statutes concerning school discipline policies; most states devolved authority for school discipline to local districts. But soon after, state after state passed not just the required laws but a rash of mandatory zero-tolerance measures. Local school districts themselves also began to adopt zero tolerance toward a wide range of behaviors, including, for example, immediate suspension for children bringing toy guns to school. By 1997, 94% of all schools had zero-tolerance policies for weapons or firearms, 87% for alcohol, and 79% reported mandatory suspensions or expulsions for possession of tobacco.[14]

School administrators began to cast a broad net, treating minor issues harshly. Even if one were to accept some justification for zero tolerance for weapons, its application became broad and subject to racial bias. A nine-year-old on the way to school in Columbus, Ohio, was found with a manicure kit with a one-inch knife and was suspended for violating the school's zero-tolerance policy on weapons. In Chicago, a 17-year-old junior shot a paper clip with a rubber band at a classmate, missed, and broke the skin of a cafeteria worker; he was expelled from school, taken to county jail for seven hours, charged with misdemeanor battery, and advised by school officials to drop out of school.[15]

In the wake of the deadly shooting at Columbine High School in 1999, schools expanded zero tolerance and armed security yet again. The federal government created the COPS in Schools program, awarding more than $750 million in grants to schools that used the funds to hire more than 6,500 school police officers. Even though mass shootings typically occurred in largely white school districts, zero tolerance and harsh policing targeted schools serving low-income students of color. While advocates for zero tolerance pointed to increasing rates of youth violence in the 1980s, the rates had leveled off in the 1990s.[16]

Zero Tolerance and Exclusionary Discipline

As zero tolerance spread, schools began to adopt mandatory suspensions for things like dress code violations, tardiness, or truancy. They suspended more and more students for "willful defiance," a subjective judgment often made by a teacher in the classroom. Vague discipline codes like willful defiance, "disrupting school," and other similar terms especially lent themselves to application in racially discriminatory ways. As a result, out-of-school suspension rates began to skyrocket, particularly for Black and Latinx students. In the early 1970s, about 6% of Black students received a suspension each year; by the mid-2000s that proportion had increased two and half times to 15%, representing over a million Black students suspended each year; meanwhile the suspension rate for Latinx students also more than doubled from 3% to 7%. The rate of suspension for white students also increased but more modestly from 3% to 5%. Consequently, by the mid-2000s, Black students were three times more likely to be suspended than white students; they were almost twice as likely to be expelled and more than twice as likely to be referred to law enforcement or arrested in school.

If we look at secondary schools, however, the extent of harsh discipline becomes even more apparent. By 2009, almost one-quarter of Black students in secondary school were being suspended each year. Black students lost almost five times as many days of instruction through suspensions as white students, 103 days per year per 100 students. A study in Texas tracked students through their high school years and found that 75% of Black students were suspended at some point during high school. Fully 83% of Black males in Texas were being suspended. Many were repeatedly suspended or suspended for long terms and the vast majority of suspensions were the result of discretionary decisions. Suspended students were much more likely to repeat a grade, not graduate, and become involved in the juvenile justice system.[17]

While popular attitudes may assume that racial disparities in discipline are a result of racial differences in misbehavior, there is little to no evidence to support this claim. In a comprehensive review of hundreds of empirical studies, Richard Welsh and Shafiqua Little concluded, "The evidence indicates that the higher rates of exclusionary discipline experienced by Black students are not the result of higher rates of misbehavior or these students engaging in a greater variety of infractions or more severe infractions." Rather, a complex set of factors including teacher perceptions and bias and the concentration of harsh discipline practices at schools with high proportions of low income and students of color, better explain racial disparities. In fact, the large majority of disciplinary referrals, suspensions, and expulsions depend upon the subjective judgment of teachers and principals. As a result, white students are referred more often for objective behaviors (e.g., smoking and vandalism) and Black students are referred more often for subjective behaviors (e.g., defiance to authority and disrespect).[18]

Schools also targeted students with disabilities for suspensions, with rates two to three times higher than other students. If we look at the intersection of race, gender, and disability, Black male students with disabilities are the hardest hit, with more than a third suspended each year. Meanwhile, about a quarter of Black female students with disabilities are suspended.

While these are national averages, zero tolerance became focused in schools serving low-income students of color, whether in urban or rural areas. Some city school systems had dramatically high rates. Memphis topped the list with 40% of Black students and over half of Black male students with disabilities suspended each year.

While exclusionary discipline finds its highest rates at the secondary level, the school-to-prison pipeline starts in preschool. Fifty thousand students are suspended from preschool each year while about 17,000 are expelled. Black students comprise 18% of the public preschool population but 47% of those suspended, making them 3.6 times as likely to receive one or more suspensions as white preschool students. Some estimates place the rate of suspension in preschool higher than in K–12 schooling, which indicates just how deep-seated the school-to-prison pipeline is in American education. Meanwhile, many districts serving low-income Black and sometimes Latinx students have dramatically high suspension rates in elementary school. St Louis and the district in which Michael Brown went to school in Ferguson, Missouri, were in the top ten nationally for highest rates, suspending nearly a third of all elementary students each year.[19]

While much attention has focused on the particularly high rate of suspension of boys of color, especially Black boys, girls of color are also targeted. In fact, Black girls are six times more likely to be suspended as white girls. Girls of color often face harsh discipline for gender specific forms of discrimination. According to Monique Morris and others, Black girls are considered over-sexualized and disciplined for the way they dress. Police arrested one girl in Texas, for example, for resisting being barred from her prom because school officials considered her dress too revealing. Educators stereotype Black girls as loud and aggressive, labeling them as "ghetto." Schools often suspend them for "willful defiance" or for violating gendered norms of behavior. Young Black girls have been suspended for throwing tantrums. Several well-publicized cases in the early 2000s concerned Black kindergarten girls arrested for throwing tantrums, some even handcuffed and placed in police cars. Girls of color also suffer from sexual harassment and assault in schools, sometimes by peers but also by security guards. School officials often turn a blind eye, and, if the girls fight back, they are suspended or arrested. As a result, Black girls make up 16% of girls in school but more than one-third of school-based arrests of girls. Police abuse in schools has parallels to police violence against women of color and to their incarceration at disproportionate rates often for gender-specific forms of racism, linking schools to prisons in the experience of girls of color.[20]

LGBTQ and gender nonconforming students of color also face harsh discipline. Schools often discipline them for violating gender roles or gendered forms of dress. Many trans and queer students report being singled out and targeted as "problem" students because of their sexual orientation, gender identity, and/or nonconforming modes of self-expression. Over 80% say they face verbal or even physical harassment by school institutions as well as their peers. When they stand up to their harassers and fight back, they are likely to be suspended themselves under zero-tolerance policies. The Genders and Sexualities Alliance Network and its partners have pointed out that zero-tolerance anti-bullying policies often ensnare trans and queer students who try to defend themselves. Meanwhile, suspending students fails to address the underlying causes of anti-gay and anti-trans bias. As a result, under zero tolerance schools continue to be unsafe spaces for trans and queer students while placing many of them on the road to jail. Consequently, while LGBTQ students comprise 5 to 7% of the youth population, they make up 15% of youth in the juvenile justice system.[21]

Studies have shown that exclusionary discipline places many students on a track to prison. Students who are suspended are more likely to fail to graduate high school and have contact with the criminal justice system. Repeated suspensions restrict learning time for students and make it difficult for students to maintain progress; they also alienate students from schooling. Consequently, the chances of a student "dropping out" of school double with just one suspension in ninth grade. Meanwhile, students who fail to graduate are five times more likely to end up in prison than those who graduate, regardless of race. Finally, out-of-school suspensions and expulsions remove students from the school grounds and place them into situations where they are more likely to come into contact with police.[22]

Police in Schools

If exclusionary discipline provides an indirect route to prison for students, policing practices in schools creates a direct route into the juvenile and criminal justice system. The rise of zero-tolerance discipline policies accompanied a dramatic increase in the presence of police in schools. Before the War on Drugs, "super-predator" mythology, and mass incarceration, police had a very minimal presence in American schools. Officers were rarely seen. In the late 1970s there were fewer than 100 police officers in U.S. schools; by 2003, however, public schools had 14,337 full-time school resource officers.[23]

Looked at another way, in 1975, only 1% of public schools had a police officer on the grounds. That proportion has now grown to encompass nearly half of all schools; 69% of secondary schools that enroll mostly students of color have police stationed on campus. By many measures, then, the rise of policing and associated repressive measures like metal detectors and searches has mushroomed in the past 40 years.[24]

The regular presence of school police shifts the focus of schools from learning and supporting students to disciplining and criminalizing them. According to a recent report by the ACLU, the stationing of police in schools has led to a dramatic increase in contact with law enforcement, an increase in student referrals to police, and an increase in student arrests. Students are removed from classes, subjected to physical restraint, interrogation, and other risks to their rights to education, due process, and equal treatment. As police presence grows in the building, teachers and school administrators begin to call in police to handle routine disciplinary issues. Meanwhile, students report abuse at the hands of police and school resource officers, who have been reported to use excessive force against students for routine matters like going to the bathroom without a pass.[25]

Punitive discipline and policing policies increasingly lead students, especially Black and Brown students, into the juvenile justice system. By the 2011–12 school year 260,000 students were being referred to law enforcement every year, and 92,000 students were subject to school-related arrests. Black students were 2.3 times more likely to face school-related arrest than white students. In 2003, while Black students comprised 16% of the juvenile population, they made up 45% of juvenile arrests. Immigrant and undo-cumented students and their families also faced an increased threat of de-portation as a result of police presence in and around schools, leading to a school-to-deportation pipeline.[26]

Racist Narratives and Implicit Bias

The justification for zero tolerance and increased policing in schools was in-timately tied to the "super-predator" demonization of youth of color. Schools needed to remove the "bad" kids from the classroom so "good" kids could learn; police and associated security measures were necessary to keep "good" kids safe from the "bad," violent kids. This myth persisted through the 1990s and into the 2000s, even though school violence and disruption had not increased and had even decreased somewhat since the mid-1980s. Moreover, there was and still is no evidence that students of color are more violent or disruptive than other students, so the racial targeting of these young people responds to myth rather than fact.[27]

The school-to-prison pipeline is reinforced by implicit bias among teachers in the classroom who are typically the ones that suspend students or call police. As noted before, there is no evidence that students of color misbehave at higher rates than white students, yet schools suspend them at three times the rate. A growing body of evidence has shown that the largely white teaching force in schools serving students of color hold unconscious biases that affect their reactions to student behavior. Implicit bias or cultural misunderstandings can lead teachers to exaggerate the disruptive behavior of Black and Brown children. In practice this means that racial disparities are greatest when teachers discipline students for subjective interpretation of behavior like "willful defiance" in contrast to more objective behaviors like smoking. One study found that teachers perceived students who used a Black walking style, defined as "deliberately swaggered or bent posture, with the heads lightly tilted to the side, one foot dragging, and an exaggerated knee bend," as lower in academic achievement, highly aggressive, and more likely to be in need of special education services.[28]

Walter Gilliam's early research showed that implicit bias affects racialized discipline practices as early as preschool. According to Gilliam, the three biggest risk factors for exclusionary discipline in preschool are big, Black, and boy, with teachers misinterpreting normal developmental behavior as problematic, aggressive, or troublemaking. Meanwhile, studies show that adults view Black girls as young as five as more knowledgeable about sex and adult topics, less in need of nurture and support, and significantly older than white girls of the same age.[29]

The Intergenerational Transmission of Poverty and Incarceration

While exclusionary discipline and policing practices form the heart of the school-to-prison pipeline system, other educational policies contribute to school pushout and place Black and Brown students on the track to jail. These policies include the resegregation of public schools that consign poor children of color to schools that fail them at high numbers. Schools serving these children have fewer resources, outdated facilities, less qualified teachers, and a Eurocentric curriculum that is not culturally responsive, and they suffer from a range of dysfunctional rules and procedures.[30]

The rise of neoliberal reforms in education in the 1990s and 2000s has also contributed to the school-to-prison pipeline. These reforms include an emphasis on standardized testing as the primary means of school accountability, the privatization of public education through the rise of corporate charter school networks, and the mass closings of schools in low-income Black and Brown communities in many cities. As No Child Left Behind and other laws and policies focused school accountability on the results of standardized tests, it gave an incentive for schools to suspend or expel so-called low-performing students, mostly students of color, to raise average scores. Many charter schools appear to have even harsher zero-tolerance discipline practices and higher rates of suspensions than traditional public schools, while they also contribute to increased racial segregation. Meanwhile, Black communities in many large cities have faced widespread school closings that remove important anchors from their communities, jobs from Black teachers, and support structures for students.[31]

Meanwhile, educational failure forms part of the larger societal system reproducing racial and economic inequality. Half of all Black and Latino children grow up in or near poverty while public institutions have systematically disinvested in the neighborhoods in which they live. As a result, low-income communities of color typically have higher levels of violence, police abuse, unemployment, and pollution with less access to decent housing, medical facilities, stores offering healthy foods, and arts programs. These conditions make it difficult for students of color to be successful in school and constitute an additional force behind school pushout.[32]

Exclusionary discipline and policing practices impact parents and caregivers as well as students. Most simply, when schools suspend students, families face additional stress to care for them while juggling work responsibilities. Parents often miss work to accompany their children back to school. When police ticket students or charge them with an offense, parents must appear in court and pay fines. Parents suffer the mental and emotional stress of worrying about the racist treatment of their children and the possibility that they will end up in prison or the victim of police and other forms of violence. Parents are the ones who end up supporting their loved ones as they struggle with racist treatment, school pushout, police abuse, time in jail and unemployment—even as the parents themselves are struggling with low-wage work, insecure housing, or threats of deportation. When parents complain to school authorities about racial discrimination or unfair discipline, they are often demonized and bullied. Sometimes, school administrators call the police on parents.[33]

Looked at from a larger systemic standpoint, we can see that the school-to-prison pipeline represents an intergenerational transmission of incarceration. In other words, parents of color are incarcerated at high levels, while schools place their children on the track to jail. By 2009, 2.7 million children had a parent behind bars. The proportion had increased from 1 in 125 children 25 years earlier to 1 in every 28 children. Two-thirds of these children's parents were incarcerated for nonviolent offenses. More than 1 in 9 Black children had a parent in prison or jail that year, a rate that had more than quadrupled in the prior 25 years. Fully one-quarter of Black children born in 1990 had a parent imprisoned by the time they reached age 14. Compared to white children, African American children are six times more likely to have an incarcerated parent. Parental incarceration has a powerful negative impact on children's physical and emotional well-being and their educational success, thereby directly contributing to the intergenerational transmission of poverty and incarceration.[34]

By the turn of the century, the school-to-prison pipeline was firmly in place. It was a new system but had grown out of historic patterns of racial domination, including the denial of educational opportunity, social control through repression and "law and order," and racial stereotyping. It was widespread and systemic, deep-seated in policy and practice, and buttressed by a racist narrative of "super-predators" as well as implicit bias. Moreover, the school-to-prison pipeline emerged as a key part of the larger "new Jim Crow" system of white supremacy, an intergenerational system of mass incarceration that keeps low-income communities of color poor and lacking in power. It was implemented through local and state policy and practiced at the school level primarily in educational systems with large numbers of Black and Latinx students from low-income communities. But it was a national phenomenon.

Dismantling the school-to-prison pipeline, then, involves more than piecemeal reform of a few misguided policies. Just as overturning the "old" Jim Crow system of segregation required a broad-based civil rights movement, confronting the school-to-prison pipeline requires a new racial and educational justice movement with those most impacted at its core. This movement needs to organize for policy change at local and state levels where zero tolerance and policing have their most immediate impact on students of color and their families. But the movement also must contend with the national forces that created the school-to-prison pipeline, including racist narratives justifying the removal of "dangerous" students of color and federal policy that pushed and incentivized state and local authorities to criminalize Black and Brown students.

In the next chapter, I discuss a framework for building a movement where organizing at local and national levels can be mutually reinforcing. In the rest of the book, I chart the rise and development of the movement to dismantle the school-to-prison pipeline as it emerged in African American and Latinx communities and worked to dismantle systemic racism at local, state, and national levels.[35]

2

"Nationalizing Local Struggles"

Community Organizing and Social
Justice Movements

To challenge deep-seated systems of racial injustice like the school-to-prison pipeline, communities most impacted by these inequities need to find ways to build powerful social justice movements. These movements must build a strong base of participation and leadership at the local level to fight for policy changes in school systems and other institutions and hold systems accountable for change. However, small, under-resourced organizing groups may not be able to build the power to create change on their own, isolated in local areas and often facing powerful opponents and intransigent officials. They need to find ways to connect across locality and, along with allies, build national movements that can support their local work and act as national change agents. This is a challenge because so many of the national alliances that support racial and social justice causes are Washington-based, professional advocacy organizations. They focus on national-level work and seldom prioritize the strengthening of local, grassroots organizing.[1]

How do community organizers build national movements with deep local roots? Put differently, how can movements combine local organizing with national advocacy in ways that support and reinforce movement work at multiple levels? Research and writings on social movements and on community organizing have surprisingly little to say on this issue. The literature on community organizing, including my own, has been relentlessly local; that is, it examines community organizing in localities with little to say about how organizing efforts connect across localities to create national movements. The modern literature on social movements has been largely focused nationally (or sometimes internationally) and, with a few important exceptions, has had little to say about how national movements support or enhance local organizing. Each literature offers important insights about the value of either local or national efforts and the processes through which they

Willful Defiance. Mark R. Warren, Oxford University Press. © Mark R. Warren 2022.
DOI: 10.1093/oso/9780197611500.003.0003

challenge injustice and create change; but we lack an integrated perspective that connects the two. By developing such an integrated perspective, I will argue, we can reconceptualize social movements as interconnected efforts across local and national levels that, when effective, reinforce each other and build the power for change at multiple levels. I will call this "nationalizing local struggles" as I believe that national movements take their energy and drive from local organizing and, at their best, lift up and spread them across the country and to the national level.

To some extent, the dichotomy in the literature has reflected the dominant reality of community organizing and national movements since the decline of the social movements of the sixties and seventies. Community organizing in its modern, post-sixties form emerged in locally constituted groups. Meanwhile, national movements became "professionalized" and centered in Washington-based advocacy organizations or alliances.

When I began to study community organizing in the early 1990s, this pattern had already been set. For the next twenty years, I wrote about organizing efforts primarily as local phenomenon, which was accurate for the most part at the time. By the late 2000s, however, I observed the rise of national alliances in the education organizing space, which reflected the emergence of educational justice movements that connected local groups with each other and to national actors like legal and advocacy groups. The school-to-prison pipeline movement appeared to me to be the most prominent and most successful and so I chose to study it. Other movements were starting to emerge in the educational field too, like the national movement against school privatization, which opposed large-scale school closings and the spread of corporate-run charter schools, or the movement against test-based accountability systems. Meanwhile, I believed there was evidence that social justice movements beyond education had also emerged that combined vibrant local organizing with national infrastructure and action, like the DREAMers and the broader immigrant rights movement.[2]

As a qualitative sociologist, I want to identify, describe, and analyze the processes through which organizers and movement builders create national movements that strengthen local organizing while acting nationally and ensure that people most impacted by injustice remain at the center. My focus is on the school-to-prison pipeline movement, which is both an educational justice and racial justice movement. But I believe that what we can learn from this movement offers lessons to other social and racial justice movements as well.

A Historical Perspective

The dichotomy between local and national in social movements may well be a more recent one. Historically, many U.S. social movements operated at multiple levels. The civil rights movement of the fifties and sixties was a national movement fought out primarily in local struggles. We know that local organizing provided the foundation for the success of the civil rights movement, a movement that led to important federal legislation and changes in segregationist policy and practice across the country. Aldon Morris identified the critical role of local movement centers while Charles Payne and others demonstrated the long community organizing tradition that undergird movement emergence. This scholarship, especially research by Morris who treated local/national dynamics extensively, has shown that local organizing did not just contribute to national power; it benefited from the connections to and support from the larger movement. The movement brought national attention to local struggles, provided a venue for sharing strategies and lessons across localities, offered policy expertise and skills training to local organizers and leaders, sometimes provided financial resources, and fostered a larger movement identity that motivated and sustained participation and sacrifice.[3]

The civil rights movement featured a rolling series of local struggles, each one learning from and influencing the other. There was an important national dimension to the movement, as local victories in any one place depended upon the victories (or setbacks) of the movement elsewhere. In terms of the framework I am developing, the local struggle of the Montgomery Bus Boycott was "nationalized," for example, and served to help launch a national movement, raise national consciousness, and draw contributions and resources from allies to the movement. Conversely, local organizers valued the media and public attention that the national movement could bring to their efforts.[4]

The civil rights movement did, of course, include important federal demands: to get the federal government to enforce the law against local white resistance and to pass the Civil Rights and Voting Rights Acts. The requirements of these acts, however, still had to be implemented locally through organizing efforts at that level. As Kenneth Andrews has shown, their main payoff was typically seen as changing the quality of the lives of people in their local communities: ending segregation and discrimination, opening opportunities in education and employment, and building power through the ballot box.[5]

The national/local dynamics of the civil rights movement were not tension free. Conflicts arose between local organizers and national leaders over control of movement strategy and the priority of placing demands on local versus federal authorities. Sometimes national leaders would try to take control of local movements. The Selma March offers an important example. Martin Luther King, Jr., and other national leaders from the Southern Christian Leadership Conference (SCLC) identified Selma in 1965 as a critical moment to advance the movement and traveled there to support a locally organized march to Birmingham led by younger organizers from the Student Nonviolent Coordinating Committee (SNCC) and the Dallas County Voters League. Local organizers felt that national leaders were usurping their local work in the service of national goals. In the end, after Bloody Sunday and a series of violent attacks on the organizers, the struggle in Selma played a key role in winning passage of the Voting Rights Act, but it also spurred massive on-the-ground voter registration campaigns in localities across Alabama and the South.[6]

Popular if not scholarly attention, though, tends to focus on the national features of the civil rights movement, centered often around the thoughts and actions of King himself, rather than appreciate its essential local character. There is a gendered component to this bias. If Black men dominated the national movement, Black women often led local organizing efforts, including women like Fannie Lou Hamer who founded the Mississippi Freedom Democratic Party and Septima Clark who set up Citizenship Schools. Ella Baker, a key advisor to SNCC, perhaps best personifies the "behind the scenes" and women-led organizing tradition of the civil rights movement. Baker criticized professional, charismatic, and often male leadership and advocated a radical democracy in which regular people would be supported to analyze the conditions of their oppression and advocate for themselves.[7]

Preexisting organizational networks among churches, fraternal societies, and civil rights organizations like SCLC, the Congress of Racial Equality, and the NAACP provided a foundation for local-national connections in the civil rights movement. These preexisting structures were part of a larger civic landscape of participatory, membership-based local chapters embedded in nationally federated civic organizations. As Theda Skocpol has shown, these federated structures were particularly effective in giving voice to ordinary Americans to influence policy at all three governmental levels with organizing at each level benefiting from efforts at lower or higher levels. Many of these civic associations incubated social movements like the civil rights movement.[8]

Skocpol and Morris both studied a time when federated structures for organizations and movements were the norm. Since the seventies, however, this type of organization has suffered a rapid decline. Instead, professionally managed advocacy groups and professionalized social movement organizations have come to dominate the citizen lobby at the national level. They typically are Washington-based and have members or followers whose affiliation is through a mailing list or Twitter account and they contain few, if any, participatory local chapters. Membership in these professionalized organizations, meanwhile, has come to favor those of higher socioeconomic status.[9]

While national movements became dominated by professional advocates focused on Washington, a rich and vibrant field of community organizing arose at the local level in the post-civil rights era. These groups were typically independent organizations, incorporated as 501(c)(3) nonprofit organizations. In the past, if an enterprising local organizer wanted to start an organization, they would do so as the local chapter of a national organization—which themselves often sent organizers across the country to set up chapters. Starting in the eighties, however, this political entrepreneur would likely start his or her own group as an independent local organization. As a result, the world of community organizations engaging members of low-income communities of color emerged as a highly fractured one. Some estimates place the number of groups as high as 6,000, but, by and large, they are independently organized and incorporated at the local level.[10]

Some local groups, especially faith-based ones, became affiliates of national networks like the Industrial Areas Foundation (IAF) founded by Saul Alinsky in the thirties or the PICO National Network (now called Faith in Action). But these were the minority. In any case, the IAF and PICO were not federations in the old sense of single organizations that operated in connected ways at local, state, and national levels. While the national networks did provide resources like trained organizers to support local groups, the groups developed issue campaigns mostly independently at local or at most state levels and were only loosely networked.[11]

As noted earlier, in the late 2000s, local organizing groups in a variety of fields began to see the need to connect. Some groups in the faith-based, institutional organizing world had preexisting connections through networks like the IAF and PICO. But, for the most part, lacking the federated infrastructure of earlier movements, these independent groups faced the task of forming alliances or coalitions if they wanted to connect across locality and operate at national levels. This was certainly true of the groups in the school-to-pipeline movement.[12]

There is a limited amount of research in the community organizing literature on these efforts. In the community organizing world, scholars have noted how groups in the PICO network worked together to help pass what became the Affordable Care Act and later tried to support immigration reform. We lack any systematic study, however, of these newer organizing efforts at the national level and any rigorous treatment of local/national dynamics.[13]

In the social movement literature, almost no studies have addressed local/national interactions either, even in the few cases where national organizations have local chapters—like the Sierra Club. The focus, if any at all, concerns how local organizing can help movements exert power at the national level to influence the federal government or shift public attitudes. None theorize the new ways movements organize in a multilevel and federated style and the ways local groups and communities ground and exert power within national movements.[14]

In a rare exception, Walter Nicholls's study of the DREAMers does address dynamics between locally emergent undocumented youth and the national, Washington-based, and mainstream immigrant rights organizations. He shows how the national groups helped give undocumented youth a venue to connect with each other and become their own political force. The newly emboldened DREAMers then set out to contend over the direction of the movement with the powerful national professionalized groups, who ultimately prevailed. Nevertheless, the bias of the movement remained on national action. When immigration reform failed at the national level, the DREAMers and the immigrant rights movement turned to local- and state-level policy change to advance their cause.[15]

Some scholars examine how movements organize at local versus national levels depending where political openings exist and relevant political authority for policy proposals lie; but few examine dynamics between the two. Overall, the social movement literature concerning the contemporary period has focused primarily on movement organizations at the national level, paying little attention to local/national dynamics and to the ways poor and working people can directly participate in the professionally dominated advocacy world.[16]

For the most part, then, we are left with the dichotomy that organizing works locally and movements work nationally and an impoverished understanding of how the two connect. Before I present a more integrated perspective, however, I examine the contributions of local organizing and national movements in more detail. I believe it is particularly important to appreciate the vital role of local organizing in fostering the participation and leadership of people most impacted by injustice if national movements are to center their involvement, their voice, and their issues.

Local Community Organizing: Centering the Most Impacted by Injustice

If movements are to have the people most impacted by injustice at their center, then they must have deep local roots. People, especially poor and working-class people of color, are most likely to get involved in civic or political action in the communities in which they live their lives and raise their children. Direct, personal, and face-to-face connections help bring people into participation. Social media connections and communications can supplement these face-to-face relationships but do not replace them. Meanwhile, the actions of local institutions like public schools have an immediate and palpable impact on people's lives and are, in that regard, the first place to engage people in political action. Well-educated and affluent elites may be able to live a more national, cosmopolitan life, but people who are the most impacted by economic and racial injustice like the school-to-prison pipeline continue to live primarily local lives.[17]

Building the Participation and Leadership of Those Most Impacted

Community organizing groups excel at building the participation and leadership of those most impacted by injustice; that is their primary purpose. An extensive body of research, including my own, has documented the strategies and processes local organizing groups use to engage people in political action to challenge injustices and advocate for policy change. They do so by engaging people as members of communities, through their relationships with other community members like parents, students, neighborhood residents, or religious congregants of various faiths. Groups use social media to enhance these connections and get their message out to the larger constituency and a broader public, but the core connections are made face to face. In fact, many organizing groups have adopted a key mechanism, called the one-on-one, relational meeting, in which organizers and participants connect with each other around their experiences, stories, values, and interests as a foundation for collective action.[18]

Whether groups use a structured one-on-one format or not, storytelling is key to participation and relationship. Organizers help participants learn how to tell their story which involves their personal experience with injustice but also the guiding family and community traditions that shape their responses to injustice. Through sharing stories in group settings, people learn more deeply about each other and form the bonds to take sometimes bold and risky action together. When people connect with each other around the issues they face, they learn that their individual problems or experiences of poverty and racism are shared concerns, caused not by individual failures but rather by the systemic inequities of public institutions. As Marshall Ganz has argued, they begin to move from a story of "I" to a story of "We" and create the foundation for collective political action.[19]

Organizing groups connect this narrative process to political education, providing history, context, and analysis that can further deepen the understanding of systemic inequities that emerges through shared stories. The front lines of raising consciousness and political education occur in local contexts as organizers employ the kind of popular education practices developed by Paulo Freire in Brazil and people like Ella Baker and Bob Moses in the US civil rights movement. Popular education is participatory education where members are actively engaged in interrogating their personal and community experiences and reflecting upon their actions as they confront systems of injustice. As a result of sharing stories and political/popular education, participants create a collective narrative that includes the systemic causes of the inequities they face, the justice of their cause, and a vision for how to act to change systems.[20]

Organizing groups foster not just participation but leadership by people most impacted by injustice. In organizing settings, people grow and develop as leaders through action, participation, and reflection. In addition to helping people learn how to tell their story in public settings, organizers provide emerging leaders with the opportunity to learn the skills of organizing, like how to run a meeting, organize actions, speak to the media, and negotiate with public officials and policymakers. They learn how to conduct participatory research and develop policies that meet their needs, and they conduct a power analysis that identifies key levers for change to achieve those policy goals. Most centrally, rather than promoting individualistic paradigms, organizing groups foster a type of leadership that is collective.[21]

Organizers also build organizations as venues through which to exert community power and sustain policy campaigns. Protests and marches bring causes to light, disrupt systems, and inspire people. They pressure public officials to act. But, on their own, protests rarely create policy change. Community organizing groups also do the patient work of building leaderfull organizations that can sustain campaigns over the lengthy process typically necessary to change policy. They protest but they also build relationships with elected officials and public administrators, as well as a larger set of allies, often combining both inside and outside strategies to win policy change and, over time, work toward transformative systemic change.[22]

Although they share the core similarities just described, there are some significant differences in community organizing traditions. The Alinsky tradition prioritizes institutional organizing, working in and through established community institutions, most typically religious congregations. Groups in this tradition often work to build broad-based, multiracial organizations. They feature intensive leadership development but can also mobilize large numbers through their institutions—with annual assemblies or accountability meetings with public officials involving sometimes thousands of participants. The Alinsky tradition makes a sharp distinction between people's personal and political life, emphasizing that organizing is an activity that occurs in the public sphere. It has sometimes been criticized as not involving the poorest or most impacted people directly in its organizing efforts and, at least until recently, not developing a systemic analysis of racial oppression to guide its work.[23]

The organizing tradition that emerged most directly from the African American civil rights movement, as well as the Chicano/a liberation movements of the sixties and seventies, has led with a racial justice framework. Some elements of this movement continue to work in and through Black churches. Many—like most of the groups in the school-to-prison pipeline movement—are more "grassroots," often led by women, and work directly with people who are the most impacted in their communities. They typically reference the tradition of Ella Baker's organizing in the civil rights movement as the foundation of their work. Like Baker, they focus on supporting everyday people to build the power to address the issues facing them in their own lives. This approach often combines personal support and community care with organizing, seeing the personal as political. It's an approach pioneered by women, especially Black women, who historically have supported families to survive injustice while resisting it.[24]

In sum, community organizing involves patient, base-building work, cultivating knowledgeable and skilled leaders connected to broader constituent networks. These leaderful organizations build the power to sustain organizing campaigns over the long run necessary to change policy and transform institutions; they also develop the capacity of communities to have a meaningful say in their future beyond any one issue campaign. Through the mentoring, personal support, and organizing training they receive, and through their participation in collective action, participants in organizing efforts often go through a transformational experience. They are no longer simply victims of injustice, or members of networks and communities where people help each other cope and survive, as important as that is. They become active change agents in their lives and the lives of their community, working to challenge systems of injustice.[25]

The Limits of Localism

Despite the foundation that local organizing brings, however, it is not enough to challenge widespread systems of racial injustice like the school-to-prison pipeline. As we saw in the last chapter, the school-to-prison pipeline spread across the country as a national phenomenon. Federal policy encouraged criminalization while the hysteria around super-predators engaged deep-seated, nationwide racist myths and drove exclusionary discipline and increased policing connected to related policies of mass incarceration. The school-to-prison pipeline was implemented locally, enshrined in school districts' disciplinary codes and policing policies. But local educators and policymakers were connected to national networks in the education field and influenced by national discourses, policy trends, and federal influence.

It is a truism to say that public education is a local affair in the United States. But the limits of localism are increasingly apparent in education policy because of two, related developments. First, the federal role in education policy has increased in importance, beginning with the passage of the Elementary and Secondary Education Act in 1965 and further strengthened through the No Child Left Behind Act in 2001. While states have the ultimate constitutional authority over public education, and state and local funding continue to comprise roughly 90% of public funding, the federal role has nevertheless expanded both in terms of the influence of its funding and its attempts to shape local policy like in test-based accountability.[26]

Second, and perhaps even more importantly, local education policymakers increasingly respond to national level discourses and actors, including policy networks and organized interest groups. The most important education trends in the United States have been national ones, like the growth of the school-to-prison pipeline. Reform trends often have powerful private foundations and national networks behind them. These reform initiatives include charter schools, high-stakes testing, private school vouchers, and mayoral control of local districts. When groups want to change local policy, they must contend with national forces as they play out in their districts.[27]

Meanwhile, many if not most of the organizing groups fighting injustice in education and other fields are small, under-resourced, and facing entrenched systems and local actors supported by powerful national networks. One survey of organizing groups working on education found that their average annual budget was less than $250,000 and each group had only one or two organizers on staff. Groups face limits in the amount of funds they can raise, relying mostly on private foundations, only a few of whom typically fund racial justice and grassroots organizing work. Consequently, while grounding their organizing locally, groups also need the support of national movements to strengthen their efforts and expand their power, as we will see in later chapters of this book.[28]

Critics of the localism of community organizing usually stress the need for advocacy at the federal level. While important, I am making a different argument: local community groups need to connect with each other and gain resources from a national movement to build the power to win at local and state levels, as well as to contend federally.[29]

In sum, an effective movement for racial equity and social justice in education as well as other policy domains needs to be grounded in strong local organizing so that it can change policies district by district or city by city. At the same time, these organizing efforts are unlikely to win in one district alone. Rather, victories in one district can serve to inspire and inform change efforts in other districts, while waging the battle of ideas nationally and at the federal level.

National Movements

National social movements make their own essential contributions to challenging deep-seated systems of racial and social injustice. First, national action is necessary to affect federal policy or influence the operations of the federal government. Moreover, when people of color face intransigent white resistance in their localities, they can appeal to the federal government or the courts if laws are violated, but they need some influence and expertise at that level to be successful.[30]

Secondly, national social movements change attitudes, challenging dominant narratives and bringing new issues of injustice to light. These cultural impacts address the ideas, values, and assumptions that undergird policies and practices. By exposing the injustice of "taken for granted" practices, movements can change public discourse in ways that support social or racial justice agendas at local, state, and federal levels.[31]

Finally, national movements give people a sense of a larger identity and inspire people to act. Even when people build a shared identity through face-to-face relationships with other community participants in organizing efforts, they may feel isolated in their locality. Feeling part of a national movement emboldens action, especially when those acts can put people at risk for state or vigilante violence and retaliation from powerful institutions and conservative communities.[32]

The Domination of Professional Advocates

National movements accomplish these tasks by incorporating larger alliances that include professional and legal advocates who specialize in lobbying, fundraising, communications work, legal strategies, and research and policy advocacy. These actors bring critical resources to social justice movements. Through combining these resources, coalitions can more effectively lobby Congress and influence the actions of federal officials; they can influence the media and shape public opinion; and they can influence other elites who drive policy in various domains including education.[33]

National alliances, however, can easily become dominated by professional advocates located in Washington. The voices of people most impacted by injustice and their direct participation are seldom present in the national world of professional advocacy politics. These advocates have technical expertise, professional status, financial resources, and personal connections to other policy elites that give them an advantage for national-level operation. They inhabit the same cultural milieu and share similar values as foundation officers and public officials. In this way, many national alliances become focused almost solely on national- or federal-level action and seldom prioritize the strengthening of local organizing. Yet, as we have seen, the participation of those most impacted cannot be built directly at the national level but requires patient and deep local organizing as a foundation to leverage national participation.[34]

To the extent that national alliances remain dominated by professional elites and focused on Washington, they are not directly accountable to communities that are the most impacted by injustice. Without the direct participation of poor and working-class people of color, the issues these organizations address may not necessarily prioritize their concerns. Walter Nicholls, for example, shows how professionalized mainstream immigrant rights groups used their better access to political, economic, and cultural resources to dominate the immigrant rights movement that had begun to emerge in local areas; they took moderate, compromising positions while the more grassroots-oriented local groups connected to working-class immigrants pushed for more radical policy change that addressed their immediate interests.[35]

Meanwhile as we will learn, it was low-income African American parents and young people in places like the Mississippi Delta that first raised the alarm about the school-to-prison pipeline. The Washington-based civil rights organizations were simply not addressing the issue at the time. Michelle Alexander has noted a similar phenomenon—that nationally based, mainstream civil rights organizations were slow to address mass incarceration, focused more on traditional issues like affirmative action, even as criminalization was devastating low-income Black communities on the ground.[36]

While the impacts of national movements described earlier can *indirectly* serve to support local organizing efforts, organizations and alliances that are dominated by elites focused on Washington, however, typically do not *directly* try to support local organizing. One of the perennial critiques of the NAACP, for example, is that the nation's premier civil rights organization lacks a strategy to build the kind of mass base necessary to challenge systemic injustice. In other words, national movements remain limited in their impact without strong local foundations, yet they seldom focus on building this kind of base.[37]

Social Media and New Movements

Recent movements that rely extensively on social media, like #BlackLivesMatter, have created new models of movement building. Some have called the types of uprisings these movements create the "whirlwind," as they can appear quickly with great force. These movements incorporate local participation in protests and rallies by ordinary people. They raise awareness, impact national consciousness, and inspire people to take action. They have challenged narratives that undergird injustice. In the case of Black Lives Matter, the movement is "unapologetically Black," targeting anti-Black racism, promoting Blackness, and pushing these issues into national consciousness. The mass protests against police violence and racism in 2020 further spurred this movement. It has shifted the racist narrative from seeing Black men as dangerous criminals to seeing them as victims of racially inspired police and vigilante violence. Leaders of these new mass protests take an intersectional approach which prioritizes the inclusion of people often left at the margins of more traditional movements, like Black women and queer women of color. These are historic movement contributions of great import.[38]

At the same time, these movements tend to be heavily decentralized and not particularly focused on building organizations. Although people most impacted by injustice participate in protests, the movements do not systematically develop these participants into leaders in intentional and strategic ways. The Movement for Black Lives has adopted a multifaceted policy platform, but its structure has not been particularly effective in achieving its radical policy objectives. In the end, as important as they are, these whirlwind movements struggle to create vehicles that engage poor and working-class people of color in the sustained advocacy necessary to effect policy change and transform fundamentally inequitable institutions.[39]

From this point of view, the analysis I present here bears some relationship to classic debates about movements versus organization. These debates conceptualize movements as "outside politics" that prioritize protest, while organizations pursue the "inside" politics of policymaking. Yet the reality is that successful social movement organizing efforts at local and national levels typically combine elements of both inside and outside politics. Both strategies have roles to play, depending on the goals of the movement, the stage of movement building, the level of resistance versus cooperation by elites, and a variety of other factors. My focus, however, is on national versus local dynamics, whatever combination of inside and outside strategies they use.[40]

Reconceptualizing National Movements:
"Nationalizing Local Struggles"

Building an effective movement, then, requires a new model that combines
local organizing with national alliances. For national alliances to prioritize
the voices and participation of low-income people of color and support rather
than cannibalize local organizing, community groups will have to find ways
to offset the greater power and control which professional advocacy organizations, funders, and researchers may have due to greater resources, technical expertise, legitimacy, and connections to policy elites. In other words,
we need new models for national movements that support, strengthen, and
spread local organizing and those new models are more likely to emerge
when people most impacted and the local organizing groups connected to
them have a larger share of power in them.

In the following chapters of this book, we will learn how community
organizers in the movement to end the school-to-prison pipeline and their
advocacy allies built this kind of new model. It took a struggle to create organizational forms that centered people most impacted and supported their
participation at national levels. These alliance structures and processes
served to support local organizing, even as local groups made a commitment to support national action. Nationally, the movement shifted the narrative away from zero tolerance and won new guidelines from the federal
government warning local districts against the school-to-prison pipeline. At
the same time, the movement provided a range of concrete supports and resources so that organizing groups could win significant policy victories at
local levels, even when they were small, under-resourced, and facing stiff opposition. The movement "nationalized" these local struggles so that groups
could learn from and inspire each other. It created a rolling series of victories
across the country with each one surpassing the previous in shifting policies
away from zero tolerance.

I learned the term "nationalizing local struggles" from Jitu Brown, an
African American community organizer from the Kenwood Oakland
Community Organization who led a hunger strike against the closing of
Dyett High School in the historically Black Southside of Chicago. Brown
became a key founder and national director of the Journey for Justice (J4J)
Alliance, composed of Black- and Brown-led community organizations
fighting against the large-scale closure of public schools in Black and Brown
communities. Brown said the J4J Alliance "nationalized" the Dyett struggle,

lifting up its victory and spreading its lessons across the country, inspiring groups to fight school closures in their localities. The J4J Alliance leveraged power at the national level as well. It worked to change the narrative about school closures, raising it as a profound issue of racial justice, and it sought to influence federal policy. More fundamentally, though, the alliance served to support and connect local struggles, highlighting victories and sharing lessons.[41]

I adopted the term "nationalizing local struggles" because I believe it best captures an alternative way to understand social movements. It suggests that national movements, while having important national-level components, are particularly effective when the local struggles of people most impacted by injustice are lifted up and spread. National movements take their energy from local struggles and can directly work to support, strengthen, expand, and spread them.[42]

In the dominant model of social movements as it currently exists in the literature, Washington-based professional actors and groups provide the resources to bring local groups together who then support a federal agenda dominated by those professionalized groups. Drawing from the school-to-prison pipeline movement, I am proposing a more complicated model. Local groups connect to each other as well as to national actors who co-create national infrastructure (e.g., coalitions) and share power in them; local victories are nationalized and spread through the movement; the national infrastructure targets Washington when possible, but mainly works to support local struggles.

The focus of scholars on the dominant model blinds us to a vibrant local organizing world that has the potential to create a different kind of national movement—a federated type movement that focuses mostly locally. This model represents a new kind of federated movement structure and process— not the chapter model of federations of an earlier era, but a complex network of independent local groups, professional advocacy organizations, national alliances, and the people that move across the field.

In what follows, we will see how organizers in the school-to-prison pipeline movement built this new kind of movement, the struggles it took to center local organizing, and the processes and procedures created to sustain it. I document how the early organizing efforts of African American parents in the rural Mississippi Delta were lifted up and helped create the beginnings of a national movement. I then trace local campaigns of Black and Brown parents and young people through Los Angeles, Denver, and Chicago, showing how local breakthroughs were "nationalized" and spread. National actors and alliances helped do the "nationalizing," and some important federal action was taken; so, the movement emerged as a complex interplay between local and national levels. But, as I learned from another African American organizer, Joyce Parker from Greenville, Mississippi, "There is no national without the local." In other words, local organizing created the foundation of the movement, engaging people most impacted by the school-to-prison pipeline and lifting their voices.

3

"There Is No National without the Local"

Building a National Movement Grounded in Local Organizing

In this chapter, I trace the rise of the national movement to end the school-to-prison pipeline from its origins in Black and Brown communities where parents and young people were the most impacted and the first to speak out.[1] Local organizing, led by parents and students of color, drove the movement as they won victories to change school discipline policies. This work set the stage for national formations that played important roles from the early days, helping to publicize and spread local victories, connect local groups, provide resources, and challenge support for zero tolerance in Washington and in the public eye. I document the struggle in the national movement to ensure that organizing groups rather than professional advocates took the lead in emerging coalitions like the Dignity in Schools Campaign. Through intentional efforts, organizers and leaders built a new model for a national movement led primarily by locally based grassroots organizers and accountable to the communities most impacted by racial injustice in education. As a result of grassroots leadership in alliance with researchers, civil rights advocates, and private philanthropy, the movement made powerful gains. It shifted educator and public support away from zero tolerance, pushed the federal government to issue new guidance that told states and districts they were violating civil rights law by engaging in racially discriminatory discipline practices, and won a rolling series of victories changing school discipline policy across the country.

Origins of the Movement in Mississippi and Other Local Communities

When Ellen Reddy and her sister Helen Johnson were organizing in the African American community of Holmes County, Mississippi, in the late

Willful Defiance. Mark R. Warren, Oxford University Press. © Mark R. Warren 2022.
DOI: 10.1093/oso/9780197611500.003.0004

1990s, they noticed teenagers and some younger children out on the streets during school time. There seemed to be more and more children every day. Finally, they approached a group of young people and, according to Reddy:

> We started to have conversations, asking "Why aren't you in school?" And they would say things like, "I got to class late," or "I got into a fight on the playground," or "I didn't hand something in." Some said they talked back to teachers and ended up in youth court where judges sent them to juvenile detention centers called "training schools."

Reddy and Johnson's group, Citizens for Quality Education, was part of a network of community organizing groups in Black communities across the Mississippi Delta called the Mississippi Education Working Group (MEWG) at the time. Organizers in the MEWG began to hear more and more stories of African American children receiving suspensions for minor behavioral offenses who often ended up in youth court. In one case in Montgomery County, students were playing around on a school bus throwing peanuts at each other, and a peanut hit the back of the white bus driver. The driver drove the bus straight to the police station where five African American boys were arrested and charged with felony assault. As a result of community pressure, the charges were eventually dropped, but the students lost their bus privileges and had to drop out of school because they had no way to make the thirty-mile journey from home. As community complaints grew in response to cases like this, the Black-led groups in the MEWG, working with the training and technical assistance provider Southern Echo, launched a campaign for the Prevention of Schoolhouse to Jailhouse, an early term for the school-to-prison pipeline.[2]

Meanwhile, Black and Brown parents and students were starting to tell similar kinds of stories to community organizers across the country. African American and Latinx parents in South Los Angeles met in living rooms to talk about their experiences with their children's schools. Working with these parents, Maisie Chin and Rosalinda Hill co-founded Community Asset Development Redefining Education (CADRE) to address harsh and racist treatment of students and their parents on school discipline issues. Meanwhile, Black and Brown students in Chicago spoke out against zero tolerance in the Southwest Youth Collaborative. Latinx families in the organizing group Padres & Jóvenes Unidos (Parents & Youth United) in Denver complained that their children were missing too much school because of suspensions for minor behavioral issues. They fell behind, often ended up leaving school, and were left out on the streets.[3]

In other words, the movement to dismantle the school-to-prison pipeline started in the late 1990s in African American and Latinx communities, where parents and young people were the first to raise the alarm. At the time, zero tolerance toward any form of student misbehavior dominated the educational system and public consciousness, as mass incarceration grew. Few were listening to these stories.

First National Gathering and Connections across Local Campaigns

On September 17, 1999, a fight broke out among students at a high school football game in Decatur, Illinois. Although the fight lasted only a few minutes, and no one was seriously hurt, seven African American boys were arrested, with four eventually charged with mob action, a felony. All seven were expelled from school for two years. The Reverend Jesse Jackson brought the incident to national attention, as his Rainbow PUSH organization led protests against the expulsions and the racist targeting of Black students with severe criminal charges.[4]

In response, the Civil Rights Project at Harvard University and a new legal advocacy organization focused on racial justice called the Advancement Project hosted the first national summit on zero tolerance in school discipline in June of 2000 in Washington, DC. In preparation for the summit, Judith Browne Dianis, co-director of the Advancement Project National Office at the time, visited local sites to investigate school discipline. In fact, she had first heard about the issue when supporting Southern Echo and its local allies in a school desegregation campaign in Tunica, Mississippi. According to Dianis, the issue of zero tolerance was new to the national civil rights community. "At the time, nobody even knew what zero tolerance was. We were like, what is this thing? What are you even talking about?"

Dianis went to Jefferson County in Florida where she found that 42% of Black students had been suspended at least once. She went back to visit Southern Echo in Mississippi where she learned about a number of cases, including one where five African American girls were suspended for five days for fighting, even though they were best friends and made up later in the day. The girls also had to appear in Youth Court where they were fined between

$150 and $200 each, given forty to eighty hours of community service, and placed on curfew for six months and probation for a year. The girls had no prior record of behavioral problems. Dianis reported at the summit that, even though data were not systematically available, it was estimated that in 1998, 3.1 million children were suspended from schools and 81,000 expelled. Twenty-five percent of all African American children were suspended over a four-year period.[5]

The national summit brought together civil rights advocates like Dianis, researchers including Dan Losen from the Civil Rights Project and Russell Skiba from Indiana University who had just begun to study the extent and harm of zero tolerance, and local organizers working with Southern Echo, Padres & Jóvenes Unidos (PJU) and other groups across the country. The summit served to bring the first national attention to the harsh and racially discriminatory effects of zero-tolerance school discipline and its connections to the juvenile and criminal justice systems. But it also served important movement building purposes. It connected various groups and actors who had been starting to address zero tolerance in isolation and helped them see that this was a national problem. This broader perspective strengthened the analysis behind local organizing. According to PJU co-director Pam Martinez:

At this conference we learned that school pushout was happening all across the country and was part of a larger systemic form of oppression for Black and Brown youth that included over policing and the criminalization of youth of color. That was groundbreaking for us and the analysis we developed subsequently about what we called the school-to-jail track would shape our organizing for years to come.

The Advancement Project proceeded to partner with PJU as well as with other groups whom Dianis met for the first time at the summit, including the Southwest Youth Collaborative from Chicago. The Advancement Project formed to practice a different kind of civil rights legal advocacy. The organization wanted to use its expertise in law, research, and communications to support the work of local organizing, while also highlighting these local struggles as a way to engage public discourse and policy at the national level. The Advancement Project began helping parents and student leaders to collect data and information on school discipline and policing practices in schools in Denver to support PJU's efforts to change district policy. Around that time, the Advancement Project launched its Ending the Schoolhouse-to-Jailhouse Track Project with partners in Denver; Chicago; and Palm Beach County, Florida.

Meanwhile, Southern Echo spearheaded the formation of the Mississippi Coalition for the Prevention of Schoolhouse to Jailhouse in 2003, which included the Advancement Project and local organizing groups across the Delta. The coalition succeeded in closing a notorious juvenile detention facility that was abusing children and got the state legislature to pass groundbreaking juvenile justice reform measures in 2004 and 2005.

In 2005, the Advancement Project and its community partners issued *Education on Lockdown*, which systematically documented and analyzed school discipline and policing practices district-wide in those cities. The report showed that zero tolerance was still on the rise. In Denver, for example, the number of out of school suspensions rose from 9,846 in the 2000–2001 school year to 13,423 in 2003–2004, mostly for minor behavioral issues. Referrals to law enforcement, typically for non-serious and non-criminal issues, rose 71% between 2000 and 2004, to a total of 1,401 referrals. Racial disparities remained striking: students of color were 70% more likely to be suspended, expelled, or ticketed than their white peers. According to Jim Freeman who worked on the report for the Advancement Project, this report was one of the very first to bring national attention to the school-to-prison pipeline.[6]

During this period, local groups like PJU began searching for ways to change school discipline policy and practice to combat the school-to-prison pipeline. In addition to PJU's Campaign to End the School to Jail Track, grassroots youth organizations in California formed a Schools Not Jails campaign and students in Chicago's Southwest Youth Collaborative advocated for changes in the school district's discipline policy, among other nascent organizing efforts.[7]

Cracks were beginning to form in the public consensus in favor of zero tolerance as the media began to report on egregious cases of school discipline abuse. In one notorious case that received national media attention, Jaisha Scott, an African American kindergarten girl, was arrested and taken from her school in handcuffs by three police officers in St. Petersburg, Florida, because she had thrown a temper tantrum. According to Dianis, Jaisha did not want to stop playing a jellybean counting game. Police officers "took her out to a police cruiser where they sat her in the back of that car for hours crying for her mommy, shackled." Meanwhile, prominent scholars like Pedro

Noguera began to speak out against the school-to-prison pipeline, adding to the efforts of researchers like Losen and Skiba to highlight the problem.[8]

In these early days, equity-oriented lawyers began to support local families and communities in the South, often filing cases on behalf of Black students with disabilities who faced extreme discipline practices or were otherwise denied educational services. The legal basis to challenge exclusionary discipline based on racial discrimination was unclear, but lawyers like Courtney Bowie with the Southern Poverty Law Center (SPLC) and others found an avenue through the Individuals with Disabilities Education Act which prohibited the denial of equal education opportunities to students with disabilities. Organizing groups like those in Holmes County and others in the Mississippi Coalition continually highlighted the intersection of race and disability, as Black students with disabilities faced exclusionary discipline and court referrals in disproportionate numbers and often experienced outright abusive treatment. In 2003 the SPLC partnered with groups in the Mississippi Coalition to force the renegotiation of the Mattie T. consent decree for the state's failure to provide adequate and appropriate services. These early legal cases helped lay the basis for later policy change through organizing efforts.[9]

Even as the foundations of the movement emerged in the early 2000s, zero tolerance remained the law of the land in school districts across the country. Educational administrators stayed committed to harsh discipline as did the national teachers unions and law enforcement organizations. Most Americans had never heard the term school-to-prison pipeline. Despite the important wins in Mississippi concerning juvenile justice reform, organizing and advocacy groups had yet to claim a victory in directly challenging zero-tolerance school discipline policies.

South Los Angeles Parents and a Human Rights Framework

When community organizer Maisie Chin and parent activist Rosalinda Hill started meeting with parents in Hill's living room on Friday nights in 1999, the African American and Latinx parents shared stories of their experiences with the schools their children attended in South Los Angeles. Story after story recounted the disconnection and disrespect they felt they received from schools. One of the early CADRE parents, Roslyn Broadnax, recounted this story:

> A teacher took my youngest son and his fourth-grade classroom to the beach for a field trip and was recorded talking to a friend on the phone. He was a Caucasian teacher and was telling them that "Yeah, I had to take them to the beach because these little N's smell. And this is the only way I think they going to get a bath."

The young son of the group's co-founder Rosalinda Hill was locked in a closet as a form of punishment. CADRE emerged out of the pain of these stories with a commitment to build a powerful movement of parents of color to address racist mistreatment of families by schools.

CADRE began systematically canvassing households in South LA, speaking to more than 4,000 parents and caregivers from 2001 to 2004. Working with a California-based advocacy group called Justice Matters, CADRE parents launched a participatory action research project where they surveyed 120 parents. These canvassing conversations and surveys documented parents' systematic mistreatment, revealing that mistreatment happened most often when the school was disciplining a child.[10]

About that time, Chin discovered a report produced by Liz Sullivan-Yuknis, who would soon co-found Partners for Dignity & Rights (P4DR), which at the time was called the National Economic and Social Rights Initiative (NESRI) with Cathy Albisa and Sharda Sekaran. The report described a human rights approach to organizing, highlighting the rights of families and communities to participate in decision-making in New York City schools. The approach resonated with the values and orientation Chin was developing with parents in CADRE and she invited Sullivan-Yuknis to LA. Sullivan-Yuknis introduced the human rights framework to CADRE and parents decided to focus on three core principles of the human rights approach: the right to dignity, the right to education, and the right to participation.[11]

Using this new framework, CADRE parents proceeded to conduct another participatory research project to document human rights violations around school discipline and held a People's Hearing in June 2006 to present their findings. In these early days, it was not popular to highlight racism and target the school-to-prison pipeline. CADRE had trouble raising funds, while more highly resourced organizing groups often focused on increasing college access among students of color. According to Chin, CADRE focused on the "black hole" of the children and their families at the bottom being sucked out of education into the juvenile and criminal justice system.[12]

Around the same time, a group of school administrators within LA Unified School District began to propose that the district adopt Schoolwide Positive Behavioral Supports (SWPBS), an approach that seeks to get at the root causes of student misbehavior and provide supports to address them, rather than suspend or expel students. CADRE decided to back the initiative because it promised to change LA schools' culture and practice of harsh discipline, and it provided family and community members with important roles in the process, including monitoring progress.[13]

CADRE became the grassroots force to push the LA Unified Board of Education to adopt SWPBS. CADRE parents came to board of education meetings and told their personal stories of harsh school discipline and its devastating consequences. They also presented the results of their participatory research surveys and cited statistics to demonstrate that Black and Latinx students were suspended and expelled at much higher rates than white students. The research and data told the big picture, while the personal stories put a human face on the data and created an urgency for the board to act. Chin says that CADRE parents were "dogged and persistent"; they attended meeting after meeting, demonstrating their determination to win meaningful change in their schools.

CADRE asked a range of legal and advocacy groups to send letters of support and received favorable media coverage. Bowing to the combination of sustained pressure from CADRE, the internal lobby among school staff, and the pressure of a special education investigation by the federal government, the board voted to adopt SWPBS system-wide in March of 2007. It was a shot heard across the country. For the first time, a grassroots organizing group led by a tenacious group of Black and Brown parents targeting racism had won a major policy change to reduce exclusionary school discipline not just in one or two schools, but district-wide in the second largest school system in the country. P4DR and CADRE worked to share this groundbreaking, parent-led victory against the school-to-prison pipeline across the country, inspiring local organizing groups to redouble their efforts. According to Chin, "all of a sudden, we were famous."

Origins of the Dignity in Schools Campaign

In addition to CADRE, Sullivan-Yuknis had been working with several organizing and advocacy groups across the country, including in New York City where P4DR was located. As they met with parents and young people, Sullivan-Yuknis says that "consistently throughout those interviews people talked about not just school discipline but more broadly the environment in schools and the way people felt treated." The demand for dignity, long an important part of the human rights framework, seemed to capture the feelings of young people and parents of color in New York, as it had in South LA.

Sullivan-Yuknis and P4DR launched an ambitious participatory research project with a range of groups in LA and New York City, leading to the 2007 report called *Deprived of Dignity*. Meanwhile, she worked closely with CADRE to develop an extensive training manual to help grassroots groups use a human rights approach to addressing school discipline and family and community participation in schools.[14]

P4DR was also a member of the Student Safety Coalition in New York City, addressing exclusionary discipline and police arrests and tickets in schools. The coalition launched a campaign to get the city council to pass a Student Safety Act to create data transparency around school discipline and policing as a first step, which it eventually won. The New York Civil Liberties Union coordinated the coalition that included organizing groups like Desis Rising Up & Moving and the Urban Youth Collaborative, as well as the educator group Teachers Unite and legal organizations like Advocates for Children.

P4DR was also part of the U.S. Human Rights Network where Sullivan-Yuknis initially met the groups in Mississippi and other local community groups. Sullivan-Yuknis came to work with Families and Friends of Louisiana's Incarcerated Children (FFLIC), for example, eventually producing a report with them to support their organizing campaigns against exclusionary discipline in New Orleans' growing network of charter schools. In other words, P4DR was emerging at the center of an informal and overlapping network of local organizing groups that were challenging the school-to-prison pipeline. By 2007 and in the wake of CADRE's victory, local groups that had been largely separated from each other increasingly began to connect.[15]

Meanwhile Rosa Hirji, a children rights attorney on CADRE's staff, chaired the Education Subcommittee of the Children's Rights Litigation Committee

of the American Bar Association (ABA) and was convening a national network of legal advocates concerned with exclusionary and racially disparate
school discipline. The Education Subcommittee had begun a Model School
Discipline Code Project in collaboration with the Chicago School Task
Force to develop a model code that rejected zero-tolerance discipline and
included positive and restorative alternatives. The Education Subcommittee
hosted a series of national teleconference calls for advocates, researchers,
and organizers to share their work around school discipline. Hirji, joined
by Sullivan-Yuknis from P4DR who became a co-convener of the network,
highlighted the CADRE victory and introduced the human rights framework as a tool for systems change.[16]

Through this collaboration, a broad network of organizations and individuals emerged and in 2006 adopted the name Dignity in Schools Campaign
(DSC), reflecting the human rights principle of dignity as central to their
vision for shifting school discipline away from punitive and criminalizing
policies toward positive and supportive approaches. The group launched a
website as a clearinghouse for research on the problem of "school pushout," a
term they chose to use rather than dropout to highlight the ways that school
policies and practices pushed students out of school. DSC also focused on
lifting up community driven solutions—like the SWPBS model supported
by CADRE in Los Angeles and the restorative justice practices advanced by
groups in Chicago, Denver, and other communities across the country.

DSC planned a conference for July of 2009 with the aim of bringing
together multiple stakeholder groups to develop and pass a National
Resolution for Ending School Pushout and review a draft of the model code
of conduct. Many of the grassroots groups who had been early organizers
against the school-to-prison pipeline participated, including CADRE; PJU;
groups in the Mississippi Coalition; FFLIC in Louisiana; Blocks Together
in Chicago; the Philadelphia Student Union; Gwinnett SToPP outside of
Atlanta; and Teachers Unite, DRUM, and Make the Road in New York City.
The conference was held at Northwestern University where Bernadine
Dohrn ran a children's rights clinic that had developed early work to combat
the school-to-prison pipeline. Local and national organizations including
the ABA Children's Rights Litigation Committee, the ACLU, Advancement
Project, CADRE, P4DR, Southern Poverty Law Center, NAACP Legal
Defense and Education Fund (LDF), National Education Association, Public
Counsel, and others contributed the funding for this first meeting, where the
Advancement Project's Judith Browne Dianis delivered a keynote address.

The spirit of deep engagement with families and students, featured in the work of CADRE but also in other organizing groups, came to infuse DSC. According to Chin, "It was learned out of a grassroots community based, organic process of listening to stories on the ground, of dialog and participation, and of putting the most affected at the center." In fact, community groups raised criticisms at the conference that the space was not friendly enough to parents and young people.

In December of 2009, following a decision made at the conference, DSC held its first Day of Action to release the National Resolution for Ending School Pushout. The event began to set a pattern for the coalition to support local organizing. According to Sullivan-Yuknis, "The Day of Action focused on using a national platform to lift up the local campaigns that folks were already doing around discipline and pushout."

Despite the attention to supporting local parent and youth organizing, DSC nevertheless seemed to be structured in the more typical national coalition manner, where community groups were involved but decision-making rested in the hands of professional advocates. According to Sullivan-Yuknis, "The core group at the time was still made up of lawyers. It was me and a bunch of lawyers." Things were about to change, but it would take a little while and intentional effort.

A Breakthrough in Denver

During the time that DSC was forming, PJU in Denver with support from its national ally Advancement Project was preparing the second major local win that would push the movement forward. Pam Martinez and PJU had taken their newfound analysis and connections from that very first 2000 conference on zero tolerance to Cole Middle School where parents had reported their children missing a large amount of learning time because of suspensions for minor infractions. Through organizing Black and Brown parents and students, PJU was able to change the discipline policy at the Denver school. The new policy put clear limits on the use of out-of-school suspensions, expulsions, and arrests, reducing them significantly in the first year of implementation.

Building on the momentum from its victory at Cole, PJU started an ambitious reform effort at North High School, a historic high school for the Latinx community. With its 58% "dropout" rate, however, the school became a potent symbol of the failure of the school system to educate Latinx youth. While organizing at North and elsewhere, PJU continued to hear stories of school pushout through suspensions and expulsions. They also learned that Denver schools had experienced a large increase in the presence of police and security guards and the placement of metal detectors and surveillance cameras in schools. Many students started saying they felt security guards made their schools feel like prisons with one student saying, "Security guards act like prison guards." Like CADRE in South LA, PJU was forthright in naming racism and focusing on racial inequities in discipline and school pushout more broadly.[17]

PJU decided to launch a bold initiative to reform discipline policy across the entire district. The Advancement Project helped PJU conduct a participatory action research project where young people surveyed and interviewed fellow students and observed juvenile court and school board proceedings. It also trained PJU leaders in how to analyze school district data, helping them file Freedom of Information requests, and then translating their research into reports and materials that other parents and students could understand and use to pressure the district for change.

An opening occurred when Michael Bennett became the new superintendent of Denver Public Schools in 2005. Bennett was willing to set up a multi-stakeholder committee including PJU representatives to rewrite the discipline policy. PJU demanded that the Advancement Project be present to provide legal advice on its behalf and Jim Freeman from the project ended up being the one to write the new code, which moved decisively away from zero tolerance.

Just hours before the school board voted on the draft in the spring of 2007, a legal challenge delayed the vote and opened the opportunity for opposition groups to seize the moment. The Denver Classroom Teachers Association (the local teachers union), for example, proposed a three strikes policy of harsh discipline, although it ultimately had to relent. Although proposals like this delayed the final vote, Denver finally passed a rewrite of its discipline policy in November of 2008, moving decisively away from zero tolerance. The new policy called for prioritizing alternatives to exclusionary discipline, establishing a pilot program to implement restorative justice programs at several schools, and explicitly called for reducing racial disparities in discipline. For the first time, a local organizing group led by youth and parents of color won the end to zero tolerance across an entire school district and the complete rewrite of its school discipline policy; and it did so by leading with an explicit racial analysis.

A Youth-Led Coalition Emerges: The Alliance for Educational Justice

PJU hit the road and traveled across the country to share its story of success with organizing and advocacy groups. Using its communications expertise, the Advancement Project helped PJU publicize its victory to a national audience. The victory spurred on nascent organizing efforts that were emerging across the country.

The role of the *jóvenes* in leading the effort was particularly inspiring to the growing number of young people who had begun to challenge the school-to-prison pipeline. Around the same time as PJU's victory, youth organizing groups from across the country met at a conference in New Orleans sponsored by the Gates Foundation. They discovered that many groups told very similar stories about their members' experiences with harsh discipline, heavy police presence, and school pushout.

Soon after this meeting, Barack Obama was elected president, and the youth groups thought it might be a propitious time to form an alliance to support local organizing and see if they could impact federal policy. According to Jonathan Stith who later became the director of the alliance, "The essential premise of the alliance was to try to influence federal policy in a way that would open up opportunities for what the organizing groups were doing locally." Nineteen groups founded the Alliance for Educational Justice (AEJ), including PJU from Denver as well as groups from Los Angeles, the Bay Area, Chicago, Philadelphia, New York City, Boston, and other localities.

AEJ began to work with groups in the DSC coalition to target Washington. DSC included base-building groups like those organizing in Mississippi, Los Angeles, and Denver, but also an array of civil rights advocacy groups with offices and experience in Washington. This network began to collaborate also with a small but growing band of researchers who had been studying racial disparities in school discipline. In 2006, the American Psychological Association had issued a report co-written by Russell Skiba critical of zero tolerance and calling for the creation of alternatives.[18]

Soon after the Obama administration took office, AEJ, DSC, and its allies prepared to try to influence reauthorization of the Elementary and

Secondary Education Act (known at the time as No Child Left Behind) to limit zero tolerance and promote alternatives like restorative justice and positive behavioral supports. They also were pushing for a Positive School Climate bill in Congress, an earlier version of which then-Senator Obama had sponsored. As the 2010 session unfolded, however, it became clear that reauthorization was not in the cards. By the end of 2010, the Republicans took control of Congress and any hopes of significantly influencing federal legislation were dashed.

Efforts to influence the Departments of Education and Justice, however, offered another opportunity. AEJ and DSC began to bring students and parents to Washington to speak directly to administration officials who proved open and interested. They were joined by researchers from the Harvard Civil Rights Project and others as well as civil rights advocates in the ACLU, LDF, and the Advancement Project, who had personal ties to many of the new officials and used these connections to open doors for parent and youth leaders to be heard. Many of these new officials had, in fact, come from the civil rights community and joined the Obama administration to advance this agenda. The combined efforts of grassroots leaders and allied advocates contributed to internal motion in the new administration. In 2011 the Department of Education (ED) expanded civil rights data collection to require all schools and districts to report suspensions and expulsions, disaggregated by race. This data would then prove to be a valuable resource for local- and state-level organizing campaigns to challenge discipline policy, as the high rates of suspensions and the racial disparities within them could now be demonstrated with hard numbers in virtually every school district in the country. Moreover, the ED's Office for Civil Rights began to investigate civil rights complaints in school discipline more aggressively using a disparate impact analysis framework, proving helpful to local organizing efforts that encouraged families to file complaints.

Funding the Movement: Atlantic Philanthropies

By 2010, a diverse movement was emerging that included a growing number of local organizing groups, national alliances like DSC and AEJ, Advancement Project, LDF, and other professional advocates based in Washington, and researchers like Skiba and Losen. In that year the Atlantic Philanthropies made a fateful decision to support this nascent movement as one of its final portfolios before sunsetting in 2016. Foundation officer Donna Lawrence, with the support of President Gara LaMarche and Vice President Marsha Smith, led the fund's decision to focus on changing zero-tolerance school discipline and Judith Browne Dianis helped convince the board to agree. Lawrence hired Tanya Coke in January 2010 to inform Atlantic's grantmaking strategy. Coke had previously led the U.S. Human Rights Fund that supported CADRE's work and P4DR's role in coordinating the first gathering of the DSC network in 2009. She was soon joined by Kavitha Mediratta, who had participated in the human rights report that Sullivan-Yuknis wrote on NYC schools. Mediratta had been the founding coordinator of the Urban Youth Collaborative's Safety with Dignity Campaign and her research on community organizing for school reform, including a time working out of P4DR's offices, had connected her to these struggles.

Mediratta and Coke wanted to work differently from the typical top-down approach of most foundations, seeking instead to partner with organizers and advocates. They sought to build a robust movement ecosystem that would help grassroots groups succeed in changing school discipline policy. They also understood that a decentralized national strategy would be required to shift disciplinary practices, given that they were set by local school districts. The strategy was designed to reframe public discourse on zero tolerance and center community organizing as a key driver of change, funding all the different pieces of the emerging movement and helping to bring the parts into better alignment.

Atlantic as well as Lori Bezahler from the Edward W. Hazen Foundation encouraged other private foundations to support movement organizing and helped launch the Just and Fair Schools Fund (later Communities for Just Schools Fund). The donor collaborative operated as a conduit for small grants to local organizing groups which the foundation saw as key to building demand and support for change at school district levels. It also funded AEJ, DSC, and the Advancement Project to amplify local organizing through national gatherings and create national level resources for the local groups to use, and it offered travel funds to bring the voices of those most affected to policymakers in Washington.[19]

The Atlantic Philanthropies also supported LDF to set up a legal strategies collaborative led by Damon Hewitt to coordinate civil rights litigation and link it to community groups. It funded a Discipline Disparities Research-to-Practice Collaboration led by Skiba and Losen to produce rigorous research to use in organizing campaigns and influence policymakers. Community organizers sat at the table with researchers to provide input on the data that would be helpful to campaigns.[20]

Grassroots organizing provided the impetus for change from the outside, but Atlantic also saw the need to build will and capacity for change in practice on the inside and create and publicize alternative models for positive and restorative approaches. Since there were about 14,000 school districts to influence, Mediratta says Atlantic settled on a strategy to create a critical mass for change through a bottom-up, top-down, and inside-outside strategy.

> The plan was to build pressure in local school districts through grassroots organizing and advocacy in a good number of places and to compliment that local pressure with direct engagement of federal leaders as well as by supporting coalitions of local players to come to Washington to put their own pressure on federal players. We hoped that if we could get the feds to focus on this issue, they would use inside channels to move districts in the direction we wanted.

Between 2010 and 2014, the Atlantic Philanthropies spent $47 million supporting all facets of the movement to end the school-to-prison pipeline. These resources were expanded as the foundation reached out and partnered with a growing number of other private funders to provide resources to the Communities for Just Schools Fund and other sectors of the movement. The strategic infusion of what amounted to unprecedented funding around an organizing and advocacy strategy proved crucial in taking the nascent movement to a new level.[21]

Organizing Groups Takeover Leadership in DSC

Atlantic Philanthropies reached out to DSC in early 2010 with an offer for significant funding—$300,000 per year with additional funds for an ally that would lead the federal work. The new group had just held its first national conference in 2009 and was undergoing a restructuring whose necessity became even clearer with the prospect of substantial funding on the table. After the 2009 conference, several of the organizers who led base-building groups working with parents and young people joined the coalition's core group, which up to that time had been composed primarily of lawyers and professional advocates. These organizers included Maisie Chin of CADRE,

Joyce Parker from the Mississippi Delta Catalyst Roundtable, and Monami Maulik from Desis Rising Up and Moving in New York. If DSC was going to be true to its human rights mission to dismantle the school-to-prison pipeline, these organizers believed it needed to be led by groups immersed in the lives of those most affected, who after all had been the first ones to speak out. According to Chin, "One of the main principles of human rights is that those who are most impacted should lead the work."

> This whole issue being lifted up at this scale came from parents and students taking the risk to tell their story. Period. No ifs, ands or buts. The strength of the work is all the stories on the ground, the actual families to which all this was happening.

The organizers pushed for transparency in all decisions and for processes that respected the ways that organizing groups operated compared to advocacy groups. For example, organizers could not make decisions on their own and often wanted to consult their group's members first, which took time. Meanwhile, Kim McGill from the Youth Justice Coalition in LA pushed the principle that DSC should deliver one-third of all funds that it receives to base-building groups in membership. The crux of the struggle, however, fell on the composition of the leadership body, that is, who ultimately would control the coalition's decision-making. The organizers highly valued having policy advocates in DSC but not as the key decision-makers. Chin, Parker, Maulik, and other organizers argued that representatives from the base-building groups should constitute the majority of the coordinating committee. According to Chin, "That led to a lot of challenging moments, as you can imagine, dealing with power and privilege inside the space."

> Those early days were not pleasant because we had to challenge a lot of advocates. Our righteousness at the time and our convictions had to do with the fact that we were accountable to our bases and we didn't feel like we could allow the coalition to be co-opted by people who had no skin in the game.

According to Maulik, a new structure was necessary to address the forces that normally lead to domination by elite advocates "with more resources, money, time or professional backgrounds and expertise, you know, the ability to be on conference calls and fly to DC," and compensate for the "lack of access to certain resources or knowledge or time that working-class people who are most affected have." According to Maulik:

> Joyce Parker would say that organizing is about the process. It's not just the end goal of the policy. There's always this tension about holding up the policy work and the outcomes with the process. The way I see it, process and outcomes are not different things. The outcome policy you're gonna get, how effective or relevant it is for people that you're working for, is not gonna happen if those people aren't a part of that process.

At retreats throughout 2010, the DSC core group struggled over a draft membership and decision-making policy that would reflect these values. It was a challenging time for many of the advocates who had devoted themselves to fighting zero tolerance and were used to a certain way of doing business. According to Matt Cregor, a key member of the original group of lawyers, accountability to those most impacted "was a value that we all recognized." When he joined LDF to work with Damon Hewitt, together they brought an emphasis on accountability to those most impacted. The move to greater accountability in the membership policy was challenging but, according to Cregor, "essential for Dignity in Schools to become the type of robust, primarily base-building coalition that it was trying to become." The new membership policy proposed a shift in the structure of the core group from individual members representing themselves to organizational members that would be accountable to their organizations and their base. Individuals could still participate in the broader coalition and serve on member committees, but they would not serve on the core group.

The turning point occurred at a meeting of the expanded core group in Tunica, Mississippi, in the fall of 2010. Organizers from base-building groups, led by Chin, Parker, and Maulik, pressed their case that DSC leaders needed to be directly accountable to those most impacted. Coming out of that meeting, DSC had a new, interim leadership group in place co-chaired by Sullivan-Yuknis and Chin, with strong representation by organizers.

The base-building groups in the full DSC membership then organized a strategy convening in Jackson, Mississippi, in March 2011 to strengthen their influence on DSC's internal structures and national campaigns. Meeting in Mississippi was quite intentional as the Black-led groups in the Delta were facing some of the most extreme racism and exclusionary discipline and had been pioneering in their struggle to challenge the school-to-prison pipeline. Chin reached out to Lori Bezahler of the Hazen Foundation, one of the first foundation leaders to support youth and parent organizing groups challenging the school-to-prison pipeline, to fund travel for the groups.

The process of revising and adopting the final membership-wide policy took until 2012, as draft policies were discussed and revised by the full membership at in-person gatherings attended by over one hundred youth, parents, organizers, and advocates from across the country. The membership ultimately decided to elect a thirteen-member coordinating committee, with a majority of seven seats reserved for base-building groups, three to four for advocacy groups and one to two for educator groups. This coordinating committee would make internal and administrative decisions regarding funding, budgeting, and staffing, but all major coalition decisions around campaign work would require a vote of the full membership body, which by this time included almost one hundred organizations. The coordinating committee also agreed that a minimum of 30% of DSC's funds would be distributed directly to member groups. Through this process DSC developed a culture of democratic decision-making that highlighted inclusive processes.[22]

There was a lot of tension through the process. According to Cregor, "A lot of it was philosophically right: the lawyers shouldn't be in charge of a campaign like this. But a lot of it felt pretty personal." Some of the original founders of DSC, like Rosa Hirji, left DSC during the transition. Others, like Cregor, stayed and supported the new policy. In the end, Cathy Albisa, executive director of P4DR at the time, reflects:

> We were borne out of a critique of the way national groups tend to function. We didn't want DSC to set agendas. Communities set agendas. The national advocacy groups could have said, "No, we're leaders, we set agendas, we don't need a governance that somehow doesn't make us the majority." But they didn't. Of course, there was struggle. It's not the way things are usually done. But I think it's profoundly wonderful that at the end of the day, everybody said yes.

DSC's Model Code of Conduct

Organizers in DSC helped solidify this new way of operating through the process of drafting the Model Code on Education and Dignity. Hirji and a group of lawyers had started working on the model code project through the ABA Education Subcommittee of the Children's Rights Litigation Committee. The code was meant to be an aspirational model for school discipline based upon positive and restorative approaches and was to be put forward as a co-authored document with DSC. The base-building groups, however, wanted the code to be more organically connected to communities experiencing the school-to-prison pipeline and struggling for change. Joyce Parker stepped forward to co-lead the model code work and insisted that DSC take it to community forums across the country for input from families and students.

Parker and Sullivan-Yuknis set out to organize forums on the code in eight communities across the country and collected feedback from families, students, and other community members. According to Albisa, this was a turning point. "It was a decision that the community rather than lawyers would be the ultimate decision-makers for what's in the model code and for DSC. It turned the document from a legal tool into a vision for the campaign." There was a lot of tension and struggle over the final authorship and ownership of the model code. The lawyers on the Education Subcommittee ultimately decided not to be a co-author of the document and Hirji eventually stepped back from the project.

DSC published the model code in the fall of 2012 in connection with the launch of a new joint Solutions Not Suspensions campaign, led by DSC and the Schott Foundation's Opportunity to Learn Network, calling for a moratorium on out-of-school suspensions. The model code document turned out to be long, with chapters asserting the right to quality and equitable education for all children; the right to dignity, participation, and freedom from discrimination; and the right to data, monitoring, and accountability. By placing a priority on participation at the grassroots level and welcoming all contributions, the model code became comprehensive and extensive.[23]

As a single read, it was quite unwieldy. As a resource to local groups, however, it became invaluable. The most widely used section featured a Discipline Code Comparison Tool that helped local groups identify their district's policies in its current code of conduct and suggest alternatives that reduce suspensions and promote positive and restorative approaches. The model code also included a substantial section on students with disabilities as the movement continued to highlight the intersection of race and disability in exclusionary discipline.

The determination to make DSC into a coalition that would support and be led by local organizing shaped DSC's financial policies as well. Joyce Parker, Kim McGill, and other leaders from the base-building groups insisted that DSC always use a portion of the funds it raised to build the capacity of local groups. That meant making materials and resources available to them, offering travel scholarships for members to attend DSC annual meetings and activities in Washington, and providing stipends to leaders who joined the coordinating committee. It also meant creating member support funds for organizing groups, which, while only in the $1,000 to $5,000 range, proved important to the many small and underfunded groups in DSC.

In the end, DSC's transition from a lawyer-dominated to an organizing-dominated alliance took place over two years. The membership and financial policies were meant to ensure that the coalition would remain rooted in and accountable to community groups connected to families and students of color. The model code process established a culture that prioritized and highlighted the voices and contributions of those most affected by the school-to-prison pipeline. DSC established its primary purpose to support local organizing and connect parents and young people across localities. At the same time, DSC built its capacity to leverage this local base to influence federal policies.

Advocating in Congress

In 2010, DSC held its first "Days at the Capitol," bringing DSC members from across the country to Washington to meet with their representatives. DSC, along with AEJ and their allies, called attention to the school-to-prison pipeline, initially as part of efforts to impact reauthorization of the No Child Left Behind Act and then on an ongoing basis to build relationships with congressional representatives like Bobby Scott, who had introduced a Positive Behavior Support bill in Congress. The Atlantic Philanthropies offered funding to LDF to coordinate federal advocacy in partnership with DSC and others. Damon Hewitt, Matt Cregor, and Eric Gonzalez came to lead these efforts at LDF.

According to Cregor, DSC was able to work with civil rights advocates with connections and reputations on Capitol Hill but bring the clout of the coalition's local base. Advocates including LDF but also people like Deborah Vagins (ACLU Washington Legislative Office), Fatima Goss-Graves and Lara Kaufmann (National Women's Law Center), and Laurel Stine (Bazelon

Center for Mental Health Law) who had ties to Congress and the administration helped open doors behind the scenes and contributed their voice and
influence to advocacy efforts.

DSC and AEJ brought Black and Brown parents and young people to
Washington repeatedly to speak for themselves to legislators. This was highly
impactful because it was rare. According to DSC Field Organizer Zakiya
Sankara-Jabar:

> Our representatives aren't used to seeing people from their districts in
> DC—the grassroots folks. We're coming in there with our DSC T-shirts
> on and that's like "wow," because unfortunately the way our government
> is, they're usually visited by wealthy lobbyists or people who are lobbyists
> working for wealthy industries. And they're suit and tied up.

The high mark for congressional advocacy came when Senator Richard
Durbin held the first congressional hearing on the school-to-prison pipeline
on December 12, 2012. According to Cregor, "DSC filled the corridors."

> Senators were running down from their offices once they saw how long
> the line was, which according to long time DC civil rights folks was better
> attended than some confirmation hearings. A young DSC member named
> Edward Ward, who had recently graduated from a Chicago Public High
> School and was now in college, was perhaps the best speaker of the group.

Two days after the hearing, twenty children and six adults were shot and
killed at Sandy Hook Elementary School in Connecticut. In the wake of the
mass shooting, the movement had to go on the defensive against a wave of
rhetoric and proposals to increase the presence of police and armed per-
sonnel in schools. Judith Browne Dianis from Advancement Project brought
DSC, AEJ, and LDF together to release a joint statement and issue a brief
taking a strong stand against increased police presence in schools. The Youth
Justice Coalition from LA initiated a youth-written statement from several
organizing groups called "You Can't Build Peace with a Piece (gun)." With
support from the DSC network, 300 youth and several hundred groups
signed the letter. Youth groups in ten cities did actions in support of the campaign. In the end, Congress did not pass any significant new legislation to increase police in schools. Intense opposition from the movement helped, but
gridlock on Capitol Hill was probably the more decisive factor.[24]

Action Camps: Creating Connections and Building an Intersectional Movement

Even as the movement played defense in response to Sandy Hook, grassroots organizing continued to build and connect. The Advancement Project secured funding from Atlantic Philanthropies for a series of Action Camps to bring local leaders together from across the country for trainings held in 2012 and 2013. Advancement Project invited AEJ, DSC and some of their individual members like PJU, Youth United for Change in Philadelphia, and the Labor Community Strategy Center in LA, to plan sessions featuring strategies that had led to policy wins. Most of the participants were youth but parents and other community members also attended.

Local organizers learned from each other, but the meetings served a networking purpose too, creating, as Scott Roberts, who led the action camp work for the Advancement Project, put it, "a pot so people could get in there and cook together." Participants built new relationships and strengthened nascent ones, both among local groups within national formations but especially across the Advancement Project, AEJ, and DSC networks. According to Dianis, "Action Camp is not just a training, it's also about how we connect young people across sites so that they are developing their own relationships so that they can see themselves as part of a bigger movement." In the end, one thousand youth and parent leaders attended Action Camps held in six locations over two years.

During the Action Camps Geoffrey Winder from the Genders and Sexualities Alliance (GSA) Network worked closely with Jonathan Stith from AEJ and staff from the Advancement Project to raise the particular issues facing queer youth of color in the school-to-prison pipeline. The GSA Network, formerly called the Gay Straight Alliance, supports four thousand GSA clubs in schools across the country, with a focus on engaging LGBTQ youth in activism. Queer youth of color had emerged as a leading component in many of the youth organizing groups as well as in the GSA clubs.

The topic came up dramatically after a series of bullying incidents led the Obama administration to issue a letter instructing all school districts to adopt a policy of zero tolerance for bullying. Winder explains why GSA Network opposed this approach.

Many people think that zero-tolerance anti-bullying policies should help LGBTQ students, but the opposite is true. These policies create a one-size-fits-all solution for any sort of code infraction. It's like mandatory sentencing: teachers and administrators don't have any options that take into account what may have gone on before an incident happened.

Often, the LGBTQ student who resists bullying gets disciplined or suspended too. In the GSA Network's view, these kinds of hostile environments make students quit school. Instead, GSA Network advocated restorative justice.

> Zero-tolerance approaches to bullying don't give students or the school a chance to repair the harm or to create a new, positive, and supportive school environment in which these things don't happen. The restorative justice approach gets at the underlying root bias and addresses it. Students and staff hold restorative justice circles, where participants share their perspectives, listen to one another, identify the harm committed, and work to resolve issues.

Winder and LGBTQ youth of color led a series of trainings and conversations across the Action Camps, pushing the need to center the experience of queer youth of color. They argued that creating a school that would be safe and supportive for these students would be safe and supportive for all.[25]

Meanwhile, groups like Power U in Miami and Girls for Gender Equity in New York highlighted the ways that the school-to-prison pipeline impacted Black girls, girls of color, and gender nonconforming students of color. They emphasized that girls and gender nonconforming students of color often faced harsh discipline for violating gender roles and for dress code violations and pointed out that Black girls were suspended at six times the rate as that of white girls. In response to the advocacy of girls of color and queer and trans youth, the larger movement increasingly moved toward an intersectional understanding and strategy, toward connecting the racial justice and LGBTQ movements, and toward greater inclusivity in the leadership of the movement and the range of issues it addressed. This intersectional approach was also reflected in emerging connections between the school-to-prison pipeline and the school-to-deportation pipeline facing undocumented students and families.[26]

Some tensions emerged between LGBTQ youth from the GSA Network and other participants in the Action Camps. Youth leaders wanted to be able to identify which gender pronouns others should use for them, which was a new practice to many attendees and required deeper discussion about gender identity. According to Roberts:

> In the final camp in Queens, we had the biggest mix of people . . . they were just not ready for the ways that the young people presented themselves, their requests to be called by pronouns that the older folks weren't even familiar with. It was a moment of education, but it was also a moment where we knew we had to get ahead of it in the next rounds because we needed all these folks to be able to work together.

While the various national formations had worked together previously, the Action Camps served to create stronger collaborations among the most prominent groups: Advancement Project, AEJ, and DSC as well as the GSA Network, contributing to a more unified national movement. The Atlantic Philanthropies then funded the groups to hold quarterly meetings to share updates and strategize together. The national groups continued to play different roles, but increasingly found ways to coordinate efforts and conduct joint initiatives for greater impact.

Rolling Victories in States and Localities

By the end of the second year of the Action Camps, the movement was in full swing with local organizing groups winning a rolling series of victories across the country. In Los Angeles, where CADRE had won the first victory in 2007 for Schoolwide Positive Behavioral Supports, the Labor Community Strategy Center secured a victory in 2011 to stop LA police from ticketing students for truancy. The Brothers, Sons, Selves Coalition, supported by another key funder of the movement—the California Endowment—went on to get the LA Unified School District to adopt a School Climate Bill of Rights which ended suspensions for "willful defiance" and promoted restorative justice alternatives. As a result, out-of-school suspensions began to drop rapidly.[27]

After PJU had won an early victory to change the Denver school district code of conduct away from zero tolerance, the group got the state legislature to pass the Colorado Smart Discipline Law in 2012 to reduce suspensions and racial disparities in discipline across the state, becoming one of the very first local groups to win policy change statewide. The next year it negotiated a new agreement between the police and school departments to end unnecessary student referrals to law enforcement, to eliminate racial disparities in discipline, and to limit the role of police in schools.[28]

As groups learned about these and other victories at the Action Camps, many were inspired to launch similar campaigns tailored to local conditions. In Boston, youth organizers in Youth on Board/Boston Student Advisory Council worked with other allies like the Boston-area Youth Organizing Project to get the school district to adopt a new code of conduct in 2013 that reduced harsh discipline and promoted positive and restorative approaches. The group also helped get new state legislation called Chapter 222 passed in 2012. The law mandated all school districts across the state to try alternatives before punitive measures. The legislation also said that schools must have an educational plan so that suspended students don't fall behind, that they must provide students with educational services if they suspend them for longer than ten days, and that they must provide special education services. The group then developed and launched a Student Rights App for cell phones through which students can access their rights in discipline cases and report abuses.[29]

In New York City, where the Student Safety Coalition first won school discipline data reporting in 2010, members of the Dignity in Schools Campaign-New York Chapter won in 2012 the removal of automatic suspensions for infractions like fighting from the discipline code and got the district to begin to implement restorative justice in schools. Over the next seven years, from the 2011–2012 to 2018–2019 school years, the total number of suspensions fell from 69,600 to 32,800 in New York City public schools, the largest school district in the country.[30]

In Chicago, a youth-led coalition of organizing groups called VOYCE with support from Advancement Project, conducted a participatory action research project to document the experiences of Black and Brown students with school discipline. VOYCE worked with allies including Community Organizing and Family Issues to win changes in the district's code of conduct. Learning from examples in places like Colorado and California, VOYCE launched a bold and successful plan to get the Illinois state legislature to pass legislation to restrict zero tolerance. SB100 banned zero-tolerance policies, limited suspensions, and promoted restorative alternatives, making it the most progressive state law in the nation at the time.[31]

Each victory built on earlier successes, so that district codes and state legislation became increasingly more progressive. Jim Freeman from Advancement Project explains the SB100 campaign this way:

> We used the law that we passed in Colorado plus some others that we worked on in Florida and some other places like Maryland and used that as a jumping off point to think about what we wanted to put forward with SB100. But then we can take it to another level, a level that we could never have done previously before those initial steps were passed.

As victories mounted, the national climate was changing, encouraging local districts and state legislators to reverse long-standing zero-tolerance positions.

Groups like Communities United that anchored VOYCE had a long history of organizing and relatively high capacity, but national connections and support helped many new and smaller groups win victories as well. When Zakiya Sankara-Jabar and Vernellia Randall founded Racial Justice NOW! (RJN) in Randall's living room in the fall of 2011, the Dayton, Ohio, group had no money and little organizing expertise. For its first two years, RJN was an all-volunteer effort. When the group joined DSC in 2013, however, it began to benefit from a variety of resources: small member grants to support the work so that Sankara-Jabar's time could be partially supported; the DSC Model Code on Education and Dignity to help the group draft and propose new language for the local district's discipline policy; and trainings by Fernando Martinez, DSC's national field organizer, and others who came to Dayton to help new members learn to organize. DSC leaders like Joyce Parker, Maisie Chin, and Gina Womack of FFLIC in Louisiana mentored Sankara-Jabar. Being part of a national coalition like DSC also provided the nascent group with a greater level of legitimacy in the eyes of local officials. DSC members and professional advocates came to Dayton on a national tour and made clear that people all over the country were watching what Dayton did. According to Sankara-Jabar, the support of DSC for a small group in a conservative area like Dayton proved crucial.

> Unfortunately, grassroots folks, parents, our voices aren't enough to be respected in any real way. That's just the way it is. But when you bring in big policy organizations who have all these lawyers, they have all these advocates and professionals, that is what gives you legitimacy, unfortunately.

Within a few short years, the group won a moratorium in Dayton schools on suspensions for students in pre-K to third grade, changed the district's code of conduct to end zero-tolerance policies, won the implementation of restorative justice in ten schools, and went on to issue school discipline report cards for school districts across Ohio.

As a Black parent directly affected by the school-to-prison pipeline, Sankara-Jabar has raised her voice at the national level in DSC, pushing the coalition to adopt even stronger language on racial justice and the impact of zero tolerance on Black children and families.

> I was forced to drop out of college because my son was kicked out of preschool. There are very real-life consequences to parents and families when our kids are kicked out of school that no one is talking about in a real substantial way. That's why I feel that it's really important for folks who are experiencing these different things in real time to actually have a voice and have leadership.

Sankara-Jabar also pushed DSC to increase opportunities for parents to participate at the national level by adopting a childcare policy to offer childcare or reimburse parent leaders for costs to attend national meetings or Days at the Capitol in Washington.

Sankara-Jabar credits the determination, perseverance, and unapologetic nature of RJN's organizing and its member parents for its victories. The group "makes no apologies for being Black and naming anti-Black racism." But she notes that none of this would have been possible without the support of DSC and other national allies.

Changing the National Conversation: Turning the Tide on Zero Tolerance

As victories mounted in localities and states across the country, the tide began to turn against zero tolerance. Local organizing groups, however, also worked in tandem with key national actors who pursued an intentional communications strategy to shift the public narrative and educator discourse away from zero tolerance. This deeply racist narrative asserted that many schools were out of control and that "bad" students were preventing "good" students from learning and preventing teachers from teaching.

The Advancement Project had long emphasized communications work and ran focus groups to help the movement understand effective ways to frame the issue. The front line in countering this narrative was highlighting the personal stories of students and parents who had faced harsh and racist discipline practices. These stories of arbitrary and excessive discipline showed the justice of their cause, demonstrating that these students and parents were not "bad" families but rather victims of an unjust system. Stories combined with a mounting research base that demonstrated profound racial disparities and harmful effects of zero tolerance. By the late 2000s, a growing number of scholars and organizations had begun projects combining research and advocacy designed to shift public and educator discourse, including the American Civil Liberties Union, the Children's Defense Fund, the Southern Poverty Law Center, and others.[32]

In 2012 the Atlantic Philanthropies opened new fronts in the communications campaign designed to influence media coverage of the school-to-prison pipeline. It funded a special journalism beat on the school-to-prison pipeline in *Education Week*, the nation's most widely read education magazine. The articles in *Education Week* and other media reported the harmful effects of zero tolerance on students and documented efforts to change district policy and move toward positive and restorative approaches. Atlantic Philanthropies also funded the Center for Investigative Journalism to report on the use of harsh discipline in charter schools. It supported Anna Deavere Smith to write a theatre piece called *Notes from the Field: Doing Time in Education*, performed across the country and adapted for television by HBO.[33]

A particular focus of the national effort to change the narrative on zero tolerance fell on teachers unions. Local teachers unions had often opposed efforts by organizing groups to end zero tolerance in their school districts while the national unions—the American Federation of Teachers (AFT) and the National Education Association (NEA)—both had official positions supporting zero tolerance. Advancement Project had been working to engage the national unions for several years. In 2012 Atlantic Philanthropies gave a $1.4 million grant to the AFT to pilot restorative justice alternatives in several cities, which got national and local union leaders more directly engaged with activists and organizing groups. DSC and AEJ leaders began to meet with AFT representatives and press their case. Lisa Thomas from the AFT was invited to join the Discipline Disparities Research-to-Practice Collaborative which presented the union with research and data to show the extent of racial disparities in school discipline and its harmful effects as well as the growing evidence that supported positive and restorative alternatives. Meanwhile, John Jackson, president of the Schott Foundation for Public Education, used his relationship with AFT president Randi Weingarten to lobby the highest levels of AFT leadership to move away from support for zero tolerance.

The AFT had its own reasons for engaging with the movement. Under growing attack by conservative and neoliberal reformers, the union needed community allies to defend public education. It opened a community engagement section and hired a team of organizers lead by Eric Zachary, a former NYC community organizer with links to the school-to-prison pipeline movement, to work with AFT locals to form alliances with community partners, and it helped launch a new coalition called the Alliance to Reclaim Our Schools that would assist these local collaborations. While the initial motivation may have been purely transactional, Thomas notes that the new relationships and conversations began to have a transformational effect on the AFT leaders' understanding and approach to school discipline.

In 2014, AFT partnered with the Advancement Project, NEA, and the Schott Foundation's Opportunity to Learn Campaign to publish a Restorative Practices Guide and held a school discipline summit for AFT locals and others, with community partners in DSC and AEJ helping to plan and lead the sessions. National AFT conferences began to pass resolutions supporting restorative practices and addressing racial disparities in school discipline. For its part, the AFT raised the need to couple an end to zero tolerance with an increase in resources for support staff and training to teachers so they could implement alternative approaches.

Another turning point occurred when the AFT partnered with Schott's Opportunity to Learn campaign to host a human rights and education conference in the fall of 2015. Movement leaders helped plan the event, took featured speaking roles, and led workshops. According to Thomas, hearing from people directly affected by zero tolerance at the meeting had a significant impact on AFT's President Weingarten:

It was there that she had her experience. I think a very clear and very stark picture of what the community partners were experiencing in terms of some of the institutional barriers and some of the issues that permeate in the day-to-day lives of people doing this work. It galvanized her to do more and to have us engage more deeply with our community partners.

At the end of 2015, the AFT issued a special edition of its magazine, *American Educator*, where Weingarten said that she and the AFT "were wrong" to support zero tolerance and called for well-supported and resourced alternative approaches.[34]

Change at the national union level did not always lead to change at the local level. As the national leadership moved away from zero tolerance, it met resistance from AFT locals. Over time, however, a growing number of AFT locals—often under intense attack by school privatizers—began to move away from zero tolerance and find ways to partner with community groups.

Similar processes of change happened across a range of institutions and associations in the world of public education, including the National Education Association, the National Association of State Boards of Education, and the American Association of School Administrators. The movement combined several strategies to shift the narrative away from zero tolerance: Advancement Project, the Schott Foundation, and others used connections at the top to begin conversations, while the Atlantic Philanthropies offered seed funding for educator groups to undertake pilot restorative justice projects in partnership with community groups. This work put institutional leaders into relationships with organizing groups where they heard directly from those most affected by harsh school discipline. Combined with research, evidence, and data, personal stories moved institutions away from zero tolerance and toward alternatives.

Meanwhile, judges, frustrated with the growing number of young people referred to juvenile courts for minor disciplinary infractions, began to call attention to the problem and advocate for alternatives. With Atlantic's support, New York State Chief Justice Judith Kaye convened a National Leadership Summit on School Justice Partnerships in 2012 where top justices and school officials from forty-five states discussed strategies to keep students in school and out of courts. The pioneering efforts of Steve Teske, chief judge of the Clayton County Juvenile Court in Georgia, began to receive wide attention, and with the National Council of Juvenile and Family Court Judges, he began training local judges on how to convene multi-stakeholder tables to reduce school referrals to courts and offer treatment services instead of punishment.[35]

The treatment of zero tolerance in major newspapers demonstrates the shift in public discourse. Between 1999 and 2012, coverage showed a dramatic swing from overall positive to overall negative views expressed about zero tolerance in school discipline. Grassroots activists were the first to name the school-to-prison pipeline in media accounts, and their narrative about racial disparities and harmful effects dominated the treatment. When the federal government began to speak out about the school-to-prison pipeline in 2011, media coverage increased dramatically but continued to use the narrative shaped by grassroots activists.[36]

The rolling victories locally, the strategic engagement with key educator groups, and the national media strategy created a profound shift in public and educator discourse. Supporters of zero tolerance were now on the defensive. In December of 2013, the *New York Times* declared the dominance of zero tolerance to be all but over as schools across the country were rethinking their discipline policies.[37]

Winning Federal Guidance to End the School-to-Prison Pipeline

As mentioned earlier, the school-to-prison pipeline movement found important openings in pressuring the Department of Education (ED) and Department of Justice (DOJ) for change. The Obama administration appointed officials who were far more favorable than those in the Bush administration to civil rights enforcement and to addressing zero-tolerance school discipline. Some of the new appointees even came from civil rights advocacy groups. Anurima Bhargava, for example, came from LDF to head the Educational Opportunities Section of the Civil Rights Division at the DOJ. Kevin Jennings came from the Gay, Lesbian and Straight Education Network to lead the Office for Safe and Drug-Free Schools at the ED.

Once again, established and well-connected advocates from Advancement Project, LDF and ACLU, and program officers in Atlantic Philanthropies worked to influence federal officials. They also helped make initial connections for the more grassroots DSC and AEJ members, who brought parent and youth leaders from local struggles to Washington to directly tell their stories. Atlantic Philanthropies and other funders like the Hazen Foundation provided targeted funds to pay for their travel.

DSC and AEJ members took every opportunity to meet with officials, tell their stories, marshal research-based evidence, and press their case. The first victory during this period occurred when the ED authorized an expansion of categories for the Civil Rights Data Collection to disaggregate data by race on suspensions and expulsions covering 85% of American schools and also include data on police presence in schools. In 2010 the department's Office for Civil Rights announced its intention to enforce civil rights violations more vigorously in school discipline cases, and local groups responded by encouraging families to file complaints.

The turning point, however, occurred in early 2011 when the ED sponsored a Voices in Action: National Youth Summit at Howard University with 350 middle and high school students in attendance. The ED had hired Alberto Retana, a veteran youth organizer from the Los Angeles Community Coalition and one of the key founders of AEJ, to lead its office of community engagement. In preparation for the summit, Retana went on a listening tour, meeting with youth from AEJ member groups across the country and bringing their views on school discipline and other issues back to the department. AEJ brought a core of seasoned youth leaders to the Voices summit, some of whom took the stage to confront then-Secretary of Education Arne Duncan and other top ED officials to push for more aggressive action. When ED officials said they were going to do a survey of youth on school climate, Retana says the youth revolted and "totally fired on them." They wanted real action, not another survey, saying, "You're the federal government and the one thing you're going to do is survey us to let us know that we're right? This is bullshit."

According to Jonathan Stith, the youth leaders asked for a meeting with Duncan and used it to ramp up the direct voice that students had in the ED. The meeting was the culmination of a long series of youth and parent consultations that moved federal officials. According to Kristen Harper, who worked on the joint initiative that the justice and education departments launched in response, the personal stories were critical to keep slow-moving agencies going, "to keep minds focused on it, to keep hearts focused on it."

Meanwhile, another bomb dropped in the spring of 2011, when the Council of State Governments presented the findings of a report on suspensions in Texas to an interagency meeting with Attorney General Eric Holder. The report showed that nearly 60% of all students in Texas had been suspended at some point in middle or high school while fully 75% of Black students had been suspended. Furthermore, the study showed that many were repeatedly suspended or suspended for long terms; that the vast majority of suspensions were the result of discretionary decisions; and that students who were suspended or expelled had a much higher likelihood to repeat a grade, not graduate, and/or become involved in the juvenile justice system. Fully 83% of

Black males had faced discretionary action and 75% of special needs students had been suspended at some point.[38]

Despite the growing evidence of the extent and harm of exclusionary discipline, the issue had still not reached a priority level to federal officials until this point. According to Mediratta from Atlantic Philanthropies who was sitting in the audience, "The Attorney General's jaw literally dropped" when he heard the report, and he left the meeting saying the DOJ needed to take action.

Holder's interest in pursuing the issue helped push Duncan and the ED to act as well. Two months later in July of 2011 the ED and DOJ announced the creation of a joint federal Supportive School Discipline Initiative, the contours of which had been informed by Atlantic and the grassroots organizations. The initiative gathered research and heard from parent and youth leaders, including many from DSC and AEJ, who kept up the drumbeat for action. On January 8, 2014, the ED and the DOJ jointly announced new supportive school discipline guidance. The guidance explicitly warned against excessive and racially inequitable school discipline practices and encouraged districts to adopt more positive behavioral and restorative justice alternatives.[39]

At the announcement event at Frederick Douglas High School in Baltimore, Holder explicitly called for an end to the school-to-prison pipeline, the first time a cabinet official had ever admitted its existence. According to Stith, for years the federal government consistently denied its existence.

> Young people and parents were told that we were crazy for naming it. So, Obama officials saying the school-to-prison pipeline existed was a huge victory. The way Arnie Duncan talked about the problem in education and school discipline, I swear it could've been written by any one of our national networks. It was almost point for point, every talking point that we had ever wrestled with them around.

The announcement that the federal government opposed zero tolerance as a key contributor to the school-to-prison pipeline marked the culmination of fifteen years of grassroots organizing that started when parents and youth like those from Holmes County in Mississippi began to raise the alarm. The guidance did not enact any new laws, but it put local districts and state agencies on notice that they would be held accountable for adherence to federal civil rights obligations in relation to school discipline and provided important guidance on positive alternatives to punitive approaches. Local groups like VOYCE in Chicago lost no time in pointing out that the federal government was on their side when they called for an end to zero tolerance. Even if policies did not change everywhere, and exclusionary practices remained embedded at the school level in many places, the tide had turned decisively against zero tolerance and the existence of the school-to-prison pipeline was widely recognized.[40]

A New Model for National Movements

By the end of 2014, the movement to dismantle the school-to-prison pipeline was in full swing. It consisted of a growing set of local organizing groups working with parents and students of color connected through national networks that included formal alliances like DSC and AEJ as well as intermediaries like the Advancement Project, and funded by the Atlantic Philanthropies and others. Local groups also connected through an increasing number of national gatherings sponsored by movement building conduits like the Schott Foundation, Communities for Just Schools Fund, and the Funders Collaborative on Youth Organizing. The movement consisted of a network of interlinked organizations but also a web of people who sometimes moved across institutions and created the relational bonds that helped coordinate and integrate initiatives. Meanwhile, AEJ, Advancement Project, and DSC were jointly facilitating a quarterly meeting where the various stakeholders in the movement met, shared information, and worked to coordinate efforts.

Although the movement's effectiveness lay in its complexity and the marshaling of a range of resources and people, the growing number of local organizing groups were its heart and soul. The direct participation of people most affected by educational injustice gave the movement its moral force and kept it accountable to needs and urgent demands of people on the ground.

Through the struggles over membership policies and processes in DSC, a new model for national alliances emerged. Following Joyce Parker's motto, "There is no national without the local," the main national formations became focused on supporting local organizing not advocating in Washington, although DSC, AEJ, and its allies did that too. Their primary role was to direct resources back to local groups, providing funds like small grants, trainings in organizing, and resources like model codes of conduct. National wins, like getting the ED to collect better data on exclusionary discipline or pushing the ED and DOJ to issue joint guidance against zero tolerance, become additional resources for campaigns at local and state levels.

The movement to end the school-to-prison pipeline is best characterized in this sense as a rolling series of local organizing efforts. Organizers with the help of national intermediaries "nationalized local struggles." In other words, when CADRE and PJU won early victories to shift school districts away from zero tolerance, their stories and strategies were intentionally lifted up and spread across the country inspiring others to take even bolder actions, each victory outpacing the other in extent of policy change.

This new model, where Washington-based professional advocates shared power with grassroots organizing groups who featured the participation of those most impacted, did not come easily or by accident. It came through the deliberate intervention by community organizers to make sure base-building groups had majority control in DSC's leadership body and in repeated negotiations in national formations to consistently forefront parents and students most impacted by injustice. Maisie Chin recognizes the work and struggle it took to create a transformative movement so that "people come to DSC and feel so respected and so part of it."

> The value of community leading, the most impacted leading, their truths being the way we frame things and not being framed by a funder or advocate—that's the story of the movement. And the leadership, the practice, the struggles it took to have that be the case and have there be a different paradigm inside DSC. I hope that's the lasting legacy of DSC and any of us who helped to build it.

4

The Prevention of Schoolhouse to Jailhouse

Intergenerational Community Organizing in Mississippi

> This chapter is dedicated to the memory of Helen Johnson who in-
> spired a movement with her passion and her anger that Black chil-
> dren were being pushed out of school while no one seemed to care.

In the opening to the third chapter of this book, we learned how African American organizers and families in Holmes County, Mississippi, became among the first people in the country to speak out against racist school discipline practices and identify the school-to-prison pipeline. In the late 1990s Ellen Reddy and her sister Helen Johnson from Citizens for Quality Education (CQE) noticed an increasing number of Black children out on the streets during school time. They learned that schools were suspending children for minor infractions and referring many to juvenile court, which sent them to detention facilities—"training schools" that abused many children. CQE and the other Black-led organizing groups in the Mississippi Education Working Group (MEWG)—later reconstituted as the Delta Catalyst Roundtable helped form the Mississippi Coalition for the Prevention of Schoolhouse to Jailhouse which spearheaded efforts to pass landmark juvenile justice reform legislation and close one of the notorious youth prisons.

In this chapter, I trace the intergenerational community organizing efforts of groups in the Mississippi Roundtable to dismantle the schoolhouse to jailhouse track from its origins in Holmes County in the heart of the old plantation South. I discuss their strategy to combine local organizing across the state with legal and advocacy groups to leverage the power to challenge deep-seated racism and entrenched white powerholders. The Mississippi groups also joined the Dignity in Schools Campaign at its founding. They helped keep the national coalition grounded in organizations in Black and Brown

Willful Defiance. Mark R. Warren, Oxford University Press. © Mark R. Warren 2022.
DOI: 10.1093/oso/9780197611500.003.0005

communities most affected by racial injustice and gained critical resources for their local organizing campaigns. Finally, recognizing that policy changes may not matter unless school systems are held accountable for authentic implementation of positive alternatives, I take a close look at the work of Roundtable member Tunica Teens in Action to build the social infrastructure for transformational change in Tunica schools and communities. The chapter ends by reflecting upon the meaning of uncovering the origins of the movement to dismantle the school-to-prison pipeline in Mississippi and highlights the lessons offered by Mississippi organizers to the larger school-to-prison pipeline movement and the country.

The Southern Origins of a National Movement

> There is not a single river in Mississippi that has not had a Black body floating in it.
>
> —Leroy Johnson, co-founder, Southern Echo

The significance of tracing the origins of the movement to dismantle the school-to-prison pipeline to African American communities in the Mississippi Delta cannot be overstated. Mississippi lies in the heart of the Southern plantation system where white powerholders have used violence to maintain white supremacy since the time of slavery. During the Jim Crow era, Mississippi African Americans faced more violence and lynching than perhaps any other place. The infamous 1955 lynching of fourteen-year-old Emmet Till, whose body was dumped into the Tallahatchie River, epitomized the violence and brutality perpetrated against Black people. According to the Equal Justice Initiative, "The lynching of African Americans during this era was a form of racial terrorism intended to intimidate Black people and enforce racial hierarchy and segregation." The Initiative's research determined that white Mississippi mobs lynched more Black people than in any other state, a total of 654 Black people between 1877 and 1950.[1]

Till's lynching and the acquittal of his murderers helped inspire African Americans to register to vote and organize, marking a key early moment in the civil rights movement. Indeed, Mississippi was not just the site of violence and repression; it was also a vital center of the civil rights movement. The Student Nonviolent Coordinating Committee (SNCC) led particularly robust efforts in Mississippi, supporting young organizers in Holmes County and across the Delta to make, according to John Dittmer, "the Mississippi movement . . . the strongest and most far-reaching in the South." Moreover, as Charles Payne and others have shown, the Mississippi freedom movement was rooted in a community organizing tradition that cultivated the participation of regular folks and long-term capacity building more than highlighting the charismatic leadership of the few.[2]

When, in 1989, Leroy Johnson, Mike Sayer, and Hollis Watkins established Southern Echo as a training and technical assistance organization to support the work of Black-led organizing groups and connect them across the Delta, the co-founders sought to draw upon this rich organizing tradition and inaugurate a new era of the movement. They saw the need for a renewed organizing effort because, despite the gains of the old freedom movement, poverty, segregation and powerlessness persisted, particularly in rural Mississippi's Delta region. In an early document, Echo characterized the post-Jim Crow period as colonialism, a direct outgrowth of earlier periods of slavery and segregation.[3]

Echo's first campaign focused on redistricting to create more opportunities to elect African Americans to public office. As a result of that campaign and subsequent organizing and mobilization efforts, the proportion of Black state legislators increased dramatically, more than doubling to constitute 28% of the seats, which provided a foundation for later policy campaigns at the state capitol. It was only in 1995 and as the result of the redistricting campaign that Mississippi formally ratified the Thirteenth Amendment to the U.S. Constitution abolishing slavery.

Echo established important operating principles that would set the pattern for the local groups and statewide alliances it assisted. Echo supported capacity building in local groups, offering leadership training, as well as research and analysis around policy issues. Echo and the local groups followed a Black-led, intergenerational community organizing model. Member groups remained independent, setting their own agendas tailored to local needs. Southern Echo distributed a significant proportion of its funds to local groups to support capacity building and organizing campaigns. Groups encouraged their local leaders to run for office as an important way to redistribute power and hold public institutions accountable to organized Black communities.

At the same time, Echo and the local groups formed regional and statewide networks like MEWG and the Delta Catalyst Roundtable so that they could impact state legislation that, in turn, would affect education, juvenile justice, and other practices at the local level. The local organizations worked in small, isolated rural communities and faced entrenched power structures. In this context, statewide networks played critical roles in constructing the power necessary to change policy and practice both locally and statewide.

Education remained close to the heart of Echo. Echo organizers learned that many adults were afraid to even raise the issue of education because school districts were often the main local employer, and people had experienced retaliation and loss of jobs for speaking up. It turned out that young people were often less afraid, and so Echo's intergenerational model combined both the experience and wisdom of older people and the energy and fearlessness of young people. Intergenerational organizing also meant that the groups were helping to raise the next generation of community organizers directly in their work.

Echo formed in a time of transition after the end of legal segregation in public accommodations and public education. Mississippi's white community had fought school desegregation tooth and nail. The state legislature came within one vote of abolishing public education in the state rather than desegregate. Grenada was the scene of some of the most violent white resistance where rampaging mobs of white men and women beat eight Black children and an adult on the opening day of desegregated schools in 1966. In the end, many whites fled integrated schools into private academies. According to Dianna Freelon-Foster, who attended the first desegregated Grenada schools as a child and is now director of Activists with a Purpose, the Roundtable member group in Grenada, the schoolhouse-to-jailhouse track in Mississippi developed as a form of resistance by the white community to desegregation. "It became the new way to deny African Americans the right to quality education."[4]

Organizers from Echo and the MEWG groups realized that the continued denial of the right to quality education through the school-to-prison pipeline and systemic underfunding was the lynchpin to the system that kept Blacks down. According to Leroy Johnson, the white powerholders believed that "anything beyond a third-grade education ruined a good field hand." In the early and mid-nineties, districts like Holmes County were spending less than $4,000 per pupil and Mississippi students were scoring last among states in standardized test scores. In Echo's view, the struggle for education was part and parcel of the struggle for liberation from systems of domination and control.[5]

Beginnings: The Prevention of Schoolhouse to Jailhouse in Holmes County

Holmes County, quite honestly, is ground zero for the whole school-house to jailhouse.

—Gregg Griffin, former organizer, Citizens for
Quality Education

When Ellen Reddy arrived in Holmes County, Mississippi, in the early 1990s, it was one of the poorest counties in the country. The county was 80% African American and rigidly segregated. Holmes County, however, had also been a vital center of the civil rights movement. Unlike other Delta counties, many African American farmers owned their own land in what was known as the Mileston area. These famers were more economically independent from white powerholders and better prepared to take the risk of speaking out and registering to vote. With the support of SNCC, Mileston farmers led coura-geous organizing drives for voter registration and racial equality. Grassroots leaders reflected the deep-seated organizing and leadership development tra-dition connected to Ella Baker and Bob Moses in the civil rights movement. The Freedom Democratic Party won its first major victory in the county in 1967 when a schoolteacher named Robert Clark became the first African American elected to the state legislature in the twentieth century.[6]

Reddy moved to Holmes County from Baltimore to join her twin sister Helen Johnson and together they launched CQE in 1996 to organize African American parents and young people. CQE was part of the MEWG network at its formation and had a close family connection to Southern Echo, as Helen was married to Echo co-founder Leroy Johnson. CQE held its early meetings in the local Mississippi Freedom Democratic Party building before it moved to the Nollie Jenkins Family Center, which Reddy and Johnson opened to provide childcare and other services to Black families. In one of its earliest efforts, CQE organized for the removal of a third-grade teacher who had been beating students and insulting their families. After filing complaints with the principal who refused to address the situation, CQE helped students write formal statements, held community gatherings to mobilize support, and met repeatedly with both the superintendent and school board. Eventually, the teacher resigned, and the principal was moved from the school into the dis-trict office as an administrator.[7]

When Reddy and Johnson noticed increasing numbers of children on the streets during school time in the late 1990s, they learned that students had been suspended for very minor behavioral infractions. Many had been referred to juvenile court by school principals and ended up in youth detention centers and so-called "training schools." According to Reddy, they found out that youth were being sent to juvenile court and to training schools for "status offenses," like truancy, smoking a cigarette on school grounds, or disobedience to a teacher, even though children were only supposed to go to training school if convicted of an actual crime. According to Reddy:

> It was like the schools were connected to law enforcement. You step out of the school straight into the jailhouse and that's why we call it "from the schoolhouse to the jailhouse." And we wanted to derail the train from that track.

Reddy and Johnson began to spend time visiting juvenile court to observe the treatment of Black children. They found that children were poorly represented by public defenders who often knew little about juvenile law and that judges were quick to refer children to training schools. They began to advise parents and youth of their rights in juvenile court and to press for alternatives to training schools. More and more, they saw Black children being trapped in the system. Even if a child got probation, it came with such strict rules and for such a long time, that the child was likely to violate the terms and be sent back to training school. One rule, for example, required a child of thirteen to be home every night by six or seven o'clock until they turned eighteen. Children also were stigmatized in small rural communities: they were identified early and often judged harshly for minor behaviors. According to Reddy:

> If law enforcement picked you up from the school, other students in the school building knew it too. There's a stigma that is attached to the family's name because you've gone to the training school. When you come back, people may say, "you're a bad ass" or those kinds of things.

During this time, Reddy and Johnson began to hear stories about the brutal conditions that children faced at the training schools. These so-called schools were supposed to provide education and support to children but typically had no programs to do so. Located far from Holmes County, families often had little contact with their children or information about what was happening to them.

One case—the Canton sisters—had a particularly profound impact on Reddy and Johnson. As Black, biracial children, Mary and Alice Canton had trouble being fully accepted in the community and were often bullied at school. They grew up with fourteen brothers and sisters in extreme poverty; their father worked long hours at farm labor and their mother was terribly ill for most of their childhood, diagnosed with terminal cancer. As pre-adolescents, they began stealing cars to joyride. Rather than receiving counseling and support, they were sent to Columbia Training School for Girls. Mary was in and out of Columbia four times where they were both physically abused. Alice recounts that the night she tried to escape, a guard punched her.

> When I try to escape, they beat me so bad. They throw me in the hole. Wouldn't let me get no phone calls. My whole right side was black and blue from my face down.

The training school left her in the "hole," a small room with no bed, for over a month and did not allow her to see any visitors. The sisters talked of guards forcing other girls to have sex with them if they wanted to be allowed to call home. The sisters became involved in the campaign to close Columbia Training School and told their stories at hearings. The school was eventually closed and, as the sisters got older, they began to reexamine their behavior and rebuild their lives. In Mary's view, "They think locking you up will change you, but it don't. It do nothing but make you ruthless." Reddy and Johnson believed girls like the Cantons needed help and support, and they never gave up on them. At one point, they included them in their mentoring group, the Princess and Queendom Initiative. According to Reddy, part of the work of community organizing groups "is to be there for young people and families no matter what happened."[8]

By the late 1990s, CQE and other MEWG members had developed a very sophisticated analysis of the schoolhouse-to-jailhouse track. In a 2000 documentary film on the growth of prisons, Reddy, Johnson, and a young organizer named Mac Epps discuss the direct connection between school pushout, zero tolerance, and youth incarceration. Johnson displays a map created by Southern Echo that shows that the state opened prisons in places characterized by critical teacher shortages and low high school graduation rates. By 2000, CQE's Youth Governance Initiative had formed a project called Schoolhouse to

Jailhouse to examine the correlation between the building of new prisons in the Delta, the high rate of suspensions, expulsions and "dropouts," and the use of high stakes testing. Meanwhile, the MEWG sponsored a summer institute at Tougaloo College on "Transforming the Culture that Moves Black Children from the Schoolhouse to the Jailhouse."[9]

In 1997 Helen Johnson had become the education coordinator for Southern Echo where she spread the message about prevention of schoolhouse to jailhouse. Johnson played perhaps the largest role in shaping MEWG's work on this issue, drawing upon her years of prior experience as a youth court officer, parole officer, and birth-to-three services coordinator for the state. Deeply moved by the injustices she saw Black children experience, and after working so long on the inside, she was excited and determined to push for change from the outside.

Johnson got an immediate response from other MEWG members who had been witnessing zero-tolerance school discipline and referrals to juvenile court and training schools too, and they were also beginning to take action. For example, in 2000 the Indianola Parent Student Group heard that teachers at the high school were punishing children for going to the bathroom during the school day, a rule violation. Students were forced to choose between a beating with a wooden paddle or a three-day suspension. The school had police officers arrest students for talking during the morning assembly. According to Betty Petty, director of the Indianola group:

> When you talk about the disciplinary beating of our children, there was paddles that had holes in them and wrapped with duct tape. They would have our children bend over. Think about a principal, 6 ft., 200-some pounds, beating on a little girl that is maybe 80 or 90, 100 pounds, the impact that that would have on that child.

The Indianola group helped parents and students organize successfully to pressure the principal to put an end to both practices. In another example, Drustella Neely, the executive director of the local MEWG group Action Communication and Education Reform (ACER) in Montgomery County at the time, reported on the group's effort to support a family whose child was wrongfully suspended in 1998.

> There was a 6th grade student who brought a razor to school with the intent of cutting one of her classmates. A friend of this child talked the child out

of cutting the child and took the razor. The child was taking it to hide it so that they wouldn't get in trouble. One of the teachers saw the child running to hide the razor and that child was caught and suspended from school for one academic year.

Montgomery County was also the scene of the incident reported in Chapter 3 where five Black teenage boys were arrested and charged with a felony for throwing peanuts on a school bus during the 1999–2000 school year.[10]

In the view of MEWG members, the schoolhouse-to-jailhouse track was not an isolated issue but was connected to lack of funding, segregation, and the myriad ways that white powerholders denied a quality education to Black students. Groups around the MEWG organized for greater funding for public education and fought resegregation efforts. Yet the campaign for the prevention of schoolhouse to jailhouse held a particular salience across the Delta, where violence and repression had been used historically to keep African Americans poor and powerless. According to Joyce Parker from Citizens for a Better Greenville, "It ain't just about suspending or about paddling."

It really is going back to there's a Black body in every body of water. There is a Black body in every lake, river and body of water in Mississippi. It goes all the way back for us historically. We're gonna have to be the one to tell that story because that is our story. That spirit of destroying the Black body.

Challenging Abuse at Training Schools

Reddy and Johnson wrote U.S. Congressman Bennie Thompson about the conditions at the training schools in Mississippi. Thompson—the only African American elected to Congress from Mississippi—had received complaints from many constituents and had been raising these concerns to state officials. Not getting much of a response, Thompson filed a complaint with the U.S. Department of Justice and asked them to launch an investigation into the Oakley and Columbia training schools. The Justice Department agreed and in 2003 issued a report revealing widespread abuse of children at the two training schools. These abuses included hog-tying with chains, shackling children to poles, and physical assaults by guards. Guards forced girls to run carrying tires and boys holding logs, and many began vomiting or were injured. According to the *New York Times* coverage of the report:

Girls at Columbia who misbehaved or were on suicide watch were stripped naked and left in a windowless, stifling cinder-block cell, with nothing but the concrete floor to sleep on and a hole in the floor for a toilet, for several days or even a week at a time. One girl had been locked in a bare cell for 114 straight days.

These were children, not criminals. The Justice Department found that at the Columbia Training School, 75% of the girls were there because of status offenses, probation violations, or contempt of court.[11]

Eventually the Justice Department filed suit against the state of Mississippi for violation of children's rights, and the state entered into a consent decree with the Justice Department in 2005 with promises of ending abuse and improving conditions. However, a federal judge had previously ordered improvements at Oakley Training School, but conditions had not seemed to change. So MEWG organizers joined with legal allies to press to close the schools.[12]

"An Unusual Alliance" around Special Needs Students

Early on, Reddy and Johnson had noticed that many students who faced suspension and referral to the training schools had special needs. They believed that most training school inmates had a mental or emotional disability, and a later Justice Department investigation estimated that between 66% and 88% had a mental disorder. In the view of Black organizers in MEWG, race and disability were intimately connected. According to Betty Petty, "A great number of schoolteachers did not understand the child's disability and would refer that child for discipline," with many ending up in the training schools.

At the time, there was no legal precedent for filing race discrimination claims for disparities in exclusionary school discipline. MEWG organizers and their legal allies did find, however, a basis for claims in the federal Individuals with Disabilities Education Act (IDEA) that gave students with disabilities legal protections concerning disciplinary actions. At the time, the state was already under the terms of the 1979 Mattie T. consent decree which required the state to provide appropriate educational services to students identified with special needs. MEWG and its partner the Southern Poverty Law Center (SPLC) argued that the state was in violation of the decree and its terms were renegotiated in 2003, with SPLC assigned to monitor progress.

The agreement required the state to improve identification and evaluation of students with special needs and the education they received and to eliminate the discriminatory treatment of Black children.

While Black-led organizing in Mississippi typically lacked alliances with the white community, disabilities turned out to be an exception to the rule. CQE began reaching out to several disability educational advocacy groups based among white parents whose children were also being mistreated in the system. These white children may not have been brutalized in the way Black children were, but they were being labeled and denied their rights. Together the Black and white groups formed a disability rights alliance called Concerned Citizens for Special Education with Helen Johnson as chair.

The group got critical support from a Black state senator named Alice Harden. In the late 1990s, Johnson began working with Harden on juvenile justice issues and their relationship to students with disabilities. Harden, who was chair of the Senate Education Committee, then worked with the group, holding hearings across the state in the early 2000s. At various times, local groups would file administrative complaints and class action suits under the IDEA Act as a key lever to press for change. Through these relationships, the predominantly white disability groups came into the larger juvenile justice reform effort under the umbrella of the Mississippi Coalition for the Prevention of Schoolhouse to Jailhouse.

Combining Organizing with Legal Advocacy: The Mississippi Coalition for Prevention of Schoolhouse to Jailhouse

The Justice Department report about abuse at the training schools validated the complaints made by CQE and the MEWG and spurred them on to launch a campaign to reform the laws concerning juvenile justice in the state. In 2003, CQE, and other members of the MEWG joined with several legal and advocacy groups to create the Mississippi Coalition for the Prevention of Schoolhouse to Jailhouse. The fact that the new coalition used the name created by CQE and grassroots organizers shows their central role in the effort. However, other partners played critical roles as well, including SPLC, the ACLU of Mississippi, the Mississippi Center for Justice, Critical Resistance South, and the Mississippi State Conference of the NAACP. SPLC set up a Mississippi office led by Sheila Bedi who played a key role in forming the

Coalition and pursuing its goals. At its founding, the coalition included just over thirty organizations and groups.

The Coalition included local groups and statewide organizations but also groups beyond Mississippi like the NAACP Legal Defense Fund (LDF) and the Washington-based Advancement Project. Judith Browne Dianis from the Advancement Project had been working with Southern Echo around school desegregation issues. Over the next several years, many of its attorneys would travel to the Delta to support the MEWG's campaigns. Dianis included examples from Mississippi in the report on the first national summit on zero tolerance held with the Harvard Civil Rights Project in 2000, attended by several organizers from MEWG groups.[13]

With this kind of publicity, the work in Holmes County and across the MEWG network started to attract national attention. Many prominent legal and advocacy groups came to Mississippi to see how they might support this work. From the point of view of MEWG, the national groups were coming to learn from their work and certainly the local groups needed their support. According to Reddy, "The national organizations took from MEWG groups the understanding around how zero-tolerance policies impact the lives of Black children and children with disabilities and can push them from the schoolhouse to the jailhouse." "And," according to Leroy Johnson, "they ran with it. They ran with it and then it became all over the country."

To build the power to change state law and reform juvenile justice, the MEWG realized it needed a combination of grassroots organizing, legal strategies, and advocacy at the statehouse but wanted organizing to drive the process. The civil rights movement had long suffered lawyers from well-funded national organizations dictating to local folks how to advance their movement. Leroy Johnson says MEWG organizers knew this history and tried hard to maintain control of the agenda and strategy.

> We were trying to figure out how to stop national folk from coming in and trying to tell us what we need to be doing while getting some support from them about the things that we wanted to do. So, it was really about us controlling our own issues, anything that was important to Mississippi and important to our communities, rather than national folk telling us what was important for us.

The Coalition set four goals and it established committees around each goal, cochaired by an organizer and a legal advocate: 1) creating a statewide public defender system for youth cochaired by organizer Joyce Parker and attorney Jennifer Riley-Collings; 2) closing the training schools with Sheila Bedi and Ellen Reddy cochairing; 3) enhancing healthy communities with Helen Johnson and attorney Mike Sayer; and 4) building the grassroots movement of parents and youth, cochaired by Reddy and Nsombi Lambright. The co-chair arrangement set the model of the alliance as a partnership between organizers, lawyers, and advocates. Tensions remained but the MEWG kept pushing for organizers to lead. According to Reddy, "We would always have to say to the attorneys, 'You can't go up in a room and represent our voices unless you listen to us.'"

The Coalition set out to reform Mississippi's archaic juvenile justice laws. To do so, the advocates brought their legal and policy expertise and the organizers engaged communities. MEWG groups with their legal allies spent many hours working with community leaders—parents and youth—to educate them about potential reform provisions and get their input. They held local meetings across the state and members contacted their representatives to advocate for reform. To demonstrate the scale of support for reform, the Coalition brought 500 students and families to march on the state capitol in July 2004. In August, it worked with allies to hold legislative hearings on juvenile justice reform and began drafting legislation for the upcoming legislative session. The legislation introduced in the 2005 legislative session was designed to end the practice of incarcerating children for status offenses and first-time, nonviolent offenders. It also called for all counties to establish community-based alternatives to incarceration and created a new monitoring unit to inspect detention centers and training schools. Meanwhile, Sheila Bedi identified the orange ribbon as the symbol of reform and the Coalition branded all materials in the campaign with orange going forward. At the same time as it crafted progressive reform, the Coalition and its legal allies worked to defeat other bills that they considered harmful to youth.[14]

The Coalition held the first of what became annual marches on the statehouse on Martin Luther King, Jr. Holiday in January of 2005. MEWG member groups mobilized hundreds of parents, young people, and community members from across the Delta and beyond. They marched, chanted, made speeches, and performed poetry. They were joined by Coalition partners and white families from the disability groups.

As organizers marched in the streets, the Coalition's legal advocates and their legislative allies lobbied for support across both parties. While white Mississippi Democrats had never been consistent allies in the cause of racial justice, the fact that they controlled both houses at the time helped with the bill's passage. Meanwhile, lawyers from SPLC and the Mississippi Center for Justice continued to monitor abuses at the training schools and file legal actions. In the end, through the combination of grassroots organizing, legal advocacy, coalition building, and lobbying at the statehouse, the Coalition was able to get the Juvenile Justice Reform Act of 2005 passed with bipartisan support in both houses and signed by Republican Governor Haley Barbour. According to Rachel Mayes, the current executive director of Southern Echo, the act was "transformative" because, among other things, it required for the first time that children receive an education while in a detention center.[15]

The Coalition built upon this historic victory to press for further reform. Working with Black State Representative George Flaggs, who chaired the House Juvenile Justice Committee, it introduced the Mississippi Juvenile Delinquency Prevention Act in the 2006 legislative session. This bill provided funding for the community-based alternatives to incarceration called for in the 2005 reform, and it established training requirements for public defenders, standards for detention centers, prohibitions on the detention of juveniles convicted of offenses that would not be crimes if committed by adults, and transitional planning for youth when they leave detention. According to Reddy, these kinds of reforms were critical because "We learned that many youth court referees were not attorneys. Some ran gas stations and sometimes held hearings determining the fate of Black youth in their gas stations."

In late 2005, the SPLC brought additional resources to the reform effort when it created and funded the Mississippi Youth Justice Project (MYJP), co-directed by staff attorney Bedi and organizer Reddy. The Coalition and the MYJP worked together to conduct community education and organizing as in the 2006 campaign, and brought two hundred parents, students, and community members out for the second annual MLK Holiday march and rally in January of 2006.[16]

Once again, the Coalition proved successful, and the act was passed and signed into law on April 17, 2006. The legislation was not just groundbreaking for Mississippi; Flaggs declared at the time that "This is the most progressive juvenile justice legislation ever to be passed in the United States," and it became a model for other efforts at reform across the country. In 2007, the Coalition continued to strengthen reform by winning full funding for a state monitoring group for youth detention centers and funding for the first time for teachers and remedial services for detained youth. In the end, the state legislature honored Helen Johnson and Ellen Reddy for the efforts at juvenile justice reform, presenting them with a plaque in 2005.[17]

Meanwhile, the Coalition had not lost sight of its goal to close the training schools. Despite the juvenile justice reforms and the consent decree negotiated with the Justice Department, reports of violence and abuse of children continued. The Coalition once again used a combination of organizing and legal strategies to press its cause. In 2005, the MEWG renamed itself the Delta Catalyst Roundtable and proceeded to hold local hearings on the training schools where children like the Canton sisters recounted their experiences. They also held marches and rallies outside the training school grounds to draw public attention to these often-forgotten places.

In April of 2006, the federal court monitor reported that the state had failed to make the improvements at the training schools agreed in a settlement in 2005. On MLK Holiday in January of 2007, the Coalition and the MYJP brought hundreds of parents, young people, and community members to the state capitol to continue advocacy for the closure of the training schools and reform of the juvenile justice system. At the end of June, the Coalition brought another hundred supporters to Jackson for a "Singing the Blues of Columbia Training School" to highlight continued abuses at the Columbia school and demand its closure.[18]

The legal strategy proceeded on several fronts. SPLC, in coordination with CQE, filed a class action administrative complaint in May of 2007 against Holmes County for violation of the rights of students with disabilities, settling in August. In May of 2007, Bedi also filed a formal letter with the state demanding the closure of Columbia when it was reported that eight girls had been shackled, some for more than a week and one for more than a month, when another girl falsely accused them of planning an escape. In June, SPLC sued the state to stop the abuse of girls at Columbia.[19]

Finally, in 2008 the state relented and permanently closed the notorious Columbia Training School for Girls and the Coalition celebrated its long-fought victory. Meanwhile, as a result of the reform efforts, the number of children in the training schools had fallen from more than 500 in 2002 to about 150 in 2007.[20]

Joining the Dignity in Schools Campaign

While the Delta Catalyst Roundtable was winning juvenile justice reform through its work with the Coalition, its members were also being introduced to the emerging national coalition to end the school-to-prison pipeline—the Dignity in Schools Campaign (DSC). They saw DSC as a large potential resource for their local campaigns. At the same time, they hoped to influence DSC, which they felt could learn from Mississippi's early and strong prevention of schoolhouse-to-jailhouse work and its model of combining organizing with legal advocacy in a true partnership that prioritized community organizing. While some national actors knew about the work in Mississippi, Betty Petty believed it important that, "By joining DSC, we came to the table to tell our own stories." According to Joyce Parker, joining DSC "put Mississippi on the map. Then others replicated some of the things that we were doing, and we were able to support them in ways that they had not built capacity for."

Parker, director of Citizens for a Better Greenville at the time, became the "network weaver" and main link among Roundtable members and between these members and DSC. In Parker's view, "If we come to the table, then we've got to come in a leadership role. We cannot come where everything is being passed down to us, decisions are being made without us." So, she joined the leadership group soon after DSC's first conference in 2009 and, as discussed in Chapter 3, allied with Maisie Chin, Monami Maulik, and other organizers as they struggled to assert the leadership of base-building groups in the new coalition. Parker had the force of ten member groups behind her when she pushed to take DSC's draft model code into communities most impacted for their input. She also pressed for DSC to follow the Roundtable's model to make available a proportion of resources raised for the coalition to support the organizing work of local members. Parker pushed hard the idea that the national is meant to serve the local even as it advocates for change in federal policy, or, as she put it, "There is no national without the local."

Roundtable members believe that the Mississippi involvement centered DSC in the experience of African Americans in the heart of American racism. According to Dianna Freelon-Foster, the Roundtable contributed strategies and coalition models, but "it's really the stories."

As the South goes, there goes the nation. We bring the South. That's rooted in the American criminal justice system and all of those systems that pertain to us as an African American people. We bring all of that to DSC.

In Parker's view, the Mississippi groups had a clarity of analysis that came from the depth of their experience.

They usually say that's just in Mississippi, but we were able to say, "No, y'all got the same problem." We were so much further ahead dealing with it and it was so blatant here. Sometimes in larger communities, it was covert. They didn't see it. But we were able to articulate, "Oh yeah, that's what that is."

While Roundtable members brought stories, analysis, and models to ground DSC, they received connections and resources in return. For example, when DSC decided to back the campaign for a moratorium on school suspensions in 2012, the Mississippi groups saw an opportunity. They had already been doing work trying to reduce suspensions and school pushout through advocating for students and families, but the campaign helped them see the possibility for policy change. Meanwhile, the national level campaign gave them more visibility and credibility locally for the policy efforts. In the view of organizer Melvin Young from Tunica, "The national recognition was very helpful."

So many times in these small communities, it seems like the local community-based organizations are the ones bringing that information in. We've had to work years to get ourselves established as being an accountable community organization that our district works with.

The groups were also able to access funding from the Schott Foundation for Public Education to support the moratorium campaign and these resources proved critical to capacity building. Some districts like Montgomery County, where organizer Al White from the Roundtable member ACER served on the school board and led the policy change, passed a moratorium. Even where others did not, the campaign increased the pressure on districts to reduce the practice of zero tolerance and widespread school suspensions.

Roundtable members also drew upon DSC for technical assistance with data about suspensions in their state and local districts to use in their campaigns. DSC representatives came to Greenville in 2015 to present a report on out-of-school suspensions produced by the UCLA Civil Rights Project as part of a national tour. The report showed that in the 2011–2012 school year the Grenada, Mississippi, school district had the highest Black/white male disparity in school suspensions in the entire country. Fully 91% of Black males had received an out-of-school suspension, compared to 13% of white male students. In other words, almost every single African American boy in the district, from kindergarten through twelfth grade was suspended that year.[21]

Roundtable members regularly participated in DSC's Week of Action against school pushout. They took advantage of the modest support funds, T-shirts, and other resources that come with participation. Meanwhile, the Week of Action highlighted the work of the Roundtable groups in their local areas. According to Freelon-Foster from Grenada:

> It is a very public activity and allowed your community to see that you were not in this alone. There were other organizations, there were other people, there were national organizations, there were other state organizations and that really helps a lot with your local work. It allows you to become more visible. It allows them to see you.

In Drustella Neely's view, "You get a certain amount of empowerment and power when you say that I am a part of Dignity in Schools. It holds clout."

Finally, the opportunity to participate in national meetings empowered students and families by taking them out of the confines of their local circumstances to connect with others and feel part of a larger movement. According to Freelon-Foster:

> Our students are smart students, they're bright students. But it gets back to who we were in the South. When you've been told all your life that you can't look a white person in the eyes, we lived in fear of that, and we accepted that all of those years. When they go to other spaces with other young people and they begin to share those stories, then it begins to empower them and uplift them. So, it's an empowerment process. A building up. It actually is a lifting up process.

By the late 2000s, the Roundtable groups and Southern Echo had developed a model to combine deep intergenerational community organizing at the local level with strong networks across the Delta and coalitions at the state and national level with legal advocacy and other organizing groups. This strategy led to important policy wins, but the groups always knew that policy change alone was not enough to challenge deep-seated racism and entrenched power structures. Changing practice required the kind of organizing that went deep into local communities, built intergenerational leadership and a social infrastructure for transformation. Tunica Teens in Action offers an important example of how Black-led organizations in the Roundtable build the kind of leadership and relationships necessary to stop the schoolhouse-to-jailhouse track at the ground level and create community capacity for educational transformation.

Tunica Teens in Action: Students Take to the Streets

Late one night near the end of the 2013–2014 school year, a group of high school seniors entered Rosa Fort High School in Tunica, Mississippi, with mischief on their minds. As a senior prank, they planned to move desks out of the school and onto the football field. Realizing that the field was one hundred yards from the school and that it would be a lot of work to carry out their original plan, they decided instead to leave a few in the hallway and go into the computer lab to move the computers onto the floor. They got ketchup from the cafeteria and smeared some on the walls and then they left.

When the prank was discovered the next morning, Principal Derrick Dace met with the parents and students involved and started a restorative process. He got the families to pay for the damage, "maybe a total of $5,000 across 24 families," and the students to do volunteer clean-up duty. But that wasn't enough for the Tunica County Superintendent of Schools, Bernard Stephen Chandler. Claiming that the students had done $30,000 worth of damage, Chandler told Dace to expel them. He also wanted them criminally charged. Dace refused. According to Marilyn Young, education director for Tunica Teens in Action (TTIA), who was also the school board president at the time, the expulsion order two weeks before graduation caused a major uproar in the community. The board supported Dace and voted to allow the students to graduate. Young said, "We told the superintendent you can't throw children away because they do something they shouldn't have done."

In August at the start of the next school year, Chandler fired Dace. Dace, a former girls' basketball coach and math teacher, was beloved by students, parents, and the broader community. The students were outraged at his firing. According to Damien Jackson, the student government president and a student leader in TTIA, Coach Dace had always helped and supported him, and he was upset. Like other students, he felt it was time to act.

> I said it's time for us to take a stand. We understand that the adults, the teachers, they can't do certain things that we can do because they can get fired. They can't voice their opinions like we can. But as youth, it's our job to speak up because we are the reason why there is a school system. We are the future of this school system.

That evening, a number of student leaders in TTIA met and decided to organize a sit-in at the morning assembly until the superintendent came to talk with them. They made signs ready for a protest. As the students gathered in the gym at the start of the day, they refused to leave for classes, as planned. When the superintendent failed to appear, however, the students changed tactics. According to Jackson, "One of my classmates said 'they don't want to listen to us. Let's march down to the superintendent office.'" Two hundred students marched several miles in the hot August sun from the high school to the district office where they tried to confront Chandler and get an explanation for the firing.[22]

Chandler, meanwhile, called the state police and told them students were rioting. Adult organizers in TTIA mobilized community support for the students. According to Ashley McKay, executive director of TTIA:

> We pulled all the old folks out that were advocates and social justice workers. They came down to stand in solidarity and to help protect our students to make sure the police didn't do things to them. They brought food, they brought water. And they did this for three consecutive days until the superintendent finally had to come out and address the school and the community.

Many teachers also supported the students, leaving with them to march on the first day. McKay, however, says they had to turn back:

Teachers were told they had to return to the school, or they would be fired. They made it halfway and then had to go back. When the student protest was over on Friday, the next Monday, the teachers held a "green-out" where all the teachers called in with the flu in support of the students.

The support of teachers and the community heartened the students. According to Jackson, "It brought us even more joy when a lot of us looked around and we saw our parents out there. My mom said, 'You go, y'all go. Y'all got to do it.'"

The students marched for three days with broad community support but to no avail. Chandler refused to back down. So, the students began to attend school board meetings. According to Young, the students were on the agenda almost every meeting and hundreds of people would attend. It was a "constant state of war, a terrible year."

Since there was no provision to recall a sitting superintendent in Mississippi, students with TTIA support began a petition drive to have the state remove him by putting the district in receivership. The students were joined by adults in the Tunica County Committee for Educational Improvement, led by retired teacher Robert Hall. According to Young, normally a state takeover is "the worst thing that can happen to our communities."

But we could not give him four years to continue down the path that we were on. So, Tunica Teens in Action had to educate our community on what a state takeover could mean and how this could be better for our history in that moment.

In January 2015, the groups took 1,100 petitions to the state board of education, and this was in a county that had less than 11,000 residents. The state conducted an investigation and found that the district was violating twenty-five of thirty-one state accreditation standards. In July, Chandler finally resigned just ahead of the expected takeover that happened later in the month.

Meanwhile, Dace had filed suit for wrongful dismissal and was reinstated with back pay in May. The students, parents, and community supporters celebrated their victory. Dace went on to serve as principal again for the next school year until the conservator put in place by the state promoted him to a position as the federal programs administrator. By January of 2017, the state claimed that the takeover was a major success, and that Tunica had the highest growth in math among low-performing districts in the state.[23]

Building Community Capacity for Caring Schools

The protests in support of Dace were only possible because of the more than twenty years of organizing by TTIA and its parent group Concerned Citizens of Tunica County, an original member of the Southern Echo and later Roundtable network. According to McKay, the executive director of TTIA who herself played on Coach Dace's basketball team and began her participation at age ten in TTIA:

> These things aren't happening overnight. Dace's relationship with community and Tunica Teens in Action didn't just happen yesterday. It's been 15 years of relationship building where you're still putting your children inside of the hands of a person that you know, that's gonna fight for them, but also let them know when they're out of place and when there needs to be some correction happening.

History and context weigh deeply in Tunica as they do across the Delta. Tunica County—at the northern edge of the Delta—is about 75% Black while the county ranked as the second poorest county in the United States in the 1990 census. The state allowed casinos in Tunica in the 1990s but the $700 million in additional revenue for local government seemingly did little to improve public education for African American students. Concerned Citizens of Tunica County formed in 1993 to fight for quality education for all students and established TTIA in 1999 to help the group become more youth-led and women-led. The youth organizing group has now eclipsed its former parent organization.

TTIA has been working to reduce suspensions and court referrals since the late 1990s. When the Mississippi legislature passed a 2003 law saying that "habitually disruptive" students thirteen and over would be expelled for three incidents of disruption in school, TTIA redoubled its efforts. It began to meet regularly with the sheriff's office, school superintendent, youth court referees, and judges to advocate and work together to find alternatives to referrals and incarceration.

Because the juvenile justice reforms pushed by MEWG required youth court referees to come from the community served, TTIA was able to help a local pastor get the position. During the student walkout, according to McKay:

> The students had been told they would be arrested if they protested, and the pastor and court referee came out to say they had the right to protest. He even marched with the students back to the high school at the end of the protest.

According to Melvin Young, this was important because it reassured parents that their children would not be arrested.

TTIA's focus on building relationships with the superintendent was credited with important gains in school improvement. According to Robert Hall, president of TTIA at the time, superintendent Jerry Gentry "bought into the TTIA model. He became a stakeholder in Tunica Teens in Action, and we were willing to do a lot of the legwork that was required to make the partnership work."

When Dace arrived at the high school as a math teacher and the girls' basketball coach, TTIA set out to build a relationship with him. Dace took on a losing team but turned it around through a combination of care and hard work. Calling practices on weekends and late at night originally alienated many parents and TTIA complained. But, according to organizer Marilyn Young and Principal Dace, they worked hard at listening to each other. When the team won a crucial game for the championship, parents from TTIA showed up with a bag full of T-shirts for the team members already emblazoned with "champions" on them. For Dace, this showed the group's support for him and confidence in the young people. According to Dace, "It's like we been family from that moment on."

> When they're for you, they're with you. But when they feel you're doing something wrong, they're not afraid to stand up and talk and let their voice be heard.

When Dace became principal, he took his caring and holistic approach with him, and continued to partner with TTIA and the community. Many of the high school students lived in low-income housing and struggled with poverty and other issues at home. Dace took his teachers on trips to visit these neighborhoods and he asked teachers to conduct home visits. Dace tried hard to address the issues facing children rather than suspend them. He wanted students to be part of the solution; so students decided together what the behavior rules would be, creating a classroom contract.

> So, they'll agree on the procedures, they'll agree on the consequences and they'll agree that we can police ourselves and the teacher doesn't necessarily have to be the one that's just doing the policing. We do it ourselves.

Dace also believed that working with parents was key. Rather than pursuing the kind of adversarial strategy or even bullying seen at other schools, Dace listened to parents first and then asked how he could help them and their child.

Partly because of the casino business, families moved to Tunica from bigger cities far away and, according to McKay, some teenagers brought gang-associated culture with them. She says students reported these concerns to TTIA staff who communicated with Dace to address the issue.

> Being able to have a person whose also community friendly inside of that building, that'll take their phone calls, that is not afraid. How many folk you know can say I call the principal after school and he answers the phone?

Jalen Dunn, a member of TTIA and one of the student walkout leaders, appreciated Dace's efforts to address issues rather than expel students.

> If a student gets to fighting or if they curse or do something in the class, disrespect or defiance, he had alternatives instead of just suspending kids and sending them home. He might have them washing tables and cleaning up. He was the father figure to some of the children. If the children don't have any clothes or any food at the house, he'll go by and he'll help the students with what they need.

Meanwhile, students who led the protest like Dunn and Jackson had been trained in leadership and organizing by TTIA for several years. The previous summer, they had attended a Freedom Summer reunion in Jackson and participated in a protest outside a Nissan plant in support of a union organizing drive by the United Auto Workers with the actor Danny Glover and civil rights veteran Hollis Watkins.

TTIA follows an intergenerational model of organizing that includes mentoring a new generation of community leaders among current students. Jackson had joined TTIA when he was in seventh grade and credits the group for helping him grow as a leader. With TTIA's help Jackson went on to Rust College, a historically Black college, where he was elected freshman class president and led a protest to improve student experience at the school.

TTIA helps many students go to college and the group promotes HBCU's (Historically Black Colleges and Universities) as often the best place for them to get support and be successful as well as learn more about the history of their community. TTIA supports students with college transition—helping with college applications as well as financial aid and housing arrangements; TTIA alumni at the college welcome the new freshmen. Alumni are expected to come back and mentor high school students, and TTIA encourages many to become teachers in Tunica.

By the time of the student walkout in 2015, TTIA had been doing almost twenty years of work to address school pushout and improve education in Tunica. TTIA helped rewrite the student code of conduct to move away from zero-tolerance discipline, worked to get PBIS adopted district-wide, advocated for an alternative school in the district, helped set up PTOs in all the district schools, and trained TTIA youth in restorative justice. All these campaigns and their resulting policy victories were important. However, they served the larger goal of building community capacity so that the actual culture of the schools in Tunica, like the high school under Dace, was humane and supportive of students and their families.

Much of this chapter has focused on the important policy victories that Roundtable groups and their allies won in juvenile justice and school discipline. However, according to Parker and other Roundtable organizers, Mississippi has often had good laws, but they are not implemented. Implementation requires holding public institutions accountable through the actions of educated and organized communities. It also requires building a social infrastructure of relationships within communities and across to educators and public officials. Roundtable members believe better policies will not matter if their communities do not have the capacity to implement them and hold systems accountable.

Lessons from Fighting White Supremacy
in Mississippi

> Mississippi is always last in everything: the poorest with the lowest
> performing schools and the greatest racial disparities. In the preven-
> tion of schoolhouse to jailhouse, however, we in Mississippi were
> first.
>
> —Joyce Parker

In this chapter, I traced the origins of the movement to dismantle the school-
to-prison pipeline to Holmes County, deep in the Mississippi Delta. African
American parents and young people in Mississippi were not the only people
of color to feel the brunt of zero-tolerance school discipline and policing
practices, but organizers in Mississippi were some of the first, if not the first,
to name the schoolhouse-to jailhouse-track, address it with a deep analysis of
the connection between education and incarceration, and begin to organize
against it. There is a through line from Holmes County to the Roundtable and
the larger national movement, one consciously developed by the Roundtable
groups and their Southern Echo partner as well as allies in DSC who recognized Mississippi as a center of gravity for the movement. In the early days,
national groups like the Advancement Project came to learn from and offer
support to the nascent movement in Mississippi. Joyce Parker herself played
a critical role in translating lessons from Mississippi to the national movement while the Roundtable groups drew critically needed resources from
their participation in DSC. At the same time, we see in Mississippi the critical
importance of statewide and national networks to support local organizing
by small community groups facing entrenched systems of racial oppression.

In Mississippi, we also see the demonstration of Parker's slogan, "there
is no national without the local." Black Mississippi parents and students
inspired organizers and families across the country with their courageous
efforts in extraordinarily difficult circumstances and their pioneering policy
changes in juvenile justice and other areas. They established models of coalition work that were shared with the national DSC coalition. They showed
how to combine community organizing with legal strategies and advocacy
work in ways that centered the leadership of groups rooted in communities
of those most affected. Perhaps most importantly, though, they provided the
national movement with deep grounding in local communities, supplying
powerful stories and analysis from the historic heart of white supremacy.

What is the significance of saying that the movement began in the Mississippi Delta? Black and Latinx people are oppressed by the school-to-prison pipeline across the country. Arguably, though, African Americans face the harshest and most brutal conditions in Mississippi in the context of historic violence and white domination. Community organizing is challenging to conduct anywhere but especially in Mississippi in small, isolated communities with a deep history and contemporary reality of white domination, threats to people who speak up, and lack of infrastructure to support organizing. It is hard to overstate the courage and determination of poor and working-class Black folks speaking up in this context and challenging white power structures.

Black parents and young people have not just spoken up. With organizers from the Roundtable network, they undertake the multiple strategies it requires to build community capacity and the power to change policy and practice to dismantle the school-to-prison pipeline. They are willing to protest when necessary, but constantly seek to be partners at the table when and where they can, including through electing members to school boards. They support students, parents. and families on an individual basis and help them advocate for themselves and their children. They also educate community members about issues and policies as they train students and parents in leadership and organizing. They mentor young people through high school and into college as they pursue an intergenerational model of organizing that connects young people to elders. While they develop policy reforms and lead campaigns to pass them, they also build a web of relationships with educators, youth court referees, judges, and elected officials to ensure genuine implementation of new policies and keep public officials accountable to communities. They do all this with precious few resources in a context of extreme poverty and racial segregation.

What Mississippi makes crystal clear is that the school-to-prison pipeline is not a matter of a well-intentioned but misguided school discipline policy. Rather, it represents the current version of the historic effort to maintain white supremacy by denying education to African Americans and criminalizing generations of young people of color and their families. The school-to-prison pipeline represents a system of domination and control that keeps Black people poor and lacking in power. At the same time, the Mississippi movement demonstrates how people most impacted by injustice living in the belly of this beast can speak out and use the tradition of intergenerational community organizing to mount a struggle to confront systemic racism. With few resources and facing entrenched opposition, the Mississippi movement made important breakthroughs and helped inspire a national movement. In this way, it made education central to the struggle for liberation and political power against criminalization and violence. In the end, the movement in Mississippi endures and offers hope for a transformed Mississippi and a beacon for the country. According to Ashley McKay:

> For us in Mississippi, we have a rich history of fight and struggle. A lot of times our history won't get told and our work will be stolen because we don't always document it. But we are a oral people. We tell our stories. We pass those stories down from generation to generation. So it may not always be written but we know the history of it.

5

Challenging Criminalization
in Los Angeles

Building a Broad and Deep Movement to
End the School-to-Prison Pipeline

In the late 1990s, African American and Latinx parents in South Los Angeles
began gathering in Rosalinda Hill's living room on a Friday evening to talk
about the issues affecting their lives. Parent after parent began to recount
stories of racist treatment and retaliation toward them when they tried to
advocate for their child. The parents, led by Rosalinda Hill and Maisie Chin,
formed an organization called CADRE—Community Asset Development
Redefining Education—becoming one of the first organizing groups in the
country to target the school-to-prison pipeline as a form of systemic racism
and a key part of the system of mass incarceration. The group became the key
community force behind a successful campaign to get the Board of Education
of Los Angeles Unified School District (LAUSD) to rewrite its discipline
code. For the first time in the country, an entire school district began to move
away from exclusionary discipline and adopt Schoolwide Positive Behavior
Supports (SWPBS)—and this in the nation's second largest school system.

In Chapter 3, we learned how the victory of CADRE parents to win
SWPBS in 2007 sparked the growth of a national movement to end the
school-to-prison pipeline and led directly to the founding of its main coalition, the Dignity in Schools Campaign, as one led by grassroots organizing groups. By that time, several organizing groups in South LA had also
begun to address the school-to-prison pipeline in other ways. The Labor
Community Strategy Center (Strategy Center) launched a campaign to
end the practice of the Los Angeles School Police Department and the LA
Police Department (LAPD) ticketing students for truancy on their way into
school if they were late. Later, the Strategy Center led a successful attempt
to get the school police to return a tank and military-grade equipment it
had received from the federal government. The Youth Justice Coalition

Willful Defiance. Mark R. Warren, Oxford University Press. © Mark R. Warren 2022.
DOI: 10.1093/oso/9780197611500.003.0006

(YJC), meanwhile, began organizing people on the other side of the school-to-prison pipeline, that is, the tens of thousands of system-impacted youth and families who had been in juvenile detention centers, jail, or prison. YJC opened FREE LA High School, provided support services and advocacy to system-impacted people and their families, and launched campaigns to change local and state policy. Eventually, CADRE, Strategy Center, and YJC joined or allied with the Brothers, Sons, Selves Coalition to get the LAUSD Board of Education to pass the School Climate Bill of Rights in 2013, a historic act that, among other things, banned suspensions for willful defiance and other minor infractions, making LAUSD the first district in California to do so.

In this chapter, we learn how these various organizing efforts represent the many fronts on which parents and students of color have found necessary to fight the school-to-prison pipeline in the vast LAUSD school system—a district with over a thousand schools and seven hundred thousand students. Organizers built a movement that is deep—intensely engaging parents and young people in transformative organizing—at the same time as it is broad—addressing a range of issues with multi-stakeholder coalitions. The movement has learned that policy changes are important but mean little unless parents and students are deeply engaged, organized for power, anchored by strong Black-Brown unity, and focused on direct participation to hold institutions accountable for systemic change for students and families most impacted by racial injustice.

South LA: Ground Zero for Mass Incarceration and the School-to-Prison Pipeline

When Black and Brown parents founded CADRE in 2001, they did so after a tumultuous decade in the life of Los Angeles. The Rodney King beating and subsequent uprisings in the early 1990s rocked the city and exposed the illusion of racial progress. The uprisings represented the culmination of mounting frustration with poverty, disinvestment, racism, police brutality, criminalization, and failed promises. The epicenter lay in South LA, also known as South Central, the historic home of LA's African American community.[1]

In the aftermath of the 1965 Watts Rebellion and by the early 1990s the manufacturing industry that had anchored the economy of South LA and offered many African Americans decent wages and benefits had gone into severe decline. Three hundred manufacturing plants closed in the 1970s and 1980s. As unemployment and poverty grew, housing and public services in South LA deteriorated. In the 1980s drugs flooded the community, crime attributed to the drug trade and gang activity increased, and tensions flared.[2]

Demographically, South LA was also changing during this time. Previously, South LA had been almost entirely Black. Yet from the 1970s through the 1990s and beyond, Latinx families, mostly from Mexico, began to move into South LA's many neighborhoods, forming a majority of the population by the 2000 census. Meanwhile company after company that had employed unionized African Americans began to replace them with the newly arriving Mexican and other Latinx immigrants whom they could pay less.[3]

South LA represented ground zero for the struggle to control historic Black and newer Brown communities through policing and mass incarceration. LAPD acted almost like an occupying military force in South LA, notorious for uncontrolled harassment and brutality. In one famous case, nearly ninety police officers raided two apartment buildings in South LA, arrested nearly forty residents and left two dozen people homeless; in the end, no one was charged with a crime. Meanwhile, in 1994 the state passed Proposition 184, the "three strikes" referendum that mandated sentencing of twenty-five years to life for three felony convictions and went on an unprecedented prison-building boom. By 2000, LA imprisoned more people, largely Black and Brown, than any city in the country, a country which imprisoned more people than any in the world.[4]

After years of disinvestment and racial segregation, South LA schools were overcrowded, underfunded, and failing Black and Latinx students at high rates. LAUSD had not built a new school in thirty-four years. Schools were so overcrowded that the district adopted year-round schedules where two-thirds of the students attended school at any one time. Some high schools had five thousand students attending overcrowded classrooms and dilapidated facilities. While California was once first in the nation in school funding, by the end of the nineties it was near the bottom in spending, adjusted for the cost of living. Studies showed that fewer than half of Black and Latinx students that entered high school in ninth grade graduated by the end of twelfth grade.[5]

LA schools were also the most heavily policed in the nation. The number of armed officers in schools rose dramatically during the 1990s and was still rising at the turn of the century, especially in certain areas like South Central

LA. While many districts hired school resource officers, LAUSD built its own school police force. Most high schools and even many elementary schools had police permanently stationed in them, where they would arrest students on-site.[6]

South LA, however, was also home to strong families and a dynamic organizing tradition. It turns out that parents and young people in South LA were some of the first to challenge systemic racism and the school-to-prison pipeline and began a journey to transform school discipline and policing policy through deep and persistent organizing. In doing so, they raised profound and disturbing questions about public education, law enforcement, and the treatment of poor Black and Brown families by these institutions in a way no one had done before; and they launched bold campaigns whose victories reverberated across the national movement to dismantle the school-to-prison pipeline.

CADRE: Redefining Parent Leadership in South LA Schools

Maisie Chin was a student at UCLA when the police assaulted Rodney King, an African American man they stopped for a traffic violation. Following the acquittal of the police officers by an all-white jury, South LA erupted in several days of uprisings against years of declining jobs and services and increasing police repression. Chin witnessed "incredible, tragic moments of violence among people of color in South LA," which launched her on a journey to racial justice organizing.

> I'm not Korean, but I saw Korean storeowners shooting at Black and Brown folks with AK47s to prevent their stores from being looted. So, it feels like all my work has been sparked, or ignited, by outrage over state violence that's very racialized, and against an economy that values property over people.

Chin saw vividly how a larger system of oppression worked to pit people of color against each other and vowed that, as an Asian American, she would never be used as a tool of racism to undermine Black and Brown communities. "I didn't know it then, but I picked a side—to challenge white supremacy."

When she left college, Chin took a position with a South LA program that tried to align K–12 and higher education institutions to improve college-going rates among students in Watts. Interacting regularly with educators, she discovered deep cynicism and profound racism toward students and their families.

> I would walk across campus and teachers would stop me and tell me what they really thought. These were exceptionally violent, dehumanizing thoughts and beliefs about students and their parents. For example, one day, a white male English teacher involved in the initiative stopped me in the hallway and told me, "These kids are all animals."

Chin's own goddaughter was a student in this same teacher's class, and she informed Chin that one day, "He told the whole class, 'I wish I was your father, so I could take you out back and beat you up, because that's what you all deserve.'"

Chin found that educators held deeply negative and racist attitudes toward low-income Black and Brown parents as well. If a parent did not come to a school meeting, teachers believed they didn't care about their children's education—not that perhaps they had to work two jobs to put food on the table, or that their trauma from experiencing racism in their own education made them hesitant to enter school grounds. Meanwhile, Chin reflected that her own immigrant Chinese parents worked graveyard shifts that meant that they were not able to attend school meetings and parent-teacher conferences. Unlike Black and Brown parents, no one labeled them as uncaring, and it never impacted her education. Chin came to understand that these race- and class-based definitions of "good" and "bad" parents were used to pit parents against each other and shut Black and Brown parents out of schools.

The Rise of CADRE: Dialogues in Living Rooms

By the late 1990s, Chin realized that the discourse in education reform circles failed to address the underlying problem of racism toward families of color. Chin felt that parents of color had a key role to play in challenging systemic racism and creating transformational change. Chin teamed up with Rosalinda Hill, a parent of Black and Mexican heritage, and they started to bring parents together to share their stories at Friday night potlucks at Hill's house on the corner of 54th Street and Van Ness Avenue. These Friday night meetings would go on for nearly ten years.

Listening and Sharing Stories

Sharing stories was critical to the emotional and spiritual work parents needed to open up about their deepest experiences and speak openly about the racism they encountered. The stories parents told were diverse, but a common thread was the profound lack of respect they felt from schools that labeled them "bad" parents and then "troublemakers" when they advocated against racist treatment of their children. Many of the parents had been involved in their children's schools in traditional ways but found that such involvement did not prevent humiliating treatment toward them. Hill, for example, was a veteran volunteer at the school where her son, who had special needs, attended. She was always on the campus and in the classroom; she was the model active parent. Yet one day in second grade, a teacher felt her son, who had an Individualized Education Program (IEP), was being disruptive in the classroom and locked him in a utility closet.

The meeting process wasn't always easy. Hill's husband Kenny was racially profiled on his job and ended up being arrested and jailed during that time, and other families faced crises too. Hill lived on the border of two gang territories, so shootings frequently occurred in front of her house. Chin and Hill persisted. They went door-to-door covering forty city blocks during those two years, just listening to parents. They found that most parents felt disregarded by the school and lacking in any real power or influence.

Although trained as a community organizer to identify targets and move issues, Chin saw the need to take time for parents to build relationships with each other. CADRE did not want to be a "parent machine that rolls out parents to everything. We were doing deeper, more liberatory work and more dialogue-based work." Searching for a deeper form of engagement turned into a two-year listening process.

CADRE finally raised a small amount of funding and was ready to open an office in 2001. The group continued conversations with parents through door-knocking and meetings, engaging over 3,000 South LA parents during this time. Working with Justice Matters Institute, a policy and research organization focused on educational justice, CADRE launched a participatory action research project in 2003. CADRE formed a Dignity and Respect Task Force composed of seven core parents who co-designed the process with Justice Matters.

Roslyn Broadnax was one of the African American parents who became highly involved in the task force. She was born and raised in South LA as one of ten children. Broadnax moved around a lot as a child because her mother could not afford to rent a big enough place for such a large family. She always felt that she was passed along to graduate high school but "did not know enough to fill out a job application." By the time she met Hill and Chin in December of 2001, Broadnax was raising sons and nephews herself in South LA. When she heard other parents telling their stories, she realized it was her truth too. Broadnax started crying because at the time,

> My nephew was telling me that his teacher would do little joke things. He would talk on the phone in the classroom to his friends and he would target certain kids. My nephew was one of them very, very dark-skinned kids he would target. He'd tell monkey jokes and gorilla jokes "Did your parents send you with a banana today?" And he'd be laughing with all his friends.

Broadnax knew she had to do something but entering the school to confront administrators brought back the trauma of her own childhood schooling experiences.

> I just didn't want to never go in there. I still had this fear of talking to authority and them shutting you down. Or using words that you don't understand to try to make you look bad. They do all that to parents.

Broadnax loved the conversations at the task force, however, and was "hooked," becoming a core parent leader with the emerging CADRE organization.

Working with Justice Matters, parents on the task force read excerpts from relevant academic literature on the subject, helped design a survey which staff administered to 122 other parents on their relationships with their children's schools, and co-analyzed the survey results, establishing the participatory approach that would shape CADRE's work going forward. CADRE parents developed a set of recommendations for action in each of three areas: cultural inclusion, genuine engagement for parents in decision-making, and accountability to the parents and community, framed in their overall demand for dignity and respect. All along the way, CADRE heard stories about families' experiences with zero-tolerance discipline and several of their demands addressed the issue, including the right of parents to receive early notice when teachers perceived behavioral issues and to monitor school discipline policy and practice without retaliation. At the time, these kinds of demands were rare as hardly anyone was talking about the treatment of parents or school discipline policy.[7]

In the wake of the report, CADRE held its first all-day retreat in the fall of 2004 to decide on its direction going forward. Roslyn Broadnax pushed parents to name systems change as their goal, rather than any one small-scale reform. When asked what system needed changing, the parents focused on what they called the "school-to-prison train" at the time. Several of the core parents and a child of one of the parents had been incarcerated. Chin realized that, while the focus of most school reformers at the time was on increasing access to college for low-income students of color, CADRE had just decided to go in a different direction. Rather than focus on equity issues at the top, CADRE would focus on the students being pushed out at the bottom. "This was the black hole, the bottom that's falling out."

Taking a Human Rights Approach

Around the same time, Chin sought out Liz Sullivan-Yuknis who was about to co-found Partners for Dignity & Rights (P4DR), then called NESRI, in New York City with Cathy Albisa and Sharda Sekaran. Sullivan-Yuknis and Albisa were using a human rights framework to analyze and address school pushout and the school-to-prison pipeline. Chin was excited because she had increasingly felt that the civil rights framework proved insufficient to understand and address the experiences of parents and to encapsulate their goal of systemic change; this was especially true given how hard it was to meet the legal requirement to not only prove discrimination but also intent to discriminate in schools. Human rights seemed to provide an integrated framework and bolder language for what CADRE parents had expressed in all those thousands of conversations.[8]

After much discussion CADRE parents decided to adopt the human rights framework and focus on the rights to dignity, a quality education, and partic-ipation. According to Chin, using their new framework,

> Parents can fight against violations of their human rights and against racist treatment. And it's all in the realm of the school that everyone has a right to attend—every parent regardless of papers, language, economic status. It's a holistic and comprehensive way of making the school a site of political struggle for racial justice.

For Roslyn Broadnax, the human rights frame emboldened her to overcome the fear that she had of confronting school administrators.

> I had never connected that our children had a human right to education. That hit me. That's when I cried. I kept crying and that became my pet peeve. That's what grabbed me and what kept me. I was able to go right back to the school. That same person that wouldn't say nothing was now ready. And I call it "getting CADRE'd."

CADRE started to infuse their organizing with human rights language, calling the humiliation students experienced with harsh, punitive, and abusive discipline a violation of the human right to dignity. The failure of schools to include parents in meaningful decision-making and to inform them of their due process rights became the denial of the human right to participation in institutions that affect their lives. The school-to-prison pipeline and pushout in all its forms represented the denial of the human right to education. CADRE knew these human rights did not have legal standing in U.S. courts. However, they gave a name and language to violations that parents felt deeply.[9]

The Campaign for Schoolwide Positive Behavior Supports

Around this time in 2005, there were student uprisings at five high schools in LAUSD and the board of education asked district officials to recommend research-based alternatives to suspensions and expulsions. Officials in pupil services wanted to recommend Schoolwide Positive Behavior Supports (SWPBS) as an alternative to zero tolerance. Learning of CADRE's efforts to confront the school-to-prison pipeline, they reached out to gain the group's support. CADRE, meanwhile, had been exploring restorative justice as an alternative and, at first, CADRE parents were not impressed with the strength of the SWPBS proposal. After much deliberation, they decided to support the proposed policy because it called for using suspensions only as a last resort, provided for the collection of data on exclusionary discipline, and included an explicit role for parents in monitoring progress toward implementation. Eddie Madison, a core African American parent leader, explains the group's reasoning.

Teachers forget that our kids live in the hood. That kid who acted out might've just seen his brother get killed in a drive-by shooting. So him shrugging his shoulders or sighing has nothing to do with the teacher or "willful defiance." We want them to get to the root core of what's going on and support that child instead of just assuming that that is a bad child, or he doesn't wanna' listen.

After documenting human rights violations and holding a "people's hearing" in 2006, CADRE parents swung into action and started going to every school board meeting, telling the stories they had collected and lobbying for the SWPBS policy. In this way CADRE emerged as the key community force behind the proposal.

Throughout this work, P4DR continued to provide support for CADRE, assisting with participatory research and working together to write a human rights training manual used widely by organizing groups across the country. P4DR and CADRE were also working together on a report on exclusionary discipline in LA and NYC schools called *Deprived of Dignity*. Meanwhile, Rosa Hirji, who was on CADRE's staff at the time, was chairing the Education Subcommittee of the Children's Rights Litigation Committee of the American Bar Association and had pulled together a national network of legal advocates concerned with exclusionary discipline. This emerging group would soon call itself the Dignity in Schools Campaign (DSC), as discussed in Chapter 3. But, at this time, it served as a conduit for connecting CADRE's human rights approach and work with parents with the emerging national conversation among academics, organizing groups, civil rights advocates, and children's rights attorneys.[10]

Meanwhile, LAUSD faced pressure from a federal court-ordered consent decree that came from the district's disproportionate suspension and exclusion of special education students. Passing SWPBS would give LAUSD a way to claim it was responding to the complaint. Hirji also helped CADRE get letters of endorsement for the proposed policy from judges, advocates, and civil rights groups around the country.

CADRE had a treasure trove of stories from their documentation of human rights violations through door-to-door interviews with parents and surveys of pushed-out students ready at hand. The organization held a people's hearing in June where a dozen parents told their stories in front of a hundred community members. CADRE invited a teacher, lawyer, and board of education member to participate, beginning to model the kind of coalition it believed necessary to transform school discipline. Monica Garcia was the newly elected member of the board of education who attended, and she would become a key ally for new approaches to discipline going forward. CADRE held demonstrations in front of the school board and testified persistently at multiple school board meetings. Garcia believes the testimony of parents was compelling.

> These are courageous mothers and fathers that are willing to talk in real time, they're talking about themselves, they're talking about their neighborhood, their street, the kid next door. It's not an academic theory or some distant reality. It is what they live.

Parents met with school board members, the teacher's union, and LAUSD staff to advocate and negotiate. Meanwhile, just before the scheduled vote in February of 2007 the SWPBS effort got a jolt of energy when the *Los Angeles Times* published a feature story on CADRE and its advocacy for SWPBS. CADRE mobilized 150 parents, young people, and community members to a board meeting to demonstrate support for the measure. The teachers union, however, called for a delay in the vote and the board acquiesced. CADRE and other supporters met with the union and, after some minor revisions to the policy, the union came out in favor. With yet another big mobilization of supporters two weeks later, the board voted unanimously to adopt SWPBS, and it became official policy on February 27, 2007. For the first time, a community organization armed with its own research and stories and led by those most impacted got a school district to move away from zero tolerance and adopt a "comprehensive, proactive, prevention-oriented, progressive framework for schools," and this in the second largest school district in the country. As discussed in Chapter 3, this victory catalyzed organizing groups across the country and helped spur the formation of the Dignity in Schools Campaign and a national movement.[11]

Focusing on Accountability: Classroom Observations and the Shadow Report

Despite its political significance CADRE knew the win would only matter if parents had the power to ensure implementation and hold the district accountable for a real change in how it treated Black and Latinx students in South Central. CADRE immediately set out to inform parents about the new policy and train them to monitor the implementation of SWPBS. A year later,

CADRE parents again went door-to-door to survey parents on their aware-
ness of SWPBS implementation in their children's schools and conducted
classroom observations. The next year, CADRE began participatory research
for a shadow report on implementation of SWPBS. The group worked with
Laura Faer at Public Counsel and Ruth Cusick at Mental Health Advocacy
Services to survey parents and students and request data from the district.
They also produced case studies of schools they believed were implementing
SWPBS with fidelity.

The 2010 shadow report indicated that the number of suspensions,
expulsions, and transfers in Local District 7 covering South LA had fallen
significantly since implementation of SWPBS but that racial disparities had
actually increased: the likelihood of African American and students with
special needs being suspended compared to white students had risen from
twice to three times as likely. The report documented some progress on implementation of SWPBS but overall a high failure rate on multiple indicators.
Many parents knew of SWPBS, but nearly half still were uninformed and
uninvited to participate. The report called for renewed focus on full implementation of SWPBS, authentic parent participation, and reducing racial
disparities, particularly in South LA.[12]

CADRE continues to train parents to monitor implementation. Parents
don their CADRE T-shirts and conduct classroom observations twice a
year. In the fall, CADRE parents conduct observations as part of Dignity in
School's Week of Action. According to organizer Oya Sherrills, "Teachers are
at first astonished to see parents this way."

> Parents learn the power of using their parenthood as a political identity to
> engage in classroom observations. To make a statement to the educational
> system that they're not passive observers, they're active observers. It's an ac-
> tion. To use your right to go into the classroom and hold your dignity and
> the dignity of the children in a way that puts us on an equal playing field
> with the system. That rarely ever happens.

Afterward, parents gather to review the observational data they collected
and create action steps. Parents work together at schools to advocate for
change, pushing for improvements but also trying to build relationships with
principals and teachers to support authentic implementation.

Building Black and Brown Solidarity

The foundation for engaging parents lies in shared storytelling. CADRE believes that schools often pit parents against each other, labeling some "bad" parents and their children as disruptors or violence-prone who need to be removed from school. As parents listen to each other's stories, CADRE encourages them to take a fundamentally nonjudgmental approach and refuse to assign blame, focusing first on root causes, which tend to be systemic as much as personal. According to Chin, "Our work is really about building solidarity across experience and creating a non-judgmental environment."

> It's very hard but a lot of our meetings are spent just trying to build a sense of commonality across the stories where people see the systemic issues threaded through the stories and they're not judging each other. They're seeing themselves as a political being or a political force if they were to work collectively.

CADRE believes that schools often encourage Black and Brown parents to blame each other. According to Chin:

> Black and Brown tension is real. Some Latino parents were saying, "The Black kids keep hitting on my kid," and the Black parents were saying, "The Latino parents are taking over," and a range of views in between. The schools often perpetuated that. They often pitted the "good parents" against the "bad parents," fearing the prospect of any unified parent voice.

CADRE believes that parents need the courage to act in solidarity even at the cost of some friendships within their own racially defined communities. Core parent Emilia Elias recounts a turning point incident in her life when her son got into a fight with an African American boy, who was allegedly the aggressor. Many other Latinx parents wanted the principal to remove the Black boy from the school and the principal was prepared to suspend him. But Elias took what she learned in CADRE seriously and argued for using SWPBS to get at the root cause of the violence, even though it threatened her friendships with other Latinx parents.

For me it was more important to say "Okay, we need to find out exactly what were the motives for this child to act this way." While the friendship that I had with Latino parents was something that was important to me, I also found that it was important for me to model and show another alternative—to find a way to teach what I was learning at CADRE. It was a very hard decision for me because as a parent you can't imagine your kids going through such things. But I also had to think about giving the child another opportunity. That was one of the hardest experiences I've ever had.

One-on-One Mentoring and Support

Organizing director Rob McGowan says the foundation for CADRE's parent organizing lies in personal interest and support. For low-income parents of color who often feel invisible, the impact can be powerful. McGowan tells parents:

> I want to know you, who you are, not just for the purpose of organizing. We're not here to fulfill our own self-interests and leave you behind. That's not what we're trying to do here. We're trying to empower individuals to change their own personal lives, their own family's lives, and in the end if enough people are doing that, then it would change the community.

Parents need to feel heard and safe to share their experiences and become, as core parent leader Leticia Arevalo says, "a part of the CADRE family."

When parents first get involved, they participate in a ten-week parent academy that focuses on self-empowerment and the processes of building community together. CADRE encourages parents to set personal goals for their development. Organizers spend a lot of time in one-on-one coaching and support. When parents set a personal goal—say to become a stronger public speaker or to learn to negotiate with decision makers—organizers scaffold their learning and development.

CADRE holds political education sessions and monitoring team meetings on a regular basis where parents learn a critical history of public education and the way the school-to-prison pipeline operates at a systemic level. Parents also build organizing skills, engage in political analysis, and learn about issues related to the current activities of the organization. The more experienced parents join the core parents team, which is authorized to make decisions for the organization. McGowan says that

> Many parents come to us feeling hopeless and powerless. I feel it. That's what we're combating the most in our organizing: to empower parents beyond the feeling of powerlessness, helplessness. Our methodology has a lot to do with self-reflection and with goal setting, stepping into their self-worth and their power.

CADRE is known for taking its time, not rushing decisions or pushing parents into actions unprepared. Organizer Edgar Ibarria speaks of the attention given to preparation.

> If a parent is ready to share a story, how can we make sure that they are emotionally prepared? We go through every little incident where they might feel their emotions triggered. Just the level of detail of guiding the parents through a story so they'll be able to say something. By the time that they are in the meeting with everybody, they are emotionally and mentally prepared for that space.

Broadnax says the organization is thoughtful and systematic about the supports parents need to be fully involved. CADRE provides childcare, transportation, and translation to every meeting, for example.

Parents report that the relationships built among them create love and solidarity, the CADRE family to which Lettie Arevalo refers. Eddie Madison explains that

> All of these ladies are my sisters. They're my family. As you can see, Lettie does not speak a lot of English and I don't speak a whole lot of Spanish, but we know how to communicate with each other. We know that we have love for each other. The well-being of her children is a concern for me. The well-being of my children is a concern for her. We're all here fighting for the same thing.

The CADRE family has become a force for parent love in the national movement to end the school-to-prison pipeline. Participation in this national movement, however, has also been valuable to CADRE. South LA parents meet other parents from across the country and share and learn. This helps create a political identity for parents that is vitally important because they are so often demonized and blamed. According to core parent Yvonne Green, being part of the national DSC is important because

> When parents unite our voices, we know that we're not alone in this struggle. We are all connected and that's how we know we're together. We listen to our voices and take whatever we hear back to our place of origin and that makes it a national struggle and a national voice.

Eddie Madison summarizes what it means for parents of color to be part of this movement.

> A lot of times the school makes you feel like you don't have any rights. CADRE let me know that as a parent you can stand up for yourself. You have rights. You have a say in what goes on at your child's school. You have a say how your child should be taught. How your child should be disciplined. CADRE has given me the inner strength to talk and to fight.

The Labor Community Strategy Center:
Ending Truancy Ticketing

In the year following CADRE's victory, children's rights and disability rights lawyers and advocates based in LA, including Rosa Hirji who chaired the group, began to convene as a "chapter" of the national advocacy network that had begun calling itself the Dignity in Schools Campaign (DSC). They invited CADRE and another organizing group—the Labor Community Strategy Center—to participate to create connections to the organizing campaigns that were happening. In the ensuing years, the original advocacy groups began to drop off, while Public Counsel and the Children's Defense Fund California (CDF-CA) became much more active. Meanwhile, the chapter added the Youth Justice Coalition as a member and began mobilizing members to attend and testify at board of education meetings. Eventually, the three organizing groups—CADRE, Strategy Center, and Youth Justice Coalition—came to anchor the DSC LA chapter with Public Counsel and CDF-CA providing technical and advocacy support. According to Strategy Center organizer Manuel Criollo, prior to any formation as DSC-LA, the groups had already began connecting with one another, especially after CADRE's victory. The groups found a strong basis for unity around their shared commitment to building a larger movement to address systemic racism.

> There was at least some level of broad unity around tackling racism and being open and frank about racism and about criminalization, and that we were trying to build a movement bigger than just policy issues around school-to-prison. That is what glued us together and made us gravitate toward each other in contrast to just forming a big tent around one issue.

One of the first campaigns DSC-LA supported was the effort by the Strategy Center to end the practice of police ticketing of students for truancy. The Los Angeles School Police Department had the practice of stationing police officers on the steps of schools and issuing truancy tickets to students arriving late for school. In other words, police ticketed students for trying to enter school. When they were just outside of school grounds, such as between a bus stop and campus, the LAPD would cite them. Both law enforcement agencies collaborated on this practice and argued that students arriving late were outside of school during school hours and therefore technically truant and in violation of the city's daytime curfew statute passed in 1995. Students, however, sometimes arrived late because they had to take younger siblings to school when normal arrangements fell through or because their bus was late. Police issued many of the tickets during sweeps of the blocks surrounding schools and students reported being handcuffed, having their bags searched, or their names entered into gang databases.

This was no small problem. During the years 2005–2009, police issued tickets to 47,000 students. The impact on students was significant. Students were charged up to $250 per ticket. Students had to miss at least one day of school, sometimes more, to appear in court and they had to be accompanied by a parent or guardian who often had to miss work. As the tickets piled up, some families ended up owing a thousand dollars or more. The most vulnerable youth—like homeless and foster youth—often had the highest fines. The courts would issue summons to students who had not paid, and, if students did not appear in court, the police would enter schools and arrest them. Many students ended up in juvenile detention centers as a result. In fact, truancy ticketing was the number one reason for police referral of students to the juvenile justice system. Unpaid fines also resulted in driver's license holds for youth even as they became adults—over the years, holds affected upward of 300,000 people.[13]

Black and Latinx students made up almost all the ticketed students. In 2011–2012, 93% of all LAUSD arrests and tickets went to Black and Latinx students. Compared to white students, Latinx students were 2.6 times more likely to be arrested or ticketed, and Black students were 4.5 times more likely. Nearly half of ticketed youth were under age fourteen and some were as young as six or seven.[14]

The Strategy Center collected hundreds of stories from students impacted by the practice. An eleventh grade Latino student told this story.

I got a ticket when I was late to school waiting for the bus. I'll be honest—I was pretty late—it was already like 9:30am, but I was going to school. I was late because I had gotten home at 11:30pm from work. Then, I had to stay up finishing a school project until 2:00am. . . . It was embarrassing being seen in the cop car by other people at school. I know I need to tell [my parents] so they can come with me to court but I am scared because they are undocumented.

An eleventh grade Latina student was illegally searched when ticketed.

My sister and I were late for school after we decided to eat breakfast at McDonalds. Two male police officers told us to meet them outside . . . One police officer searched our purses and the other searched us. I was really shocked that I was being searched. I know that I could have said that I do not consent to the search, but I was too afraid to tell the officers that. . . . They escorted my sister and me to school in the police car and took us to the Dean's Office. The officer asked for our names and then gave us tickets . . . My parents cannot afford these tickets![15]

Founded in 1989 by Eric Mann, the Strategy Center's mission is to develop consciousness, leadership, and organization among oppressed peoples to build local, national, and international social justice movements. In the early 2000s Strategy Center organizers started a union for public bus riders and began to talk with students going to school on buses. As organizers heard about the high fines students were receiving, the group adopted the view that truancy policies were an important part of the larger system that was criminalizing Black and Brown students in LA. At the same time, the Strategy Center was developing its analysis of mass incarceration as a new form of racial control; mounting a campaign against truancy ticketing seemed to be a way to directly address the issue. The Strategy Center built a coordinating committee to explore these issues headed by lead organizer Damon Azali with Barbara Lott Holland, Eric Mann, Patrisse Cullors, and Alex Caputo Pearl in 2003.

Taking Action with Students in Schools

In 2006–2007, the Strategy Center established its first Taking Action Clubs in LA high schools, starting with some of the young people it met on the bus campaign. Many of these students had experienced harassment at the hands of police officers. Abel Navarro, a Latino student of Mexican heritage and a student leader with the Taking Action Club at Hawkins High School, said the police stop him at least once a week when he rides his bike to school or home, and it takes a toll on him.

> The police assume I did something bad or that I was running from something bad, or they just assume that something bad has to come from someone going at a fast pace. Honestly, being a young teenager, who wouldn't want to go fast? I'm always going fast. They'll just hold you there on the street until they get a call about a crime. If they don't get a call, they'll eventually say, "All right, well you're free to go."

Michael Davis, an African American student leader of the Taking Action Club at Manual Arts High School, called the practice of police picking up students for truancy and dropping them off at school in police cars "public humiliation."

With students leading the effort, the Strategy Center launched the Community Rights Campaign (CRC) in 2006. The campaign's slogan became: "Hey LAUSD! I'm pre-med, pre-job, not pre-prison!" The CRC's demands included ending truancy/tardy tickets and stopping the criminalization of Black and Brown students by the Los Angeles School Police Department. To be in alliance with CADRE, Public Counsel and other organizations demanding positive school discipline and ending zero tolerance at LAUSD, the CRC also added the demand for "counselors not cops." With support from Public Counsel, the CRC surveyed 1,000 students about their experiences with truancy ticketing, treatment by police, and other issues related to the school-to-prison pipeline. CRC petitioned the LA police for ticketing data and began to work with legal advocates like Ruth Cusick who had moved to Public Counsel and the ACLU of Southern California who represented students unfairly ticketed and helped the Strategy Center analyze data and produce reports.[16]

Strategy Center organizers combined personal support and mentoring of student leaders with political education. According to organizer Ashley Franklin, mentoring happens in one-on-one meetings with youth leaders where the personal becomes political, and "Young people become a part of your family."

> One-on-ones is checking in on how they're doing in life and how they're doing politically, creating plans of where you want them to go, reading together, growing together and sharing with one another.

The Strategy Center teaches young people about the connection between contemporary experiences and historical oppression. According to organizer Zoe Rawson,

> We hold political education sessions with students about what does it even mean that it's a curfew, which is a very loaded term in terms of the legality to stop youth of color during the day, in the street, for nothing other than being in a public place. It has historical connections to criminalizing freedom of movement for people of color which has connections to slavery and the Black Codes.

Franklin says that political education helps students see, "there's something much larger happening in the world. It helps young people's imagination just go."

Like CADRE, the Strategy Center also sees building Black and Brown unity as necessary to make the kind of structural changes it seeks. Manuel Criollo explains that the Strategy Center attracts young people who are questioning the racial divisions they see in their community and are looking for ways to connect. The group emphasizes the role of anti-Black racism even as it addresses racism toward Latinx people and others.

> We get very specific to the histories of resistance of each individual community, especially Chicanos in the Southwest, even when we uplift the unique role of Black struggle in the United States. You'll see me doing presentations

in Boyle Heights in the middle of a Chicano-Mexican neighborhood and I talk about how central the struggle against slavery was for establishing the right to education.

The national civil rights organization Advancement Project also helped young people use data to create maps showing ticketing concentrated in the heavily Black and Latinx South and East LA areas. Meanwhile, students wrote petitions and organized rallies. They gave testimony about their experiences with truancy ticketing at community forums, at meetings with the police, and eventually at city council hearings.

The Strategy Center led a concerted campaign over several years to end truancy ticketing and scored several partial victories along the way. As a result of CRC organizing with Youth Justice Coalition, CADRE, and other allies in DSC-LA, in May 2010 then School Police Chief Mike Bowman announced that school police would start to limit ticketing. In 2010 Juvenile Court Judge Nash, frustrated with truancy tickets flooding his court, set up a truancy task force to recommend alternatives. In April 2011 newly appointed School Police Chief Steve Zipperman announced a plan for police to severely restrict truancy ticketing. Finally, on February 13, 2012, LA City Councilor Tony Cardenas offered a motion to revise the municipal code to essentially end police ticketing of students for truancy once and for all. Students attended the historic council meeting dressed up in either caps and gowns or orange prison jumpsuits to dramatize the choice before councilors. The policy was passed unanimously.[17]

Ending Citations and Returning the Tank

Building on the victory against truancy ticketing, the Strategy Center extended its campaign to include police ticketing and arrests of students for all infractions in school. The CRC along with DSC-LA had already issued a report in 2010 documenting cases of police abuse and violation of student rights, noting that with 340 sworn officers and 147 school safety officers, LAUSD had the largest school police force in the country. In 2012 the CRC with the Center for Public Integrity reported that between 2009 and 2011, police issued more than 33,500 citations to lower-level juvenile court with more than 40% going to children 14 years of age or younger. Officers often arrested or cited students for nonviolent and rather minor violations, including possessing alcohol or marijuana on campus. Students led the new campaign against arrests and citations, using skills honed in the truancy campaign. The coalition won a series of victories culminating in August 2014, when LAUSD announced it would end the policy of arresting or citing students for minor infractions, referring students to interventions instead.[18]

Just after this victory, Strategy Center organizers traveled to Ferguson, Missouri, to support African American activists protesting the killing of Michael Brown. They faced police with armored vehicles—tanks—received from the federal government under its 1033 program, where the military provided excess equipment for free to local law enforcement agencies. When these organizers returned to Los Angeles, they discovered that the LA school police had received an armored vehicle and military grade equipment from the 1033 program too—including three grenade launchers and sixty-one semi-automatic assault rifles.[19]

Questioning why LAUSD needed military weapons and the message it sends to students and their families, the Strategy Center launched a campaign to get the school police to return the tank and weapons and issue an apology for accepting them in the first place. Laura Aguilar, a student leader with the Taking Action Club at Manual Arts High School, said students felt the campaign was important because:

> These are weapons that are used in war. It tells us the warfare now is towards people of color. . . . They're meant for destruction. I don't want their presence to be the destruction of my community.[20]

The Strategy Center drew on its movement connections to bring national attention and support to this local campaign. At DSC's annual meeting held in LA in 2016, participants joined a march against the 1033 weapons organized by the Strategy Center outside the school district offices. Members of DSC, AEJ, and other groups put pressure on the Obama administration to cancel the program entirely, nationalizing this initially local struggle. As a result of pressure from advocacy groups, the Obama administration agreed to restrict the program but declined to cancel it entirely. However, after a heated eighteen-month campaign, LAUSD did finally agree to return the weapons, end participation in the program, and issue the apology, becoming the first school district in the country to withdraw from the 1033 program. The victories of the Strategy Center against policing practices and the 1033 program had a significant national impact, spurring on the school-to-prison pipeline movement to challenge the presence and practices of police in schools.[21]

Youth Justice Coalition: Organizing System-Impacted Youth and Families

Campaigns led by young people with the Strategy Center ended truancy ticketing and reduced other forms of ticketing and arrest of students. What happens to the educational and life trajectories of young people, however, who have been or are still being arrested in community and school settings? The Youth Justice Coalition (YJC) formed in 2003 to address the issues facing young people like this, that is, system-impacted youth and their families.

That includes young people like Tanisha Denard. Denard lived three miles from her high school and often arrived late because she missed her bus, or it was full and drove by without picking her up. She started getting truancy tickets.

> At that time, I wasn't familiar with the court system. I didn't know. I thought it was a ticket and then I can go to class because the first ones that I got, nothing ever happened. But over time, they became warrants for you to appear in court which I didn't even know I had to do.

The police eventually came and arrested her at school, and she ended up in a juvenile detention center for a month. Upon her release, she had five days to re-enroll in a school or face return to detention. Fortunately for her, Tanisha received a flyer from YJC as she left the detention center telling her about the group's FREE LA High School, designed for young people impacted by the system. Tanisha enrolled before the deadline. She eventually graduated and became an organizer for YJC working to reform the detention system and move funds from policing to youth services.

Founded originally by a group of people impacted by the criminal justice system, the YJC's mission is to "dismantle policies and institutions that have ensured the massive lock-up of people of color and the consistent violation of youth and communities' Constitutional and human rights." According to co-founder and organizer Kim McGill:

We woke up right away to the fact that LA County locked up more people than anyplace else in the world, has the largest juvenile hall system in the world, largest probation department in the world, largest county jails in the world, largest sheriff's department in the world, largest court system in the world, and deports more people than anyplace in the nation.

YJC made ending the school-to-jail track one of its top priorities. According to McGill, the coalition was distinctive for its focus on the "back end" of the track.

A lot of people who have been pushed out of school haven't necessarily experienced the jail side of the school to jail track, where maybe the criminalization they've experienced is searches in classrooms and ticketing and truancy sweeps. Our organizing has also addressed what it means when you get locked up and you can't come back to your home school or you can't come back to your entire district. Or, based on a gang allegation, you're expelled from the school or district just because of what you wore or what you're assumed to be.

Nationally, 80% of people in prison do not have a high school degree and the large majority struggle with access to jobs, housing, and services when they re-enter their communities after incarceration. YJC tries to avoid the term "gang," using "neighborhood affiliation" instead, because the group believes that youth of color are often labeled and criminalized in a racist manner as gang members and the phenomenon is misunderstood.

FREE LA High School

In 2007, YJC opened FREE LA High School to be a force for liberation for young people. The school serves youth aged sixteen to twenty-four as an alternative to incarceration and as a re-entry program for youth coming home from lockups. FREE LA High School follows principles aligned with liberatory education and a community organizing philosophy. Learning is culturally relevant and project-based, and the courses promote critical thinking. Every Friday, students take "street university," where they gather in circle to talk about issues in their lives and build relationships; they also circle up by gender identity and sexual orientation. They learn about YJC campaigns and organizing skills and they end by creating "dream boxes" or maps through which they envision their future.[22]

FREE LA High School is located in YJC's Chuco's Justice Center building, which is a youth and community space the group makes freely available for artistic, educational, and movement-building gatherings. YJC named it after Jesse "Chuco" Becerra, one of YJC's youth organizers who was murdered in September of 2005. YJC runs a Welcome Home program through the center that supports young people returning from jail or prison, providing services and advocacy. YJC organizer Dayvon Williams, who was jailed as a teenager for residential burglary and found YJC when he returned to the community, helps run the program.

> Welcome Home provides resources for clothes, food, bus passes, resources for jobs, and some housing programs as well to help people get back up on their feet. We go with families to see court officials and we organize and work on bills at the Board of Supervisors, Police Commission meetings, and Sacramento.

YJC also offers a wide variety of educational and training classes to families and community members. Thousands of youth have learned about their rights and what to do if the police stop them.

Transformative Justice

YJC offers a form of restorative justice that it calls transformative justice. YJC believes restorative justice as typically practiced is often compromised when used in the court system and schools and ends up assigning blame rather than creating transformational change in systems. In McGill's view, "How can we restore something we never had in the US since colonization?" Transformative justice is "about transforming the individual and the environments that we live in."

> We believe that it's not just about determining the harm that was caused and repairing that harm but also looking at the root causes that led to the conflict in the first place and seeing that both sides have been harmed and both sides have also harmed others and how do we address the root causes, how do we heal the community and school factors that led to it.

FREE LA school uses transformative justice or TJ circles to handle disputes that arise between students and among members of the community and rule violations like coming to school high on drugs. According to Joey Reyes,

> We don't ticket students. We don't fine them. We don't criminalize them. We always say "No, we need a circle." We hold a transformative justice circle so we can address the issue and then we go from there.

Abraham Colunga, who was formerly neighborhood affiliated and spent eleven years in jail, is the school's peacebuilder; he says that when a fight breaks out in a regular school, "School cops get involved. The aggressor gets expelled and the other person gets suspended."

> Here, we put them into separate rooms. If they're too hot in the moment and want to be left alone, okay just chill out. Once both parties are able to comprehend and not be mad, we'll go straight into an emergency TJ circle. We figure out what the problem is. Who is harmed and what to do to repair the harm—on both sides.

Stacey, the school's therapist, says that YJC's organizing approach connects healing and justice, that is, healing is part of the process that helps young people fight for justice which is necessary to end the systemic causes of trauma.

Some students at the school come from different neighborhood affiliations and the school serves as a safe space to reduce conflict. According to math and science teacher Oscar Moreno:

> I've seen rival gang members here playing basketball together, talking side by side. And they're not talking about killing each other, just talking about social justice, life, things that they could relate to each other. Like "Oh you've been harassed by police? I've been harassed by police."

YJC involves youth in campaigns for policy change at local and state levels. All students at the school participate but some become more involved and join LOBOS (Leading Our Brothers and Sisters Out of the System). LOBOS members receive a small stipend and work as organizers with other students and system-impacted youth in the community. In 2015 YJC led an effort with Strategy Center and DSC-LA to win amnesty for youth who had received a total of 245,000 tickets for fare evasion on public transit and led the effort to pass state legislation decriminalizing fare evasion for minors. YJC also helped push the LA County Board of Supervisors to pass an ordinance that required LA County juvenile facilities to ban the practice of placing youth in solitary confinement and, if deemed necessary for physical safely or a "cooling off" period, sharply limiting the time allowed. Former LOBOS and now organizer Dayvon Williams feels passionately about working on campaigns like this because he experienced solitary confinement himself.

> I have epilepsy. While I was in the cell, I started coughing up, throwing up, shaking a little bit. The officers came to the window yelling, "Something is wrong with him! Something is wrong with him!" I said I have epilepsy, but they thought I was lying, and they placed me in solitary confinement for about two weeks.[23]

YJC has also leveraged its base of participants and allied with other organizations to advocate for state legislation in Sacramento. This is a big commitment as the drive from LA to the capitol takes six to seven hours or more; in 2015, YJC brought youth to Sacramento twenty-seven times. In this way the group helped pass a state law that ended discrimination against system impacted youth coming home from lockups so that young people would have a right to go back to their home school or to a comprehensive high school.

YJC has also organized to challenge the "war on gangs" which YJC sees as a war on youth and communities of color, including working to end the use of gang databases and gang injunctions. By 2015 more than sixty-five thousand young people—96% of whom were Black or Latinx—had been placed in the LA County gang database, often without their knowledge and without clear justification. Injunctions have been used to restrict freedom of motion and association of suspected gang members, a group that includes thousands of innocent young people. Police can arrest a young person in the database if they find him or her in the presence of another suspected gang member, even if neither knew they were in the database in the first place.[24]

YJC then spearheaded the LA for Youth campaign that calls for 5% of all city and county spending on law enforcement to be diverted to youth and educational services. At the county level, these funds would be enough to pay for 70 youth centers and 650 youth workers as well as 35,000 additional youth jobs and internships. Over 100 organizations co-sponsored the campaign.

Leveraging its pioneering local work, YJC has made important contributions to the national movement to end the school-to-prison pipeline. As discussed in Chapter 3, when the Sandy Hook school shooting happened in 2012 and President Obama called for more money for school police, YJC led a process to create a collective response from youth of color across the country called "You Can't Build Peace with A Piece (gun)." Within a few months, over three hundred young people and scores of allied organizations signed the statement and used it to push back against increasing police and military presence at schools. In addition, FREE LA has served as a national model for building a police-free school that uses transformative justice to create a safe and supportive environment for students.[25]

It's hard to exaggerate the meaning that YJC and FREE LA High School has had for its students and especially for the LOBOS. Juan Pena says he came to the United States from Mexico speaking no English and was placed in an English-only class with no language support. When he acted out because he could not understand what was happening, he became a target of teachers. One teacher, for example, told him, "You're not gonna' be shit, you're gonna' be a bum." When falsely accused by a white student of drug possession in fourth grade, a police officer handcuffed him. In later years, he was repeatedly suspended, physically assaulted by school staff, and eventually expelled. Then he discovered FREE LA school, which gave him a new lease on life. He got his degree and now works on organizing campaigns as a LOBOS.

> I'm still alive. Honestly, I didn't think I was gonna' be alive this far. I'm now thinking about what I do with my life. I'm about to be 23 years old. I got to do something with my life. I got to go to school. I got to step up to the plate even more. YJC has opened up my eyes a lot.

The Movement Grows: The School Climate Bill of Rights

As the movement grew in LA and across the country, new actors entered the field. In 2011, two private foundations—the California Endowment and the Liberty Hill Foundation—sponsored the creation of a Brothers, Sons, Selves (BSS) Coalition of youth organizing groups in Los Angeles. The coalition included the Strategy Center as well as Inner City Struggle (ICS) in East LA and Community Coalition in South LA. ICS and Community Coalition had years of experience organizing young people to address education issues, including getting LAUSD to ensure that all secondary schools offered the "A to G" courses required to pass in order to be admitted to a four-year state university. These groups had seen their campaigns as challenging the school-to-prison pipeline broadly understood as systemic inequities but had not focused on changing school discipline policy before.

In 2011, the BSS Coalition decided to launch a campaign for a school climate bill of rights that would include a ban on suspensions for willful defiance, a highly subjective and vague category prone to racially biased application. CADRE became a strategic partner to the campaign and other DSC-LA groups like Public Counsel, YJC, and the Children's Defense Fund also supported the campaign, with YJC eventually joining the BSS Coalition. Young people led the campaign, testifying at board of education meetings, mobilizing their peers for rallies and actions, working with the media, and lobbying board members. The coalition got strong support from board member Monica Garcia and, as the tide was turning nationally against zero tolerance, from some officials within LAUSD as well. With ten member organizations and a larger support network bringing a range of resources to the effort, BSS was able to win the historic bill of rights on May 14, 2013. The bill bans suspensions and expulsions for willful defiance, requires schools to exhaust all alternatives before suspending a student for any cause, requires schools to implement restorative justice as well as SWPBS, and includes language to limit the role of police in schools. The bill also includes data-reporting requirements and provides for the rights of parents to receive training and be included in SWPBS.[26]

On another front, DSC-LA and other groups sought to advocate for use of the additional funds that came to the district when the state passed the Local Control Funding Formula in 2013. The formula increased resources to school districts serving low-income students, English language learners, and foster youth; it also provided more autonomy on spending decisions to local districts while requiring greater transparency and engagement with local communities. In response, DSC-LA and other LA groups worked to ensure the additional funds did not go to policing but rather to restorative justice and positive supports for students. At the time, LAUSD spent $60 million per year on school police and only $7 million on restorative justice.

According to Angelica Salazar from the Children's Defense Fund, DSC-LA and its allies have excelled at pursuing an inside-outside strategy, organizing from the outside to put pressure on the board of education and building relationships with sympathetic elected officials and administrators.

> DSC-LA is very astute in understanding the need for a certain kind of re-lationship building. It's not that you compromise your ideals; it's that you build with clarity and you know what you're going to disagree on before you even get to the meeting. You know where there's room to negotiate. And you know how to neutralize these very powerful political figures when you have your reports or when you have your actions.

By the mid-2010s, the movement to dismantle the school-to-prison pipeline in LA consisted of an ecology of organizations, each with a particular focus or constituency, often supporting each other and amplifying the impact of the movement. Organizing groups like CADRE, Strategy Center, YJC, ICS, and Community Coalition work deeply with parents and students, building leadership and community pressure for change; meanwhile, Public Counsel, the Children's Defense Fund, and ACLU of Southern California bring legal, research, and professional advocacy expertise and resources to the table in strategic alignment and when invited by organizing groups.

As the movement continued to grow, the BSS Coalition and its partners joined groups across the state to get the California State Assembly to pass AB420 in 2014. The act made California the first state in the nation to ban in- and out-of-school suspensions for students in kindergarten through third grade for willful defiance or disruptive behavior and to ban expulsions for all students for willful defiance and other minor infractions like dress code violations. Some sponsors, like the BSS Coalition, felt the legislation did not go far enough because it stopped at third grade and lasted for only an ini-tial three years, so it withdrew its approval at the end. The bill nevertheless represents a historic step toward reducing exclusionary discipline in the nation's largest state and inspired state-level campaigns in other localities like VOYCE's SB100 campaign in Illinois.[27]

Meanwhile, organizing against the police presence in schools continued to deepen and expand. CADRE and other veteran DSC members played a key role in bringing seventeen organizations together across the state to form a DSC-California chapter that focuses on ending the presence of police in schools entirely and centers the work of the Black Organizing Project (BOP), whose goal was to eliminate the Oakland School Police Department by 2020. When mass protests erupted in 2020 against the police killing of George

Floyd in Minneapolis, the police-free schools movement gained momentum. DSC-California groups like BOP and Coleman Advocates in San Francisco leveraged years of police-free schools organizing to win their demands. Coleman Advocates ended the school district's contract with the city police department while BOP won the elimination of the school district's police department. Groups in LA were not able to completely defund school police but, through a resolution proposed by Monica Garcia, the board of education cut the $70-plus million school police budget by 35% or $25 million. In 2021, the board cut the budget by another $25 million.[28]

A Dramatic Drop in Suspensions and Continued Push for Accountability

As a result of over fifteen years of organizing, beginning with CADRE's campaign for SWPBS, the number of suspensions fell dramatically in Los Angeles. In the 2007–2008 school year, LAUSD students lost 74,765 instructional days due to out-of-school suspensions. By the 2016–2017 school year, that number had dropped to fewer than 5,600 days. Meanwhile, by 2016–2017 LAUSD had conducted "train the trainer" programs in alternatives to suspensions like community-building circles at 459 district schools with plans to implement restorative justice in all schools by 2020.[29]

Although still high, police ticketing and arrests have also decreased, at least on record, reducing contact between students and the criminal justice system. Between 2014 and 2017 the number of arrests by LA school police fell by about 10% and citations dropped by almost half. Meanwhile diversions to alternative programs increased, roughly tripling. By another measure, the number of juvenile arrests in Watts in the heart of South LA fell from forty-six per thousand youth in 2011 to fifteen per thousand in 2017.[30]

Organizers and advocates nevertheless remain concerned with the extent and depth of change in school climate and the treatment of students of color and their families even with dramatically lower suspension rates. Organizers fear that students of color may be pushed out of classrooms into hallways or detention rooms even if they are not officially suspended. Meanwhile LAUSD continues to invest relatively small resources into promoting restorative justice and it lacks sustained efforts to train teachers in positive approaches to discipline beyond a one-time effort. In response, organizers continue to advocate for use of the additional funds from the Local Control

Funding Formula to support restorative justice and SWPBS and have pushed for more extensive and sustained teaching training programs to better prepare teachers in positive approaches.

In this light, CADRE continues to monitor implementation of SWPBS and to train parents to hold schools and the district accountable for genuine changes in treatment of students and their parents. In 2017, ten years after LAUD adopted SWPBIS, CADRE along with partner Public Counsel issued its second shadow report where it found continued and large racial disparities in school discipline. At the twenty schools in South LA in which CADRE parents are active, Black students were 7.5 times as likely to be suspended as their white and Latinx peers. The parent-led study found severely limited implementation of SWPBS with little family and community participation. Schools in which CADRE parents advocated for inclusion fared better than South LA schools as a whole where fully 94% scored limited or insufficient in family and community collaboration. The pattern of persistent racial disparities in exclusionary discipline holds across LA and the state as well. Meanwhile, despite the decline in arrests and ticketing by school police, racial disparities continue in that area as well.[31]

In CADRE's view, a key cause of the continuing school-to-prison pipeline remains the attitude of educators toward parents of color from low-income communities, as much as their attitude toward students. Speaking of teachers, Maisie Chin asks, "How can you love the child but hate the parent?"

> Teachers come with their preconceived notions before they step into the classroom, assuming reasons for people's poverty, assuming reasons why people aren't getting out of poverty, assuming or judging or stereotyping what poverty does to people. That's the racism towards parents of color in general, parents of color in poverty specifically. I don't know how you love the kids and hate the parents, but that seems to be what is still happening to this day.

So, CADRE remains focused on deep work with parents, elevating their stories and experiences. According to Chin, validating the stories of parents is a political strategy that challenges deep-seated, systemic racism.

> Parents embody all the history and the trauma, and they can also embody all the political possibilities of transformation. It's going to be up to them. No one else really has skin in the game to do that kind of work. We believe

parents can be the shape shifters who can and will call forth the better angels in our schools.

Conclusion: A Deep and Broad Movement

The experience of organizing groups working to end the school-to-prison pipeline in Los Angeles shows the value of a movement that is both deep and broad. When parents began meeting in Rosalinda Hill's living room, they catalyzed a movement with deep roots in Black and Brown families and a broad reach across issues and institutions. Such a combination proved powerful to challenge the school-to-prison pipeline in the second largest school district in the country, with an entrenched bureaucracy that had been failing Black and Brown children for decades and a militarized police force that criminalized children and incarcerated more people than any city in the country.

CADRE's deep work with parents anchored the movement in the experiences of families most impacted by systemic racism. Black and Brown parents were the first to raise the alarm and identify the school-to-prison pipeline when nobody else was paying attention. Their stories were and remain compelling. Their questions speak to the heart of systemic racism in public education and our larger society. CADRE's deep engagement helped parents overcome the "blame game," where schools blame "bad" kids and "bad" parents. CADRE's fundamental principle—to not judge the parent—disrupted that narrative and brought together Black and Brown parents caught up in "divide and conquer."

This kind of deep work with parents is incredibly complex and requires focus and commitment over the long term. It involves personal engagement, efforts to address trauma that families experience from poverty, racism and criminalization, mentoring, and support to parents who are changing their lives as they emerge as leaders in their community. It also involves relationship building, political education. and training in organizing skills. There are no shortcuts but doing this work creates a group of powerful parents who are focused, knowledgeable, and persistent. While observers often count numbers at rallies and policy victories, CADRE is "passionate and persistent," as Roslyn Broadnax says, providing what it takes to create not just policy wins but meaningful change in deep-seated systems of injustice.

At the same time, we also learn that to combat the school-to-prison pipeline requires a movement that is broad in two, related ways: in the range of issues and institutions that it targets and in the partnerships and coalitions formed to engage those issues and institutions. While CADRE remained focused laser-like on ending zero tolerance and implementing SWPBS and restorative justice in schools, the Strategy Center targeted truancy ticketing and police arrest and abuse of students in and around schools. Meanwhile, YJC challenged police abuse in communities, court practices and conditions in juvenile facilities, and built a school for system impacted youth. This is an extraordinary array of issues and targets, yet all seem necessary to dismantle the school-to-prison pipeline, which involves interlocking systems of oppression.

Organizing and advocacy groups have also found a way to support each other's campaigns and partner together to form longer-lasting coalitions like DSC-LA, DSC-CA, and the Brothers, Sons, Selves Coalition. These coalitions have drawn on the strengths of each group to leverage resources for change. This larger movement ecology and infrastructure includes the variety of organizing groups involved, each bringing personal stories and testimonies of parents and students. It also includes a range of legal and advocacy groups like Public Counsel, ACLU, and the Children's Defense Fund, which provide expertise in data, legal support to families, and political connections.

Local organizing in Los Angeles has had an impact far beyond the city's perimeter. In many ways the work of organizing groups in LA has been "nationalized" and has had a significant impact on the movement to dismantle the school-to-prison pipeline. CADRE's victory for SWPBS in 2007 inspired organizing across the country and became a key impetus for the formation of the Dignity in Schools Campaign. Its deep work with parents and advocacy by Maisie Chin herself influenced DSC's decision to prioritize leadership by groups working with people most impacted in DSC and the coalition's deeply democratic decision-making culture.

The Strategy Center was one of the early groups to address the role of the police in the school-to-prison pipeline; its truancy ticketing victory and campaign to end the 1033 military equipment program helped move the national movement toward a call for police-free schools. Meanwhile, YJC's focus on police, courts, and the juvenile system and its response to mass shootings have worked to connect the largely school-oriented movement to the law enforcement and criminalization system. Its transformative justice program has been a model for groups looking for restorative approaches that lead to systemic change.

In the end, the LA movement shows that dismantling the school-to-prison pipeline takes policy change in schools and policing systems that results in lower rates of exclusionary discipline and police ticketing and arrests. Policy change is not enough, though. The culture of public education has to shift to respect Black and Brown parents and students and to recognize and value community power, parent power, and student power. Culture change comes through deep organizing with people most impacted by injustice. According to Kim McGill:

> The vision is different when it's led by people most impacted; the demands are more forceful, less watered down. You're less likely to compromise or settle for hollow victories or smaller victories. Movements that matter are built from the ground up, not from the top down.

6

From the Local to the State

Youth-Led Organizing in Chicago

In 2013 a group of high school students from some of Chicago's poorest communities launched a bold plan to pass legislation to end zero-tolerance school discipline across the state of Illinois. After two years of intense organizing, Governor Bruce Rauner signed Senate Bill 100 and the students celebrated their improbable victory. SB100 bans zero-tolerance discipline policies, which required schools to suspend or expel students for certain behaviors, limits the arbitrary use of suspensions, and promotes alternatives to exclusion such as restorative justice. Moreover, SB100 applies to all publicly funded schools including charter schools. SB100 represented the strongest state legislation designed to dismantle the school-to-prison pipeline at the time. Organized into VOYCE—Voices of Youth in Chicago Education—students co-wrote the legislation, mobilized their peers to demonstrate support for the act, built a diverse alliance including parent organizing and advocacy groups, and led the lobbying effort to pass the bill, traveling on a weekly basis to the state capitol almost four hours away to tell their stories and press legislators to pass the bill.

In this chapter, I tell the story of VOYCE and the processes it uses to build the voice and leadership of students who are the most impacted by racist school discipline and policing practices. I highlight the organizing strategy used to pass the SB100 legislation—a combination of personal storytelling, participatory research, and alliance building. I also illuminate the ways that VOYCE connected to the national movement to dismantle the school-to-prison pipeline and how its SB100 campaign both was helped by and influenced that movement. By doing so, I seek to solve a puzzle: How did a relatively small and under-resourced coalition made up mostly of youth of color from low-income communities, who were too young to vote, lead passage of what at the time was the most progressive state law on school discipline in the country?

Willful Defiance. Mark R. Warren, Oxford University Press. © Mark R. Warren 2022.
DOI: 10.1093/oso/9780197611500.003.0007

Mass Incarceration, Public School Failure, and Resistance

In the late 1990s, high school students in Chicago working with a group called Generation Y of the Southwest Youth Collaborative began speaking out against zero-tolerance school discipline practices. They surveyed 350 fellow students and issued one of the very first reports in the country about harsh and racist school discipline policies. Called *Suspended Education*, the report documented a sharp rise in the number of suspensions for minor offenses, such as tardiness and skipping classes, and advocated alternative policies designed to keep students in school and learning.[1]

In many ways, Chicago in the early 2000s represented ground zero for the criminalization of African American people. Black boys and young men bore the brunt of state violence, but Black girls and women as well as Latinx people were also disproportionately targeted. Michelle Alexander highlighted Chicago in *The New Jim Crow*, her seminal work on racism and mass incarceration. Alexander reported that fully 90% of people sentenced to prison for drug offenses in Chicago were African American. So many Black men were criminalized by the mid-2000s that 55% of adult Black males and 80% of the adult Black male workforce in Chicago had a felony record. Zero-tolerance policing was often justified because Chicago neighborhoods exhibited high levels of violence and one of the nation's highest murder rates. Yet the racist application of policing practices seemed to do little to stem intercommunal violence and instead subjected young people to further abuse at the hands of the state. In a famous case, police commander Jon Burge was accused of torturing more than two hundred African American men over a twenty-year period to coerce false confessions. Burge led a group of officers called the "Midnight Crew" whose methods included beating, suffocation, burning, and electrical shock to the genitals, sending scores of innocent Black men to prison. Burge operated with impunity, reportedly referring to his electric shock device as his "n-gger box," which was on open view in his office for many years for any visitor to see.[2]

During this time, Chicago also became known as the home of so-called "dropout factories," that is, high schools concentrated in low-income Black and Latinx communities with very low graduation rates. In many of these high schools, fewer than half of entering ninth graders graduated with their peers four years later. In one of the more extreme cases, only 89 of the 479 students that enrolled in Sullivan High School on Chicago's North Side in

2002 graduated four years later. VOYCE got its start when students joined forces to develop their own solutions to the so-called dropout crisis, which they would later reframe as school pushout.[3]

By the mid-2000s public schools in Chicago were in crisis. As the result of a systematic process of disinvestment, Chicago schools had outdated facilities, failed to offer important support services like nurses and counselors, and often lacked libraries or art and music classes. In the relentless pursuit of raising test scores, the district had so focused on instruction in core subjects that it abolished recess for all students across all schools, including young elementary school children. Rather than invest in low-performing schools, the district began to close them in large numbers and sanction the opening of charter schools in their place. In 2013, the board of education voted to close 47 schools, at the time the largest single closure of schools in the nation, bringing the total to 111 closed schools since 2001. The closed schools were largely in Black neighborhoods, where they performed vital community support roles. Eighty-eight percent of students affected were African American. Closing them seemed to lead to more disruption in students' lives with little evidence that displaced students did any better. Meanwhile, many students now had to cross gang territory to attend their new schools, further increasing their risk of danger and violence.[4]

At the same time, Chicago was also home to a rich tradition of resistance and grassroots organizing. Saul Alinsky, sometimes called the "father" of American community organizing, began his work in the 1930s in the neighborhoods surrounding Chicago's stockyards. Meanwhile, in the 1960s, Chicago became a key center for the Northern civil rights movement and its more radical Black nationalist forms. As a sign of both the strength of the movement and the violence of the state's repressive actions, Chicago police murdered the Black Panther Party leader Fred Hampton in his bed in Chicago in 1969, along with Mark Clark, another Panther leader. Although the media played up the Panther Party's militant tactics and advocacy of armed self-defense, the organization had deep roots in Black communities where it organized people to demand jobs, housing and education, and offered needed services like a free breakfast program.[5]

As the Black Power and other movements of the sixties and seventies waned, community organizing in Chicago persisted and adapted through the 1980s and 1990s and into the early 2000s. Many groups across the city became engaged in addressing the failures of public education, and youth organizing emerged as a strong and vital force. By then, however, an important shift began to take place. A new generation of young organizers of color stepped into leadership of community organizing groups, like Jenny Arwade and Raul Botello from Communities United, called the Albany Park Neighborhood Council at the time. These new leaders increasingly came to reject several features of Alinsky style organizing of the eighties and nineties, in particular its nonracial approach. Instead, organizers of color wanted to explicitly highlight racism as a critical cause of the conditions Black and Latinx young people faced in schools and in their treatment by the police and directly confront racial inequities.

VOYCE Beginnings

Seven Chicago community organizing groups came together to form VOYCE in 2007 because they believed that students had to build power at the citywide level to create much-needed changes in the school district. Communities United became VOYCE's anchor organization, where the coalition was housed and administered, but the coalition also included the Logan Square Neighborhood Association, the Southwest Organizing Project, Kenwood Oakland Community Organization, Brighton Park Neighborhood Council, Organization of the Northeast, and Target Area Development Corporation. Most of the founders of VOYCE had been organizing young people for several years, learning how to combine youth leadership with adult guidance, but others were new to youth-led work. All the groups believed, however, that young people most directly impacted by educational inequity were in the best position to develop meaningful, long-lasting solutions.

VOYCE formed specifically to organize high school students to develop student-centered solutions to the so-called dropout crisis. Funded by a grant from the Gates Foundation and supported by an experienced researcher named Catlin Fullwood, VOYCE youth conducted a participatory action research project to address the dropout crisis. At the time, Chicago Public Schools (CPS) had a graduation rate of less than 50%, one of the lowest in the country. Jenny Arwade, co-director of Communities United, says the research proved powerful, and "We came to see it as a key youth development process that's the foundation of something longer-term."

This was an entirely new way of having really community-owned research that we thought was very powerful. . . . It was also really energizing to the young people who felt like this was exactly what they hoped would be happening in schools, that they would be able to engage in a deep level of critical thinking around issues of concern to them.[6]

Fifty-two young people participated in the year-long project, designed to reveal the experiences of dropping out from the student point of view. Some VOYCE youth had thought about dropping out of school themselves. Maria Degillo, for example, got involved in Communities United after tragedy struck her family. Degillo and her parents came to Chicago after waiting thirteen years for a visa, but they had to leave her older brother behind in the Philippines. He died three years later from cancer caused, they believe, from alcohol abuse due to depression. Two days later, his visa came through. In the wake of his death, Degillo, who had graduated in the top ten of her class in middle school, fell into depression and started cutting classes in high school.

> One day I was caught cutting class. They told me to bring my mom in the next day. The woman laughed and started looking through my paperwork. She said, "Oh, you know you're seventeen. You might as well drop out." Next thing I know, I was in the counselor's office and the counselor was telling me, "You know, high school is not for everyone." I was just crying the whole time. I didn't know what to do. I never thought about dropping out before. They ended up transferring me to an alternative school.

Degillo still did not get the help she needed to deal with her depression, so she continued cutting class in the alternative school and felt labeled as a problem. She got connected to VOYCE, which provided her the support so lacking in school.

> When I first got involved, the organization provided me with a safe place to articulate how I felt and to understand that the hate and the injury that I feel shouldn't be towards myself. It should be towards the system that targets young people of color and low-income families of color.

In VOYCE, Degillo and other youth leaders started to ask, "Why are we dropping out?"

> I did the ethnographic observations, the data analysis, the codings; that was such an eye-opening process of understanding how a lot of things that I hate

about myself are things that were created by the systems that I'm involved in. I used to think, "I'm the young person and I'm the problem." I stepped out of that and I started understanding, well, "Why do I think that way?"

In other words, Degillo and other students started to see low graduation rates as a systemic problem of school pushout rather than an individual problem of students dropping out.

In the end, VOYCE members surveyed 1,325 students and conducted in-depth interviews with 208 students, 110 teachers, and 65 parents. They also visited successful schools in six states. VOYCE students identified lack of trusting relationships as a key part of the problem but also heard concerns by students about harsh school discipline policies. The students issued their report in 2008, calling for school administrators to help build trusting relationships between peers and staff and for an end to the use of harsh discipline policies. The head of CPS at the time, Arne Duncan, agreed to partner with VOYCE to pilot freshman orientation seminars and personalized four-year graduation plans across the district's high schools.[7]

Unfortunately, the changes were too late for Maria Degillo. Since her depression was never treated, she continued to cut classes and eventually dropped out of the alternative school. She stuck with VOYCE, though, and found a new path. VOYCE became her place to recover.

> I was able to talk about my story. I was able to be powerful. I was able to engage other people. And I was surrounded by people who knew that I wasn't stupid. I had a voice. I had something to say. I was worth listening to, and that to me was healing.

Degillo remained involved in VOYCE and eventually got her GED. She enrolled part-time in college while working for VOYCE as an intern and later organizer for the SB100 campaign.

During the campaign, VOYCE also became committed to leading with a racial analysis and naming racism explicitly in its work. Prior to this period, many community groups working on education had shied away from focusing explicitly on racial inequities, believing it to be divisive or unproductive in gaining broader support for group demands. Part of the reason for the shift, as noted earlier, was that organizers of color now led organizations like Communities United and believed that the root causes of systemic failure needed to be analyzed along racial lines. Another reason, according to Jenny Arwade, was the role of youth.

> Young people were leading it with brutal honesty about what's really happening to them. And racial disparities and race was a key public narrative that our young people put forth. This was before Black Lives Matter and a lot of the public education folks felt very uncomfortable with young people saying that [Mayor] Rahm Emanuel doesn't care about Black people, young Black students. When Black students with disabilities are being suspended nine times more than their white counterparts, then that's their reality.

VOYCE and Youth-Led Organizing

The member groups in VOYCE organized students in local high schools, but they also engaged youth through neighborhood connections. While VOYCE focused on educational injustice, member groups also involved young people in a variety of campaigns like immigrant rights and the "Fight for 15" to raise the minimum wage to $15 per hour. Many VOYCE youth leaders brought in other family members, so some young people got involved as early as middle school. Over the years, VOYCE had chapters or otherwise worked with students at 8 to12 schools, with 100–150 core participants at any one time and hundreds engaged in outreach efforts or attending larger actions of the coalition.[8]

VOYCE offered young people training in the skills of organizing, providing opportunities for voice, participation, and leadership to students most impacted by inequities and injustices in schools. VOYCE students were not necessarily "A" students. They had suffered from the effects of poverty, racism, and immigration restrictions and often struggled in schools that lacked resources and culturally relevant curriculum and with teachers who stereotyped them as slow learners or troublemakers. VOYCE created a safe space for these students to heal as the coalition engaged them around their interests and concerns, honored their experiences, and scaffolded their development. Every year VOYCE held a retreat where youth members gathered, usually outside of the city, to share and bond. According to Christian Diaz, youth organizer for Logan Square Neighborhood Association (LSNA) at the time, at the retreats:

High school students sit together around a campfire and talk about what they're most proud of or what their greatest fear is. They really bond and build relationships that carry the work. Young people sit in a circle and it's done through a restorative justice framework. Every person gets to speak. Every person feels heard. It's a cathartic experience for young people to be vulnerable with each other because those places just don't exist in our city much less in our schools.

Kenwood Oakland Community Organization (KOCO) organizer Jitu Brown explains how his group mentored and supported students in a variety of ways.

We helped create individualized graduation plans for our young people. We organized a set of activities like college visits and career days. We brought in speakers to the VOYCE meetings so that the young people could learn about the community.

Young people in VOYCE lead their own campaigns. Speaking of the Southwest Organizing Project (SWOP), youth leader Jose Mancilla says:

We are truly youth-led although we need some guidance. We're the ones that come up with what to do in every community; how to speak about the SB100 bill; and then we're the ones that host the meetings. We do all of everything. When we break out into groups, we have somebody in charge of the groups. We have the chair for the meeting which is youth; everything is youth in the meeting.

Adult staff, however, manage the member organizations and provide advice and training to youth so they can lead campaigns. They helped young people conduct a power analysis to guide their campaigns. Over the years, adult staff raised on average $750,000 annually to support youth-led organizing in VOYCE. Arwade emphasizes the need for youth and adults to build trust and explains how Community United fosters youth-adult collaboration.

For us it's about how we create mutual spaces of respect and joint learning where we are really sharing each other's experiences. Young people have lived experiences and creative ideas and all these other things that they bring to the table, their relationships and networks with other young people. As adults, we bring fifteen years or more of organizing experience.

Our strategy is to bring the best of both of these worlds to actually create a winning strategy.[9]

VOYCE worked hard to help young people build relationships across neighborhoods and across Black and Brown communities often seen as rivals. According to Raul Botello, co-director of Communities United, VOYCE's first campaign to address the dropout/pushout crisis helped unite students who were all affected.

Young people chose the dropout rate or school pushout as the definitive kind of bridging for all the young people from different schools. That was the one time where young people felt like, "Wow, I have so much more in common with folks from the North Side or the South Side." It crossed geography and race and gender and sexual orientation.

LSNA organizer Christian Diaz says that seeing commonalities across communities helps students avoid self-blame and appreciate the systemic causes of dropping out.

Students say, "We don't deserve to have a good school because the students don't care about their education and we're all messing up and we deserve to be punished." But when you have youth from different backgrounds and from different parts of the city sharing the same stories with each other, then I think it elevates their consciousness. They start to realize that this is much bigger than just me and my high school. This is a problem that's really affecting all youth of color in our city who go to neighborhood schools.

Juliet Alejandre, another LSNA organizer, says sharing stories affirms young people. "It was very cathartic as people were being heard and affirmed, and that was beautiful."

Youth leaders in VOYCE say they found support and community in the coalition and its member groups. They felt accepted and also grew and developed. Youth leader Esmerelda Corrado says:

Communities United helped me out of my shell. I was shy all the time, I didn't speak up. I would always stay home, but they told me there is a lot more to the world than you think, and it opened my eyes a bit. This is what keeps me coming and staying here with the community.

According to youth leader Juan Padilla:

> Here in Communities United we created this culture where we have community agreements and one of them is called Be a Croissant Not a Donut, which means be open minded like a croissant and not closed minded like a donut. I describe myself with that because I feel like I was able to open up my mind.

Jonathan (Jade) Aguilar, a trans young woman, participates with Communities United:

> Because I was finding myself in a hole, not being accepted by my family because of who I am. I got the opportunity to come here, and people actually validate me as a woman even if I don't look like a woman and that's just very comforting. I used to go to church, and I found myself being not my authentic self because I had to hide who I was. Communities United gave me the opportunity to be who I am and just show that I have good stuff to bring to the table.

Many young people like Carlil Pittman featured in the Introduction chapter, as well as Jose, Esmerelda, Juan, and Jade went through transformational experiences through their participation in VOYCE, becoming change agents in their lives and in their communities.

Dismantling the School-to-Prison Pipeline in Chicago

VOYCE began its campaign to address exclusionary discipline in CPS as a result both of organic "bottom-up" concern from its youth members and "top-down" inspiration from connections to other groups. VOYCE members and their own friends had been subjected to harsh and racially targeted zero-tolerance policies at schools. Through their work on the dropout crisis, VOYCE students became concerned about zero tolerance and high rates of suspensions as a systemic problem. In other words, VOYCE's focus on the school-to-prison pipeline developed organically from its constituents and their organizing efforts.

Meanwhile, other organizing groups had already been working to end zero-tolerance school discipline policies in Chicago and advocate for restorative justice alternatives. Community Organizing and Family Issues (COFI) and Blocks Together had both been involved in a successful effort to remove zero tolerance from the district's official code of conduct in 2006, although the practice of racially inequitable and harsh discipline continued. In fact, the number of suspensions continued to rise. The groups went on to build community- and parent-led restorative justice programs and peace centers in public schools and continued to advocate for changes in district policy and practice.[10]

At the same time, VOYCE was immersed in national networks of organizing groups working on educational justice issues. Communities United was a founding member of the Alliance for Educational Justice (AEJ), for example, which included twenty-eight youth organizing groups from across the country including Padres & Jóvenes Unidos (PJU) in Denver. Many of these groups had begun to speak out against zero tolerance and the school-to-prison pipeline. As discussed in Chapter 3, PJU won a groundbreaking victory in 2008 to change discipline policies districtwide away from zero tolerance and went on the road to publicize its victory. Pam Martinez, co-director of PJU, came twice to Chicago to share the group's strategies with VOYCE and other groups. Meanwhile, private foundations began to make funds available to organizing groups to address exclusionary school discipline and VOYCE was able to secure support from the Just and Fair Schools Fund when it formed in 2010.

Replicating its earlier strategy, VOYCE launched another participatory action project, this time with assistance from the Advancement Project. In *Failed Policies, Broken Futures*, VOYCE reported that the rate of out-of-school suspensions in Chicago had quadrupled from the 2001–2002 to the 2007–2008 school year, when 23% of all high school students were suspended, mostly for willful defiance or disruptive behavior. Moreover, in the 2009–2010 school year, Black students were nearly four times more likely to receive an out-of-school suspension than their white peers; one out of four Black males were suspended at least once.[11]

VOYCE youth also targeted the impact of policing and school-based arrests, often for minor infractions, on students. At the time, Chicago had police substations located in high schools. These were not security officers or school police but regular Chicago police officers who were permanently stationed in schools and could arrest and book students right in school buildings. VOYCE reported that in 2009 there were 4,500 school-based arrests of Chicago students, 78% of which were for minor infractions. Students who were arrested were 50% more likely to leave school before graduating than students who were never arrested.[12]

Powerful personal stories accompanied these statistics. The report cited the story of Juan, a VOYCE member who in May 2010 was in the second semester of his senior year at a high school on Chicago's north side. Police arrested him outside of school two months earlier for writing graffiti, but he was working hard to improve his grades and graduate on time. One day the security guards called Juan in for questioning about an incident concerning graffiti in the school, because the police computers in their office showed that he had been arrested before. They asked him to name the tagger, but Juan didn't know who it was.

> They said that since I didn't give them his name, they were going to punish me instead, for this one-inch-sized tag that I had made like two years ago, before even my first arrest. I told the assistant principal that I'm doing better in school and I only got a few weeks left to graduation. But all he did was look me in the eye. He didn't answer me; he just left the room.

Juan was handcuffed and taken to the police station, where he spent six hours in an empty cell. He returned to school after a three-day suspension, only to find that his suspension had been extended to two weeks, the maximum length at the time before expulsion. He saw the grades that he had raised to A's and C's drop back to F's again. And as an undocumented student, he now has a record that will make it harder to apply for citizenship.[13]

While the report drew from local stories like Juan's, VOYCE youth also tapped their national networks, visiting thirteen high schools that had implemented alternatives to zero tolerance in various cities and drawing some of their recommendations from model efforts in Denver, Baltimore, and Boston. In the end, VOYCE recommended a complete rewrite of the code of conduct to end harsh and racially inequitable discipline practices and to create the foundation for learning by investing in social and emotional supports for students.

In addition to pushing from the outside, VOYCE proceeded to work with the district administration to try to revise the student code of conduct and to lobby for the creation and support of more positive and restorative approaches to discipline issues. It joined a code of conduct revision process that included other groups that had been organizing for an end to zero tolerance like COFI. VOYCE youth expressed their views in the process which also drew from the model code of conduct developed by the national Dignity in Schools Campaign with the participation of COFI, as well as from efforts to redraft discipline rules by PJU and others.

During this time, VOYCE launched a campaign in response to excessive fines that the Noble Charter School network was charging students. Jamie Adams, a VOYCE student leader, had been personally affected by unreasonable fines when in eighth grade at an ASPIRA charter school. To enter her school, students had to pass by security guards who scanned them with a metal detector wand on their way in. They had to bring a clear book bag to school and wait while guards searched it, making Jamie feel like "I was in jail."

> One time I had a pack of gum in my book bag and apparently they classified that as candy, and they said that it would be a distraction to students. They sent me to the office and, without talking to me and without talking to my parents or anybody else they automatically said, "You know what, you have to pay a dollar per piece of gum that's in your book bag or you can't graduate." I was in eighth grade and it wasn't too far from graduation. So, I had to pay the fees.

Aside from the principal of the issue, for many students from low-income families like Adams, every dollar counts.

> I come from an extremely low-income family. Yeah, that three or four dollars might not have been a lot, but that money could have been used for something else—buying medication or going toward paying bills. It's not like we have money to just throw away.

Researching the issue, VOYCE youth found out that the Noble network had generated $188,000 in fines in the 2011–2012 school year alone. Noble fined students $5 for minor infractions like missing buttons on uniforms and up to $280 for "disrupting the classroom." If students had multiple infractions or couldn't pay the fines that mounted up, Noble required them to attend "behavior modification" classes that cost $140. Supported by their national partner, the Advancement Project, VOYCE helped parents file suit against unreasonable fines. At the same time, the coalition organized to get Noble to change its policy. Working with Parents United for Responsible Education,

VOYCE rallied hundreds of families at district headquarters and acquired prominent media coverage that showed the network in a negative light. On April 11, 2014, VOYCE and its ally announced that the Noble network had agreed to stop fining students entirely. With this victory, VOYCE became one of the first organizing groups in the country to directly confront a charter network around harsh discipline policy and win.[14]

VOYCE was mainly concerned, however, with discipline policy in the district's schools that the large majority of students attended. Although zero tolerance had been removed as official policy in 2006, VOYCE did not see much difference in practice as no limits were set on how harshly students could be punished for minor infractions and little priority was being placed on alternative approaches. VOYCE noted that in 2011 the district spent $51.4 million on school security guards, fifteen times the amount spent on college and career coaches. Through its advocacy work in alliance with COFI and participation in the district's code revision process, CPS adopted another new code of conduct in 2012 that began to set some limits on suspensions. Despite this progress, though, VOYCE youth became increasingly frustrated as they saw the changes in CPS coming "too little and too late" and not penetrating deeply into change in practice at the school level. Part of the problem was turnover at the top of the district's leadership. The district's CEO changed hands four times from 2009 through 2012.[15]

Meanwhile, VOYCE began to hear about the efforts of organizing groups in other localities to take their campaigns to dismantle the school-to-prison pipeline to the state level. In 2012, PJU leveraged its 2008 district-level victory to end zero tolerance in Denver to launch an effort to pass the Colorado Smart Discipline Law to reduce suspensions and racial disparities in discipline across the state. This began a rolling series of state initiatives, each one building on lessons of the previous ones to create even more progressive legislation, in places like California, Massachusetts, and Maryland.[16]

While senior organizers like Arwade and Botello were perhaps in the best position to learn from other groups and conduct overall strategic assessments, VOYCE youth also attended national convenings and learned about cutting-edge organizing campaigns. Carlil Pittman, for example, discusses how the SB100 campaign was inspired by campaigns in other states.

> In Baltimore, they passed something that was very similar to SB100 and I'm like, "Can I get the information? This is exactly what we're trying to do." It was working for them. So being able to see that, this is working over here in

Baltimore, this is working in New York City, this is working in Maryland. We could bring this back to Chicago and show this works; we need to try this.

Meanwhile, in January of 2014, VOYCE youth went to California for a learning exchange with the Gay Straight Alliance Network (now Genders and Sexualities Alliance Network). According to Jamie Adams, these trips had a big impact on young people like herself. They learned that the school-to-prison pipeline

> wasn't just in Chicago, it was in Illinois. Oh, it's not just in Illinois, it's in Wisconsin too. Oh, it's in California. It's in Mississippi. It's in Oakland. It's in Florida. It's all over the country. When hearing the stories of other young people and actually building relationships with them, it's broadened my perspective of how this world works and how organizing works.

VOYCE youth heard about how local groups launched the statewide campaign for Proposition 47 to reduce criminalization of young people of color in California and came back inspired to try to make change at the Illinois statehouse.

In the end, frustrated with the slow pace of change in Chicago and encouraged by victories in other states, VOYCE launched a bold campaign to change school discipline laws across Illinois, which became the campaign for SB100. VOYCE leaders thought that changing the state law would increase the pace of reform at the district level in Chicago. They were also excited, however, to take on the challenge of leading a big statewide campaign.

Launching SB100

VOYCE membership had shifted somewhat over time, so at the launch of the SB100 campaign, the coalition included anchor organization Communities United along with SWOP, LSNA, KOCO, Action Now, and the Brighton Park Neighborhood Council. VOYCE partnered again with the Advancement Project who sent Jim Freeman to help write a bill that would end zero-tolerance school discipline and promote positive and restorative alternatives. Freeman had experience supporting campaigns for local and state level changes in other localities including Denver. Using his attorney expertise,

Freeman drafted the proposed legislation, developing the content in partnership with VOYCE youth. Youth leaders brought their own ground-level expertise, their ideas for policies that would help them, and their dreams for a better future for themselves and their communities. VOYCE students from the different member organizations debated alternatives and consulted with young people from their groups, until they reached a consensus. According to Jose Sanchez, the VOYCE organizer who worked closely with youth, "Every point that we had around the bill had an origin with a young person that had been impacted by it."

> One of the things that we included in the policy was that counselors are no longer allowed to counsel students to drop out. That's because a lot of the youth from LSNA talked about having to stay home a couple of days because they needed to take care of siblings, going back to school and the counselor saying, "Well, you should drop out and maybe go work and then get your GED at some other time."

In the end, students felt strong ownership of the bill. According to Jamie Adams, "There was no part of this bill that we didn't have our foot in."

VOYCE had a solid base of youth leaders but knew that it needed a broader alliance to build the power to pass state legislation. VOYCE staff reached out to a wide set of groups to establish the Campaign for Common Sense Discipline. The coalition included eighteen organizations, including parent organizing groups like COFI; restorative justice organizations like Alternatives, Inc.; as well as state-level advocacy groups like the ACLU, the Illinois Safe Schools Alliance that advocated for safe and supportive schools for LGBTQ students, and the disabilities advocacy group Access Living. According to Karen Lynn Morton of COFI, "The coalition was something that this state has never seen before."

> You had African American and Latino women and a youth group all working together, saying the same thing—that the school-to-prison pipeline is real and that our children are being suspended in mass numbers. I think they had to take notice.

VOYCE then turned to cultivating allies and advocates in the state legislature where Democrats held a majority in both houses. VOYCE found a key sponsor for the bill in Senator Kimberly Lightford, the assistant majority leader, chair of the Black caucus, and chair of the Senate Education Committee. An African American, Lightford had been concerned about the issue of zero-tolerance school discipline and its impact on Black students ever since the 1999 incident in Decatur, Illinois, where seven Black football players were expelled for a fight during a football game. African American state representative William Davis sponsored the bill in the House, but Lightford led the overall effort on the inside.

The legislation VOYCE developed for the 2014 legislative session and sponsored by Lightford and Davis required all publicly funded schools in Illinois to publish data on exclusionary school discipline disaggregated by race. The second part of the bill included restrictions on zero-tolerance practices and the promotion of alternatives. As the 2014 session unfolded, it became clear that VOYCE would have to split the bill and concentrate on passing the data requirements first. SB2793, the data transparency bill, did pass in 2014 and the new data it made available helped make the case for eliminating zero tolerance in the next legislative session.

Building on the victory in 2014, VOYCE and its allies proposed SB100 in the 2015 legislative session. Its key provisions included a ban on zero-tolerance policies that require automatic suspensions or expulsions for specified infractions, limitations on suspensions, a bar on fines and fees for discipline, and the promotion of positive and restorative alternatives.

Using the clout of her leadership positions, Senator Lightford con-vened a table that included groups supportive of SB100 like the Chicago Teachers Union but many that were initially opposed, including the Illinois School Management Alliance representing school administrators, principals, and school boards, as well as state attorney's offices and law enforcement. Some school districts, like CPS, also originally did not sup-port the law.[17]

Lightford argued that change was coming, and traditional opponents of reform in school discipline policy would do better to be at the table, rather than be forced to accept policies to which they had not contributed. It turned out that the management alliance had filed its own school discipline bill, which provided an additional rationale for Lightford to create a negotiating table. Given Lightford's standing and staunch support of school discipline re-form, opponents felt compelled to attend and try to negotiate to defend their interests.

From the point of view of VOYCE and Lightford, this table became the place to hammer out a version of the bill that could win enough support to pass. William Davis explains that the strategy was to move opponents to neutrality.

> Lightford worked and negotiated the bill ultimately to get to a point where groups were neutral on the bill. We figured they wouldn't like it; but if we could get them to a point where they were neutral, that that would be the goal and that would help us to ultimately pass the bill.

Lightford also worked to ensure that VOYCE youth were present for all negotiations. This challenged the insular, "buddy-buddy" culture at the statehouse, according to Jenny Arwade.

> People were so outraged that we would have young people in the negotiations in Springfield because it is such a lobbyist culture: it's very much like you go up the elevator, everyone's smiling, complimenting each other's jewelry. It's very insular and unhealthy. You were only supposed to have two reps per organization, but Lightford would always let us bring however many people we wanted. And they were furious.

The presence of youth changed the dynamic at the table.

> Lightford would refer back to the young people's stories. If somebody said something outrageous, she'd be like, "But this young person just said that this happened to them. You're saying they're lying." Because we brought the real experiences of young people, she was able to ground her work in their experiences.

The Power of Personal Stories

VOYCE brought a busload of students nearly every week throughout the spring 2015 session to the statehouse to tell their stories and lobby for the bill's passage. Students made a big commitment as the journey was nearly four hours each way; they missed class and other responsibilities, had to fit in homework assignments during the trips, and take make-up tests. Speaking of the dedication it took, Amina Henderson-Redwan says. "No teenager wants to get up at five in the morning and do work. It was tiring, but it had to get done." Maria Degillo, the former VOYCE student leader and now organizer, says students were deeply committed.

These young people woke up at five in the morning to drive three hours down to Springfield to go straight into the lobby and just run around, chasing legislators, just for a second to be able to tell their story. I mean, talk about passion, right?

Joel Rodriguez from SWOP says that the staff from member groups had to make a big commitment too, as bringing significant numbers of youth to Springfield every week took a toll on under-resourced organizing groups.

VOYCE students told their personal stories at legislative hearings and in one-on-one meetings with legislators. For example, Amina Henderson-Redwan talked about being arrested and suspended from school. She had gotten into an argument with another student, and both were brought to the dean's office. Amina asked to leave so she could let off steam and not "get physical" with the other student. But the dean refused and called a security guard who put Amina into a chokehold.

I said, "You know what, let me just walk away." Instead, the guard grabbed me and choked me up against the wall, so I had to hit him. The police came up and arrested me and sent me to the juvie center. They said I had to stay in there for 12 hours and couldn't go back to school for ten days. But luckily my principal was lenient and let me come back after maybe the fifth or sixth day.

Juan Padilla told this story:

In my eighth period gym class I was playing badminton with a friend, and she threw a badminton racket on the ground. It bounced back and hit my teacher's leg. He sent her to the discipline office. He wanted to go to the police station within the school and tell them to arrest her, but my principal saw that this was obviously absurd. But she ended up getting a five day out-of-school suspension—that's a full week of school. When she got back, she didn't know how to catch up with her classes and she felt like dropping out.

At first, youth leaders found approaching legislators to be very intimidating. They "prepped endlessly" at the beginning, but over time, learned the ropes and grew more confident. According to Jamie Adams:

My first time I went I was extremely nervous. But after talking to the first couple senators and legislators, you get more comfortable with it, and then by the end you know the Capitol like the back of your hand. You know where this person is. You know where this building is. You know the shortcuts.

Still, it was not always easy. According to Esmeralda Carreno:

Our trips to Springfield were fun and adventurous but when we are in the Capitol, we have to be professional about it. We can't just run around. We have to know what we were doing. So, we would always prep and some-times we would prep again while we were walking to the office. Some of the legislators were tough honestly; they would ask challenging questions like, "Why is it important to me? Isn't this only a Chicago thing?"

VOYCE youth came so often to Springfield that they became well-known fig-ures. Staff would help them track down legislators, sometimes ushering them through back doors. According to Jamie Adams, "The secretaries were really supportive, and they always had candy for us. It was really cool [Laughter]."

VOYCE youth met one on one with individual legislators to gain their commitment to support the bill. Once that commitment was made, young people would take "selfies" or photos on their smart phones with the leg-islator and post them on social media. Posting selfies built momentum for the campaign and also served as a record of the legislator's commitment for which they could be held accountable. Carlil Pittman describes the process VOYCE developed.

We'd all have a paper with the different senators or representatives that we need to hit up and we'd split the list up. If they supported the bill, we asked to get a picture with them. "You say you support our bill, so we put it on social media and that way we can hold you accountable for it." And the sen-ator holds the phone up and we all squeeze in the picture.

Personal stories proved powerful in influencing legislators. The stories coun-tered the narrative that justified zero tolerance, that is, to keep "bad" kids out of class so the "good" kids could learn. The stories revealed that students were being disciplined unfairly for relatively minor offenses. The students in front of legislators did not appear to be bad kids at all. They were articulate, well-informed, and civically engaged young people. Legislators saw them as "impressive" kids who they could feel good about supporting, "great kids" as Senator Lightfoot called them.

> You could relate to them as young people. You could believe that they had a dire commitment to transform and change the way the state law reflected them. They were not shy about standing up to the administrators. They were always still very polite and professional, but they were very good debaters.

The personal connection VOYCE youth made with legislators also gave moral urgency to the cause. Legislators had to face young people who had been victimized and seemed to deserve support. These students and their friends could not wait. They demanded action right away. According to Jenny Arwade:

> When one student Tony shared his story about being arrested three times in school, our legislators were emotionally moved. They felt very connected to him. So now, when we're working with them in Springfield, it's not just, "Oh, here's the group coming down to Springfield." They remember the stories that are driving the work, which creates a different dynamic.

Supporting the legislation also allowed legislators to feel they were on the right side of a justice issue. Legislators, for example, often initiated the process of taking selfies with VOYCE youth leaders. They smiled broadly, feeling good about supporting these bright and positive young people.
Reflecting on the role of students and their stories in the campaign, VOYCE youth leader Jose Mancilla says that young people brought passion.

> The youth are the key to everything because the legislators see that it's the youth's passion. It's their story, it's not the organizers' story. It's their stories.

Juan Padilla says youth demanded to be heard, "To express what they are thinking and what makes them angry and why they are here and why this matters to them." Raul Botello says the stories gave legislators the courage to act.

> I think the personal storytelling really mattered for our champions, because any time it became very difficult during negotiations, Lightford would

pivot back to one of the stories. So, it really gives the legislators courage to be emotionally invested in making those tough decisions, when moving the bill forward or making a yea versus a nay.

Winning Passage of SB100

Personal stories are powerful but could be dismissed as isolated events. A second key element to VOYCE's strategy was to show the widespread nature of exclusionary discipline and its disparate impact on students of color. From 1992 to 2009, Illinois' out-of-school suspension rate more than tripled. By the time of the campaign, Illinois had some of the highest suspension rates in the country. VOYCE pointed out that Illinois students were losing more than one million instructional days to out-of-school suspensions, the vast majority for minor infractions. VOYCE showed that the problem was not confined to Chicago but was spread across the state. VOYCE wanted to demonstrate that it was a statewide issue implicated in most of the districts that legislators represented. VOYCE mined data released by the U.S. Department of Education's Office for Civil Rights and showed that many districts in Illinois had extremely high suspension rates. For example, there were forty-seven out-of-school suspensions for every one hundred students in Thornton Township in South Holland, thirty-six for every one hundred in Proviso Township in Forest Park, and thirty per one hundred in Thornton Township in Calumet City.[18]

VOYCE did not shy away from issues of race and, in fact, intentionally highlighted racial disparities in school discipline. It turned out that Illinois had some of the highest racial disparities across American states. VOYCE pointed out there were thirty-two out-of-school suspensions per one hundred Black students and only five per one hundred white students in Illinois, or more than six times as many. Illinois was suspending the highest proportion of Black students of any state in the country with a quarter of African American male students in the state receiving a suspension each year.[19] According to Representative Davis, the racial disparities provided an additional motivation for legislative support.

I think at the very least not being scared to have a conversation about race is important and was important with regard to this bill. There had to be a recognition that there is disproportionality as it relates to students of color and the discipline that is enacted in schools and unfortunately the statistics bear that out,

In order to strengthen its case and appeal to more conservative legislators, VOYCE brought several other arguments to bear. Perhaps the most important was to highlight the economic costs of exclusionary discipline. Districts lost money when they excluded students and the cost of incarceration far exceeded educating students. VOYCE even called its initiative the Campaign for Common Sense Discipline to try to appeal to legislators on many levels.

The common denominator across legislators, however, was their response to VOYCE youth who met personally with them and told their stories backed up with data. Legislators found VOYCE students to be very well informed and that appeared to incline them to support their cause. VOYCE youth could tell their personal stories, and they could also cite statistics about the extent of exclusionary discipline and its cost. According to Representative Davis, "It probably is a combination."

> It's the stories that they told. While those were personal stories, they also did some research. They had statistical data to show the disproportionate impact of suspensions and expulsions, particularly for students of color. Members like to think we're smart and we like to think that we're learned . . . so we say, "Well, is there any data to support it?" So they were prepared . . . not only with their stories, they had data to show it as well.

One by one, VOYCE youth won legislators to their side, both Democrats and Republicans. Meanwhile, they continued to bring pressure to bear from their allies, with representatives from the Campaign for Common Sense Discipline speaking at committee hearings and lobbing their legislators. The wider alliance reassured legislators that VOYCE had broader support for school discipline reform.

VOYCE youth were able to leverage another resource that came from the national movement, that is, the joint guidance issued by the U.S. Departments of Education and Justice in January of 2014 discussed in Chapter 3 The movement had successfully lobbied the federal government to move away from support for zero-tolerance discipline policy, a process that included visits to Washington by VOYCE youth leaders. The ensuing joint guidance highlighted the harmful and racially disparate effects of zero tolerance and recommended that school districts find alternatives like restorative justice and positive behavioral supports. VOYCE argued that their proposals were now in line with the latest guidance from the federal government, as well as with changes that were occurring in state policy across the country.

By late April, with the original opponents moved to neutrality at Lightford's negotiating table, the bill was put to a vote. SB100 passed the Senate in April by a vote of thirty-eight to sixteen. It passed the House in May by a vote of seventy-three to forty-one and was signed into law by Governor Bruce Rauner on August 24, 2015, to take effect in September of 2016. Rauner, a Republican, was something of a maverick and had campaigned on promises to address issues facing the Black community. Signing SB100 could be a way to fulfill part of his commitment at low financial cost.

As passed, SB100 included the following provisions:

- Bans zero-tolerance policies, where school administrators are required to automatically suspend or expel a student for particular behaviors, unless required by law (for weapon or drug possession);
- Allows suspensions of three days or fewer only if a student poses a threat to others or disrupts the school environment;
- Allows suspensions longer than three days, expulsions, or disciplinary transfers to alternative schools only if other options, such as restorative practices, have been exhausted;
- Bans fines for disciplinary infractions;
- Prohibits school staff from encouraging students to drop out of school; and
- Promotes alternative restorative approaches.

Several factors coalesced to support passage of the bill. Democrats had a majority in both houses of the state legislature and were open to a message of reforming school discipline. The bill's legislative sponsors were well positioned in both chambers and Senator Lightford held enough clout to corral potential opponents. These opponents were caught off guard when the bill was introduced and were never able to mount an effective opposition. The powerful Chicago Teachers Union had recently elected a reform slate to its top officer positions, and they came out in support of the bill. The Republican governor was inclined to fulfill part of his election promise to the Black community by signing the bill.

More broadly, a changing political context also contributed to passage of SB100. The national trend was moving away from zero tolerance, as discussed in Chapter 3, and this helped create momentum for passage. The federal guidance warning against zero tolerance produced an even more favorable public and educator climate for ending zero tolerance. By 2015, spurred on by Black Lives Matter, growing activism and political dynamics made many Democratic officials more reliant on mobilized voters of color and responsive to decriminalizing demands. Even some Republicans became open to some forms of decriminalization as conservatives came to appreciate the high cost of mass incarceration.[20]

While all these factors contributed to the passage of SB100, the bill's key promoters were nevertheless VOYCE youth who traveled weekly to Springfield and told stories of their lived experience with the school-to-prison pipeline and its real-life consequences. According to many participants, the passion, leadership, and energy of the young people provided the key force for passage of the bill. Senator Lightford, reflects this consensus when she says that when legislators "can put a face with the statistics, it makes a difference."

> The 2012 study from the federal civil rights data showed that Illinois suspends proportionately more African American students than any other state in the U.S. Someone can tell you that or you can read it, but when you have students come to say, "I'm one of those students," that has an impact.

Lessons from Youth-Led Organizing in Chicago

Following passage of SB100, school districts across Illinois began to revise their codes of conduct to align with the new state law, reducing zero tolerance across the state, and the number of suspensions fell. The total number of in-school suspensions across Illinois declined from about 190,000 in the 2014–2015 school year to about 160,000 in the 2018–2019 school year, while the number of out-of-school suspensions fell by one-third from about 150,000 to just over 100,000. This drop mirrored the trend of falling suspension rates in Chicago following the changes in the code of conduct and then the continued impact of SB100. The number of suspensions fell in Chicago from about 25,000 in the 2016–2017 school year to just over 20,000 in 2018–2019. This is significant evidence of the impact of VOYCE and other parent and youth organizing groups and their advocacy allies in shifting the narrative and practice of public schools away from zero tolerance. Nevertheless, as in other places where suspensions have fallen as a result of organizing efforts, racial disproportionality continues.[21]

This chapter has shown the power of young people who are most impacted by educational injustice leading a campaign to dismantle the school-to-prison pipeline in a state with some of the highest suspension rates and largest racial disparities in the country. It's a remarkable story because, as noted at the beginning of the chapter, VOYCE represents a group of students of color at a relatively small set of high schools in one city who themselves cannot vote; yet VOYCE played the key leading role in getting reform legislation applying to the entire state passed at the statehouse, legislation that was the most progressive in the country at the time. Like in Los Angeles and Mississippi, we see how the movement conducted deep and broad organizing.

We learned how youth-led organizing facilitated by adult organizers deeply engaged students, helping them build relationships, think critically, and develop as leaders capable of telling their stories, analyzing data, crafting legislation, and lobbying legislators from across the state. While the initiative was youth-led, it involved a partnership with adult staff who raised funds, mentored youth, taught political education and organizing skills, facilitated connections with other allies in Illinois and across the country, and led strategy development conversations. The partnership combined the wisdom, experience, and connections of seasoned adult organizers with the energy, experience, analysis, and perspectives of young people who lived the school-to-prison pipeline every day. In the end, though, young people made key decisions about SB100 and provided the passion that moved legislators to act.

We learned about the power of personal storytelling by youth leaders to change the narrative about zero tolerance, provide moral urgency to action, and create a personal connection that helped move legislators to support their bill. Stories proved critical but VOYCE combined them with data that showed the widespread nature of harsh and racially disparate discipline policies. They built a larger coalition to bring other allies and more resources to bear on the campaign. They negotiated and proved willing to compromise to pass the core provisions of their legislation. At the same time, context mattered. Senator Lightford played a critical role in bringing potential opponents to the negotiating table while the Democratically controlled legislature and a supportive governor helped the cause of change.

Finally, we learned that we cannot understand the SB100 campaign as a purely local or state phenomenon. VOYCE was enmeshed in a range of alliances and networks that formed part of the national movement to end the school-to-prison pipeline. These networks directly and indirectly provided important support to the campaign, from foundation grants to model codes of conduct and from legal advocates with bill-writing expertise to federal guidance warning states and districts away from zero tolerance. In fact, the original idea to launch the SB100 campaign came from the local/national interface. In other words, while SB100 emerged organically from the experiences and concerns of youth of color and their families in Chicago, the campaign was also inspired and shaped by groups in other localities like Denver and California that had pioneered statewide campaigns.

Just as VOYCE benefited from the national movement, we also learned that VOYCE's impact goes beyond the SB100 policy win, as important as that is, to both local and national levels. The leadership developed by young people in VOYCE has translated to other issues and campaigns. VOYCE youth leaders in KOCO, for example, played a key role in getting the organization to take direct action to stop the closing of Dyett High School on the South Side of Chicago—one of the few successful campaigns to stop school closings in Black communities. According to Jitu Brown, an organizer from KOCO and national director of the Journey for Justice Alliance, two students who had become leaders in VOYCE challenged KOCO to act, which eventually led to a historic hunger strike and the decision to reopen the school, a victory that reverberated across the country.[22] According to Jawanza Malone from KOCO, the young people's impact was national.

> While VOYCE started as a program to impact the school-to-prison pipeline, the development of those young people who were a part of VOYCE led to this national movement against school closings and privatization that is touching communities around this country.

In fact, Raul Botello says that Communities United sees the kind of youth organizing practiced in VOYCE as a way to cultivate a new generation of community leaders over a twenty-year horizon.

> The school-to-prison pipeline, understood simply as a discipline code and restorative justice, is a very immediate, hands-on issue. But it's really a new form of structural racism that will take a long-term struggle to defeat. We need to give young people the opportunity to develop as leaders and build a leadership pipeline to have a long-term impact on the school-to-prison pipeline and structural racism.

As in our examination of organizing efforts in Mississippi, Los Angeles, and elsewhere, we learn that the national movement to end the school-to-prison pipeline consists of an interlocking set of local struggles that intentionally learn from and inspire each other. The national movement publicized VOYCE's victory on SB100 around the country and it inspired other local groups to redouble their efforts to push for greater change at local and state levels. VOYCE youth leader Jamie Adams speaks to the importance of organizing groups connecting across localities because "It's like fighting a giant spider."

> You fight with one leg of it, it has seven other legs. You can't just defeat one part of it and think it's done. This change needs to happen everywhere and that's what the Alliance for Educational Justice (AEJ) works on. VOYCE does it locally. AEJ does it nationally. Other groups do it at their local level and then we come together and collaborate to kill the head of the spider.

Adams reflects on the school-to-prison pipeline as part of a war on youth.

> All the issues that we work on like racial systems, homophobic systems, the school-to-prison pipeline, school closings, budget cuts. It all comes down to attacking young people and attacking youth. It's a war on our young people and unfortunately it's a battle that we have to fight. We have to fight for our education. So that's our main focus, that's our hash tag: #EndWarOnYouth.

Adams speaks of organizing as her calling and describes the impact it has had on her.

> I love organizing. I love doing this work. I love going to rallies. I love talking to young people and seeing thoughts moving inside of their head. I'm going to be the first girl that graduates high school in my family, and I'm gonna be the first one to attend a university and go to college.[23]

7

The Movement Spreads

Organizing in Small Cities, Suburbs, and the South

By the time VOYCE youth won their SB100 victory in Illinois in 2015, the movement to end the school-to-prison pipeline was in full swing. The rolling series of victories occurring across the country, each one building on the one before and inspiring others to further efforts, comprise one indication of the movement's maturity. The entrance of new organizing groups into the movement, often outside of the biggest cities and sometimes in conservative areas, constitutes another indication of this movement flow. These new groups were typically small and under-resourced, and many addressed racial inequities in suburban areas with newer populations of students of color. Yet now they could tap the resources of the national movement to support their efforts.

In this chapter, we discuss examples of the development and spread of the movement to new localities and to new constituencies. We start in the Midwest in Dayton, Ohio, where we see how Black parents tackle the school-to-prison pipeline in a conservative area without a strong infrastructure of local support for community organizing. The case of Racial Justice NOW! in Dayton illustrates how new, small groups of parents and young people can have outsized victories in part because of the strength and support of the national movement.

We then go to the South as well as to Southern suburbs. The South has a particularly repressive and violent racial history rooted in slavery and Jim Crow segregation, as well as distinct social, political, and cultural features as we first saw in Chapter 4 on Mississippi. Examining racial inequities in education in the South is critically important because the majority of African Americans live in the South and a full majority of public school students in the South live in or near poverty. We start in New Orleans and then travel to Gwinnett County in suburban Atlanta, ending in Henrico County and other suburban counties outside of Richmond, Virginia, the capital of the old Confederacy.[1]

Willful Defiance. Mark R. Warren, Oxford University Press. © Mark R. Warren 2022.
DOI: 10.1093/oso/9780197611500.003.0008

Dayton, Ohio: Black Parent Organizing in a Midwestern City

In the Introduction to this book, I tell the story of Zakiya Sankara-Jabar's journey to racial justice organizing. Sankara-Jabar's African American son had been repeatedly suspended from pre-school. When she did some research about Black boys and education and talked with other Black parents in Dayton, Ohio, Sankara-Jabar learned that his experience was all too typical. She took the bold step to co-launch Racial Justice NOW! (RJN) with Professor Vernellia Randall in 2014 as an unapologetically Black organization dedicated to organizing Black parents to dismantle the school-to-prison pipeline and educational racism.

At the time, Dayton was not untypical of many small- to medium-sized cities in the Midwest. Like many others, deindustrialization hit Dayton with a vengeance and the loss of good-paying manufacturing jobs and the flight of more affluent white residents to the suburbs left Dayton largely poor; the highest concentrations of poverty lay in West Dayton, heart of the Black community. In 2010, Dayton Public Schools were almost 70% Black with nearly 100% of students considered poor or low-income. Metro Dayton was also a fairly conservative area, as suggested by the largely Republican group of state legislators that represented the area.[2]

The school-to-prison pipeline is pervasive in cities like Dayton. At the time that RJN began its work, Dayton's out-of-school suspension rate was four times the state average. While Black children made up 64% of the district's students, they accounted for 80% of those suspended. Black boys with disabilities were the most suspended and expelled in the school district. While poor Black boys were suspended the most, even middle-class Black boys were suspended at higher rates than any other group. A 2017 report showed that Black boys had the worst academic outcomes of any group, regardless of income.[3]

Stories That Ground the Organizing

Families of color often struggle in school districts like Dayton. They fall under the radar screen of the media, while popular and scholarly attention often focuses on big cities like Chicago, New York, or Los Angeles. Meanwhile, nascent organizing efforts struggle without a particularly robust field of private philanthropy accustomed to funding grassroots groups. Yet their struggles are no more real. As Sankara-Jabar began to reach out to Black parents, these are some of the stories she heard.

Iris Blanchard knew her youngest daughter was free spirited and independent minded, even from an early age. She wasn't disrespectful, she just wanted to be herself and do things her own way. In the suburbs, this would be encouraged. In Dayton Public Schools, teachers labeled her Black daughter as misbehaving and punished her. Starting when she was three years old and in a pre-K program in a public school, Blanchard says,

> I would get constant phone calls saying that she couldn't sit in the classroom properly, she was out of control, and that maybe this is not the school for her. You know, she shouldn't be here.

The school wanted to put her on medication, but Blanchard refused. She tried placing her daughter in a private school but that was no better. Her daughter continued to struggle into high school where she had a low GPA and was barely making it through. After a sports game, the students were getting rowdy, and a police officer said that her daughter "was being disrespectful."

> He slammed my daughter to the ground, basically busted her head. She had a big old knot on her head. She had to go to the hospital. She had on contact lenses so it kind of scratched her eye right where she hit on that concrete. That could have killed her.

After the incident, Blanchard took a different tack. She had always tried to get her daughter to behave and that seemed to make things worse. Instead, she decided "to let her be who she is."

> That's when I started seeing a positive change in her personality and that's when I became more of an advocate, like "Y'all need to back up and let her be." Once I became even more of an advocate, that's when I really again saw the change in her behavior. Blossoming!

Her daughter decided she wanted to achieve and raised her GPA to 3.5 or a B+. She graduated, got her real estate license at age 18, and is now in community college. RJN brought Blanchard to Washington to tell her story at a policy meeting at the White House, and Blanchard began helping other parents in Dayton know their rights through RJN.

Yamika Leeger Stephens adopted her nephew at age one, after he suffered the death of his mother and traumatic experiences with his birth father. She admits that when he entered kindergarten, he had some behavior issues. The school, however, wanted him tested and encouraged medication. While acknowledging the issues, Stephens feared the school was not prepared to support a Black boy who didn't fit into "the box." As a first-time mother, though, Stephens was not sure what to do and was afraid that her Black son would be labeled early on—to his detriment.

> I was just trying to figure out what these things are and what questions I should ask. What rights do I have as a parent? Can I come in with some support? It was so hard being a new parent and figuring out what the needs are for him and understanding the language that teachers and administrators use when they're talking to you about your child.

Stephens met Sankara-Jabar through a community connection.

> She shared with me her experience with her son, and I shared an experience with my son. That was the connection there. I just started coming to the monthly meetings. The meetings helped me to see that I need to and can do so much more and be so much more as a parent. I have a son who's a Black child. So whatever teacher he may have, there's always an implicit bias.

Stephens did have her son assessed. Learning from other parents in RJN, however, she got a counselor who helped him deal with his trauma and whose mantra was "pills don't make skills." The counselor set up a positive behavioral program in coordination with the school. RJN meetings opened Stephens up "to be a little bit more active and assertive" and to have a team accompany her to any meetings with the school. By third grade her son had learned to manage his behavior; he was doing well and reading at a fifth grade level. Stephens continued to be involved in RJN because she has developed a commitment to the community.

> If my child has experienced this, how many other children has experienced this? And where does that lead our children? Where does that lead our boys? Well, we know where it's led them. Behind bars. Being a mother is

so much more to me now. I'm not just one child's mother, but a mother to a community.

Alugu McClendon's son suffered from ADD and bipolar disease. He had a lot of trouble in school, being bullied by children and reacting by bullying other children. McClendon could not find mental health services for him in the school or community. In the end, her son damaged some property and McClendon had to call the police. The boy served some time in a juvenile facility; when he came out on parole, she continued to struggle to get services. Finally, he got the opportunity to attend a residential program that helped him enormously. But when he returned home, the charter school he had attended refused to accept him back.

> They just said he wouldn't be a good fit. And, you know, that's hurtful for a child to hear who's trying to do better. As a mother, I actually fought back tears because I didn't want them to see how much that hurt and I didn't want my son to see that either. It was just a terrible experience.

McClendon heard about Sankara-Jabar's advocacy and found support and assistance from her and the RJN network. "Sometimes you just need somebody that you can vent to or talk to and express how you feel, what you're going through." With support from RJN, she was eventually able to place her son in a public high school where he began to do well.

Sankara-Jabar heard story after story like these, of Black parents who did not know their rights and felt isolated and frustrated with their inability to get services, who wanted supportive rather than punitive treatment for their children from schools, and who were "suffering in silence." Many of these parents lacked connections to formal organizations and needed to be reached through informal networks in the community.

> You have to be able to meet people where they are, the parents who usually won't come out for a meeting. We've built the relationships through networks, which makes them more comfortable to tell me something very personal about what they are going through. That's not easy. It's tough for parents, especially in a climate that blames poor, working class parents for everything that's wrong with our children. It does not make it easy for us to share.

From Personal Support to Collective Advocacy

At first, many of these parents required personal support and help with advocacy. As they built trust with RJN, they began to tell their stories publicly and participate in the group's organizing campaigns, which took off quickly. RJN repeatedly took parents like these to school board meetings where they testified about their experiences. Personal stories proved powerful, but the group also marshaled the data that Professor Randall amassed showing the widespread extent of exclusionary discipline and its racially disproportionate impact on Black children. At the time, Dayton was one of only three districts in the state that allowed suspensions for pre-K students.

RJN also worked to build relationships with board members and school officials. Although the superintendent was initially skeptical of RJN, Sankara-Jabar met repeatedly one on one with her, eventually holding regular monthly meetings. According to Sankara-Jabar, the superintendent came to see the value of RJN's initiatives and ended up supporting the group's proposed moratorium on pre-K suspensions and other reforms. She appointed Sankara-Jabar to the district's policy committee and placed a representative from RJN on the student code of conduct committee as well as on the district's accountability panel.

Since funding from private philanthropy proved unavailable, RJN remained a volunteer organization for its first four years. In the fifth year, through its connections with the Dignity in Schools Campaign (DSC), the national coalition challenging the school-to-prison pipeline, the group started to receive some small funds including a partial stipend so Sankara-Jabar could spend more time organizing. Eventually, a DSC connection to the Communities for Just Schools Fund resulted in a grant that allowed Sankara-Jabar to take a paid position as executive director, which greatly expanded the group's capacity. While DSC remained RJN's steadfast partner, the group also expanded its capacity by joining the national Journey for Justice Alliance focused on school privatization and creating partnerships at the state level with the Ohio Poverty Law Center and Advocates for Basic Legal Equality.

RJN quickly scored a series of impressive victories. RJN won a moratorium on pre-K suspensions in Dayton, Ohio, schools; changed the district's code of conduct to end zero-tolerance policies; and won the implementation of restorative justice alternative programs in eight schools. RJN got the district to establish an Office for Males of Color, modeled on the successful program from Oakland, California, only the third in the country at the time. RJN also issued school discipline report cards for 1,100 school districts across Ohio, causing an uproar when it gave "F" grades to many so-called high performing districts for exhibiting large racial disparities in exclusionary discipline. RJN also served as a key force behind passage of an Ohio law in 2018 that barred suspensions and expulsions for students in pre-K through third grade who committed minor infractions.[4]

National Support and Local Contributions

RJN leveraged deep roots among Black families to win these victories, but it's hard to see how RJN could have had the impact it did without the national movement. In addition to the crucial connection to funding, DSC provided RJN with its model code of conduct, full of ready-made data, analysis, policy language, and alternative programs to adapt and use locally. DSC also sent Fernando Martinez, its national field organizer, to conduct trainings in organizing skills with RJN parents. DSC provided the small, young organization with the legitimacy that comes from being part of a national organization. DSC made it clear that RJN had important national supporters who were watching what happened in Dayton. DSC members came to Dayton to issue the group's national report on charter school accountability and came again as part of its national tour to support local organizing. Sankara-Jabar was strategic in leveraging this support.

> We made sure to plan the tour around a school board meeting. We also had a big event over at Dayton Boys Prep. The superintendent came and brought all her executive staff and we had two board members there. It was huge. The local teachers union was there and so was the Ohio Education Association.

Through DSC, Sankara-Jabar built a relationship with the Advancement Project, which connected her to the National Education Association (NEA), of which the Dayton teachers union was a member. She invited NEA representatives from their pilot restorative justice project to come to Dayton to help train teachers. DSC also gave RJN members the opportunity and funds to come to Washington, DC, during its Days on the Capitol to meet with Ohio Congressional representatives to share their stories and advocate for support. Being part of a national movement helped RJN parents feel less isolated and more determined to press their demands on the district.

DSC also gave Sankara-Jabar leadership opportunities that expanded her skills and expertise. DSC staff and several key leaders mentored her as a new organizer and executive director. Among them, Sankara-Jabar highlights the support she received from Joyce Parker, an African American woman like herself and key DSC leader from Mississippi.

> Joyce helped me to speak up more. You don't realize that women and people of color and Black people, we're socialized to be quiet, to stay in our place. That's the opposite of Joyce. I think she had to learn that. But she was the one that helped me be more assertive and to speak up.

Within six months, Sankara-Jabar took a position on DSC's Coordinating Committee and joined several leadership subcommittees. She became DSC's national field organizer in 2017.

Sankara-Jabar also had an impact on DSC. Along with other members, she pushed DSC to have a stronger focus on anti-Black racism. Without minimizing its impact on others, she pushed the campaign to be consistently intentional to highlight the disproportionate impact of the school-to-prison pipeline on Black boys, on Black students with disabilities, on Black LGBTQ students, and on Black girls. As a parent herself, she also pushed DSC to provide childcare or a stipend to cover childcare costs at all campaign-sponsored events.

Rooted in her own personal experience as a Black mother and in the stories and experiences of other Black parents, Sankara-Jabar was able to leverage resources from the national movement to empower a small organization to impact school discipline policy across Dayton and the state. Reflecting on the trajectory of RJN, Sankara-Jabar says it all started because "two Black women came together and said our children are suffering and we are not gonna be quiet about it."

New Orleans: Combating the School-to-Prison Pipeline in a Privatized System

When Verna Carr's African American son was eight years old, she suspected he had a learning and perhaps emotional disability and needed an Individualized

Education Plan (IEP). The elementary school he attended in New Orleans, however, refused to have him assessed. Carr tried for years to get him help. He struggled in and out of school and by middle school ended up "in the wrong crowd." He was arrested at age thirteen when he accompanied an older boy on an armed robbery. Even though he was just a child, officers brought him into juvenile court in shackles.

> He was shackled from the ankles with a chain wrapped around his waist all the way up to his wrists. I took sick when I saw that. I cried and cried and cried. All of a sudden, a Mr. Johnson, came up and wrapped his arms around me and said, "It's gonna be okay, I'm gonna help you through this."

It turns out that Mr. Johnson was with an organization called Families and Friends of Louisiana's Incarcerated Children (FFLIC). When her son was released after serving several months, Carr got help from staff and leaders from FFLIC. With FFLIC's assistance, Carr was finally able to get a disability assessment for her son, which diagnosed him with ADHD, partial schizophrenia and bipolar disorder. At that point, however, Carr says, "The system came at me." The officer at the disability hearing claimed she was an unfit mother, even though she was working hard to support her family and had been trying to get her son help for five years. "They made me feel less than a mother."

> When my son was going to court, I was there every day, every hour. I'm talking getting fired off my job, getting write-ups because they don't care about a mother that's working and trying to be there for her kids at the same time. I'm talking lights off. I'm talking water off. I'm talking trying to get food in the house.

With FFLIC's support, she refused to have her son sent to an alternative school for offenders and enrolled him at a charter high school. Nevertheless, she found that her son was labeled and harassed at every turn.

> If my son moved too fast, the security was putting handcuffs on him. If my son talked too loud, they were calling the police. When he would act up, security would put handcuffs on him and threaten to fight him. He's a 15-year-old boy and security's a grown man!

Carr built a team, including FFLIC members, to help her advocate and mentors and counselors to support her son. She worked hard to build relationships with school administrators and teachers, some of whom did support her son, to keep him in school and learning despite the harassment. Things never went smoothly but by the spring semester of his senior year, he was on track to graduate. Meanwhile, Carr started going to FFLIC trainings and became a team leader with the organization, helping to advocate for and with other parents and support organizing campaigns.

> FFLIC made me stronger for the next kid that's gonna walk through those doors with those shackles, so I can take that mother in my arms and say, "It's gonna be okay." Through FFLIC and with my fight and my heart and my passion for my son, it became a passion for all these kids.

Carr's story exemplifies the harsh and even brutal criminalization of African American children in New Orleans. It is perhaps not surprising that FFLIC's entrée to dismantling the school-to-prison pipeline started with its work to reform a violent and inhumane juvenile justice system. As it transitioned to incorporate campaigns against zero-tolerance discipline policies, New Orleans became ground zero for the charter school movement and FFLIC's local work attained national significance. Indeed, FFLIC, a statewide organization based in New Orleans, sees itself as a movement-building organization operating on local, state, and national levels simultaneously, each level reinforcing the other.

From the Back End to the Front End of the School-to-Prison Pipeline

When Gina Womack became office manager for the Juvenile Justice Project of Louisiana (JJPL) in 1999, she was horrified to learn about the brutal conditions facing the more than two thousand children incarcerated in juvenile prisons in the state. Shackling, beating, and other forms of abuse were common for children as young as thirteen. Parents were separated from their children and their rights routinely violated. Womack helped JJPL found FFLIC for parents and families who needed support but also wanted to change the system that was abusing their children. FFLIC worked with lawyers in JJPL on a campaign to close the notorious Tallulah Correctional

Center for Youth, which the *New York Times* said was possibly the worst juvenile facility in the nation. Tallulah incarcerated children as young as eleven. According to FFLIC:

> Aside from failing to provide adequate medical or mental health care, proper food, appropriate education or other rehabilitative treatment, confined children were routinely and brutally beaten, intimidated with force and humiliation, encouraged to fight-it-out with each other, maced and placed in isolation for weeks or months at a time.

After several years of organizing and advocacy, FFLIC, JJPL and its allies got the state to pass a historic juvenile justice reform act in May 2003, which closed Tallulah and led to a 75% reduction in the number of young people in prison.[5]

When Hurricane Katrina devastated New Orleans in 2005, FFLIC had already begun to expand its focus from the "back end" to the "front end" of the school-to-prison pipeline. After Katrina the state dissolved the New Orleans public school district, laid off seven hundred teachers, and replaced the district with a patchwork of state-run public schools, locally run public schools, and an increasing number of charter schools. Many children had to travel long distances across the city to get to school. The number of security guards and metal detectors increased and, if anything, harsh and racially inequitable school discipline practices seemed to worsen. Many students told FFLIC that schools felt like jails. Recounting the views of one student, FFLIC organizing consultant at the time Ashanna Bigard described John McDonogh High School this way:

> They had barbed wire. They had six-foot-high gates and another foot of barbed wire. The school actually looked like a detention center for really violent young people. There was security outside of the gate as you enter and two more security guards and a police officer at the door. You went through the metal detector and took off your shoes and belt and they searched your book bag. Another police officer patted you down. The girls had to pull out their bras and shake them.

Working with Liz Sullivan-Yuknis at the New York-based Partners for Dignity & Rights (called NESRI at the time), FFLIC issued a report in 2010 on harsh discipline and policing practices in the Recovery School District.

The report revealed that with a 98% African American and almost 80% low-income student population, more than one in four students had been suspended in the 2007–2008 school year—twice the state and four times the national average. In the report, FFLIC called for an end to zero tolerance at local and state levels and the establishment and funding of positive and restorative alternatives.[6]

According to the Womack, excessive suspensions for minor infractions impact the whole family, "ripping them apart."

> The kids are getting sent home a bunch of times. Parents throw their hands up, saying "I'm trying to work, I got multiple kids, you getting sent home from school." The kids can't go back to school unless the parents come. Parents sometimes have lost their job because they got to go back to school over and over. Sometimes the parents just don't go because it's a choice to keep their job.

Schools then report parents to child services for neglect of duty, and this can lead to family break-up or criminal charges. In this way, minor infractions lead families into the court system.

Confronting a Privatized School System

Over the years, the proportion of charter schools expanded in New Orleans so that by 2019 the entire system consisted exclusively of charter schools, creating a privatized school system. Many African American parents and students report that charter schools combine strict discipline with a regimented, test-oriented curriculum with little cultural relevancy. After firing long-term teachers with roots in the community, the charter system came to rely on Teach for America teachers who were typically white and from outside New Orleans, and who only commit to teach for two years. According to Bigard, the post-Katrina educational system is designed "to further dehumanize an oppressed and traumatized population." Schools became rigid factory-like environments designed to increase test scores regardless of the needs of young children, who are then punished for normal activities. Bigard says that schools "take away the things that are culturally significant to children."

They replace them with punishment and discipline where you have children believing that they are bad or a discipline problem because they need
to use the bathroom, or they get hungry, or they get tired. They convince
our babies that something is wrong with them because they're human.

The privatized, charter system in New Orleans has a fragmented structure with thirty-eight different charter boards governing about eighty local
schools. FFLIC finds it challenging to try to make systemic change and hold
schools accountable in a balkanized school system where the large number
of separate boards of directors of charter schools or networks are unelected.
In addition, according to Bigard, teacher turnover remains high and so does
turnover of administrators. Years of relationship building goes down the
drain when a principal leaves.[7]

The Black women in and around FFLIC's leadership have years of experience with education, child development, and culturally appropriate methods
to address trauma and healing. Yet they feel profoundly disrespected by a
charter-dominated school system that hires outside teachers and pays outside consultants, while ignoring the expertise in the community. The emphasis on drill and kill methods and on strict discipline runs counter to the
research on child development. Apparently, according to Bigard, educators
don't believe this research applies to Black children.

Charter schools say, "Well these veteran educators, they don't want to follow
our culture." We say, "If your culture is damaging to our children, you're not
gonna make me an overseer on a plantation." Veteran teachers from New
Orleans did not invent best practices, but we know what they are: Children
between zero and eight need to play with each other to build the brain syn-
apsis to have self-regulation.

Bigard concludes that charter schools "do the opposite of what children need
and then wonder why they explode."[8]

FFLIC joined DSC soon after its founding and played an important role
right from the beginning. DSC held its first official annual meeting in New
Orleans, and FFLIC's education organizer Damekia Morgan joined DSC's
Coordinating Committee when it reconstituted to include base-building
groups. FFLIC contributed to and then used DSC's Model Code of Conduct
in its work to advocate for change in local codes of conduct and state legislation; it helped write and endorse the DSC's National Resolution to End

School Pushout and adopted DSC's Solutions not Suspensions Campaign framework. FFLIC also participated in DSC's Week of Action every year to help bring national attention to conditions in New Orleans and Louisiana. Womack notes that DSC's prepackaged materials were incredibly helpful for a "barebones" organization that does not have the capacity to create everything from scratch. FFLIC also sent parents and youth members to Washington to meet with congressional representatives and federal officials as part of DSC's Days at the Capitol. Morgan says the trips to DC constituted an important growth opportunity for parents and young people who struggle for respect in their local education system. They learn how the legislative process works, claim a seat at the table, advocate for policies they want, and feel a sense of "exercising their power in those spaces."

FFLIC was one of the key groups that helped DSC write its Accountability Guidelines for School Pushout and Charter Schools and used these guidelines to advocate with local charter schools and networks. As more and more charters formed, and it became increasingly difficult to organize for change in each one, the need for state action became greater. Using the 2010 report, FFLIC began to work with African American State Senator Sharon Broome to advocate for passage of state laws to end zero tolerance. In 2011 FFLIC worked with a task force and got the legislature to pass legislation ending suspensions for "willful disobedience"; the Republican governor at the time, however, vetoed it. According to Womack, the state teachers association and even some of the school management associations in the task force supported the legislation, but later declined to endorse the reform. Even as the group continued to work to ban suspensions for willful disobedience and "disturbing school," FFLIC did get a law passed and signed in 2015 ending suspensions in pre-K to third grade for dress code violations.[9]

FFLIC continues to organize for change in a variety of ways. It developed a curriculum for peer-to-peer training of parents in Positive Behavioral Intervention and Supports. It advocates for changes in codes of conduct and suspension policy in individual schools, charter networks, and even with the Orleans Parish School Board. Meanwhile, FFLIC continues to conduct individual advocacy to support families and build a base for its policy efforts. As with RJN in Dayton, parents like Verna Carr who gained critical support from FFLIC for their children often become leaders in the organization, supporting other families and participating in organizing campaigns by testifying about their experiences and attending hearings and campaign events.

FFLIC expanded its work to support the creation of Black Men Rising, a group dedicated to supporting boys and young men struggling in the education and justice systems and to helping them advocate for themselves. Antonio Travis founded the group with several Black male friends from his high school. They all graduated and went to college, so are counted as successes by the school; but they quickly realized how poorly prepared for college they were. Following a scripted regimen at the high school, told what to do all the time, and required to walk in straight lines in the hallway, Travis did not know how to take charge of his own education when he got to college. Travis dropped out of Talladega College in Alabama and returned to New Orleans. He reached out to Womack who was the aunt of one of his best friends and to his mentor Ernest Johnson who worked for FFLIC and got involved.

> They gave me a platform to voice my frustrations. They said, "Look, what are you mad about? Use our platform to voice it." Because of what happened to me in my charter school and what was going on in my community, I just felt like this was a perfect opportunity to be real and authentic about it.

Travis and his colleagues built Black Men Rising as a mentorship program that creates a strong and positive community among Black boys and young men. The group works in schools and juvenile centers and participates in FFLIC's policy change campaigns as well. Travis became DSC's youth representative to the National Youth Alliance of Boys and Men of Color, which supports organizing groups across the country. FFLIC gave Travis a platform and he is ready to run with it.

> I'm not patient. I don't have a plan set out for when I'm 60 or 70. I don't know if I'll make it that long. There's too many barriers. A lot of young men of color think the same way—we instant and we just try to go. We're ready to go, we're ready to do it. Just put the resources where they need to go so we can light it up!

Within a few years of helping to found Black Men Rising, FFLIC also sponsored a Black Girl Rising group to address their particular needs in schools and juvenile centers.

Despite all its work "on the front end" to stop the school-to-prison pipeline, FFLIC never lost its commitment to children on the "back end," those incarcerated in detention facilities and their families. In 2017, FFLIC launched its Stand in Love campaign where it organized a thousand people to send Valentine's Day cards to young people locked in prisons and juvenile facilities. During the COVID-19 pandemic of 2020, it became a key force advocating for the health and safety of young people incarcerated in juvenile and adult facilities.

Black Women Lead

The Black women in and around FFLIC at the time of the interviews express a sharp critique of racial oppression and a commitment to building a community of support. Speaking of teachers in the city's schools, Bigard says, "If you screamed at dogs like they scream at our 5-year-old children, somebody would do something." When Black women call that out, however,

> We're told we are ignorant because ultimately what people want is compliance to white supremacist culture. We need to be emulating whiteness and if we're not, then we're uneducated, ignorant and a threat.

According to another key Black woman leader, Ruth Idakula, FFLIC organizing is rooted in historic relationships of cultural resistance to white supremacy.

> Relationships are the solidarity or the glue in terms of cultural resistance that happened here—also in Africa in terms of colonialism, but here in terms of slavery and Jim Crow and the massive incarceration that is happening right now. And that is where our organizing actually comes from.

According to Morgan, FFLIC's organizing is designed "to fight against a system that was created to oppress us." FFLIC creates a space for Black women to be themselves.

> It's been hard to experience the level of oppression we face in this city. I know that I couldn't do this if I didn't have an Ashanna to call or Ruth to call or Gina, to talk about this. I love Gina for the fact that she fights to keep FFLIC here because in this city, we don't have this space. People don't have

a space where I feel my true self and I can be who I am divinely meant to be without my oppressions holding me down.

Idakula sums up the organizing spirit of FFLIC and its Black women.

What I love about being in New Orleans and being in the presence of these other three Black women [Womack, Morgan and Bigard] is that we are passionate about our children and we are very clear that we need to fight for our children. We have a relationship based on that commitment and organizing is about relationship. Even if FFLIC did not exist, we would still do this work. It's just our life's work.

Gwinnett County, Georgia: Challenging the School-to-Prison Pipeline in a Changing Suburb

The scene at the Gwinnett County Board of Education meeting in April of 2017 struck me as a throwback in time. The board members were all white and middle-aged or older, and seemed frozen in the past. They sat on a dais raised high above floor level at the head of a large assembly room, looking down on the attendees. They devoted the first part of the meeting to celebrating student and teacher achievement and virtually all the recipients were white. Then, Black parents and community members from the Gwinnett Parent Coalition to Dismantle the School-to-Prison Pipeline (SToPP) rose to protest a recent case of police brutality against a sixteen-year-old Black high school boy. In breaking up a fight between students, one school resource officer handcuffed the boy while another slammed him to the ground leaving him bloodied. DSC members from across the country who were in town for their annual meeting also spoke in support and signaled national attention to the events in Gwinnett County.

The Black community members in attendance called for an investigation of the incident. The school board and superintendent sat there stone-faced. Not a single board member or school administrator responded in any way. I was sitting with a group of high school students from Boston who attended as part of the DSC delegation. The students were shocked and distraught that there was not at least some response to a charge of assault let alone a willingness to investigate the incident. I was also upset and angry. The school administration denied any wrongdoing to the news media, but at the meeting itself apparently felt no need to respond at all.[10]

Origins of Gwinnett SToPP: A Directly Impacted Family

Marlyn Tillman moved to Gwinnett County, a suburban community outside of Atlanta in the summer of 2001. She came from Montgomery County, Maryland, a racially diverse and affluent community with a progressive school system. Tillman felt good about bringing her children to the positive Black mecca of Atlanta, owning a modest home, and being able to send her children to a well-resourced suburban school district with a national reputation. The problems, however, began right away. In the third week of school, she started receiving phone calls that her eighth grader was wearing gang colors, in this case the blue swag of his favorite sports team—the University of North Carolina Tar Heels. Tillman was shocked to hear there were gangs in Gwinnett County and told the school administrators that she would have never moved to the area if she'd known. They backtracked immediately and tried to assure her that there were no gangs in Gwinnett County. Yet they continued to claim he was wearing gang colors and had to change clothes. According to Tillman, "The only gang my son knew was the book club."

The school suspended him in his second month. Tillman's son was struggling with the move to Gwinnett and leaving his father behind in Maryland. He got into a fight when another boy threw food on a shirt that his father had given him. Tillman agreed that hitting the other student was not appropriate, but she challenged the suspension. Her son needed help and patience adjusting to the move, not punishment. She tried to meet with the principal who refused to talk with her.

Tillman was unclear what the rules for behavior were. She asked for a copy of the school's code of student conduct. A school official wanted to read it over the phone to her, as it was not available in print version. She objected and demanded that the district print and distribute copies of its code of conduct to families, which they eventually did.

Tillman appealed the case to the state superintendent of schools, which got the attention of the principal, but the suspension still stuck. Meanwhile, her son continued to receive a series of after-school detentions and disciplinary infractions. The next suspension happened at the beginning of his sophomore year in high school. Tillman was used to parents advocating for their children and a school system that was responsive. She could negotiate in Montgomery Schools and find a "workable point" to agree on. She found that in Gwinnett County, however, "There were no workable points."

> If you don't have those connections, you're getting nothing. This is a plantation system. You don't see the physical vestiges, but the structural ones are very much in place. Education for them is a privilege because they understand that if they let you be educated, you might do what they don't want you to do and you're no longer controllable. They use it as a system of control.

When the school suspended her son again for a dress code violation, administrators refused to let him go to his Advanced Placement class; but he was allowed to participate in football practice after school. That said it all to Tillman.

> I told them, "You let him run up and down that field like a monkey. But you made sure that he missed his learning for the day. You had no problem taking the most valuable thing from him." They said, "Oh, Miss Tillman, it's not that way. Don't say it that way." But I responded, "No, you let him run up and down the field like a monkey and I'm gonna say it that way every time I say it." I said it then. I say it now. It goes through me still now when I say that.

Tillman called it an example of racial profiling: the school was trying "to break his spirit and get him to assimilate to what they wanted."

Around this time, Tillman learned about the district's tribunal system where students were sent for behavioral violations and could be expelled from their school and sent to a special disciplinary alternative school. Tillman realized that the school was escalating her son's discipline status, treating minor infractions like dress code violations as more serious (gang-related) ones. Fearing the school was putting him on the road to a disciplinary alternative school, and with support from the American Civil Liberties Union (ACLU) of Georgia, Tillman filed suit. She charged that the dress code was vague and subject to biased application. Settling out of court, she was able to get her son's record changed and some revisions made in discipline practice regarding dress code violations.

Through her connection to the ACLU, Tillman learned more about the larger systemic issues behind her son's experience—the school-to-prison pipeline. She teamed up with Jennifer Falk who was an organizer with the Gwinnett NAACP branch at the time and held a series of community meetings with parents. An initial core group from these meetings formed the Gwinnett Parent Coalition to Dismantle the School-to-Prison Pipeline (SToPP) in 2007.

The group ran straight up against a school board and administration that was not used to grassroots organizing and direct advocacy, especially by parents of color. In fact, Gwinnett schools held itself up as a national model and rarely received criticism of any sort. The district's superintendent won Georgia Superintendent of the Year in 2005 and was one of four finalists for the national title. A local newspaper quoted him as responding, "The very name of the (coalition) is degrading to teachers and educators who work diligently to educate students."[11]

According to Falk, "We were really pariahs for using that name." Tillman says the superintendent would work with the new group but only if it changed its name, which Gwinnett SToPP refused to do. The founders felt naming the school-to-prison pipeline was necessary to signal their determination and avoid being coopted by the powerful school system.

> When they have tensions and issues within the community, Gwinnett tries to sequester it by bringing you in closer, loving up on you, giving you a little bone. Then, if you still want them to keep giving you this tiny bone and you want them to say they're working with you, then you can't say anything, and you can't do anything big. If you want to be their friend, that's how you be their friend. We decided we didn't want to be their friend that badly.

Challenging the School-to-Prison Pipeline in a Changing Suburb

At the time of its founding, Gwinnett SToPP confronted a school system that hadn't seemed to have changed much since its early days as an almost all-white and affluent suburban system. In 1970, Gwinnett County had only 72,000 residents who were almost entirely white. But the county population grew rapidly and Black, Latinx and Asian-American families started moving in. By 2008, white children were a minority of the school population. By 2018, Gwinnett's school system itself had about 180,000 students, making it

Georgia's largest district, with a racial breakdown of about 32% Black, 30% Hispanic, 23% white, and 11% Asian. Yet, as of 2018, Gwinnett County had yet to elect a single county commissioner or school board member of color. The superintendent, a white man, had served since 1996, making him one of the longest running and most influential superintendents in the state or country. The district, however, is a two-time winner of the Broad Prize, which recognizes efforts to reduce achievement gaps among low-income and students of color.[12]

Gwinnett SToPP remained unimpressed by awards from outside institutions while racial disparities in school discipline and academic achievement continued unabated. In the 2017–2018 school year, Black students continued to receive in- and out-of-school suspensions and be placed in disciplinary alternative schools at disproportionate rates. In 2019, Gwinnett schools empaneled another committee to study racial disparities in school discipline when data showed an increase in disciplinary hearings as well as suspensions in the system.[13]

The nascent group faced the challenge of what appeared to be an intransigent and entrenched administration and school board, and a larger Southern cultural context that worked through relationships. According to Falk, "It's a very Republican community and everyone has been on the school board forever." If you didn't have the relationships with powerholders, and most of the newer people of color did not, then you didn't get access to resources. The culture also expected deference, which historically maintained deep racial inequities, and was hostile to direct, determined and assertive advocacy. Falk says "Community organizing is a dirty word here. Standing up and marching is a dirty word. It's not something you do in polite society."

Meanwhile, Tillman found that many Black families thought they had made it when they moved into the suburban community.

> They are shocked that they receive the treatment they do. There was also
> a faction who thought that you shouldn't make waves because you are in
> Gwinnett; it's a nice community and you don't want your child targeted.

Falk refers also to the fear of speaking out, saying, "People felt uncomfortable being vocal, assertive and everyone was afraid for their child to be affected."

In this context, the support of the national movement proved essential. Around the time Gwinnett SToPP formed, Tillman discovered the nascent

DSC network, and the group attended the coalition's first official meeting in Chicago in 2009. The national connections she made strengthened the resolve of the new group. Tillman says it let members know that "we ain't crazy. This stuff is really going on. It was just very re-affirming." Over the years, the group made use of DSC's model code of conduct, Week of Action materials, and other resources.

National connections also helped Gwinnett SToPP acquire funding to support its work. The local area simply lacked private foundations that understood organizing and were willing to support a grassroots organization led by families of color. Gwinnett SToPP was able to get financial support from the DSC members fund and from funders it met through DSC like the Communities for Just Schools Fund.

Making Gains and Preparing for the Long Struggle

In its early days, despite intransigence from the school board, Gwinnett SToPP was able to work with a new district executive director for discipline to rewrite parts of the student code of conduct. Drawing from the section on policing in DSC's model code of conduct, the group targeted the vagueness in the code's language on the kind of conduct that warranted contact with school resource officers. The group then developed training to go with the revised handbook, to inform parents of their rights.

Gwinnett SToPP also sought to improve conditions in the discipline alternative schools, which the group labeled pre-prisons, and make data more available and policies more transparent at those facilities. At the time, the district listed more than 170 infractions, often very minor ones, that could land a student in an alternative school. Although students with disabilities made up 11% of the student body, the group found that they represented 27% of the students facing disciplinary panels like the tribunal system that could transfer a student to an alternative school. As a result, Falk says, "Special education bled into all we did," and Gwinnett SToPP began to provide support and advocacy to families when a child with an IEP entered the tribunal system.[14]

Currently, Gwinnett SToPP sponsors a variety of initiatives to build a base of parent leaders, influence a wider network of allies and stakeholders, and engage with willing educators and administrators in the school system and policymakers at the state legislature. The Parent Leadership Initiative offers parents and their allies a monthly workshop for eight months on the workings of the school-to-prison pipeline as well as on advocacy skills and policy alternatives.

To build and influence a wider network, Gwinnett SToPP sponsors a Finding New Directions program where parents and a diverse variety of stakeholders meet monthly to discuss the school-to-prison pipeline and alternatives to keep students in school and learning. Participants review sections of the student code of conduct and advocate for revisions, with school officials sometime participating alongside parent advocates. Gwinnett SToPP also plays the role of supporting a wider regional and statewide network of community organizations and advocacy groups like the ACLU working to address racial inequities in public education.

When necessary, Gwinnett SToPP has also filed civil rights complaints or threatened legal action. According to Kathleen Burch, an attorney with the ACLU, legal strategies are an important part of the tactical toolkit in the South, and particularly in a place like Gwinnett County with an entrenched, largely white political establishment.

> They're picking on the disenfranchised, the weakest link. Children don't vote. The people who are being pushed out are young minorities. You're talking about a segment of the population that historically people in power have tried to disenfranchise. So, if those who are making the rules don't think they're gonna lose in court, there's no incentive to change the rules.

Tillman says that the relationship with Gwinnett Schools continues to be adversarial. Nevertheless, the group finds ways to work with individuals and departments within the district and influence policy in a more positive direction. Tillman has occasionally served on committees appointed by Gwinnett Schools to address discipline reform and worked collaboratively with school officials to revise policy and practice, like abolishing the quotas where school resource officers were required to have a set number of "contacts" with students every day. In the wake of the 2020 mass protests, Gwinnett SToPP redoubled its efforts to address police abuse of students and launched a campaign to remove them entirely from Gwinnett schools.

Reflecting on Gwinnett SToPP's history, Tillman argues that its biggest achievement is building parent leadership. According to Regina Butler-Streets, one of these parent leaders, change in a place like Gwinnett will be a long struggle, but will happen.

Marlyn [Tillman] is a change agent. Through the organization, we create more change agents that are then able to penetrate the school system and at some point eventually change that system.

Another parent leader, Sabina Oakley says that in addition to winning some important reforms, "Without Gwinnett SToPP being here, the school system would be much worse than it is."

According to Pamela Perkins Carn of the Interfaith Children's Movement, a close partner to Gwinnett SToPP, the group "is small but mighty." Gwinnett SToPP tries to build bridges where it can but "is not being nice about it. They have the audacity to speak truth to power."

Gwinnett County's education system has a national reputation for being one of the best systems in the country. It's a challenge when you're calling to task a system that has this type of reputation. Maybe it makes you not so welcomed every day in all spaces. It's David against Goliath. Gwinnett County Schools is a Goliath. It's big and it's imposing. And there you have Gwinnett SToPP and parents really calling on it to be what its reputation says it is. That's not easy.

Richmond, Virginia: Challenging Racism in Special Education

On the third day of my visit to Henrico County, a suburb outside of Richmond, Virginia, I attended an IEP meeting between school staff and a Black parent whose African American daughter was bullied by a boy who was touching her inappropriately. School officials had told the ninth-grade girl that "the boy just probably likes you." The girl had been diagnosed with depression and PTSD the previous summer and had been suspended seven times in middle school; she was sent to detention several times already in her first year in high school. She needed help and support but instead was facing a potentially hostile, bullying environment.

The mother came with two parent advocates, Kandise Lucas and Lorraine Wright, to demand that the school conduct an investigation and issue a report, as required by law. At the start of the meeting, Lucas pointed out that the meeting was in violation of the law because the official conducting the meeting was an administrative intern and therefore not qualified to officiate at an IEP meeting. The school officials objected to the presence of advocates and a tense, even hostile, atmosphere ensued.

I was deeply disturbed to see the level of indifference on the part of school staff. If the mom hadn't brought the advocates, she would have faced a wall of school officials alone. The assistant principal who eventually arrived to legally conduct the meeting looked bored. School staff entered and left the room seemingly at random. Only the school psychologist showed an ounce of concern. When Lucas said the girl's file was incomplete and had some errors, not a single staff person felt it necessary to look at the file, let alone correct the errors. When the girl herself entered halfway through the meeting, no one greeted her or asked her how she was doing. The meeting ended without school staff committing to an investigation or to any change in support for the child.

In the Introduction to this book, I recounted the story of an African American boy in Henrico County Schools who was assaulted by a school resource officer on the grounds of his middle school, handcuffed, and dragged through the mud. I attended a meeting of school officials with the boy's parent where she was insulted and ended up having to settle for the replacement costs of his clothes. I was shocked by the violence of the assault on a child and the intransigence of school officials. This second case, although less physically violent, may be even more disturbing though. It suggests the complete normalizing of exclusionary school discipline toward students of color with disabilities, the routine violation of student's legal rights, the indifference of educators toward students of color, the stonewalling toward parents, and the hostility toward parent advocates who assert the rights of the child and her family.

Violating the Rights of Children and Families

Kandise Lucas left her position as a special education practitioner for Henrico County Public Schools in 2007 when the district refused to renew her contract because, according to Lucas, of her relentless advocacy as a district employee for students with disabilities and their families, specifically economically disadvantaged families of color in the eastern part of the county. Lucas felt she could no longer in good conscience administer a program that she believed did not provide proper support for children and their families in need. Lucas began to advocate for parents with children with disabilities

to help them get the support and services to which they were legally entitled, co-founding an organization called Advocates for Equity in Schools
with Lorraine Wright. Lucas and Wright witnessed clear patterns confirming
the violation of the rights of students with disabilities, particularly African
American children. Several years later Wright created the grassroots movement I Vote for Me, premised on self-advocacy and the protection of human
rights. The pair continued parent advocacy work with families. Here are
some of these families' stories.

When Michelle Williams's African American son was in high school in
neighboring suburban Chesterfield County, he suffered from anxiety and
depression, was diagnosed with ADHD, and was in the process of being
evaluated for autism. He had an IEP but was repeatedly suspended for
missing school due to behavioral challenges and lack of culturally competent behavior intervention supports. Meanwhile, her son was bullied by
other students, and, despite the pleas of Williams, "The school ignored it."
He tried to commit suicide several times during these years. When I met
her, Williams's son was suspended and had been out of school for sixty-five
days. She believed the suspension was illegal because he had a behavior intervention plan that had never been updated and utilized even though it
was three years old. She brought advocate Lucas with her to a Manifestation
Determination Review meeting with school officials. According to Lucas,
the school could not remove the son from school if it hadn't implemented
the IEP plan correctly. The school objected to the presence of the parent
advocate. In fact, Lucas had advocated for Williams's oldest son a couple
of years earlier and had been arrested for trespassing when she and
Williams asserted the parent's legal right to be accompanied by an advocate. Chesterfield Schools dropped the charges, but Lucas filed a complaint
charging retaliation with the U.S. Department of Education's Office for Civil
Rights (OCR). OCR settled with district, agreeing to the basics of Lucas'
complaint. It confirmed the rights of a parent to the support of an advocate and required all district officials to receive professional development in
proper responses to parent advocates and their right to protection against
retaliation.[15]

The long struggle took a toll on the parent, however. Williams was hospi-
talized as a result of the anxiety and severe stress she was under.

That's the side of the pipeline to prison that no one gets to see: the sleepless
nights, the tears, the multiple emails. When your phone rings and it's the

school and you don't want to answer because your anxiety is up here. You can't sleep because you know that you're all your child has.

Williams could not get a resolution with the school system for her son's situation. She ended up filing a due process complaint with the Virginia Department of Education and a discrimination complaint based upon race and disability with OCR. Williams' youngest child at six years old then began having trouble with the school. She believes "they're labeling and targeting a whole family," pre-judging a child based on the behavior—and stereotyping—of older siblings.

Williams, like many other parents that work with Lucas and Wright, has become an advocate for other parents and for change in the school system. Wright says that Williams was one of the parents that was instrumental in getting the former superintendent of Chesterfield pushed out of that district.

He was so ridiculously non-compliant. They were arrogant and they were just violating civil and human rights all over the place. So she kept coming back and she kept coming back. That's why we want parents to know: never underestimate the power of one to impact the lives of many.

At the time of my interview with her, Williams said her son "is taking it day by day."

He's a child that deserves an education, an appropriate education with the right supports. You ever look at someone and see they may be smiling, but you can sense that their soul is dead on the inside? My son has been like that for a long time. But he's now in recovery. He has hope now that he has a voice.

Pakistani-American Zaib Lakhani has Down Syndrome but his mother has advocated for him to be included in regular education classes. In ninth grade at his high school in Henrico County, school staff took him out of class and told him to clean the cafeteria. His mother, Zahra, would not have minded if all students were expected to help clean the high school to learn about community responsibility. But, instead, the school singled out Zaib and a few special needs students to clean rather than learn. Zahria believed this incident represented a larger pattern in the way the school treated her son. She saw the brilliance in her child and wanted to encourage him. Instead, she says,

The school had broken down to him in various ways that you are not who you think you are. You are a child with limited possibilities and your dream of being with peers without disability is not going to fly here and you have to stay in your box.

She complained to the school, but the practice continued. Eventually, she paid for a billboard to advertise the treatment of students like Zaib by Henrico schools. She turned over an audio recording of school officials making the cleaning assignment to a local TV news station who reported on it. Afterward, according to Lakhani, she was banned from the school grounds. She brought Lucas to her son's next IEP meeting where the school tried to have Lucas arrested for trespassing. Despite mistreatment, Zaib continued in high school and has become an advocate for himself, testifying at Virginia Board of Education meetings and setting up his own blog on educational justice. Zaib knows that the way the school treats him is wrong and wants to fight for his right to education, declaring "I am me. I am educated to my friends."[16]

Training Parent Advocates

Over the years Lucas and Wright have advocated for more than one hundred families and trained three to four times as many people to be advocates for their children and others. Lucas explains the process.

> We've created what we call advocacy teaching labs. For instance, if there's an IEP meeting, we conference all the parents in. We have our little device and no matter who has an IEP meeting, we conference everyone in. Parents can listen and learn and offer feedback.

Training in rights and mutual support among parents is key, according to Frank Thornton, president of the Henrico NAACP at the time. Thornton believes that the school system tries to isolate parents. Typically, a Black parent will be alone at a meeting, facing a table surrounded by mostly white school officials with degrees and laptops.

> It's very intimidating for the parent. Quite often if a parent doesn't understand something, they don't volunteer to say they don't understand. They feel like they have to go along with what the school says.

Lucas and Wright have faced retaliation for their efforts to advocate for parents. Lucas has been arrested seven times for her advocacy work in three counties throughout Virginia, mostly for trespassing on school grounds while supporting a family. Lucas was acquitted in all cases until she was convicted for trespassing in 2018 at Colonial Trail Elementary School in Henrico County because she refused to leave the parent alone on school grounds with hostile administrators when asked by a principal whom she accused of racial discrimination. While she served no jail time, she was permanently banned from entering Colonial Trail Elementary School by a Henrico County Circuit Judge. According to Wright, "They try to discredit her."

> Criticizing her tactics, saying she's rude. All of that is to divert your attention from what the school should be focusing on—compliance to federal law in order to properly serve these already so disenfranchised students.

Lucas believes that the retaliation against parents and their advocates when asserting their right to an education for their children today is like what happened in the civil rights movement when powerholders retaliated against Black people asserting their right to vote. Lucas says, "If you're not upset and outraged, something is wrong with you, not me."[17]

Like Gwinnett County outside of Atlanta, Henrico and other suburban Richmond counties had been largely white; they formed part of the resistance to school desegregation during the time of the civil rights movement. In fact, Richmond and Virginia were centers of what was called "massive resistance" by whites to desegregation efforts. Black families began moving into Henrico County in the nineties, however, and, more recently, Latinx and Asian American families have grown in number. Henrico became a "majority-minority" district and by 2018 its school population of 50,000 was 38% white, 36% Black, 10% Hispanic, and 11% Asian. Twelve percent of its students have disabilities.[18]

Data reported by the school district demonstrated that, in fact, Henrico schools discipline students of color and those with disabilities at high rates, much higher than white students and those without special needs. In 2014–2015, 12% of African American students received a short-term suspension at least once while only 2% of white students were suspended—a rate six times as high; meanwhile, over 13% of students with disabilities were suspended while just under 5% of students without disabilities were suspended. A 2012 report found that Henrico schools had the third highest rate of all districts in the country for suspension of Black male students with disabilities; 92% had been suspended at least once in the 2009–2010 school year. Virginia was in the top ten of states suspending the highest proportion of Black students with disabilities.[19]

At the 2014 DSC Days at the Capital, Lucas and Wright suggested DSC conduct a tour to many of the highest suspending districts identified in the 2012 report and the tour came to Henrico in 2016. DSC representatives from five cities spoke at school board meetings in both Henrico and Chesterfield counties and held press conferences and interviews, lending national credibility to the local effort. Meanwhile, joining DSC expanded the capacity of the local groups, offering access to resources like the model code and the opportunity to attend meetings to learn about federal policy. In fact, within a couple of weeks of joining, Lucas and Wright had the opportunity to meet with U.S. Senator Chris Murphy from Connecticut, one of the legislators most concerned about exclusionary discipline in Washington. The new members seized leadership opportunities so they could both contribute to and learn from the national movement. Both Lucas and Wright became federal liaisons with the responsibility to share information about federal policy changes with DSC members in their region. Lucas also became a consultant for DSC on the Every Student Succeeds Act, working with the NAACP Legal Defense Fund. Wright was elected to DSC's Coordinating Committee, serving two terms as cochair. Wright also served as the DSC consultant to collaborate with the University of Massachusetts Boston to co-create a toolkit containing resources for groups resisting the school-to-prison pipeline. Meanwhile, Henrico members have pushed DSC to address special education in even more explicit and intentional ways than it had, including in its strategic plan.

Change has come slowly in suburban Richmond, but some reduction in suspension rates began in 2011. In 2015, Henrico schools changed its code of conduct to try to move away from exclusionary discipline and rates continued to fall. The police changed its arrest policies in 2015 to reduce arrests for minor infractions. Yet racial disparities and disparities for students with disabilities continued at high levels. Fully half of all Black students with a disability received a short-term out-of-school suspension in the 2016–2017 school year; two-thirds of economically disadvantaged Black boys with a disability were suspended. Advocates believe that the core of the problem persists—the inequitable treatment of students of color with disabilities and the denial of the rights of students and their families.[20]

As in many other Southern communities, advocates in Virginia try to use the courts to gain leverage over intransigent local officials. Even if they don't win, the legal costs involved put some pressure on districts to change. In the context of fighting suits filed by parents, usually with support from Lucas, Henrico schools hired a former state secretary of education to review the school system's special education program. The consultant's 2018 report criticized both the school's lawyers and the family advocates for unnecessarily heightening adversarial relations. Nevertheless, it seemed to support the central claim raised by families and advocates, finding that the district continued to discipline students with disabilities and students of color with disabilities at higher rates than their peers and that the extent of disproportionality was high compared to similar jurisdictions. The report recommended improving parent engagement and closing the racial disparity gap through racial bias training for teachers, amending the code of conduct for students, and developing a plan focused on race and culture to reduce exclusionary discipline practices in elementary and secondary schools.[21]

Advocates have also used appeals to state-level governance to pressure local districts. In fact, Richmond area advocates believe change is required at the state level because, as Wright argues, the problem is pervasive across the region and state.

> You can't possibly have the same sort of instances from district to district unless it's standard operating procedure. These are not anomalies. These are not just happening by happenstance. There is a culture that's endorsed. There is an environment that's created. The Virginia Department of Education has to address it.

Conclusion: Multi-Level and Multi-Pronged Strategies

In the end, Lucas, Wright and parent advocates have pursued multiple strategies to pressure recalcitrant districts to end racially discriminatory and harmful disciplinary practices against students of color and those with disabilities. We have seen these kinds of strategies followed across the cases discussed in this chapter. Groups consciously work at multiple levels—local, state, and national. Small groups simply cannot amass the resources and power necessary if they operate only at the local level, particularly in the

South, in suburban districts with newer communities of color, and in smaller cities in conservative areas. The national movement has provided these groups with critical resources: reports on school discipline data relevant to their districts, training in participatory research, model codes of conduct, and connections to funding. Just as importantly, the national movement has provided local participants a chance to connect across localities, where they share with and learn from other groups, come to better appreciate the systemic nature of racial oppression, feel inspired by meeting activists across the country, and engage in federal policy advocacy. The national movement intentionally makes its presence known in these local areas, shining a spotlight on districts unused to much attention.

Local groups also pursue a multi-pronged strategy, including parent advocacy, awareness raising, policy advocacy, and legal filings to push school systems to change and be held accountable to the rights of students of color and those with disabilities and their parents. The strategies are designed to disrupt a resistant, racialized system in which communities of color have little political power. Progress has been faster in some places and slower in others, but multi-pronged and multi-level strategies are making a difference. In the end, according to Kandace Lucas, "We are snatching kids out of the school-to-prison pipeline."

It's almost as if you can get this visual: The school is pushing them in and we're trying to snatch them out. That's what it comes down to.

8

The Movement Expands

Police-Free Schools, Black Girls Matter, and Restorative Justice

As the movement to end the school-to-prison pipeline matured, new constituencies came forward to raise their voices about their needs and new ways to address the school-to-prison pipeline rose to the fore. In this chapter I build upon the earlier discussion of the police ticketing campaign in Los Angeles to examine campaigns against police violence in schools and the rise of the movement for police-free schools. In Chapter 3, I discussed the work of the Genders and Sexualities Alliance Network to address the needs of queer students of color and link together the LGBTQ and educational justice movements. In this chapter, I recount efforts by Black girls, girls of color, and gender nonconforming students to take an intersectional approach and assert their voice and particular issues in the movement. Finally, families and students cannot change deep-seated systems of racial injustice on their own or win authentic implementation of restorative justice alternatives without the participation of teachers in the classroom. I end the chapter by examining efforts by community organizers to ally with teachers and teacher unions. I discuss the work of teachers, like those in Teachers Unite in New York City, who colead school-site organizing campaigns with students and parents to foster deep changes in school culture and climate, and in relationships and power.

Police-Free Schools

On October 25, 2015, Niya Kenny filmed a white school police officer body slamming her classmate, a Black sixteen-year-old girl named Shakara, to the floor at Spring Valley High School in Columbia, South Carolina. Deputy Sherriff Ben Fields placed Shakara in a headlock, flipped her desk over, and then dragged and threw her across the classroom floor, all for allegedly refusing to hand over her cell phone. Yet it was Niya and Shakara who were

Willful Defiance. Mark R. Warren, Oxford University Press. © Mark R. Warren 2022.
DOI: 10.1093/oso/9780197611500.003.0009

arrested, charged with "disturbing school," and sent to juvenile detention. One student present at the time described the impact on students.

> I've never seen anything so nasty looking, so sick to the point that you know, other students are turning away, don't know what to do, and are just scared for their lives. That's supposed to be somebody that's going to protect us. Not somebody that we need to be scared of, or afraid.

Meanwhile, the video went viral, aired repeatedly on television stations, and led to a national outcry about police abuse of Black children in schools. For young people and youth organizers with the Alliance for Educational Justice (AEJ), the incident demonstrated what they long knew: police did not make schools safer. Rather, police formed a key part of the system that criminalized students of color and should be removed from schools.[1]

AEJ dubbed the incident #AssaultAtSpringValley and swung into action. Youth members of AEJ, led by the Urban Youth Collaborative (UYC) in New York City, started writing love letters to Niya and Shakara to show their support. When released from detention, Niya attended a Youth Power conference sponsored by the Funders Collaborative on Youth Organizing in Durham, North Carolina, where students from UYC as well as the Philadelphia Student Union and Power U Center for Social Change in Miami called her on stage and read the love letters to her. They linked arms and welcomed Niya into the movement.

AEJ worked with Color of Change and local groups to collect 150,000 signatures on a petition to have the charges against Niya and Shakara removed. They delivered the petitions on the alliance's second annual "End the War on Youth" day. In January of 2016 Niya and a group of youth leaders from New Orleans testified at a hearing of the United Nation's Working Group on People of African Descent and called for the removal of police from schools, a position the international group subsequently endorsed in its recommendations to the United States. Finally, in September the charges against Niya and Shakara were dropped. Nevertheless, Officer Fields was never charged with criminal wrongdoing, although he was fired from his position.[2]

Reflecting on the significance of her actions, Niya says:

> That day everything was going down, I felt like I did the wrong thing. I kept telling myself, "You should have just sat down and just been quiet."

But speaking up and being arrested and everything, it just brought so much awareness to the school-to-prison pipeline. Honestly, if I could go back, I wouldn't change anything. It was like the universe brought me there that day.

According to Maria Fernandez, a long-time youth organizer who coordinates the Advancement Project's police-free schools work, "Police violence in schools was not new."

But the assault at Spring Valley, however horrific it was, energized a movement around criminalization that goes beyond suspensions. That changed everything for everyone. It woke people up to what is happening. It made people more willing and ready to fight the fight around school police.[3]

The Assault At Campaign: #EndWarOnYouth

When George Zimmerman was acquitted of the 2012 fatal shooting of African American teenager Trayvon Martin, youth members of AEJ from across the country were attending a Free Minds Free People's conference in Chicago. Fifty young people huddled together in the hotel room of AEJ's national director, Jonathan Stith. According to Stith, "Young people were really scared, they were terrified, they were heartbroken. It was just a lot of emotion in the room." The young people consoled each other but also committed to taking action to fight for justice. Within a week AEJ mobilized a delegation of one hundred youth members to go to Tallahassee, Florida, and stand with the Dream Defenders and Power U Center for Social Change when they occupied the Florida State Capitol building, demanding an end to the state's "stand your ground" law used to justify Zimmerman's actions. Stith says the action helped shape a new direction for AEJ.

That was a real powerful movement building moment for us where we met that moment and we were like, "Y'all are not alone in this struggle." Young people ultimately understood that Trayvon could have been all of them or any one of them.

The next year, Black residents of Ferguson, Missouri, took to the streets to protest the shooting by a white police officer of unnamed African American

Michael Brown. Youth organizers affiliated with AEJ came to offer their support and organizing expertise. In that summer of 2014, they faced armed police with tanks in the streets of the city. Returning to their hometowns, they realized that their student members in schools were facing the same police as Black residents in Ferguson. Police shootings in the streets, and the role of police as a repressive and controlling force in Black communities, had a direct parallel to police presence and assaults of students of color in schools. Stith explains how Ferguson pushed AEJ to broaden its focus on school discipline and educational justice to demand an end to what it called the war on youth.

> It seems like young people are dying every day and getting shot down by police. We're a movement building alliance, so it became clear: our stuff is bigger than education. School is our base. We believe schools transform society and society can transform schools. Coming back from Ferguson, young folk were saying it feels like there's a war happening to them, that they're dying every day, that it feels ever present.

The alliance subsequently developed an analysis that students of color were facing state sanctioned violence, launching its campaign to #EndWarOnYouth. AEJ started a rapid response initiative labeling instances of police abuse at schools with the hashtag #AssaultAt and providing support for victims of police assaults and local organizations across the country.

The rise of awareness of racist police violence and the militant response by the Movement for Black Lives emboldened AEJ members and other school-to-prison pipeline organizers. Before Ferguson, according to Stith, demanding police-free schools was seen as unwinnable. "But with Black Lives Matter happening, the question of police is up and people have gone to Ferguson. They came back ready to fight." The two movements—Black Lives Matter and educational justice—interweaved as it turned out that many Black Lives Matter activists had been trained in organizing when they were members of youth organizing groups. Patrisse Cullors, for example, was trained as a youth leader in the Bus Riders Union by the Labor Community Strategy Center discussed in Chapter 5 before she co-founded the Black Lives Matter movement. For their part, Stith and other AEJ organizers ended up writing the education platform of the Black Lives Matter movement.[4]

AEJ's rapid response #AssaultAt campaign brought national focus to the move toward police-free schools, as it highlighted case after case of police violence across the country. In May of 2016, a Philadelphia school police officer assaulted Brian Burney, a youth member of the AEJ affiliated Philadelphia Student Union (PSU), for trying to go to the bathroom without a pass. When the officer refused to let Brian use the restroom, Brian threw an orange at the wall out of frustration. Officer Maciocha punched Brian twice in the face, slammed him down on the floor, and put him in a chokehold; he was later diagnosed with a concussion. #AssaultAtBenFranklin recorded and publicized the case and supported PSU in a campaign to demand justice for Brian and then a larger call for diverting funds that support more than four hundred police officers in schools to pay for counselors, nurses, and restorative practices. After weeks of protests and rallies, PSU won a commitment from the district to reduce the size of the school police force and create a complaint system for students and parents, only the second school police force in the country to establish such a system. Meanwhile, Black parent organizers from the Journey for Justice Alliance came to Philadelphia to stand with young people, helping to build a consensus against the presence of police in schools in the wider educational justice movement.[5]

#AssaultAtREACH supported the campaign of the Baltimore Algebra Project when a school police officer slapped and kicked a Black male student for being late to school. #AssaultAtRoseville helped the Youth Organizing Institute when a school police officer in Wake County, North Carolina, was recorded body slamming a fifteen-year-old Black female student, Jasmine Darwin, then jerking her limp body up by the arm and dragging her out of camera view.

By 2018, AEJ was able to identify 61 cases of police violence in its #AssaultAt campaign; by 2020, it had identified 145 incidents. While AEJ was able to document and support many of these students and groups, the alliance believed the cases represented only the tip of the iceberg of police abuse of students. AEJ helped link the struggles together and, by doing so, took up the wider call for the removal of police from schools as the next iteration of the movement to end the school-to-prison pipeline.

Laying the Foundations for Police-Free Schools

AEJ was not alone in its call for police-free schools, as momentum in this direction had been building for a while. Beginning in the late 1990s, students of color had been criticizing the heavy police presence in schools, as well as metal detectors and searches, charging that their schools felt like jails. From the early days of the peanut incident on a school bus in Mississippi

described in Chapter 3, community groups had been concerned with excessive and unwarranted police arrests of schoolchildren, and the topic was cov-
ered in the Advancement Project's report called *Derailed: The Schoolhouse
to Jailhouse Track* in 2003. In Chapter 6, we saw how the Los Angeles-based
Labor Community Strategy Center launched a campaign to stop police
ticketing of students in 2007, and later got the LA School Police to return
military grade equipment and a tank to the federal government. In opposition to the call for more armed police in schools after the mass shooting
at Sandy Hook Elementary School in 2012, the Los Angeles-based Youth
Justice Coalition initiated a national campaign called "You Can't Build Peace
with a Piece (gun)" that included scores of youth groups across the country
and was endorsed by DSC and many other groups in the school-to-prison
pipeline movement. In 2013 Padres & Jóvenes Unidos (PJU) in Denver became the first community group in the nation to broker a written agreement
between police and a school district to limit the role of police in schools to
serious threats to school safety.[6]

In 2012, responding to the murder of Raheim Brown by a school police officer, the Black Organizing Project (BOP) in Oakland became the first community organization to win a formal complaint system for police abuse in
schools for students and families. Recognizing the limitations of this kind
of reform, BOP built on its victory to launch a campaign for police-free
schools. In doing so, BOP became a national leader in the call for the complete removal of police from schools—setting the goal of 2020 as the year for
establishing police-free schools and inspiring organizing groups across the
country to make this bold demand.[7]

Nevertheless, while many organizers in the school-to-prison pipeline
movement long opposed a police presence in schools, many people in the
communities their organizations served were so used to the presence of police in schools, and the justification that police were necessary for student
safety, that it took time to convince them that police should not be stationed
in school. Young people were at the forefront of the call for police-free
schools, while parents were sometimes more hesitant, concerned about police brutality but also worried about the safety of their children. From the
early days of organizing for the removal of police in Oakland, BOP organizers
like Jackie Byers recognized that

> Some people within our own communities feel like they need police, that
> it's a necessary evil in our schools. When we began to challenge that, we

got a lot of pushback. Folks were asking for alternatives. They wanted us to guarantee one hundred percent that we would keep all children safe without police. We have to figure out how to shift the narrative that police keep Black children safe. That is still a struggle.[8]

DSC went through a careful two-year process of internal discussion before it adopted its position calling for the removal of the regular presence of police from schools. Many pathbreaking groups in the police-free schools movement like BOP, Coleman Advocates, and PJU were also members of DSC and the coalition had long been critical of the role of police in schools; it included policies on reducing school policing in its 2012 Model Code on Education and Dignity and fought against efforts to increase the presence of armed security in the wake of the Sandy Hook massacre. Nevertheless, the position was new to some members. DSC's Counselors Not Cops platform, drafted by DSC members and staff including veteran core leader Harold Jordan of the Pennsylvania ACLU and DSC Campaign Coordinator Natalie Chap, called for the removal of police from schools and for promoting safety through positive measures that supported rather than criminalized students and for using restorative justice, peacebuilders, and a range of intervention specialists. DSC also called for districts to make agreements with police departments to clearly limit the rare instances when outside police could enter schools and to protect students' rights if they did. DSC launched its Counselors Not Cops campaign in 2016, providing groups with a set of resources to support campaigns to remove police from schools. DSC featured the new campaign in its Week of Action that year, with local organizations adapting the demands to their context and needs. Some, for example, called for reductions in police or limitations to their role in schools as a step on the road to full removal.[9]

By 2017 the movement for police-free schools was in full swing. AEJ developed a partnership with the Advancement Project that provided research and analysis, political education, and strategic communications to support local groups responding to police assaults. The partnership sponsored the first national meeting for police-free schools in 2017 with Black Organizing Project, Coleman Advocates, the Strategy Center, Power U, and El Puente. In September of 2018, the partners issued *We Came to Learn*, a report on school policing and an accompanying action kit for local organizations. Once again, the national movement built upon initiatives started at the local level and helped spread those model campaigns across the country. It then created national-level resources to strengthen organizing efforts adapted to local conditions and helped create a sense of a national movement to embolden local efforts. In December of 2019, the National Campaign for Police Free Schools adopted a resolution calling for the abolition of police, declaring themselves abolitionists.

> Police Free Schools means dismantling school policing infrastructure, culture, and practice; ending school militarization and surveillance; and building a new liberatory education system. We believe removing police from our schools is a seed for removing them from our communities. We are abolitionists, grounded in our respective freedom traditions together. #PoliceFreeSchools, like abolition, is a practical organizing tool and a long-term goal.[10]

Although community organizations had a growing number of compelling stories of abuse at the hands of police, the movement was hampered in its early days by a lack of systematic data about the presence of police in schools and their interactions with students, including assaults and arrests. However, the U.S. Office for Civil Rights began requiring schools to report the relevant data for the 2015–2016 school year. In 2019, the ACLU published its analysis of the 2015–2016 civil rights data collection, revealing that nearly half of all public schools were patrolled by police. The report revealed that 1.7 million students attended schools with police but no counselors; 3 million attended schools with police but no nurses; 6 million attended schools with police but no school psychologists; and fully 10 million students attended schools with police but no social workers. The report found that schools with police were more likely to criminalize students, with 3.5 times as many student arrests as those without police. Overall, there were over 230,000 school-based referrals to law enforcement and 61,000 school arrests that year. Students of color and those with special needs were disproportionately criminalized, with Black students three times as likely to be arrested as white students; in some states they were eight times as likely. Black girls were particularly criminalized with arrest rates four times that of white girls. Meanwhile Black and Latino boys with disabilities constituted 3% of students but made up fully 12% of school arrests. Other research showed that LGBTQ students were twice as likely to be arrested and detained for a nonviolent offense compared to their peers while immigrant and undocumented students also suffered from enhanced surveillance and threats of deportation. The ACLU report concluded that most arrests were not for violent behavior but for minor misbehavior, while other research also suggested that arrests were for infractions like "disturbing schools" or "disorderly conduct."[11]

Contrary to the defenders of police in schools, there proved to be no evidence that the presence of police makes schools safer. Despite the tremendous growth in school resource officers in schools across the country, no systematic studies have shown they have increased safety. An increasing number of studies, however, have shown the harmful effects of police in school, making schools less inclusive and more prone to racialized disciplinary measures. Instead of police, movement organizers called for restorative justice and the presence of peacebuilders in schools, as groups increasingly piloted these approaches. In Chapter 5 we saw how the Youth Justice Coalition (YJC) created a police-free school in Los Angeles using transformative justice and peacebuilders.[12]

Meanwhile, the movement for police-free schools and justice reinvestment campaigns fueled each other. Justice reinvestment calls for diverting funds from policing and criminal justice into support services, education, and community programming for youth. As described in Chapter 5, YJC campaigned to remove funds from law enforcement to fund youth services in Los Angeles. Padres & Jóvenes Unidos in Denver, Communities United in Chicago, and Make the Road New York worked with former Advancement Project staff member Jim Freeman to produce a report called the $3.4 Trillion Dollar Mistake, documenting the full costs of thirty years of mass incarceration. The groups issued a call for diverting these funds from criminalization to investment in youth, community, and educational services in support of local campaigns. Meanwhile, the Urban Youth Collaborative worked with the Center for Popular Democracy to issue The $746 Million a Year School-to-Prison Pipeline, a report that documented the full costs of policing and disciplinary policies in the city's schools and called for a Young People's Social Justice Agenda to divest from criminalization and invest in education and youth services.[13]

While, prior to 2020, no district had removed police from schools, the number of partial victories—reducing police presence in schools and limiting its role—continue to mount. In the fall of 2017, as a result of a community-based organizing campaign, Toronto district public schools removed police from the forty-five high schools where they had been stationed. While Toronto is a Canadian rather than U.S. case, the victory nevertheless inspired the American movement by showing that a large, urban school district can operate safely without police.[14]

Mass Protests Tip the Balance

When the mass protests against police racism erupted in 2020, the movement built on the foundation it had laid over the previous years to quickly push school districts to remove or defund police in schools. In short order, youth and parent organizing groups that had fought for years to push back against police in schools in Minneapolis, Denver, San Francisco, Portland, Milwaukee, and several other cities won historic victories as school districts ended their contracts with school police; some places like Los Angeles cut the school police budget significantly. The Black Organizing Project scored a major victory when it got the Board of Education to eliminate the Oakland Schools Police Department; reallocate funds previously used for sworn police officers to student support positions; and launch an inclusive, community-driven process to adopt a revised student safety plan.[15]

For many observers, the police-free schools movement seemed to emerge out of nowhere. In fact, however, it had been carefully prepared over the years by youth and parent organizing groups and nurtured by the national movement to end the school-to-prison pipeline. Organizing groups had been active in almost every city that defunded or removed police from schools in 2020. They had proposals in hand, had built relationships with sympathetic officials, and had educated a base of young people and parents ready to mobilize quickly.

According to Jonathan Stith, when young people and parents of color first started naming the school-to-prison pipeline and calling for an end to zero tolerance, "we were called crazy. Nobody believed us. After years of organizing, ending zero tolerance and the pipeline became the official position of the U.S. government. Now, police-free schools are the next frontier."

Black Girls Matter

While #AssaultAtSpringValley helped catalyze the police-free schools movement, it also opened space in the movement for the assertion of the experiences and voice of Black girls and girls of color. According to Maria Fernandez, "It birthed a conversation around Black girls, Black girls and policing, and Black girls and school discipline." The school-to-prison pipeline movement had always supported students of color across gender identities. Nevertheless, when gender was specified, Black and Brown boys sometimes received special attention, and Black boys were recognized as facing a particular crisis in educational failure and incarceration. In the wake of the killing of Trayvon Martin, then President Obama launched the My Brother's Keeper initiative that focused on supporting boys and men of color. While boys of color needed this attention, many girls and women of color believed that it nevertheless contributed to the historical erasure of their experiences. Meanwhile, taking an intersectional approach, the founders of the Black Lives Matter movement highlighted the leadership of women of color and queer women, serving to inspire women and gender nonconforming activists to assert that "Black girls matter" in the school-to-pipeline movement.

Reproductive Justice Is Restorative Justice

The Power U Center for Social Change in Miami, the area where Trayvon Martin grew up, became one of the first organizing groups to develop a particular line of work with Black girls and gender nonconforming students of color to assert their voice and experiences with criminalization in schools and communities. Ruth Jeannoel, director of organizing for Power U at the time, pushed the group to recognize "the ways in which Black girls are subjugated simultaneously by patriarchy, white supremacy and heterosexism, especially in school," and to incorporate reproductive justice into its restorative justice work.

> I'm a Black mother and I'm doing this through my lived experience. One of the pillars of reproductive justice is the right to raise our children in safe and healthy communities. Another is the right to autonomy over our bodies. We had been doing campaign work on restorative justice for 10 years. At the time it was important to push to bridge the two. I felt the connection and knew I had to see how the rest of my team felt about it.

This was a new framework and Jeannoel got some pushback from the group. But the organizers started asking girls about their experiences and the new framework resonated.

> A lot of stories we heard were about how girls were getting suspended, bullied, having to fight back, around their bodies—someone snapping someone's bra multiple times. So many had experienced sexual assaults and

harassment in schools that led to pushout. The group came to see the inter-section of restorative and reproductive justice, if we really wanted to center Black girls and gender nonconforming youth.

In 2015 the group formed the Miami Black Girls Matter Coalition with S.O.U.L. Sisters Leadership Collective, Miami Workers Center, and the Dream Defenders and held the first Black Girls Miami Summit. The coalition organized a town hall in the spring of 2015 attended by three hundred Black girls, community members, and decision makers. Since the voices of Black girls often got silenced in gender-diverse settings, Power U and the coalition created spaces for Black girls and gender nonconforming students to share their stories with each other, birthing the "Black girls matter" circles. This process created strong collective bonds and prepared the girls and gender nonconforming students to tell their stories in public.

Their testimonies included a range of experiences with personal and systemic violence. Many Black girls reported being stereotyped as loud and aggressive and disciplined as "defiant." Others talked about stereo-types of Black women as over-sexualized and being disciplined for the way they dressed. Many gender nonconforming students reported harassment over their dress or use of bathrooms assigned by gender binaries. Girls talked about sexual harassment or abuse by security guards and by their peers. One girl said she would hear teachers tell female students that "they were going to be whores" because of the way they dressed. She reported that there was "one security guard who, if he saw you by yourself, he'd tap you on your butt. I snatched the broom from him and hit him and I got written up."[16]

At the town hall, the coalition outlined a far-reaching program of policy demands to address the needs of Black girls. These included divesting re-sources from policing to invest in better-resourced schools with supportive and race-conscious counselors and teachers, restorative justice programs, and high-quality and culturally relevant curriculum that includes crit-ical thinking. The coalition also demanded comprehensive sex education in schools that included a queer lens, including conversations on consent and options other than abstinence, as well as a set of demands to respond to the needs of young parents, including access to breastfeeding, midwifery, and doula support. Finally, the girls demanded safe and inclusive spaces for LGBTQIA + students, including gender neutral bathrooms and respect for gender identity.[17]

In the end, Power U and the coalition argued that by addressing the concerns of the most marginalized students along intersecting lines of oppression, the movement would be creating solutions—like safe and supportive school climates free of physical and sexual harassment—that worked for all students. According to Jeannoel, the movement must address oppression in all its forms to obtain true freedom and liberation. "An essential part of freeing Black boys is centering the experiences of Black girls and gender nonconforming young people, so all will be free."

Power U worked to spread its message to the larger national movement. The 2015 town hall was co-sponsored by national civil rights organizations including the Advancement Project and the African American Policy Forum and was publicized widely. In 2015 Power U helped host the last of the series of Advancement Project-sponsored Action Camps where youth and some parents from across the country came to share strategies and receive organizing training. Power U organized a plenary session on Black Girls Matter and led workshops during the camp. It went on to partner with the Advancement Project to conduct a participatory action research project and produced a report in 2017 called *The Hidden Truth* on the failure of Miami-Dade County Schools to develop meaningful alternatives to suspensions in their Student Success Centers. The report included a detailed section on the experiences of Black girls and gender nonconforming students and featured a grading rubric that included reproductive justice alongside restorative discipline practices, becoming one of the first reports from the grassroots movement to address these issues. Power U used the report for its organizing, but it also served as a model for groups across the country to highlight how Black girls matter.[18]

The Schools Girls Deserve

Girls for Gender Equity (GGE), based in New York City, emerged as another organizing group that was at the forefront of the grassroots movement to organize girls of color and gender nonconforming students to assert their voice and leadership. According to Kate McDonough, director of organizing at the time, GGE works to ensure that girls and gender nonconforming students of color have the opportunity not just to name the problem but also create their own solutions.

GGE is very intentional about naming institutionalized racism and sexism and homophobia and transphobia and making sure that those who are the most marginalized and most impacted are at the center of our work and are really driving the work.

GGE launched the School Girls Deserve project and worked with over one hundred girls and gender nonconforming students of color to document the issues they faced and imagine schools that would support and empower them. They conducted a participatory action research project on their experiences with school pushout and collected many stories. They found that girls who were the recipients of harassment often ended up being disciplined for resisting it. McDonough explained that "sexual harassment is completely and totally normalized in schools."

When young women are being harassed, they either won't report it, or they feel like nothing will happen if they do. Girls who are being sexually harassed to the point that they fight back, then get in trouble for fighting back. They could be harassed and finally have had it and they punch the person or scream at them and say, "Stop looking at me," and they'll be disciplined for that.

Cristina Powell, a biracial high school student and member of GGE's Sister in Strength leadership group, described the various participatory activities they used in the project, including Vision Sessions to imagine the school that girls deserve and employing art to collectively display their ideas. In other words, they "drew the schools they wanted." At many events during the course of the campaign, the group had policymakers go through a metal detector simulation so they could experience something like what students faced in schools every day. GGE youth then presented their holistic vision for the schools they deserved: well-resourced schools with safe and inclusive environments free of punitive discipline and sexual harassment, without high-stakes standardized testing, and with culturally relevant curriculum that featured the history and contributions of women of color and trans and queer people, staffed by teachers who understood their experiences. According to McDonough, girls also wanted and deserved

a culturally competent sex education that included needs of LGBTQ students, a curriculum that talked about relationships, that talked about power and privilege, that allowed for young people to really think through their identities, and that addressed sexual harassment and consent.[19]

As part of the campaign, GGE demanded that the NYC Department of Education and the City Council hire Title IX Coordinators to protect cis and trans girls and gender nonconforming youth from sexual harassment in schools. GGE also initiated New York City's first Young Women's Initiative focused on girls and women of color, which developed a holistic program to meet their needs and was endorsed by the City Council. Powell said it was important for girls and students of all genders to assert their voice in the halls of power like this, "to be at the table when education decisions are being made."

GGE is an active member of DSC and brought its intersectional perspective on girls and gender nonconforming students of color into that coalition. GGE advocated for DSC to use people's personal pronouns at its meetings and helped participants new to this practice understand why it is important to affirm people's identity in this way to create an inclusive environment. McDonough believes educational justice movements must "examine how we may unintentionally recreate the oppressive structure that we're trying to tear down."

> Are we creating a safe space for trans young people to be there? Do we not just say our pronouns but make an effort to really learn people's pronouns and use them? Do we make sure there are gender neutral bathrooms in the space? Sexual harassment does happen in movement spaces, so how do we make sure that our own gatherings reflect the schools and communities that we want and that we're fighting for?

Meanwhile, researchers and advocates connected to larger educational and racial justice movements also began to highlight the systemic and personal experiences of girls of color with exclusionary school discipline and police, as well as sexual harassment and the policing of gender roles. The African American Policy Forum, led by Kimberlé Crenshaw, issued one of the first reports in 2015, entitled *Black Girls Matter*. Crenshaw and colleagues analyzed U.S. civil rights data and showed that in 2011–2012, while Black boys were three times as likely to be suspended as white boys, Black girls were six times as likely to be suspended as white girls. In New York City, they were ten times more likely. The report also discussed the consequences of sexually harassing behavior, physical and sexual assault, and bullying. The next year

Monique Morris, co-founder of the National Black Women's Justice Institute, published the book *Pushout: The Criminalization of Black Girls in School* and brought even greater public attention to the issue.[20]

McDonough has seen a lot of progress in the inclusion of girls and gender nonconforming students in the school-to-prison pipeline movement. They see their concerns included in almost all the movement's messaging.

> For a while a lot of the school-to-prison pipeline conversations, and this still does happen, is mostly around young men: straight, Black, boys. We had to say, "We're not advocating for you to stop talking about boys." Because sometimes folks would get mad, and they saw it as like an either-or. What we're just saying is that girls, and queer and trans youth, and owning that all of these identities can exist in one person, are impacted by this as well. It doesn't have to be an either-or. It can be a both-and.

Jeannoel, who went on to found Fanm Saj, Inc., says that, as a mother of two Black girls,

> I want schools to be a place where they can learn without the threat of being pushed out or excluded; where they can speak up without being silenced and where their needs, hopes and dreams are heard and valued.[21]

Educators in the Movement: Restorative Justice

While parents and young people have been the key drivers of the grassroots movement to end the school-to-prison pipeline, they have long known that they cannot transform public education on their own. They need to find ways to create authentic partnerships with teachers in the classroom and administrators in the school building if they want to change the culture and climate of schools, let alone create teaching and learning environments that help students thrive and be successful in their lives. Yet many teachers have been complicit in the school-to-prison pipeline, discriminating against students of color with a range of gender identities and punitively disciplining them. As we saw in Denver and Los Angeles, local teacher unions initially opposed changes to school discipline procedures to reduce suspensions. In fact, when parents and young people first started naming the school-to-prison pipeline and calling for its end, both national teacher unions had official positions supporting zero tolerance.

Shifts in Teacher Unions

We saw in Chapter 3, however, that the two national unions, the American Federation of Teachers (AFT) and the National Education Association (NEA), gradually shifted their positions through advocacy by movement actors, eventually rejecting zero tolerance and endorsing alternatives like restorative justice. While many local unions continued to resist change, others slowly and gradually embraced alternatives as organizers leveraged national union support to push for change locally. Meanwhile, reform slates began to win elections to some local union offices and this newer leadership began to support change agendas; the Chicago Teachers Union, for example, supported VOYCE's campaign to end zero tolerance through SB100. As the national movement won the narrative against zero tolerance, teachers and their local unions became at least open to alternative approaches. Attacks on public education and teachers unions by school privatizers also pushed unions to form alliances with community groups. Teacher unions, though, made sure to combine support for alternatives to exclusionary discipline with demands for greater resources and training for teachers to implement them.[22]

In 2014, the Advancement Project formed a partnership with NEA, AFT, and the Schott Foundation to produce a restorative justice guide for teachers. The Advancement Project had been engaging with the national unions for several years to move them away from zero tolerance and wanted to create resources to support restorative justice as an alternative. According to Lisa Thomas from the AFT, resources like the guide are critical because

> it doesn't take a whole lot of training to write a referral and put a kid out of the classroom; but it does take additional supports and additional training on responding to behavior that is disruptive to learning for not only the student that's engaging in these behaviors but those around him as well as for the educator.

While the guide from national unions encouraged many local affiliates to change policy, it did not require recalcitrant locals to do so. That would take local advocacy and organizing.[23]

Denver emerged as one of the first places where organizing groups and teachers unions partnered to implement restorative justice as an alternative to exclusionary discipline. Padres & Jóvenes Unidos's (PJU) campaign in 2008 to revise the student code of conduct to end zero tolerance was one of the first in the nation where an organizing group won pilot restorative justice programs in schools as an alternative to exclusionary discipline. While the NEA affiliated Denver Classroom Teachers Association initially opposed that 2008 reform, over the years the relationship between the organizations shifted. Six years later, PJU was able to partner with the district, the teachers association, and the University of Denver to create the Denver School-Based Restorative Practices Partnership with support from the Advancement Project and the NEA. Funds from the NEA supported resources for expanded implementation of restorative justice at three schools where teachers and community members were already working together. The schools were also supported to mentor additional Denver schools to implement restorative justice. Meanwhile, the partnership sought to impact the national movement. It hosted regular visits by delegations from other districts. In 2016, NEA published a report based upon best practices in Denver to help spread what it considered a strong model to other districts.[24]

According to Daniel Kim, director of organizing for PJU, things changed so much that while discipline policy used to be the flash point of divisions between PJU and the union, it had become a "bridge." This bridge developed, PJU co-executive director Ricardo Martinez says, because national attacks on public education and labor unions means that teacher unions have to find allies—"And that's us." PJU pushed the union to see the need not just to defend public education but to transform it. "That means they have to change too. And one of the first things to change is around zero tolerance." By 2020, the Denver teachers' association had moved so far that it endorsed the resolution to end the school department's contract with Denver Police.

PJU was worried that teachers would not see restorative justice as a wholesale change in school climate and culture but simply as a way to teach life skills. According to Martinez, "When you look at racial disparities, the problem is not the student behavior, it's the adult behavior."

We have to address the inherent racism of this country and how it plays out. Our effort is not that something is wrong with the student. Our fight is that there's something wrong with the adults and the system. So, we're giving the adults a better set of methodologies and tools to address their behavior.

The partnership was intentionally located at PJU, as Dwanna Nicole who managed the project for the Advancement Project, explained, "to keep families and students at the center of the work" and make sure it was sustainable.

Leadership changes and staff changes. But if you have a community that understands and cares and knows what is happening in that school, then that's actually how you create sustained practice throughout time.

From organizer Kim's point of view,

We're the ones who have the most at stake in seeing real changes to the practices in every building and in every classroom. We're the ones who are going to make sure that this is not just some checking of a box or is not just some flavor of the month thing, but that it actually works because our students and families are the ones who need it to work, who need it to change.

Meanwhile, NEA began hosting monthly sessions run by the Advancement Project for its members and others to receive hands-on training in restorative justice. The NEA required schools to bring teams to the sessions and include a community member to help increase the capacity for authentic implementation of restorative justice upon the participants' return. Unlike many professional development models, the NEA approach was deep and extensive and involved personal work in restorative circles. According to Nicole,

There's no PowerPoint and no one is standing at the front of the room teaching; there are no notes. You're learning because you're doing it. Because participants feel it themselves and because they share their own stories in a circle, it affects them personally.

Teachers quickly learn that restorative circles are not simply a tool to use with students when they get back to their school.

They realize that it's really about them. They came there thinking about how they were going to help their students but what they realize is that they actually needed it. They needed a space where they could talk about some of the harm that has been done to them and some of the harm that they have committed.

As movement organizing won restorative justice alternatives in districts across the country, many school systems began to implement these programs on their own. While pilot projects in Denver and elsewhere proved promising, many in the school-to-prison pipeline movement remained deeply concerned that by removing restorative practices from an organizing context, its real promise could be gutted. Organizing groups promoted restorative justice to transform school climate and culture and to build respectful relationships between teachers and students and their families. They worried it could become deficit-focused and understood and practiced simply to change "bad" student behavior rather than an agent for systemic change. Even more, organizers worried that restorative justice could become another program implemented down onto school communities and teachers without authentic buy-in by teachers and participation by families and students. Meanwhile, professional nonprofit organizations seemed to be monopolizing funding for trainings. These outside trainers often helicopter in, conduct training in how to hold a circle for example, and then leave without creating deep transformation in relationships and culture. When schools implement restorative practices in superficial ways, it might fail and discredit the whole idea. According to Nicole:

> Sometimes people were just given a video to watch and then expected to go keep a circle. Some people were just reading books and keeping circles. It was something but it wasn't restorative justice. They were calling it restorative justice and teachers were now saying, "It doesn't work. We tried it and it didn't work."

School-Site Organizing for Deep Culture Change

Teachers Unite in New York City directly took up this challenge: to organize teachers to create deep and transformative changes in school culture and climate—and in relationships and power—through partnerships with students and families. Sally Lee founded Teachers Unite in 2006 with other teachers who saw the need for an organization of teachers independent of the local union. The NYC United Federation of Teachers (UFT) had a history of opposing the demands of communities of color dating back to its opposition to Black community control of schools in the sixties. Lee explains the group's mission this way.

> We started Teachers Unite with a mission to organize democratic school chapters under the principles of equity, voice, diversity, and action, with an eye toward changing society and building a center for radical teacher organizing. . . . We founded TU to try to build analysis and power among an intergenerational group of educators with a vision of democratically transforming the UFT into an ally in fights for racial and economic justice in schools and communities.[25]

From its beginning, Teachers Unite focused on ending the school-to-prison pipeline. Working with Partners for Dignity & Rights (called NESRI at the time), Teachers Unite produced *Teachers Talk: School Culture, Safety, and Human Rights* in 2008. The group surveyed over three hundred middle and high school teachers in NYC and found that teachers were often critical of harsh discipline policies and wanted support for students rather than punishment. Almost two-thirds of teachers felt that armed police officers in the school never or rarely made students feel safe. Teachers Unite joined the Student Safety Coalition and later the New York chapter of DSC, where the organization put into practice its mission to partner with student and parent organizing groups fighting for racial equity. The chapter worked to end zero tolerance and shift the district away from exclusionary discipline practices.[26]

Teachers Unite embraced restorative justice early on as an alternative to exclusionary discipline and its members began to implement it in the schools in which they taught. The group believed that only school site-based organizing, in which teachers patiently build a consensus for change and create meaningful partnerships with students and parents, could lead to transformative changes in schools. According to Lee, parent and student organizing groups play a key role in winning policy changes. However, while necessary, policies "will not meaningfully change the experiences of young people in schools,"

If there is no buy-in from or support from their teachers. Districts under fire are too happy to offer multimillion-dollar contracts to nonprofit vendors who nominate themselves to train staff, usually without adequate plans or any educator input... Our members end up frustrated by being stuck in the middle of a co-opted agenda that cares nothing about centering the voices or experiences of young people and their families and does nothing to build power or reflection among school staff.

Elana "E.M." Eisen-Markowitz, a member of Teachers Unite, helped lead a process to grow restorative justice at her high school. She explains that Teachers Unite uses both restorative and transformative justice as terms for their work, "although transformative justice perhaps more accurately acknowledges the role and history of institutional oppression and emphasizes that we must move forward rather than attempt simply to restore what was there before."

> Both restorative and transformative justice are concerned with the *process* of growing justice as well as the result of the process. If restorative justice is to shift school culture and policies, we knew we needed to create a sustained organizing process at the school site so that all staff, families, and students could embrace restorative justice as a transformative strategy.

Eisen-Markowitz helped form a restorative justice action team at her school that included eight teachers, four students, and two parents who planned a schoolwide process of education, professional development, and critical self-reflection. They used role plays, surveys, and community-building circles to create models of transformational healing and safety; and they supported individual faculty members as they moved to change practice in their classrooms. In the meantime, they helped the School Leadership Team rewrite the school's Comprehensive Education Plan to focus on addressing racial disparities and increasing parent involvement. In the end, the teachers at the school affirmatively voted to adopt restorative justice. They agreed to have the school hire a full-time coordinator who would hold a unionized position (as opposed to contracting with an outside agency) and ensure that the slow and complex process of transforming culture would be institutionalized in the school community. Reflecting on this careful and extensive process, Eisen-Markowitz says:

School-site organizing, like true transformation and healing, is slow and neither linear nor hierarchical. It looks different in different places. It's based on a decentralized cycle of leadership development that requires many different invested leaders who learn from and challenge one another.

In response to requests from DSC members and others, Teachers Unite produced a documentary and online toolkit called *Growing Fairness* that featured deep and sustained models of restorative justice drawn from the practice of Teachers Unite members like Eisen-Markowitz. The documentary and toolkit helped Teachers Unite advise organizing groups looking to find ways to work with teachers in their local areas around restorative justice and efforts to address racial discrimination and other issues in schools.[27]

While Teachers Unite remained one of the few educator groups in DSC, community organization members also pioneered models of community-based restorative justice that influenced the larger movement. Community Organizing and Family Issues (COFI) in Chicago created parent-run restorative justice programs called peace centers in a range of Chicago schools beginning in the mid-2000s. According to parent leader Lynn Morton:

Our peace center model is still the only one where parent and community members from that community are the facilitators of peace circles and restorative chats and family group conferencing. It's a model that is grounded in the philosophy that the community is for the parents and the parents have what the community needs to make it better.

While mainly focused on parent leadership, COFI also runs community-based peace centers where young people co-lead restorative circles with parents and other community members. Over the years, COFI has trained thousands of parents in what it calls Family Focused Organizing and in restorative justice, spreading its influence across the state of Illinois. COFI has also created several guides for parent engagement and parent-led restorative justice programs that have been widely used and cited and which have spread its model to DSC members and across the larger movement. COFI connects its work with parents in schools and peace centers to organizing efforts where parents have worked to change the district's student code of conduct and win implementation of community schools across Chicago. COFI also supported statewide legislation like SB100 sponsored by VOYCE and discussed in Chapter 6, and then created a parent guide for its implementation.[28]

In the wake of the passage of SB100, VOYCE, for its part, started working with the Chicago Teacher Union's Quest Center to incorporate restorative justice into the professional development program in classroom management that it provided to Chicago teachers. VOYCE, with funding from the Robert Wood Johnson Foundation, formed the Safe Schools Consortium Initiative as a partnership with the Chicago Teachers Union and Alternatives, Inc. to develop a restorative justice guide and pilot professional development work in four schools.

To create restorative practices that transformed school climate and culture to be supportive and nurturing for students, VOYCE engaged youth leaders in contributing to the teacher guidebook and in implementation of pilot projects at the school level. In speaking of young people's influence on the guidebook, Walter Taylor from the QUEST center, says:

> The youth were saying, "You need to do things with us and not to us and not for us." So, the guidebook should be full of things where teachers are doing things with the students. Not a lesson where they are being lectured to and where the students are taking more of a leadership role in the work, for example, facilitating the talking circles.[29]

A Complex Movement Emerges

From its beginning the movement to end the school-to-prison pipeline contained diverse constituencies and addressed diverse issues. For many years, though, it seemed particularly focused on ending zero-tolerance school discipline practices. As the movement won victory after victory in toppling exclusionary discipline policy at local, state, and even federal governmental levels, however, new issues and constituencies came to the fore. While building in the background for many years, the movement for police-free schools erupted in 2020 and won a string of victories to remove police from schools. Black girls, girls of color, and gender nonconforming students, always a critical part of the movement, asserted their leadership and particular needs. Both new developments gained inspiration from the Movement for Black Lives and the attention it brought to intersectional organizing and the leadership of women and queer people of color. The movement faced the challenge of supporting and including these diverse issues and constituencies, but they also served to energize and renew the movement as well.

Meanwhile, restorative justice emerged as perhaps the key alternative to exclusionary discipline in the movement to end the school-to-prison pipeline, so the stakes became high to show it works to create safe and supportive school environments. Yet, movement organizers think it will only be effective when it forms part of authentic and deeper school transformation processes. This requires the movement, whose vitality came from student and parent organizing, to engage in long-term processes of implementation. Organizers are pressed for time and resources and are challenged to support these kinds of implementation projects. Yet they represent an exciting new phase with great promise to achieve dignity and respect for students and families.

Implementing alternatives also places schools and teachers at the center of change efforts. The teacher-activists in the movement received a shot in the arm from the energy of the 2020 mass protests, which came in the wake of a steady rise in teacher organizing through the mid-2010s. Consequently, the foundation for a broader movement with stronger alliances between students, parents, and teachers has emerged. Veteran teacher organizers like Lee and Eisen-Markowitz in Teachers Unite believe the time has come for the movement to support community building more strongly at the school level. When they think about making systemic change, Lee and Eisen-Markowitz "envision working with young people, families, neighborhoods and communities to flourish at the school site."

> Deep and sustainable transformative justice needs to be built school by school. We need to recognize the harm committed by our colleagues and act to transform relationships while we create processes and structures for those harmed to imagine new solutions. An educational justice movement guided by principles of democracy and equity needs to support members of school communities to lead the way.

Conclusion

Organizing and Movement Building for Racial and Educational Justice

When African American parents and community organizers in Holmes County, Mississippi, first spoke out and called for the Prevention of Schoolhouse to Jailhouse in the late nineties, zero tolerance was the law of the land. In fact, exclusionary school discipline and the presence of police and security officers in schools were still on the rise. Black and Brown communities were firmly in the grip of a system of mass criminalization that particularly targeted boys and young men of color in and out of school, while also trapping students with disabilities, girls, LBGTQ, and gender nonconforming students in the system as well. School systems routinely suspended and expelled students of color with the justification that they had to remove the "bad" and dangerous kids so the "good" kids could learn. District and state school administrations, a wide range of educational associations, and the major teachers unions all accepted or promoted zero tolerance. It was the dominant ideology at the time, enshrined in local, state, and federal policy. Virtually no one had heard of the school-to-prison pipeline in those days, let alone recognized its devastating impact on students of color and their families.

Beginning with the voices of parents and young people of color in places like the Mississippi Delta, Chicago, Los Angeles, and New York, a new movement emerged to challenge zero tolerance and associated policing practices. Organizing groups working with parents and students joined with allies at local, state, and national levels, creating a powerful movement. This movement highlighted both the extent and harm of exclusionary discipline as well as its racially disparate impact. In other words, it named racism and showed how zero tolerance targeted students of color and those with special needs.

By the mid-2010s the movement to dismantle the school-to-prison pipeline had spread across the country, with organized groups in almost all large cities, some of their suburbs, many medium-sized cities and a few rural areas, particularly in Mississippi. In other words, established groups

Willful Defiance. Mark R. Warren, Oxford University Press. © Mark R. Warren 2022.
DOI: 10.1093/oso/9780197611500.003.0010

seemed to be concentrated in mid-large cities and in suburbs—where there are concentrations of people and some resources to support organizations. Informal groups of parents and young people, however, also took action in various places, including smaller cities and rural areas. We only have anecdotal evidence for these more informal initiatives, and they may be more difficult to sustain. They are highly significant, however, since we need to understand that the broader movement includes organized groups as well as networks of people who take action in less formal settings.

Over the course of twenty years, the movement shifted public and educator discourse decisively away from zero tolerance, changed school discipline policy to limit exclusionary discipline in districts and states across the country, and promoted alternatives like restorative justice. By 2018, over fifty of the largest school districts and more than half of the states had revised policies to reduce exclusionary discipline. The movement even pushed the federal government under the Obama administration to acknowledge the existence of the school-to-prison pipeline and issue guidance to school districts to reduce exclusionary discipline and seek alternatives that kept students in school and learning. As it developed, the movement incorporated new voices and issues, including those of girls of color and LGBTQ and gender nonconforming students of color, and inspired educators to develop restorative and transformative justice alternatives in their own school communities in alliance with parents and young people. By targeting the school-to-prison pipeline, the movement challenged one of the most important mechanisms—if not the most important mechanism—for the reproduction of poverty and lack of power for communities of color and the defense of white privilege and white supremacy.[1]

By the end of the 2010s, these reforms were beginning to have a significant impact on suspension rates across the country. Nationally, from the 2011–2012 school year to the 2015–2016 school year, the out-of-school suspension rate fell from 5.6% to 4.7%. The rate for African American students fell from 9.7% to 8.0% while the rate for Latinx students fell the most—by 30%.[2]

The impact was especially large in places like California where organizing groups won reforms adopted and implemented more aggressively. As discussed in Chapter 5, in 2013, a coalition of local groups capped ten years of organizing and got the Los Angeles Unified School District to ban suspensions in all grades for willful defiance as part of a comprehensive package of reforms that included the expansion of restorative justice alternatives. The next year, the state banned suspensions for willful defiance for grades K–3 and extended it to grade eight in 2019. The state began to include suspension rates as a measure of school success in its accountability requirements, creating further incentive for schools and districts to reduce the use of exclusionary discipline. Meanwhile, districts across the state expanded restorative justice and counseling supports.

As a result of these and other changes, the number of out-of-school suspensions dropped 46% in California from a cumulative total of 709,702 in the 2011–2012 school year to 381,845 in 2016–2017, while the number of expulsions fell 42%, from 9,758 to 5,657. From the 2011–2012 school year to the 2018–2019 school year, the overall out-of-school suspension rate in California fell from 5.8% to 3.5%; the rate for African American students declined from 13.8% to 9.1%, while the rate for Latinx students fell from 6.1% to 3.6%. As noted in Chapter 5, Los Angeles suspensions fell dramatically to just 0.7% by 2018–2019. In the 2007–2008 school year, LAUSD students lost 74,765 days due to out-of-school suspensions. By the 2016–2017 school year, that number had dropped to fewer than 5,600 days.[3]

Other districts in which organizing groups and their allies had won changes in policy also witnessed significant declines in exclusionary discipline. In New York City, the nation's largest school district, out-of-school suspensions fell by over 50% from 69,000 in the 2011–2012 school year to the 2018–2019 school year. The average length of suspensions also fell, to 5.8 days in the 2018–2019 year compared to 7.5 days the year before. In Chicago, the total number of suspensions fell by about 20% from 2016–2017 to the 2018–2019 school year.[4]

While suspension rates fell, there is some evidence that school-based arrests and referrals to law enforcement appeared to increase. From the 2013–2014 to the 2015–2016 school years, arrests grew 3% while referrals grew 17%, with some states reporting a doubling of arrest rates.[5]

By the late 2010s, however, there emerged a serious conversation about the presence of police in schools and innovative campaigns calling for police-free schools. With the mass protests following the police killing of George Floyd in Minneapolis in 2020, the campaign gathered momentum. Minneapolis Public Schools canceled its contract with the city's police department and a number of districts followed suit, including St. Paul, Denver, San Francisco, and Portland, among others. These districts were located mostly in places where the grassroots movement to dismantle the school-to-prison pipeline had been organizing for several years to end the presence of police in schools and so were best prepared to seize the moment to win the long-sought policy change. Oakland entirely eliminated its School Police Department, culminating a ten-year organizing campaign by the Black Organizing Project.

How did a group of relatively small, resource-poor community organizations working with parents and students in low-income communities of color build a movement that has achieved such substantial gains? In this conclusion, I highlight the features documented in this book that help explain the growth and success of the movement. I then elaborate the lessons of this study for building a national movement with deep local roots. I offer a new way to think about national movements as "nationalizing local struggles," and I discuss the ways in which this movement also leads us to rethink local organizing. I end by returning to the challenges organizers continue to face in building a movement powerful enough to fully transform deep-seated systems of racial inequity and educational injustice, particularly in an era that has witnessed the rise of white nationalism and the Trump presidency.

Key Elements of Organizing and Movement Building

The movement to dismantle the school-to-prison pipeline exhibited several key elements and pursued a number of effective strategies that help explain the growth of the movement and its success. Each of these elements had a distinctive impact, yet many were interrelated. In fact, it is perhaps in the combination of these elements and strategies that we can best explain how a small but determined set of organizing groups and their allies challenged zero tolerance and changed school discipline policy in states and localities across the country.

Participation and Leadership by Most Impacted

Local organizing groups centered the experiences and participation of those most impacted by the school-to-prison pipeline, that is, students and parents of color in low-income communities. Parents, students, and the organizers who worked closely with them in these communities were the first to speak out against the school-to-prison pipeline at a time when few others were listening. They named zero tolerance as racially targeted against their children and communities, directed especially but not exclusively against Black boys and students with special needs. They raised the alarm over increased policing; students cried "Our schools feel like jails" and parents and students highlighted abuse of their children by police officers and security guards in schools. Over the years, the people most impacted by injustice continued to be at the forefront, speaking out along intersectional lines, as Black girls and other girls of color, LGBTQ, and gender nonconforming students of color highlighted the forms of repression they faced. Most recently, students and parents began demanding more culturally relevant curriculum and calling for investments in public schools rather than privatization, highlighting the fact that a range of interrelated and.oppressive school policies and practices push students of color out of school and onto the pipeline to prison.[6]

Students and parents brought their direct experiences and stories to launch the movement. For the first ten years of movement building, little systematic data on exclusionary discipline or school policing was available. Prior to 2011, the federal government did not collect universal data on suspensions and expulsions for all schools and districts and did not collect such data on policing and school-based arrests. During this time, the stories of people most impacted proved crucial to the start of the movement, which eventually helped push the Office for Civil Rights to require all schools and districts to report school discipline data. Parents, students, and community organizers persevered even when few listened. As momentum began to build and data became more available, personal stories continued to anchor the movement. As will be discussed, the movement consistently combined stories and personal testimony with data to advocate for an end to exclusionary discipline with elected officials, educators, and the public.

At times, the movement made use of social media to spread and amplify the stories and the voices of those most impacted, to highlight cases of abusive and discriminatory punishment and gain public support, and to keep local groups connected. The #AssaultAt campaign launched by the Alliance for Educational Justice (AEJ) made extensive use of social media to publicize cases of police abuse of students, like those in Spring Valley, South Carolina, and others, when the mainstream media ignored them. Student leaders in VOYCE from Chicago took selfies with state legislators and posted them on social media when they committed to support the group's legislation called SB100. Youth organizing groups highlighted social media strategies; but parent organizing groups and intergenerational coalitions like the Dignity in Schools Campaign (DSC) also featured Twitter storms and other techniques as ways to bring local members together to advance common campaigns.

As reforms began, students and parents organized to hold systems accountable for change. In Los Angeles, for example, CADRE continued to train parents to enter schools to monitor progress. They issued accountability reports on a regular basis. Other groups with pathbreaking victories like Padres & Jóvenes Unidos in Denver also persevered over many years, issuing accountability reports and continuing to advocate for meaningful change. While educators and public officials often claimed progress by lowering out-of-school suspension rates, as important as that is, parents and young people asked the harder questions: Were students still being pushed out of class to the office or to "holding pens" even if not sent home? Did lower suspension rates reflect a transformed and supportive school climate for students and humane treatment of parents? Why were racial disparities continuing even as suspension rates fell? In other words, the voice and participation of those most impacted remained critical to holding the movement and school systems accountable for real change.[7]

Scholars of critical race theory have long understood the power of counter-storytelling by people of color as a force to challenge racist narratives and institutional racism. Scholars of social movements and community organizing have also highlighted stories as a way for participants to connect with each other and narrate the justice of their cause. In this book, we see how the participation of people most impacted brings the power of these stories directly into organized movements and policy reform campaigns. By prioritizing the voices and participation of parents and young people of color to policymakers, the movement adopted a critical edge and claimed a moral force that demanded and increasingly received a response from public officials. The direct presence of people most impacted telling their stories in legislative assemblies played a critical role in winning legislation or new policies to end zero tolerance.[8]

Building a Racial Justice Movement

Parents, students, and community organizers built the movement to dismantle the school-to-prison pipeline movement as an educational justice *and* racial justice movement. From the beginning, organizing groups highlighted racial disparities in school discipline and named students of color as the target of criminalization by police and security apparatus in schools. Many groups like CADRE and others affiliated with DSC charged schools with violating the human rights of students and families and found in the human rights framework a powerful platform to address racial oppression and white supremacy.

When groups in the Mississippi Roundtable talked about the school-to-jail track as the new form of racial oppression and CADRE named systemic racism, these were radical moves at the time. The world of education reform in the early 2000s, including most community organizing groups engaged in school reform efforts, did not frame their work as confronting racial discrimination and inequity, let alone systemic racism. Groups were told that it was more effective to talk in universalistic, race-neutral terms, even if everyone tacitly knew that students and families of color in low-income communities faced the greatest crisis in public education.[9]

As discussed in Chapter 2, the field of community organizing was shifting in the early 2000s, with organizers of color taking leadership of established groups like Communities United in Chicago or starting new groups like Padres & Jóvenes Unidos in Denver or CADRE in Los Angeles. These organizers believed that real change would not occur without exposing the root causes of school pushout and criminalization as racist systems. The organizers of color who came to lead emerging community groups in the school-to-pipeline movement, working predominantly with Black and Brown parents and students, decided to speak their truth as they saw and experienced it.

Today, highlighting racial disparities may not seem particularly bold. When organizing groups took this stand in the early 2000s, however, it was not a popular position. This was before the attention given to mass incarceration and the "new Jim Crow" and before the rise of Black Lives Matter and the mass protests against police violence and killings in 2020. When Barack Obama was elected in 2008, there was even widespread talk of a post-racial America. In many ways, the early movement to end the school-to-prison pipeline was pathbreaking in targeting racism and criminalization and presaged the racial justice movements like Black Lives Matter that would follow and intersect with it.

Establishing itself as a racial justice movement shaped the school-to-prison pipeline movement in important ways. First of all, it turned out, as we saw in the story of VOYCE and SB100 in Chapter 6, that targeting racial disparities proved to be an effective strategy. This was particularly true as the Movement for Black Lives grew, and national consciousness shifted. The school-to-prison pipeline movement increasingly named the centrality of anti-Black racism as well as intersectional forms of oppression. In this way, the movement was able to make stronger connections between exclusionary discipline and mass incarceration and between police abuse in schools and police abuse in communities. The demand of young people in AEJ to #EndWarOnYouth and to end state violence against youth of color created a framework to connect with the Movement for Black Lives. Meanwhile, the framing of racial justice provided the movement with a longer-term vision and agenda for systemic transformation even as it worked on more immediate policy initiatives.

The civil rights movement of the fifties and sixties was a multi-issue racial justice movement. Since that time, however, the organizing world has become more siloed, with groups variously targeting housing, education, economic rights, immigration, and police violence among other issues. In part, community groups are responding to the structure of the policy environment. In other words, if groups want to create policy change with limited resources, they concentrate their efforts on the relevant political targets which are, themselves, typically siloed by policy domains. They are also responding to the priorities of private foundations which normally fund groups to work in one policy domain. Nevertheless, the racial justice framing of the school-to-prison pipeline movement pushes against this silo-ing with an intersectional understanding that multiple issues and systems feed racial oppression and defend white supremacy, reproducing poverty, criminalization, and lack of power for communities of color.[10]

An Intergenerational, Diverse, and Intersectional Movement

As the school-to-prison pipeline movement grew, it emerged as an intergenerational movement among young people, parents, and older community members and one that included a diverse group of participants across communities of color, particularly Black and Brown communities. This diversity provided the movement with additional strength by incorporating a broad base and heightened credibility. It also allowed the movement to address a range of issues led by different constituents. For example, many participants pressed for an intersectional approach that addressed the particular experiences of people and groups at the juncture of multiple forms of oppression. At various times, Black girls and trans and queer youth of color have pushed their concerns onto the movement's stage and taken important leadership roles. Groups increasingly connected advocacy to end the school-to-prison pipeline with advocacy to stop the school-to-deportation pipeline facing undocumented students and their families.

Within this diversity, Black women and women of color feature prominently in leadership of the movement. They lead many of the local organizing groups and play a prominent role in national alliances like DSC. Through their leadership positions, Black women and women of color played a strong role in shaping the approach to organizing at local and national levels, as highlighted in Chapter 7 and will be discussed later in the chapter.

There have sometimes been tensions in building such a diverse and intersectional movement, particularly when so many constituencies and communities feel marginalized and silenced by the larger society. Youth feel silenced and often disrespected by older adults, but parents of color also feel marginalized and unheard. Black participants have asserted the centrality of anti-Black racism, while Latinx communities sometimes believe that their experiences with racism are not well understood or fully appreciated. Older participants initially struggled to accept and practice the use of personal pronouns that gender nonconforming youth have insisted upon. Black girls have felt silenced while others worry about taking the spotlight off Black boys. Meanwhile, Indigenous communities have not been well connected to the national alliances, even though they experience high rates of school pushout and criminalization.[11]

One of the most enduring challenges appears to be creating spaces where both young people and parents feel heard and fully included. There are cultural differences between the two groups that take time and attention to address. Fully intergenerational spaces appear to emerge more often at the local level where students and parents connect more regularly in organizations and campaigns and develop closer relationships. At the national level, the majority of participants in DSC have been adults and the coalition has struggled to create venues where youth feel fully included. Young people have always been members of DSC, though, and have served on leadership bodies over the years. AEJ was created as a youth-only space—although adult organizers committed to supporting youth leadership play key roles.

Overall, though, the movement has succeeded in creating spaces where people connect to each other, listen, and learn. Participants appear to appreciate the need to understand other people's experiences even as they assert their own. Eventually, for example, the use of personal pronouns became established practice in the movement. Latinx organizers, for their part, have come to highlight the fact that Black students are the most disproportionately disciplined even as they critique how the school-to-prison targets Latinx students. DSC and AEJ, among others, often partner in movement work and represent an intergenerational alliance in that way.

In the end, movement leaders push against an either-or perspective that pits groups and people against each other and instead take a both-and approach. As we saw in Chapter 8, appreciating the issues that Black girls face does not necessarily detract from also targeting how the school-to-prison ensnares Black boys. Highlighting anti-Black racism can be combined with critiques of anti-Latinx racism. The movement speaks to the ways the school-to-prison pipeline impacts both students and their parents and incorporates the direct interest both groups have in challenging systemic racism and educational injustice. Achieving this kind of unity takes work and constant attention, and it remains an ongoing project. The energy and power created by the diverse, intergenerational and intersectional movement, however, helps explain its growth and success.

Stories and Data

Organizing groups pursue a range of strategies to advocate for policy change. The combination of three elements—stories, data, and alliance building—appears widely practiced and important to successful campaigns. I documented in more detail in Chapter 6 how VOYCE utilized these strategies in the campaign to pass SB100 in the Illinois legislature, but I found this combination used by groups at local, state, and national levels across the country.

As discussed earlier, organizing groups center the voice and participation of students and parents who have directly experienced the school-to-prison pipeline. As such, they bring powerful stories to ground the movement. Organizers help participants tell their stories as ways to make sense of their experiences; as they share these stories, they come to see the systemic nature of the injustices they face. Students are particularly vulnerable to retaliation in school settings and parents worry about reprisals against their children if they speak out. As they share stories, participants connect to each other and build the kind of solidarity necessary to gain the courage to take risky action. When students and parents tell their stories in public, they offer a compelling refutation of the racist narrative that undergirds the school-to-prison pipeline—that schools need to remove the "bad" kids so the "good" kids can learn. When they offer personal testimony to school boards, state legislators, and federal officials, they shed a human light on systemic oppression and make an urgent case for action.[12]

Personal stories, as powerful as they are, can be dismissed as exceptional individual experiences. Organizing groups combine stories with data to show the widespread nature of harsh and racist school discipline and policing practices and their harmful effects. VOYCE, for example, was able to influence Illinois state legislators in part because the coalition showed that school suspensions were high and racially inequitable across the entire state, not just in big cities like Chicago. When Attorney General Holder heard about the Council of State Governments study that showed that 75% of Black students in the state of Texas had been suspended at some point in secondary school, he was reportedly compelled to act.

Alliances and a Broader Movement Ecology

In addition to marshaling stories and data, organizing groups also built alliances across groups and with legal, advocacy, philanthropic, and research organizations, creating a broader movement ecology which, in turn, enhanced the power of organizing. Alliances occurred at local, state, and national levels and they brought critical additional resources to the movement, including financial resources, legal, communications and lobbying expertise, additional research capacity, political connections, and the legitimacy that comes from professional status. Several national intermediaries played key roles in these alliances, including the Advancement Project, the NAACP's Legal Defense Fund (LDF), and the American Civil Liberties Union. Many focused at the federal level and undertook national communications work, but the Advancement Project provided expertise and support to local organizing efforts as well. LDF worked with local groups in DSC to get states to include school discipline as a measure of accountability in implementation of the Every Student Succeeds Act. Partners for Dignity & Rights (formerly NESRI) provided infrastructure support to anchor the DSC coalition. The Discipline Disparities Research to Practice Collaborative brought organizers together with scholars to create an agenda designed to advance the research base for ending the school-to-prison pipeline.

The support of private philanthropy also proved critical to movement success. The decision by Atlantic Philanthropies to deliver millions of dollars to the movement, with a priority on parent and youth organizing, created a turning point. The foundation not only supplied organizing efforts with critically needed resources; it also encouraged other foundations to fund the movement and, as discussed in Chapter 3, it helped the movement coordinate efforts focused on grassroots organizing, communications, research and advocacy, thereby helping to build the infrastructure for a national movement. Other national foundations also funded and helped create movement infrastructure, including the Ford and Kellogg Foundations and the Schott Foundation for Public Education. Meanwhile the California Endowment funded in-state efforts while a range of local foundations supported organizing groups and campaigns in their areas. The Edward W. Hazen Foundation provided seed grants for new and emerging groups across the country. The donor collaborative Communities for Just Schools Fund played a critical role in bringing new funds into the field and directing grants to local organizing groups that may not have had the capacity to attract awards from national foundations. More recently, philanthropic organizations concerned with public health have supported the movement.

Research showing the widespread and systematic nature of the school-to-prison pipeline also provided a valuable resource to support the movement's policy demands. Student and parent leaders collected data in participatory action research projects. The work of scholars and researchers, however, produced a growing body of evidence on the harmful and racially disparate impact of zero tolerance and demonstrated the effectiveness of alternatives. Meanwhile, the expertise and status of established researchers added legitimacy to research findings and movement campaigns.

The expertise, status, and political connections of a larger network of professional legal and advocacy groups helped create openings with public officials and members of the education establishment and provided them with expert advice in terms with which they were familiar. These professional connections and inside forms of lobbying combined with pressure from the outside by parents and students to create an effective force for policy adoption and implementation. In cases where inside and outside strategies faced roadblocks, lawsuits also helped pressure recalcitrant local districts, particularly around the treatment of special needs students.[13]

Changes in the Political Context

At various times, the movement benefited from changes in the political context at the same time as it contributed to these changes. The election of Barack Obama created openings at the federal level. The 2010 midterm elections closed off the possibility of congressional action but kept open the opportunity to influence the administration. The education policies of the Obama administration, however, represented a mixed bag to most education justice organizers. The administration supported the continuation of high-stakes testing and promoted the expansion of charter schools. Nevertheless, the Department of Education hired staff in the Office for Civil Rights (OCR) who were sympathetic or committed to racial justice issues, while the Department of Justice hired staff in its Educational Opportunities Section in a similar way. In fact, many civil rights advocates took these positions in order to promote change. Movement leaders persistently lobbied these administrators for change, with doors opened by professional advocates and lawyers who had personal connections. In response, OCR moved to require all schools and districts to report data on school discipline disaggregated by race, which provided an evidence base for advocacy across localities and states. Persistent advocacy eventually played a critical role in getting the Departments of Education and Justice to issue joint guidance warning against zero tolerance. The guidance helped provide a favorable context for local organizing efforts, which claimed that the federal government was on their side.[14]

Local efforts, however, often had to confront resistant administrations in school districts, including many in Democratic-oriented and liberal-minded cities. Chapter 3 documents how the movement shifted public understanding and support away from zero tolerance, raising awareness of the negative and racially disparate impact of exclusionary discipline practices in education associations, among education researchers and policymakers, and with the national teachers unions. As zero tolerance was increasingly discredited, a new political context opened that proved favorable to local and state level campaigns for discipline reform.

The growing attention to mass incarceration that occurred in part around the publication of *The new Jim Crow* by Michelle Alexander and in part as a result of criminal justice reform organizing, helped create public awareness of the criminalization of people of color and increase public recognition of the harm of zero-tolerance policies. The rise of the Movement for Black Lives raised consciousness around anti-Black racism and police violence. Public awareness of state violence and persistent racism in American society helped create more favorable responses to the school-to-prison pipeline movement's demands and sympathy for targeting racial disparities. Meanwhile, through the decade of the 2010s, many Democratic elected officials felt the need to be more responsive to the decriminalizing demands of mobilized voters of color.

The Black Lives Matter movement inspired organizers and leaders in the educational justice movement, helping them to feel connected to a national racial justice movement. As discussed in Chapter 8, these leaders emboldened their demands as they tied police abuse of students of color in schools to police abuse and violence toward young people of color in communities. At the same time, the school-to-prison pipeline movement itself raised consciousness on racial violence and criminalization and supplied the Movement for Black Lives with leaders and activists trained as young people in educational justice organizing.

In 2016, the rise of white nationalism and the election of Donald Trump changed the political context again. Trump appointed Betsy DeVos as Secretary of Education and the department proceeded to rescind the federal guidance on school discipline that warned against zero tolerance. It began to resurrect the discredited position that schools needed to suspend the "bad" students so the "good" ones could learn. DeVos also restricted civil rights enforcement while she promoted private schools and moved the federal government away from commitments to racial equity. Trump built his campaign on appeals to racism, restricted immigration and escalated deportations, sent children to detention camps on the border, and fostered a law enforcement and repressive movement. He lifted the restrictions that the Obama administration had put on the 1033 program that provided surplus military equipment to local law enforcement including school police. The rise of right wing and racist movements across the country emboldened Trump and was encouraged by his policies and pronouncements. In the end, the Trump presidency and the Republican control in Congress closed off any hope of further progress on school discipline and policing at the federal level, although the movement continued to work with sympathetic congressional representatives preparing future legislation.[15]

Meanwhile, the 2018 shooting at Marjorie Stoneham Douglas High School in Parkland, Florida, reignited calls for more armed police in schools, with a sympathetic Trump administration then in place. In response, several states passed laws increasing the presence of police or school resource officers at schools. As a result of its strong base and broad alliances, however, the movement was able to hold the line on school discipline policy for the most part at local and state levels and zero tolerance did not reestablish itself. New fronts even broke out in the movement during the Trump era with the focus on girls and gender nonconforming students of color and on organizing against the school-to-deportation pipeline.[16]

In 2020, during completion of this book manuscript, mass protests against anti-Black racism and police violence changed the context again, this time in ways favorable to the movement. Groups like the Black Organizing Project and others had persevered in campaigning against the presence of police in schools through the Trump era. In 2020, the police-free schools movement capitalized on the openings created by the protests to finally begin to defund and remove police from schools.

With the election of Joseph Biden as president at the end of 2020 and a Democratic-controlled Congress, new openings are occurring for the movement again at the federal level. The movement is pivoting to back federal legislation like the Counseling Not Criminalization in Schools Act with old and new allies in Congress, and it is working with a new set of more favorable officials in the Departments of Education and Justice to eliminate federal support for school police and to strengthen federal guidance and policies to reduce exclusionary and racially inequitable school discipline. Meanwhile, the movement continues to push forward with renewed energy for police-free schools and restorative and transformative justice alternatives at the local level.[17]

Rethinking Social Movements: "Nationalizing Local Struggles"

The movement to dismantle the school-to-prison pipeline can best be characterized as one that nationalized local struggles. From its beginnings in rural Mississippi to the victories of CADRE in Los Angeles and Padres & Jóvenes Unidos in Denver, and the ongoing series of victories like those of VOYCE in Illinois and the Labor Community Strategy Center in Los Angeles, the movement publicized and spread local successes, creating a rolling series of policy victories across the country. National alliances and intermediaries helped publicize these successes and supported tours by organizers where they shared their strategies and policy wins.

Until the early 2000s, organizers from independent community groups working on education issues rarely had the opportunity to connect across locality. Starting in the mid-2000s, however, organizers and leaders met in a rapidly expanding series of venues sponsored by national alliances and intermediaries. These included regional and national gatherings of AEJ, annual meetings of DSC and their Days at the Capitol, the Action Camps hosted by the Advancement Project, conferences held by Communities for Public Education Reform early on and later ones sponsored by the Communities for Just Schools Fund, the Schott Foundation for Public Education, the Funders Collaborative on Youth Organizing, and a wide variety of other funders and intermediaries. Organizers and leaders learned from each other at these venues and gained the ideas and inspiration necessary for small groups to launch bold campaigns against powerful targets.

The national successes of the movement came first from the bottom up, as local organizing campaigns in places like Los Angeles and Denver were lifted up and spread across the country. After 2008, the movement did undertake action at the national level by trying to influence the federal government and to shape national public opinion and policy trends. However, two distinct and highly related aspects stand out. First, organizers made sure that people most impacted and the organizations that worked directly with them were centered in the movement and held decision-making power. Second, the national movement prioritized supporting and expanding local struggles, even as it undertook national-level work.

It took a series of intentional struggles to create a movement structured in this way, as I described in Chapter 3. These were struggles over power and over who would control the movement. First, organizers in the emerging DSC pushed for the coalition's internal processes to give majority decision-making power to local organizing groups rather than professional advocates and to foster widespread participation in decision-making. DSC's membership policy provides for the majority of seats on its leadership body—the coordinating committee—to be representatives from base-building groups who organize people most impacted. Meanwhile, major policy decisions require extensive consultation with the entire membership. In addition, when participating in national actions, like its Days at the Capitol in Washington, DSC provides funds to bring members most impacted to directly participate. Overall, DSC prioritizes processes that maximize inclusiveness and democracy. This makes it hard for the coalition to act quickly; but when it does act, it includes the majority of its members who are connected to parents and young people.[18]

Second, while simultaneously operating as a national force, the movement prioritizes the support and strengthening of local organizing. DSC has established several practices to reflect this priority. The coalition focuses on creating resources like the Model Code on Education and Dignity that member groups can use. It offers trainings in organizing skills and policy analysis for members of local groups. It redistributes roughly one-third of its budget to support member groups and provides additional materials and resources in conjunction with its annual Week of Action and other activities. It offers stipends to groups who participate in national planning activities and provides travel scholarships and childcare cost reimbursement to groups that bring parents and students to national meetings and actions.

DSC has the most clearly formulated policies to center organizing and those most impacted and it is by far the largest national formation in the movement. Once DSC shifted power to base-building groups, however, it seemed to set a template for the larger movement. Meanwhile, some of the national intermediaries, like Advancement Project, had already been committed to community lawyering, that is, to offering legal expertise to support local communities rather than exerting control over their agendas, as they believed had often happened in previous civil rights struggles.[19]

Pushed by grassroots organizers, other professional advocates and their organizations came to see the advantages of building more authentic partnerships in this new way as they came to appreciate the key role that organizing groups and local struggles played in building an effective movement. One of the enduring contributions of the school-to-pipeline movements may be this new way of operating and new kind of partnership relationship. It may also best be understood as a work in progress, an enduring struggle.

Tensions remain and equitable partnerships are constantly negotiated. The system appears to be set up to favor professional advocates and re-create their power in movements. Private foundations are often prepared to give the national, professionalized groups larger grants while continuing to offer small grants to local groups. Professional advocates can often respond quickly to events and issue statements with the support of well-resourced communications departments that put them in front of media coverage. Grassroots coalitions like DSC have participatory membership policies that often require extensive discussion before making decisions. Meanwhile, influential elites including those in public office often look first to professional advocates whom they know or who have status and reputations. A mainstream elite culture shared by lawyers, professional advocates, policymakers, scholars, and the media can serve to exclude people most impacted at the ground level, that is, the parents and students who participate in and lead local struggles for justice. It is now more established to have people most impacted at the table, but it remains a struggle for authentic participation and real power.[20]

Despite these ongoing tensions, though, professional advocacy and organizing groups in the school-to-prison pipeline movement have found a way to continue to work together, often in complementary ways. The movement features a division of labor, with some groups focused on lobbying, communications, and legal work and others on supporting grassroots organizing and the voice and participation of parents and students. Advocacy groups often play a more inside game, using their relationships to get federal officials to meet with movement activists, for example. DSC, AEJ, and some other intermediaries also play a role in this inside game as they build relationships with officials; but they are the ones who can bring grassroots parents and students to these meetings and hearings to offer their testimony and demand action as people directly impacted. Partnerships and division of labor can occur at the local level too, as when the Advancement Project helped VOYCE youth write the legislation that became SB100 and assisted them with their advocacy efforts at the statehouse.[21]

The result is a new kind of federated movement that operates at local, state, and national levels, with lines of mutual reinforcement between them. At times, the movement marshals its forces to push the federal government or issues national statements, like the one in response to threats of increased policing in the wake of the tragic Sandy Hook school shooting. For the most part, though, the action takes place in local communities and sometimes at the state level. It is these struggles that are "nationalized," that is, lifted up, supported, and spread across the country, making local struggles national ones.

This local-national dynamic is also not tension free. Local groups have limited resources and must decide if participating in national activities is worth the time and effort. It remains challenging for groups to build strong relationships across long distances. Time and money remain limited for travel, so personal contact is intermittent. Social media supplements the face-to-face relationships built at in-person meetings but does not replace them. Even online meetings take up precious time when small local groups have so many pressing demands.

Moreover, parents and young people often struggle to achieve direct and meaningful decision-making power at the national level. The movement consistently brings parents and young people to movement-building meetings and to public events to speak for themselves and to testify. That is critically important. Most parents and young people directly impacted, however, do not typically have the time to participate consistently and over the extended period it requires to build relationships and acquire the experience and expertise to strategize at the national level. Instead, organizers and staff usually represent local base-building groups on leadership bodies and in strategic planning and decision-making spaces, even in the most grassroots spaces like DSC.

Many of these organizers and staff members are parents or youth of color themselves, of course, and the organizers work closely with parents and youth. Even if parents and students do not consistently participate in leadership bodies, groups like DSC include those most impacted in major policy decisions. While writing its Model Code on Education and Dignity, for example, DSC leaders traveled to local settings to gather input and feedback directly from parents and students. Member groups are also supposed to consult with parents and students when they vote on major decisions. These are critically important processes. Yet much of the work to shape strategies and policies occurs in the smaller and more regular meetings of leadership bodies, alliances, and one-to-one conversations among movement leaders. In these settings, organizers and staff of base-building groups, rather than parent and youth members themselves, predominate.

Local groups accountable to parents and youth, nevertheless, retain control of their own agendas. In this paradigm of federated movement, national alliances cannot dictate to local organizations or require participation in national activities. This is an important accountability measure to ensure that the movement remains responsive to the experiences and voices of those most impacted by injustice.

In this way, the federated character of the school-to-prison pipeline movement is more decentralized than the movements of earlier times, like the civil rights movement. The civil rights movement, of course, was not a monolithic, hierarchical organization. It was a complex interaction of local movement centers, national federated organizations like the NAACP and the Southern Christian Leadership Conference (SCLC), and shifting alliances among these organizations. Nevertheless, the national leadership of the federated groups could and did undertake strategic planning, allocate resources to certain local or national struggles and campaigns, and sometimes usurp control in local situations.[22]

By contrast, there are no national organizations with local chapters in the school-to-pipeline movement. That is not to say that none of the more powerful national advocacy groups or alliances—or private foundations for that matter—do not try to influence local organizations or shape movement priorities. They do so, however, by offering resources and opportunities rather than by issuing directives. The availability for funding for certain kinds of work, for example, can be an important influence on local decisions. Nevertheless, local groups remain free to withhold their participation if they do not support these agendas. In this study I found many examples of local groups taking advantage of opportunities but little evidence that they felt controlled by national actors.

This structure makes the movement more democratic, but it also means that it cannot move quickly as a unitary force. The school-to-prison pipeline movement cannot decide to focus strategically on a place like Selma as the civil rights movement leadership in SCLC did in 1965. It can nevertheless act in concert, even if the process to consensus is slower. National cooperation typically happens when local initiatives catch fire across groups. For example, the larger movement joined and spread the "You Can't Build Peace with a Piece" campaign launched by the Youth Justice Coalition in Los Angeles when youth groups across the country quickly signed on as a way to protest the threat of increased armed security in schools in the wake of the school shootings at the Sandy Hook Elementary School. Later the movement adopted a campaign launched by the Labor Community Strategy Center to get the Obama administration to end the federal 1033 program that provided military equipment to local police departments.

In the end, the school-to-prison pipeline movement is more bottom-up than top-down. There is less central direction and more local autonomy. National actors tend to amplify and spread struggles initiated at the local level, rather than directly create or influence them. "There is no national without the local," as DSC leader Joyce Parker is fond of saying. The local/national dynamic, in other words, has a strong grounding in the local where the foundation of its power is generated. The larger movement is best understood as a series of interconnected local struggles with an important but loose national infrastructure.

It may be that because political authority for public education remains primarily at the local and state levels, that a locally focused movement is more likely to emerge in education than other policy domains. The immigrant rights movement, for example, has an incentive to target federal action, the seat of primary authority. Yet, even in that movement, organizing for "local citizenship" rights and conditions of life remain critically important to working-class immigrants on the ground. In reality, all policy domains—from access to healthcare and housing to policing, economic and climate justice, and queer and trans rights—include a mixture of authority at various governmental levels.[23]

Consequently, this new model of building and understanding social movements has much to offer to the broader struggle for racial and social justice. While the control of most social movements remains in the hands of professional advocates focused on Washington, the school-to-prison pipeline shows that an alternative is possible, one where local organizers share power with professional advocates and where a national movement directs its primary attention to supporting and spreading local struggles. It requires, however, an intentional and ongoing struggle to create and sustain a truly federated movement and craft a set of policies and procedures to keep people most impacted at the center of the movement.

Rethinking Community Organizing

In the modern era, community organizing has been understood as a local phenomenon. This study suggests that this perspective is far too limited and increasingly out of date, certainly in the educational justice and racial justice field. While there is no national without the local, there would be far less organizing and success locally without the national movement that supports and spreads it. While some scholars have criticized the limits of localism, their attention has typically been on the need for local groups to connect to undertake national or federal action. While important, I am suggesting a different perspective: we need to pay attention to the ways that groups connect nationally to strengthen their local organizing.[24]

The spread of the school-to-prison pipeline movement across the country and its impact in so many localities are impossible to understand without appreciating how groups learned from and were inspired by each other. The development and delivery of resources by national groups like DSC to local campaigns appear critical for small, under-resourced groups in conservative areas to win the kind of changes they have won. Even relatively larger community organizations, like Communities United and the VOYCE coalition it sponsored in Chicago, benefited in numerous ways from the national movement. In fact, VOYCE got the initial idea to target the Illinois statehouse with the SB100 school discipline campaign from groups who had been advocating for change at the state level in California. It received legal and research support from the national office of the Advancement Project and youth members were inspired to persevere in their local campaigning through connections to a larger youth movement facilitated by AEJ and a range of national intermediaries. The national "win" to get the U.S. Office for Civil Rights to require all school districts to report discipline data and the issuing of guidance against zero-tolerance school discipline by the federal government became important resources for the local SB100 campaign. None of this support from the national movement would have been decisive without deep organizing by local groups like VOYCE; but a full understanding of local organizing for educational justice now requires attention to its interconnection with a national movement. We can see this trend as well with the local groups who combined into the national Journey for Justice Alliance to strengthen their local campaigns against large-scale school closings in Black communities.[25]

The findings from this research on the school-to-prison pipeline movement also open other lines of inquiry in the community organizing field. It challenges notions that the power of community organizing comes mainly through its ability to mobilize large numbers of community members and potential voters—what we might call broad organizing. Instead, this study shows the power generated through deep organizing, that is, the intense work with people most impacted by injustice to build their leadership and bring their voice to organizing campaigns.

Several scholars have emphasized that all forms of effective organizing include some balance of broad and deep organizing. Cultivating the voice and participation of people impacted by injustice plays a key role and is even definitional to the organizing tradition. Groups in the Alinsky organizing tradition, like the Industrial Areas Foundation (IAF), do patient relationship building and leadership development work with participants, as I have documented in my own work. Its organizing was deep in that sense. Treatments of the power of community organizing, including my own, though, have typically stressed its ability for large-scale mobilization to win policy change. A key part of the Alinsky legacy of institutional organizing, for example, concerned working with faith-based and other existing organizations that could leverage turnout of large members—being broad-based. I documented this approach in a study of the IAF in the 1990s, whose local affiliates could bring thousands to large actions and meetings called "accountability nights" with public officials. Meanwhile, social movement scholarship and public commentary have also appreciated the power of protest movements domestically and globally, ones that mobilize large numbers, like Black Lives Matter or the 2020 protests against racist police violence.[26]

There appears to be a different balance of broad and deep in the movement to dismantle the school-to-prison pipeline and new dimensions to deep organizing. In these organizing campaigns, we see the even greater power of personal storytelling by a small number of committed and persistent people who are directly impacted by injustice. Many of these participants lack strong connections to institutions and most of the students are not even old enough to vote. CADRE won its early victory against exclusionary discipline in Los Angeles, the second-largest school district in the country, through this kind of deep organizing. It brought scores of parents out to board of education meetings, not thousands. But those scores of parents understood deeply the nature of the struggle and were prepared to be insistent and persistent. Groups like CADRE work intensely with participants, building skills, knowledge, and capacity through political education, relationship building, mentoring, and personal support. We have seen that organizers combine storytelling with data and alliance building, and that campaign success depends as well on a variety of factors in the political context. Mobilizing demonstrations of broad support remains important at certain times. Nevertheless, the foundation for campaign success across the country rests in deep and persistent organizing that features the voice and participation of those directly impacted by injustice, not necessarily large turnouts.[27]

The organizing in the school-to-prison pipeline movement is also deep in some new ways. It features a key role for political education to help participants connect their personal experiences to an analysis of systemic racism. It also incorporates central elements of the Black women's tradition of racial justice organizing as discussed in Chapter 2. This tradition has long combined organizing with community care, supporting participants holistically in their lives as they become engaged in community action. As noted earlier in this chapter and in Chapter 7, Black women and women of color lead many of the groups and national alliances in the school-to-prison pipeline movement. They offer assistance to families and to young people and support them in advocacy around their own experiences with the school-to-prison pipeline. They meet them as whole persons not just as leaders or public actors. As people feel supported in their own struggles, many become participants in the organizing campaigns, telling their stories and participating in meetings and actions; some also become advocates for others, building the organization's network of members and supporters.[28]

As a newer dimension of deep organizing, many groups increasingly address the trauma experienced by parents and young people through the violence and abuse of the school-to-prison pipeline and as a consequence of poverty, racism, and criminalization. Organizers and leaders who proposed restorative practices originally as an alternative to discipline and punishment in schools are now promoting healing practices within their organizations. This "healing justice" approach centers healing within a critique of systemic causes of trauma and action to confront them. Yet, in a departure from traditional forms of community organizing, organizers work to create healing spaces within their organizations, making extensive use of the arts and healing practices, drawing from Indigenous and other traditions.[29]

There are tensions in these elements of deep organizing as well. Groups are stretched thin with few resources and time to address trauma, provide support to members, and help them to advocate for themselves and their families, even as they organize bold and ambitious issue campaigns. Many groups help parents and students become advocates and support networks for others, so that staff do not have to do everything; but it also takes staff time and attention to help others develop the capacity to advocate. In the end, though, this holistic and caring approach is necessary to develop a deep base of participants and leaders who address the trauma they have suffered even as they challenge the system that caused it.

Deep organizing produces policy change, but it is also vital for culture change. As we saw in Chapter 5 on Los Angeles and elsewhere, policy change will not automatically transform the practice of educators who hold deeply ingrained stereotypes of students and parents of color and habits of punitive relationships. If we want systemic transformation, the culture of public education has to shift to respect Black and Brown parents and students through the assertion of parent and student power by people most impacted by injustice and the creation of new equitable relationships.

Challenges Facing the Movement

Despite the important successes of the movement, it faces significant challenges to achieve its goal of dismantling the school-to-prison pipeline. Access to funding remains an ongoing challenge as the priorities of foundations shift and change. Overall, private philanthropy offers little support to grassroots organizing and to work that explicitly targets racial inequities and educational injustice.[30]

The movement faced a particular challenge when the Atlantic Philanthropies completed the spend-down of its endowment and ended its multimillion-dollar grant program to the school-to-prison pipeline movement. Meanwhile, the Ford Foundation reoriented its funding to educational justice organizing and the W.K. Kellogg Foundation ended the part of its racial equity program that had supported many of the organizing groups. In response, groups redoubled their efforts and sought out new sources of support, including from the public health community where they argued that the school-to-prison pipeline should be addressed as a public health issue. Nevertheless, the movement continues to struggle to acquire the funds necessary to mount ambitious campaigns at multiple levels.

The Persistence of Racial Disparities

As discussed earlier, despite the gains of the movement in reducing suspension rates, including those for Black and Brown students, racial disparities continue to persist. In fact, they have hardly budged. Policy changes have reduced the amount of discretion teachers in the classroom or school administrators have to suspend students and this change has kept tens of thousands of Black and Brown students in classrooms instead of out on the streets. When they do suspend, however, educators continue to target Black and Brown students at the same rate of disproportionality compared to white students as before.

On average, Black boys continue to be suspended at three times the rate as white boys, and Black girls at six times the rate as white girls. Looked at by another measure, Black secondary students lost 103 days per 100 students enrolled, compared to 21 for whites, nearly five times as many; Black boys lost 132. Some districts continue to have dramatically high rates of suspensions and high racial disparities. In Grand Rapids, Michigan, Black middle and high school students lost 740 days per 100 students, compared to 166 days per 100 white students. However, a recent analysis of California data charting days of lost instruction from 2011–2012 to 2016–2017, shows some narrowing of the Black/white racial gap as Black students experienced the greatest decrease; nevertheless, racial disproportionality remains high as Black students continue to lose almost four times as many days of instruction as white students, about the same as in 2011–2012.[31]

A similar pattern occurs in more affluent and diverse communities: school systems have lower suspension rates, but they target students of color disproportionately when they do suspend. Groups have tried to highlight implicit bias as one reason for the continuation of racial disparities and push school districts to address it. Despite the persistence of racial disparities, of course, tens of thousands of students of color now remain in school rather than being suspended. Nevertheless, the movement has yet to create an effective strategy to address racial disparities that reverses deep-seated bias and racist practices systematically at all levels of the school system.[32]

Authentic Implementation of Alternatives: Transforming School Climate and Culture

As discussed throughout this book, organizing groups have faced the challenge of translating policy victories into deep transformative change in school climate and culture. They have won the implementation of restorative justice in many schools yet remain concerned about the authenticity of these programs. In principle, schools should be able to implement restorative justice programs with fidelity. The role of organizing groups should be to hold schools accountable for authentic change. Many groups in the movement, like CADRE in Los Angeles, prioritize this kind of accountability work and play a key role in continuing to push for systematic change.

In the end, though, restorative justice seems more likely to be a force for transformation of school climate and culture when connected to organizing processes that enter schools directly. As discussed in Chapter 8, organizers believe that restorative justice can be easily coopted by school districts that hire outside training firms to conduct professional development with teachers who have no meaningful buy-in or say in the process. Restorative justice becomes yet another program imposed down on schools that are underfunded and where teachers feel unsupported or resist change. In this context, restorative justice programs may not have much of an effect; when they are perceived to fail, it can serve to discredit the whole movement.

This book has featured several groups who, among others, have offered models where teachers and parents build authentic restorative justice alternatives through school-based organizing efforts. The Youth Justice Coalition in Los Angeles has developed a transformative justice model; Teachers Unite in New York City works with teachers who partner with students and families to lead change efforts; and Community Organizing for Family Issues in Chicago sponsors parent-led and sometimes student-led restorative circles in schools. In these cases, restorative justice becomes a catalyst for a larger and deeper effort to transform schools into places where educators treat students humanely and help students empower themselves, while welcoming and collaborating with families. Many activists prefer the term transformative justice because it signals the kind of transformation that this approach is meant to create in relationships between schools, students, and families: one that will lead to equitable and liberating education.

Yet organizing groups have too few resources to devote to ongoing engagement with individual schools, while also trying to build parent and student leadership and organize issue campaigns. The number of organizing groups is far too small to engage directly in more than a small number of schools. Yet all students need restorative justice and comprehensive alternatives to harsh discipline. In the end, the school-to-prison pipeline movement continues to try to generate models of restorative justice that can be spread across schools and school districts even as it struggles for strategies that promise deep change on a widespread basis.

Intersectional Organizing Across Issues and Movements

While the school-to-prison pipeline movement has been effective in part because of its sharp and persistent focus on school discipline and, more recently, policing, organizers know that zero tolerance is only part of a larger set of policies and practices that push students out of school and into the criminal justice system. Even authentic implementation of restorative justice will only be fully effective to the extent it serves as a catalyst for a systematic changes in how schools operate. Public schools serving students of color in low-income communities are chronically underfunded, have out-moded facilities and outdated equipment, with less qualified teachers than those in more affluent communities, and offer a curriculum that is not cul-turally relevant to the lives, histories, and traditions of the communities of which students are a part. These schools typically teach a rote curriculum focused on increasing test scores rather than hands-on learning and critical thinking. Moreover, many of the schools in Black communities are under threat of closure, as part of a neoliberal gentrification process that is pushing Black people out of cities. When corporate-oriented charter schools open in their place, these schools often feature even stricter discipline practices. Increasingly participants in the school-to-prison pipeline movement are coming to see that public education was created and continues to work to support the system of white supremacy and requires complete transforma-tion. Challenging school discipline and policing may be keys to unlock the larger system, but that larger system still needs to be addressed.[33]

Meanwhile, a range of other racialized social and economic processes out-side of the educational system per se also serve to push students of color out of schools. These include lack of affordable housing, low-paid and insecure work for families, environmental racism, criminalization, intercommunal violence, food insecurity, and the lack of a range of services that support whiter and more affluent communities including healthy food options, arts and cultural programs, reliable transportation, and access to high-quality healthcare and dental services. Students living in these deeply inequitable circumstances are much less prepared for and supported in learning com-pared to their more affluent peers and less likely to graduate high school. The concept of the school-to-prison pipeline captures the comprehensive system that reproduces poverty and white supremacy, but changes in school disci-pline and policing only address part of the larger picture.[34]

The school-to-prison pipeline movement has been increasingly looking for ways to connect issues both within the educational justice movement and across to other allied movements that address the range of inequities that con-tribute to school pushout. DSC joined with the Journey for Justice Alliance and other groups fighting school closings in Black and Brown communi-ties and advocating for the establishment of sustainable community schools that feature culturally relevant curriculum and support services for students and families. The campaign for police-free schools involving AEJ and the Advancement Project and led by Black and Brown youth and families in orga-nizing groups connects the school-to-prison movement to the Movement for Black Lives and for defunding police in communities. Groups fighting the school-to-prison pipeline like Youth Justice Coalition in Los Angeles, Padres & Jóvenes Unidos in Denver, and Communities United in Chicago are working in coalition with labor unions, criminal justice reform groups, and others to advocate "justice reinvestment" that moves funds away from police and criminal justice systems and puts them into public schools, youth jobs, and community supports. DSC and other groups highlight the school-to-deportation pipeline to connect educational justice with immigrant rights.[35]

Despite these promising initiatives at intersectional organizing and solidarity, there are pressures that keep organizing groups siloed and focused on single issues. Private foundations often fund in issue streams. Low-resourced groups seeking to make immediate improvements in the lives of poor families of color feel the need to focus on one issue; to do so, they must target public institutions that are themselves often siloed by issue or policy area—like a school committee. Building the kind of trust, shared understanding, and mutual interest in solidarity required for connections across issue-based movements takes time and attention that is in short supply for small, under-resourced groups. Nevertheless, organizers in the school-to-pipeline movement know that groups are likely to fail separately if they cannot find ways to connect and build the broader power to win together.[36]

Closing Thoughts in the Time of Mass Protests

As I drafted this conclusion in the summer of 2020, mass protests were occurring across the country against the police killing of George Lloyd and against anti-Black racism and violence in all its forms. The country was in the middle of a pandemic that has sickened and killed Black, Indigenous and people of color, and poor people at higher rates than white and affluent people, once again, exposing the systemic racial and class inequities in our nation. The rapid shift to online learning has also disenfranchised low-income students of color and exacerbated racial inequities in educational access. Meanwhile, the adoption of new surveillance apparatus by school systems threatens progress made in removing police from schools.

I know that these words will be read a year or more after the main wave of protests may have ended. I believe this study, undertaken in an earlier moment in time, offers some enduring lessons for communities organizing to end mass criminalization and white supremacy and for their allies in the cause of racial and educational justice. We know that mass protests spark a response and catalyze change. We know less about the deep and sustained organizing work that lays the foundation for the emergence of mass protests and persists after they recede to continue to press for policy change and institutional transformation.

Communities need to be persistent and marshal a range of resources and strategies to transform racist policies and then hold systems accountable for authentic implementation. Nowhere is this more apparent or challenging than in our educational and criminal justice systems which intersect to form the school-to-prison pipeline. Mass protest can help shine a spotlight on injustice, mobilize new activists and win public support for change agendas. Changing policies and transforming deep-seated systems of injustice, however, will also take organization, leadership development, and complex alliances at local, state, and national levels. In other words, it will take organizing and the kind of movement building that supports and strengthens organizing.

Black people who experience state violence by the police and school systems challenge us to confront the most profound questions facing our society and democracy. Police killings represent the tip of an iceberg of a much broader and deeper system of state violence and mass criminalization in which the school-to-prison pipeline plays a central role. The daily physical and social-emotional damage caused by the school-to-prison pipeline ruins the lives of tens of thousands of young people of color and turns our schools into pre-prisons. The abuse of Black and Brown parents who speak up to defend their children crushes the spirit and denies their human rights and our common humanity.

I hope readers will leave this book with a renewed commitment to confront the systemic racial oppression that denies the promise of American democracy to Black communities and communities of color. At the same time, I also hope readers will appreciate the transformative power of people most impacted by injustice organizing for change. The parents and students who anchor the movement show us the possibilities for education to be a force for the liberation of peoples. Liberatory education occurs when parents and young people share their stories, analyze the systems that oppress them, learn about their history, and take action to create a just and equitable society.

Public education lies at the heart of our democracy, for better or worse. Currently our educational system reproduces racial inequities and serves to maintain white supremacy. Yet public education also has the potential to be a force for the liberation of peoples. Access to quality and empowering education, as well as the power to determine the nature of that education, has been the precious demand of African Americans and other oppressed people fighting for their freedom throughout history. The Black and Brown parents and students at the forefront of the movement to end the school-to-prison pipeline are creating a new chapter in this historic movement. They hold out an urgent vision for what education for liberation and democracy can and must mean in our time: the dismantling of white supremacy across our institutions and the reimagining of public education and our human community.

Acknowledgments

First of all, I would like to thank the students and parents who form the heart of the movement to dismantle the school-to-prison pipeline. Their stories, their experiences at the hands of school and police authorities, their struggles, their insights, and their hopes and dreams fill this book. Their commitment to racial equity and educational justice inspires me and animates this book. I am honored they have put their trust in me to tell, as best as I can, a collective story of their movement.

Many of these parents and students work together in member groups of the Dignity in Schools Campaign (DSC) and the Alliance for Education Justice (AEJ), who were my partners in this project. I deeply thank DSC, AEJ, and their many member groups for working with me as I conducted research on the movement to dismantle the school-to-prison pipeline and wrote this book. They provided advice and guidance through all the stages of research and writing. I have been on a journey in researching and writing this book, and I appreciate all of the people who have taught me and let me join their journeys.

DSC established a subcommittee whose members met regularly with me to design the project and provide feedback as I conducted the research and developed the themes in the book. They also read and provided feedback on drafts of the manuscript and contributed so much to this book in so many ways. I give my deepest thanks to these committed DSC members: Liz Sullivan-Yuknis, Maisie Chin, Harold Jordan, Marsha Weissman, Lorraine Wright, Zakiya Sankara-Jabar, and Joyce Parker. Many other staff and leaders from DSC also helped me with this project and contributed to this book, including Tafari Melisizwe, Lakita Jackson, Natalie Chap, Nancy Treviño, Teena-Marie Johnson, Letha Muhammad, Sally Lee, Marika Pfefferkorn, Hashim Jabar, and Al White.

I would also like to thank Jonathan Stith from AEJ who partnered with me on this project too and provided advice, guidance, and insights throughout the process.

Many organizers and leaders hosted me in my fieldwork visits to their localities; they are partners in this project as well. They shared their stories, gave their insights, and connected me to parents, students, and allies in their local movements. In Chicago, these folks include Jenny Arwade, Raul Botello, and Maria Degillo from Communities United, Nancy Aardema from Logan Square Neighborhood Association, and Jeff Bartow and Joel Rodriguez from the Southwest Organizing Project. I give a special thanks to Maisie Chin who hosted and shepherded my research in Los Angeles, but I also thank Roslyn Broadnax from CADRE, Manuel Criollo, Ashley Franklin and Zoe Rawson from Labor Community Strategy Center, and Maritza Galvez from the Youth Justice Coalition. I rode across the Mississippi Delta with Joyce Parker of Citizens for a Better Greenville who hosted my visits, but so many other special people hosted me as well, including Ellen Reddy and Janice Harper of Nollie Jenkins Family Center, Diana Freelon-Foster of Activists with a Purpose, Betty Petty from the Indianola Parent Student Group, and Marilyn and Melvin Young and Ashley McKay of Tunica Teens in Action. Other hosts include Zakiya Sankara-Jabar from Racial Justice NOW!, Gina Womack from Families and Friends of Louisiana's Incarcerated Children, Marlyn Tillman from Gwinnett SToPP, Lorraine Wright from I Vote for Me, Kandise Lucas from Advocates for Equity in Schools (now called Advocates for Justice), and Pam and Ricardo Martinez from Padres & Jóvenes Unidos.

I thank Judith Browne-Dianis, Scott Roberts, and Maria Fernandez from the Advancement Project; Dan Losen, Matthew Cregor, Jaime Koppel, and Lori Bezahler, who all advised me and helped shape this project. Ruth Idakula, Damekia Morgan, and Ashanna Bigard contributed to this book as well.

I have many scholar friends and colleagues who have helped and supported me during this project. Many of them participate in the Urban Research Based Action Network and I have learned so much from them about community engaged research for social justice. These special friends include Karen Mapp, John Diamond, Tomni Dance, Jose Calderon, Vajra Watson, Tim Eatman, Ron Glass, John Rogers, Sean Ginwright, Veronica Terriquez, Michelle Fine, Celina Su, Julio Cammarota, Ben Kirshner, Michael Johnson, and many others. Through the years, I have been honored to have the support of scholars whose work has inspired me, including Theda Skocpol, Bill Wilson, Sara Lawrence-Lightfoot, Bob Putnam, Joyce King, Bill Ayers, and Jeannie Oakes.

I would like to thank the many doctoral students in public policy at the University of Massachusetts Boston who helped me and contributed to this project. I have learned so much from them. Luke Krupscznk helped design the research. Lindsay Morgia, Jeffrey Moyer, Andrew King, Patricio Belloy, and Trevor Aldridge conducted the lion's share of the coding of the transcripts. Lindsey Morgia and especially Mary Krebs worked closely with me and the Dignity in Schools Campaign to produce a companion Toolkit of resources for community organizations working to dismantle the school-to-prison pipeline. I would like to thank Andrew King for suggesting the title "Willful Defiance," Emma Tynan for help in disseminating the lessons of the book, and Bianca Ortiz-Wythe for her support and colleagueship.

I would like to thank the deans of the McCormack Graduate School, David Cash and Rita Kiki Edozie; and the chairs of the Department of Public Policy and Public Affairs, Christine Brenner and Michael Johnson, for supporting me in this project. I'd also like to thank the many staff members at UMASS Boston who helped me, including Michael Gaughan, James Stark, Shaleah Rather, Rashelle Brown, Chayaphon Klinthong, Andrea Ward, Brandynn Holgate, Lisa Greggo, Jamie Tull, Chris Brindley, and Melissa Quashie.

I would like to thank 19 the Agency for the graphic on the cover of the book (student with backpack and raised fist) designed originally for DSC's Week of Action and the Labor Community Strategy Center for the photo of the group's joint 2016 march with DSC against the 1033 program, which provided military-grade equipment to the Los Angeles School Police.

I would like to thank the many foundations that financially supported the research for this book. These include the Edward W. Hazen Foundation, the Ford Foundation, the W.K. Kellogg Foundation, the NEA Foundation, and the Nellie Mae Education Foundation. The Schott Foundation for Public Education supports the People's Think Tank, which I helped co-found and is assisting in efforts to disseminate the lessons lifted up in this book. I would also like to thank Kavitha Mediratta from the Atlantic Fellows for Racial Equity Program for her support and help as well as Jaime Koppel and Thena Robinson Mock at Communities for Just Schools Fund (CJSF), Marianna Islam and John Jackson at the Schott Foundation, and Sanjiv Rao and Claribel Vidal at the Ford Foundation. I also thank Patrick St. John, Andrea Garvey, Kefiana Kabati, and the whole team at the Schott Foundation as well as the People's Think Tank Steering Committee for their support.

I launched this project while holding a College Board Fellowship at the Hutchins Center for African & African American Research at Harvard University and a John Simon Guggenheim Memorial Fellowship. I wrote most of the book while a fellow at the Center for Advanced Study in the Behavioral Sciences at Stanford University. I thank Henry Louis Gates, Jr., and Margaret Levi and their teams for their support, and I appreciate my fellow scholars for their encouragement and community.

My editor and friend James Cook, Emily Mackenzie, and the good folks at Oxford University Press worked with me to make the book a strong piece of scholarship, a contribution to public understanding and education policy, and a resource for movement building. I thank them.

A different version of the material from Chapter 6 appeared in "'Our stories are powerful': The use of youth storytelling in policy advocacy to combat the school-to-prison pipeline," co-written with Jeffrey S. Moyer and Andrew R. King, which appeared in the *Harvard Educational Review*, volume 90, No. 2 (Summer 2020).

We lost so many friends and colleagues over the past few years, but I would especially like to honor the memory and spirit of Allison Brown from CJSF and Thomas Nikundiwe, whose vision and passion for educational justice inspires all who were fortunate to know them.

I would also like to appreciate Najma Nazy'at, whose contagious energy and deep commitment to young people animates this book.

When I think about my commitments to organizing and my journey to racial justice, I always come back to my father. He taught me that working people must fight for their rights to get anywhere in this world. With his staunch support for the civil rights movement, he set me on a path to antiracist and multiracial organizing that I have carried the rest of my life. I would also like to thank my mother for her love and support as well as my extended family.

My wife and partner Roberta brings her passion for children and their families, her commitment to justice, her brilliant mind and her joyful spirit to our journey together through life, love and organizing, with our hearts entwined. She has shaped this book—and me—in profound ways with her passion, her insights, and her support; I have no words to thank her enough. Meanwhile, our beautiful daughters, Sade and Imoh, dazzle me with their creativity and passion for life and teach me every day with their own journeys in and through racial justice.

Community Engaged Research Methods

In the Introduction to this book, I discussed my approach to conducting community engaged research for the study on which this book is based and highlighted some of the challenges I faced. In this appendix, I provide additional details concerning the research design, data collection, and analytical methods I used. I hope this discussion will help readers better understand and evaluate the findings and conclusions presented in the book. I return at the end of the appendix to a consideration of the dynamic tension inherent in community engaged research and its promise for rigorous scholarship that is responsive to the racial and social justice demands of our time.

A Qualitative, Multiple Case Study Design

The purpose of the study was to document and analyze the development of the movement to dismantle the school-to-prison pipeline with a focus on the relationship between local community organizing and national movement building. There has been little research on this specific movement and not much scholarship generally on the local/national relationship in racial and social justice movements. Consequently, I chose a qualitative, multiple case study design because that is an appropriate strategy for building knowledge and theory in a new area of research. Case studies allow researchers to develop contextually grounded and richly detailed analyses. Qualitative case study research is a particularly good method for identifying processes; in my study, it allowed me to describe and examine the processes through which organizers built a movement and the movement achieved its results. I took a strongly inductive approach. I sought to build new knowledge for the field through close ethnographic methods. The result is a study that is part historical narrative and part analytical description.[1]

I chose a multiple case study design because this strategy allowed me to study several local organizing sites as well as develop a case study of the national movement—and then examine the interconnections between them. I chose local sites in the Mississippi Delta, Chicago, and Los Angeles to include regional diversity as well as places of significance for the development of the national movement. I choose the Mississippi Delta because I wanted to trace the movement to its earliest organizing in local communities. I also chose the Mississippi Delta to include a Southern site and a more rural one. I chose Los Angeles because it was central to the emergence of the national movement and the formation of the Dignity in Schools Campaign (DSC), because I wanted to include a very large urban district on the West Coast, and because organizing groups had won multiple policy changes over many years that had led to some of the most dramatic declines in rates of exclusionary discipline. I chose Chicago as a Midwestern city and one where organizing groups had won the most significant state-level victory at the time—SB100. This selection of cases also provided me with the chance to examine diverse constituencies and organizing approaches that feature in the larger movement: intergenerational organizing in Mississippi, parent organizing and youth organizing (separately and in coalition) in Los

Angeles, and youth organizing in Chicago, as well as diversity in organizing across Black and Brown communities.

To include a wider representation of local organizing and examine the interplay with the national movement in diverse local contexts, I also conducted shorter field-work visits to other sites. In consultation with my community partners in DSC, I chose Dayton, Ohio, to examine how a small, under-resourced group won significant victories quickly. I chose New Orleans to analyze organizing in a Southern city and one dominated by corporate charter school networks. I chose suburban Atlanta and Richmond to include organizing in suburbs with newer populations of students of color. I included Denver because its victories played critical roles in the development of the national movement.

To study the movement at the national level, I focused on the two main alliances composed of grassroots organizing groups—DSC and the Alliance for Educational Justice (AEJ). I also incorporated the role of other key national intermediaries, including the Advancement Project and NAACP Legal Defense Fund, and a range of movement participants like researchers and foundation officials. I conducted many of the interviews in Washington, DC, and New York City, but also traveled to the sites of various national meetings and conferences to conduct observations and interview participants at these locations.

I created a research schedule that would align with the interactive processes I wanted to study. I conducted multiple, typically week-long visits to each of the main research sites, rotating across the local sites and interspersing these with observations and interviews at the national sites. This sequencing helped me investigate the relationships among organizing efforts across localities and between the local and national movement. I was able to follow up at local sites on issues and findings from the national level or from other local sites.

Data Collection and Analysis

For each case study, I conducted in-depth, semi-structured interviews, observed a variety of meetings and activities, and reviewed relevant documents. I interviewed the executive director(s) and organizers from each group; leaders (parents, young people, and others); educators and public officials with whom they engaged; allies and sometimes opponents; and independent observers or actors. These interviews were designed to reveal organizing and movement processes from multiple perspectives. I had a general template of interview questions to help provide consistency across participants and sites; however, I tailored individual interviews to the particular knowledge or role of each interviewee. On average, each case involved about thirty formal, in-depth interviews of one-hour duration. The shorter cases included four to six in-depth interviews each. I also conducted focus groups in the main local sites so that I could include a wider variety of parents and young people. In total, I interviewed 140 people and conducted 13 focus groups which included an additional 50 parents and youth leaders. The interviews and focus groups were recorded and professionally transcribed. Unless otherwise noted, all quotations from individuals in this book come from these interviews.

I observed a variety of organizational activities in local and national sites. I observed internal organizational meetings, training and political education sessions, direct action events and public meetings, as well as several multiday conferences sponsored by national alliances. These observations were designed to see organizing in action, to better understand the role of various kinds of participants, and to reveal dynamics in the relationships between various participants. It is difficult to meaningfully count the number of observations I conducted, since they varied so much in length and character—from a one-hour meeting to a three-day conference. On average, though, I conducted formal observations of about a dozen events in each site, for a total of more than fifty events representing two hundred hours of observation across the study. I took detailed fieldnotes for each observation.

In addition to the formal interviews and documented observations, the study also includes insights from countless informal observations and conversations with participants while in the field. I spoke informally with a wide variety of participants during the fieldwork and listened to many conversations among participants between meetings. These informal conversations provided valuable information and context that enriched the study.

Finally, I collected and reviewed a variety of documents in each research site. These included organizational leaflets and annual reports, data on the relevant education systems and schools, as well as newspaper articles and other publications about organizational activities. These documents helped me understand the history of the groups in each case as well as their internal dynamics and public activities. I cite these documents in footnotes in the text, where appropriate. Unless otherwise noted, the data sources for the other claims in the accounts come from the interviews and observations.

I began data analysis while still collecting data through a process of journaling. The journals gave me the opportunity to reflect on what I was learning, identify key emerging insights, and develop some initial themes and lines of analysis. After the period of formal data collection ended, I proceeded to more formally and systematically analyze the data collected in each case and across the cases. My analysis drew primarily from the interviews and the fieldnotes, supplemented with information from relevant documents. I used maxQDA, a qualitative data analysis software system, to help me code and analyze the interview material. A research team of graduate students conducted most of the initial coding of the interview transcripts with my guidance and participation. We compared coding practices to try to create a uniform approach.[2]

I then worked with these "first order" codes, combining and integrating them to create the larger themes for the analysis presented in the book. I used process tracing to link organizing processes to outcomes in terms of the organizing itself (how did it impact participants? How did it build a movement and shape the way movement alliances worked?) and in terms of policy (how did it lead to changes in policy or practice?). In order to increase the accuracy of the analysis, I triangulated data sources by checking wherever possible what people said in interviews against what I observed and what was stated in published accounts. As I drafted the manuscript, I systematically reviewed the materials for each case again to make sure the themes identified were supported by the data.[3]

Since I chose groups I thought were strong, and because I relied often on information provided by participants, I knew my bias would be toward seeing the positive side of the work of organizing and movement groups. Consequently, I intentionally looked for tensions, problems, and unmet challenges during data collection. I also sought to interview people who would be independent and sometimes critical of the groups. During data analysis, graduate students and I searched for discrepant data and alternative interpretations of emerging patterns in the analysis. I weighed all these data and alternatives in an effort to produce a balanced and nuanced account of local organizing, national movement building, and their interconnections.[4]

Dynamic Tension in Community Engaged Research

As discussed in the Introduction to this book, I believe it is important to build a collaborative relationship with the organizing groups I study. Just as organizing gives voice to those typically silenced by racial domination, I wanted to ensure that participants spoke through my research. I discussed the research project with key leaders from each organizing group. I agreed that I would seek to understand their organizing work from their point of view, to reveal the motivations and analysis underlying their work, and their goals as they understood them. I agreed that their voices would hold a prominent place in the book.

The book does more than tell the stories of participants, however, as important as that is. Through engagement and constant dialogue, I crafted a narrative analysis that includes the diverse views of participants but also combines and integrates them and sets them in context. During the project, I was in constant dialogue with movement participants as I collected data. I shared emerging analysis and drafts of the chapters with groups and responded to their concerns and incorporated their insights. A subcommittee of DSC read and commented upon the larger manuscript. Participants corrected errors, challenged some aspects of the analysis, and made others more nuanced and complete. I listened closely to this feedback and discussed the issues raised thoroughly. I believe this engagement process made the analysis presented in this book more accurate, nuanced, and rigorous.[5]

Documenting and analyzing movement-building work through deep partnership with organizers, parents, young people, and community members is exciting and powerful work. At the same time, it requires constant dialogue, self-reflection, and relationship building. As a while male university professor working mainly with people of color, I had to constantly reflect on my positionality and work to ensure our partnership was equitable.[6]

The resulting work in the form of this book reflects a dynamic tension. On the one hand, it is a collective product that reflects our partnership and consensus-building work. We created this together and I am deeply indebted to my partners for their commitment to this project and their faith and trust in me. On the other hand, as a trained researcher, I am the person who conducted the project; I initiated plans, engaged extant scholarship, conducted the interviews, analyzed the data, and drafted the book. In the end, I am responsible for the arguments and analysis presented in this work.

I believe, though, that the dynamic tension in our partnership creates rigorous and energetic scholarship that represents the integration of diverse perspectives so necessary to movement building. Our society faces a profound challenge to confront anti-Black racism and historic racial and social inequities. Scholarship that is detached from communities struggling for change and limits itself to the concerns of the academic community will not produce the kind of research that is required to contribute to a more just society.

For too long, parents, young people, and members of Black, Indigenous, and communities of color have been treated as passive objects of supposedly enlightened researchers, policy professionals, and educators. At worst, elites have seen them as dangerous or problems to be "fixed." The movement to dismantle the school-to-prison pipeline demonstrates the profound contributions that people most impacted by injustice make to our understanding of racial inequities and educational failure and to strategies to address them. Community engaged scholarship seeks to create a dynamic, participatory, and inclusive process of knowledge production that works to transform the power hierarchies that reproduce white supremacy. It models the kind of dialogue, relationships, and collaborations we need to respond to profound inequities and contribute new ways forward toward liberatory education and a democratic and just future.

Notes

Willful Defiance

1. See Mississippi Code Title 37, available at: https://codes.findlaw.com/ms/title-37-education/ms-code-sect-37-11-18-1.html, *Pushed out* (Sullivan and Morgan 2010), "South Carolina legislature repeals racist 'disturbing school' law for students," Sarah Hinger, *ACLU Speak Freely*, May 21, 2018, available at: https://www.aclu.org/blog/racial-justice/race-and-inequality-education/south-carolina-legislature-repeals-racist; and *How America outlawed adolescence* (Ripley 2016).
2. See *California Department of Education News Release*, January 14, 2015, available at: https://www.cde.ca.gov/nr/ne/yr15/yr15rel5.asp. See also *The unequal impact* (Losen and Martin 2018), and on Black male suspensions in California, see *Get out!* (Wood, Harris III, and Howard 2018).
3. As quoted in *Speaking up and walking out* (Rojas and Wornum 2018: 20–22). The non-profit is Youth on Board.
4. On California trends, see "Suspension, expulsion rates fall sharply in California, but racial and ethnic disparities remain," Carolyn Jones, *EdSource*, November 1, 2017, retrieved from: https://edsource.org/2017/suspension-expulsion-rates-fall-sharply-in-california-public-schools-but-racial-disparities-remain/589722. For Los Angeles, see "School discipline data reports-suspensions, 2016–2017 school year," LAUSD, http://schoolinfosheet.lausd.net.
5. I use the term parent in this book to include extended family members and other caregivers who raise children.

Introduction

1. See "Dayton Public to limit suspensions," Jeremy P. Kelley, *Dayton Daily News*, June 18, 2014, available at: https://www.daytondailynews.com/news/dayton-public-limit-suspensions/uM7yB628rYnS1OBX1uQNnL/; and "Law will change Ohio school safety, behavior, suspensions," Jeremy P. Kelley and Laura A. Bischoff, *Dayton Daily News*, July 8, 2018, available at: https://www.daytondailynews.com/news/laws-will-change-ohio-school-safety-behavior-suspensions/Z4zV9fc5dNu0LrbxOoitrJ/.
2. See Chapter 6 for an extensive discussion of the SB100 campaign.
3. See Chapter 5 on Los Angeles and Chapter 6 on Chicago for further details.
4. See Chapter 4 on Mississippi for further details.
5. See *A world of hardship* (Cookson 2020).
6. See the Conclusion chapter and other places for details on the impact of the movement.

7. See *A match on dry grass* (Warren, Mapp, and Community Organizing and School Reform Project 2011).

8. For an early critique of the nonracial approach of organizing groups in the Alinsky tradition, see *Beyond the politics of place* (Delgado 1997). For an extended treatment of the multiracial organizing work of the Alinskyite Industrial Areas Foundation, see *Dry bones rattling* (Warren 2001). On the shift to racial equity by the former PICO network (now called Faith in Action), see *A shared future* (Wood and Fulton 2015).

9. For a discussion of the role of community engaged scholarship in educational equity, see the articles in the special issue of *Urban Education* I co-edited, entitled *Research confronts equity and social justice* (Warren 2018b).

10. On researcher positionality, see *Race, culture, and researcher positionality* (Milner 2007), *Black feminist thought* (Collins 2000), and *Qualitative educational research* (Luttrell 2010); see also *The formation of community-engaged scholars* (Warren, Oh, and Tieken 2016).

11. *Lift us up! Don't push us out!* (Warren 2018a).

12. The Toolkit on Organizing to Combat the School-to-Prison Pipeline is available at: www.dignityinschools.org.

Chapter 1

1. See, for just one example, *The school-to-prison pipeline* (Mallett 2016), which offers a detailed treatment of its causes and includes a comprehensive set of policy recommendations but does explicitly discuss it as a racist system of domination and control tied to mass incarceration. On nexus, see *The right to be hostile* (Meiners 2007); see also *First strike* (Sojoyner 2016) and *The prison school* (Simmons 2017). For a discussion of school discipline policy as nets of social control, see *Trouble at school* (Irby 2014).

2. *From the war on poverty to the war on crime* (Hinton 2016). See also *The first civil right* (Murakawa 2014) and *Pillar of fire* (Branch 1998).

3. *The flat world and education* (Darling-Hammond 2010).

4. As documented in *The flat world and education* (Darling-Hammond 2010).

5. *The new Jim Crow* (Alexander 2010). On the increase in drug-related incarceration, see *Criminal justice facts*, available at: www.sentencingproject.org.

6. *The new Jim Crow* (Alexander 2010).

7. For a historical discussion of the myth of Black criminality, see *The condemnation of Blackness* (Muhammad 2019). *Body count* (Bennett, DiIulio, and Walters 1996: 27). "Jogger's attackers terrorized at least 9 in 2 hours," David E. Pitt, *The New York Times*, April 22, 1989, retrieved from: http://www.nytimes.com/1989/04/22/nyregion/jogger-s-attackers-terrorized-at-least-9-in-2-hours.html?pagewanted=all.

8. On the impact of deindustrialization, see *When work disappears* (Wilson 1996). On mass incarceration as social control under neoliberalism, see *Punishing the poor* (Wacquant 2009b). For a historical account, see *Why mass incarceration matters* (Thompson 2010).

9. For an overview, see *Incarceration and social inequality* (Western and Pettit 2010b). On racial discrimination throughout the criminal justice process, see *Report to the United Nations* (Sentencing Project 2018). For a more extensive treatment, see *The new Jim Crow* (Alexander 2010); see also *The growth of incarceration in the United States* (Travis, Western, and Redburn 2014).

10. *The new Jim Crow* (Alexander 2010); see also *Prisons of poverty* (Wacquant 2009a) and *Golden gulag* (Gilmore 2007). On the experiences of formerly incarcerated people, see *Homeward* (Western 2018) and *National inventory of collateral consequences* (American Bar Association 2013).

11. See, for example, *Golden gulag* (Gilmore 2007) and *Who's looting whom?* (Page and Soss 2020). On racial capitalism, see *Black Marxism* (Robinson 2000).

12. On the association of race and education, see *From the war on poverty to the war on crime* (Hinton 2016) and *Incarceration and social inequality* (Western and Pettit 2010b). For the North Carolina study, see *Toolkit* (School Justice Partnership North Carolina 2019).

13. See *Incarceration and social inequality* (Western and Pettit 2010b).

14. See *The Gun-Free Schools Act of 1994* (Cerrone 1999), *Zero tolerance for children* (Sughrue 2003), and *Are zero tolerance policies effective in the schools?* (Skiba et al. 2006). On the early foundations for zero tolerance, see *The history of "zero tolerance"* (Kafka 2011). On the early actions of police as a repressive force in schools, see *Bullies in blue* (French-Marcelin and Hinger 2017) and *We came to learn* (Advancement Project and Alliance for Educational Justice 2018b).

15. See *The dark side of zero tolerance* (Skiba and Peterson 1999).

16. For a brief, critical history of school policing, see *We came to learn* (Advancement Project and Alliance for Educational Justice 2018b). On youth and trends in school-based violence, see *Beyond suspensions* (U.S. Commission on Civil Rights 2019).

17. Unless otherwise noted, data from this section on suspensions comes from *Are we closing the school discipline gap?* (Losen et al. 2015); on days of instruction lost, see *Lost opportunities* (Losen and Martinez 2020). The Texas report can be found in *Breaking schools' rules* (Fabelo et al. 2011).

18. See *The school discipline dilemma* (Welsh and Little 2018); see also *Do Black students misbehave more?* (Huang 2018). On the social construction of discipline and the widening and deepening of nets of social control, see *Trouble at school* (Irby 2014).

19. See *A first look* (Office of Civil Rights 2016) and "New data reveal 250 preschoolers are suspended or expelled every day," Rasheed Malik, Center for American Progress, available at: https://www.americanprogress.org/issues/early-childhood/news/2017/11/06/442280/new-data-reveal-250-preschoolers-suspended-expelled-every-day/.

20. See *Pushout* (Morris 2016), *Black girls matter* (Crenshaw, Ocen, and Nanda 2015), and *The effects of zero tolerance policies on Black girls* (Hines-Datiri and Carter Andrews 2020). On police violence against women of color, see *Invisible no more* (Ritchie 2017).

21. See *LGBTQ youth of color* (GSA Network n.d.), *Power in partnership* (Advancement Project, Equality Federation Institute, and GSA Network 2015), and *Two wrongs don't make a right* (Advancement Project, Alliance for Educational Justice, and GSA

Network 2012). On the overrepresentation of LGBTQ youth of color in the juvenile justice system, see *We've had three of them* (Irving 2010).

22. See *Sent home and put off track* (Balfanz, Byrnes, and Fox 2014), *Breaking schools' rules* (Fabelo et al. 2011), and *Punishment and inequality in America* (Western 2006); for a comprehensive treatment, see *Prelude to prison* (Weissman 2015).

23. "Beyond fear" (Hirschfield and Celinska 2011).

24. As reported in *Cops and no counselors* (Whitaker et al. n.d.); see also *Bullies in blue* (French-Marcelin and Hinger 2017).

25. For the ACLU report, see *Cops and no counselors* (Whitaker et al. n.d.).

26. See *Juvenile arrests 2003* (Snyder 2005), *Bullies in blue* (French-Marcelin and Hinger 2017) and *We came to learn* (Advancement Project and Alliance for Educational Justice 2018b). See also *The school to deportation pipeline* (Hlass 2017). According to data from 2017–2018, Black boys were 2.4 times as likely to be arrested in school than white boys, while Black girls were 3.7 times as likely to be arrested as white girls; see *Data snapshot 2017–2018* (Epstein et al. 2020).

27. See *Are zero tolerance policies effective in schools?* (Skiba et al. 2006).

28. *The effects of African American movement styles* (Neal et al. 2003); see also *The color of discipline* (Skiba et al. 2002) and *Discipline policies* (Losen 2011).

29. *Do early educators' implicit bias* (Gilliam et al. 2016) and *From Preschool to prison* (Chakara 2017).

30. See *Dismantling desegregation* (Orfield and Eaton 1997), *Whither opportunity?* (Duncan and Murnane 2011), *Educational inequality and school finance* (Baker 2018), *Inequitable opportunity to learn* (Cardichon et al. 2020), and *So much reform* (Payne 2008).

31. On the incentive to push out students to raise test scores, see *Race, inequality and educational accountability* (Darling-Hammond 2007). On the impact of charter schools on segregation, particularly in certain districts, see *Charter school effects on school segregation* (Monarrez, Kisida, and Chingos 2019); for a comprehensive assessment, see *Choosing charters* (Rotberg and Glazer 2018). On the increasing evidence concerning zero-tolerance discipline and charter schools, particularly "no excuses" schools, see *NEPC review* (Torres and Golann 2018) and *The irony of rigor* (Waitoller, Nguyen, and Super 2019). On school closings, see *Ghosts in the schoolyard* (Ewing 2018). On neoliberalism in education more broadly, see *The new political economy of urban education* (Lipman 2011).

32. See *Stuck in place* (Sharkey 2013) and *The effects of poverty* (Yoshikawa, Aber, and Beardslee 2012). On intentional government policies that segregated Black communities, see *The color of law* (Rothstein 2017).

33. See, for example, *We interrupt this crisis* (CADRE and Justice Matters 2004) and *More education* (CADRE 2006).

34. See *Collateral costs* (Western and Pettit 2010a) and *Parental imprisonment* (Wildeman 2009). On the impact on children, see *Parental incarceration and children's wellbeing* (Turney and Goodsell 2018) and *Mass incarceration and children's outcomes* (Morsy and Rothstein 2016).

35. For a more extensive treatment of the school-to-prison pipeline as a form of structural racism tied to mass criminalization and racist social control, see *The school-to-prison pipeline* (Heitzeg 2016). For a personal account that makes similar connections, see *Being bad* (Laura 2014). For additional reading on zero-tolerance discipline and the school-to-prison pipeline, see *Disrupting the school-to-prison pipeline* (Bahena et al. 2012), *Closing the school discipline gap (Losen 2015), The school-to-prison pipeline* (Kim, Losen, and Hewitt 2010), *Ending zero tolerance* (Black 2016), and *The school-to-prison pipeline* (Mallett 2016). For a powerful treatment concerning the lives of African American youth in Chicago, see *Unequal city* (Shedd 2015). For a recent comprehensive review of school discipline and policing policies and their impacts, see *Beyond suspensions* (U.S. Commission on Civil Rights 2019).

Chapter 2

1. Citations for the claims made in this introductory section of the chapter can be found when they are discussed in more detail later in the chapter.
2. See *A match on dry grass* (Warren, Mapp, and Community Organizing and School Reform Project 2011). Other treatments of community organizing as a local phenomenon include *Streetwise for book smarts* (Su 2009), *Community organizing for stronger schools* (Mediratta, Shah, and McAlister 2009), *Learning power* (Oakes and Rogers 2005), and *Black social capital* (Orr 1999); see also *Youth activism* (Kirshner 2015). On the emergence of national educational justice movements, see *Transforming public education* (Warren 2014). On the movement against school privatization and high-stakes testing, see *Slaying Goliath* (Ravitch 2020). On the immigrant rights movement, see *The DREAMers* (Nicholls 2013).
3. See *I've got the light of freedom* (Payne 1995) and *The origins of the civil rights movement* (Morris 1984). On the local and national policy impact of the movement, see *Freedom is a constant struggle* (Andrews 2004) and *Local protest and federal policy* (Andrews and Gaby 2015).
4. See *The origins of the civil rights movement* (Morris 1984, chapter 2) and *Parting the waters* (Branch 1988).
5. *Freedom is a constant struggle* (Andrews 2004). I consider the movement to be a national rather than regional one; see *Sweet land of liberty* (Sugrue 2008).
6. See *Pillar of fire* (Branch 1998) and *In struggle* (Carson 1981).
7. See *Ella Baker and the Black freedom movement* (Ransby 2003); on Septima Clark, see *Freedom's teacher* (Charron 2009); and on Fannie Lou Hamer, see *For freedom's sake* (Lee 1999).
8. See *Diminished democracy* (Skocpol 2003), *A nation of organizers* (Skocpol, Ganz, and Munson 2000), and *What a mighty power we can be* (Skocpol, Liazos, and Ganz 2006).
9. See *Diminished democracy* (Skocpol 2003); see also *Bowling alone* (Putnam 2000), *Mobilizing interest groups* (Walker 1991), *Social movement organizations* (Edwards and Foley 2003), and *The unheavenly chorus* (Schlozman, Verba, and Brady 2012).

For a different view, see *Replacing members with managers?* (Walker, McCarthy, and Baumgartner 2011) and *How do members count?* (Foley and Edwards 2002).

10. See *The influence of organizational structure* (Walker and McCarthy 2007). For another argument that racial justice movements fractured after the demise of the civil rights movement, see *Black political organizations in the post-civil rights era* (Johnson and Stanford 2002).

11. On the IAF, see *Dry bones rattling* (Warren 2001); on PICO see *Faith in action* (Wood 2002); see also *Organizing urban America* (Swarts 2008). The rare exceptions prove the rule. National People's Action, for example, helped local affiliates combine efforts to pass the Community Reinvestment Act in 1977 and the ACORN network undertook some jointly coordinated campaigns around living wages, for example; but these national efforts were not sustained; see *Organizing access to capital* (Squires 2011) and *The people shall rule* (Fisher 2009).

12. For documentation of the increasing alliances of faith-based organizing groups at local, state, and national levels, see *Building bridges* (Wood, Partridge, and Fulton 2012) and *A shared future* (Wood and Fulton 2015).

13. On PICO's national efforts, see *Higher power* (Wood 2007). The network now called Faith in Action also adopted a racial equity frame and launched a campaign to address violence in local communities; see *A shared future* (Wood and Fulton 2015). One journalistic study of the ACORN organization, *Seeds of change* (Atlas 2010), documents the organization's national work and an interdisciplinary volume, *The people shall rule* (Fisher 2009), treats some aspects of local-national relationships, but does not systematically analyze the processes using a theoretical lens. A few studies have examined some of the state-level efforts of community organizing groups; see *Dry bones rattling* (Warren 2001) and *Community organizing for stronger schools* (Mediratta, Shah, and McAlister 2009). Some, like *Community organizing and regionalism* (Kleidman 2004) and *Going regional* (Rusch 2012), have shown the difficulty of local participants asserting power even at the state level, let alone the national level.

14. A few studies on the border between community organizing and social movements, however, do discuss some ways that state-level or national formations can support local organizing—supplying funding sources, policy expertise and information, opportunities to connect across localities, and connections to policymakers; see *Grassroots coalitions and state policy change* (Post 2011) and *A shared future* (Wood and Fulton 2015). On the Sierra Club, see *Leadership, membership and voice* (Baggetta et al. 2010).

15. See *The DREAMers* (Nicholls 2013). Other studies of the immigrant rights movement address both local and national aspects, but don't theorize their relationship; see, for example, *Rallying for immigrant rights* (Voss and Bloemraad 2011). See, however, the related discussion of networked versus hierarchical organizations in the environmental justice movement in *Networks and mobile arrangements* (Schlosberg 1999).

16. See *Geography and social movements* (Miller 2000).

17. On localities as the first place to engage people in political life, see *Everyday politics* (Boyte 2004). There is an extensive literature on the role of place-based institutions in the lives of people and their communities and in fostering civic and political

participation. On the importance of the structure of neighborhood life, see *Civil society reconsidered* (Sampson et al. 2005); on the role of religious congregations, see *Congregation and community* (Ammerman 1996); on the Black Church in particular, see *Streets of glory* (McRoberts 2005); on community-based youth organizations in the lives of young people, see *Urban sanctuaries* (McLaughlin, Irby, and Langman 1994); and on schools as anchors of communities and democratic institutions, see *Schools and urban revitalization* (Patterson and Silverman 2013) and *Why community matters* (Longo 2007). On the factors that promote participation of people of various race and socioeconomic statuses, see *Voice and equality* (Verba, Schlozman, and Brady 1995). Social ties are important to political participation even when mainly organized through social media; see *Social networks and protest participation* (Larson et al. 2019).

18. For a comprehensive treatment of the processes of community organizing, and for further references on this extensive literature, see *A match on dry grass* (Warren, Mapp, and Community Organizing and School Reform Project 2011). On the relationship between online and in-person organizing, see *Re-engaging social relationships* (Speer and Han 2018).

19. On story and narrative, see *Leading change* (Ganz 2010) which also discusses the transition from "I" to "We"; on the development of political consciousness of Black women through shared experience, see *Black feminist thought* (Collins 2000).

20. On popular education, see *Pedagogy of the oppressed* (Freire 2000 [1970]) and, in the African American organizing tradition, see *Teach freedom* (Payne and Strickland 2008).

21. For a useful treatment of the skills and practices of community organizing, see *Collective action for social change* (Schutz and Sandy 2011).

22. For the classic comparison of organization and mass protest movements, see *Poor people's movements* (Piven and Cloward 1977). On the relationship between mobilizing and organizing, see *How organizations develop activists* (Han 2014).

23. On the development of the Alinsky tradition in its modern version, see *Dry bones rattling* (Warren 2001). On the development of a racial equity analysis within the PICO network (now called Faith in Action), which emerged from the Alinsky tradition, see *A shared future* (Wood and Fulton 2015).

24. For a comparison of Alinsky and feminist organizing models, see *Community organizing or organizing community?* (Stall and Stoecker 1998). On the African American civil rights organizing tradition, see *I've got the light of freedom* (Payne 1995). On the role of Black women in the civil rights tradition, see *How long?* (Robnett 1997). On the Chicano/a movement tradition, see *Youth, identity, power* (Munoz 2007); see also *Mexican American women activists* (Pardo 1998).

25. On the processes of individual empowerment in the context of community power, see *Community organizing* (Speer and Hughey 1995).

26. On the increasing role of the federal government and the continued obstacles to the influence of federal education policy as a result of local and state control, see *Collision course* (Manna 2010). State-level education funding and policy also plays

an increasingly important role vis-à-vis local districts; see *Education, equity, and the states* (Dahill-Brown 2019).

27. On the nationalization of local education policy, see *Outside money in school board elections* (Henig, Jacobsen, and Reckhow 2019). On the changing politics of education policy, including the importance of interest and advocacy groups organized nationally, see *The end of exceptionalism* (Henig 2013). On the impact of charter school lobbies, networks, and policy trends on one local area, see *Charter schools, race and urban space* (Buras 2014).

28. The survey is reported in *Mapping the field* (Mediratta and Fruchter 2001). On the limits of foundation giving to racial and social justice organizing, see *Social justice grantmaking* (Lawrence 2005), *Short changed* (Pittz and Sen 2006), and *The revolution will not be televised* (Incite! Women of Color Against Violence 2007). For a more recent treatment, see *Decolonizing wealth* (Villanueva 2018).

29. For a critique of the limits of localism stressing the need for national power, see *Contesting community* (DeFilippis, Fisher, and Shragge 2010).

30. On the relationship of local organizing and the national civil rights movement affecting federal policy, see *Local protest and federal policy* (Andrews and Gaby 2015). For a comprehensive discussion of the role of national advocacy groups in policy-making and implementation, see *Advocacy organizations in the US political process* (Andrews and Edwards 2004). For a broader review, see *The political consequences of social movements* (Amenta et al. 2010), and *The consequences of social movements* (Bosi, Giugno, and Uba 2016).

31. For a recent comprehensive review, see *The cultural impacts of social movements* (Amenta and Polletta 2019).

32. For a useful review, see *Collective identity and social movements* (Polletta and Jasper 2001).

33. The social movement literature has largely neglected the role of alliances and alliance building. For a rare treatment, see *Strategic alliances* (Van Dyke and McCammon 2010).

34. On the dominance of elites, see *The unheavenly chorus* (Schlozman, Verba, and Brady 2012). For a related discussion of the role of professional consultants in dominating what are apparently grassroots movements on the left and right, see *Grassroots for hire* (Walker 2014). For a discussion of the mutuality of professional advocacy groups and grassroots movements, see *Replacing members with managers?* (Walker, McCarthy, and Baumgartner 2011).

35. See *The immigrant rights movement* (Nicholls 2019) and *Going national* (Nicholls, Justus Uitermark, and van Haperen 2020).

36. *The new Jim Crow* (Alexander 2010: 11).

37. As just one example of the recurrent criticism of the NAACP, see *How to save the N.A.A.C.P. from irrelevance*, Melissa Harris-Perry, *New York Times*, May 30, 2017, available at: https://www.nytimes.com/2017/05/30/opinion/melissa-harris-perry-naacp.html.

38. On whirlwind movements, see *Uses of a whirlwind* (Van Meter 2010). On #BLM, see *Making all Black lives matter* (Ransby 2018) and *A herstory of the #BlackLivesMatter*

movement (Garza 2014). On intersectionality in the leadership of new movements, see *A new political generation* (Milkman 2017).

39. For a nuanced assessment of the strengths and limitations of the Movement for Black Lives, see *From #BlackLivesMatter to Black liberation* (Taylor 2016). Most assessments, however, have stressed the movement's positive contributions to broadening participation, rather than focus on questions of leadership development, organization, and policy outcomes; nevertheless, many at least note the need to combine social media with more traditional forms of organizing to create policy change; see, for example, *Scaling social movements* (Mundt, Ross, and Burnett 2018).

40. For the classic treatment that dichotomizes movements and organizations, see *Poor people's movements* (Piven and Cloward 1977). For another treatment, see *Let the people decide* (Fisher 1994). Newer research indicates growing interest in movement building among organizing groups and the blurring of lines between the two; see *Building power* (Wood, Partridge, and Fulton 2012). For a discussion of the interplay between inside and outside strategies, see *Contentious politics* (Tilly and Tarrow 2015).

41. See *#FightForDyett* (Brown 2018) and also *Death by a thousand cuts* (Journey for Justice Alliance 2014).

42. Social movement scholars have examined diffusion, but have not particularly focused on the spread of organizing across localities; see, for example, *Diffusion and scale shift* (Soule 2013).

Chapter 3

1. The title of this chapter comes from Joyce Parker of Citizens for a Better Greenville and a co-founder of the Dignity in Schools Campaign.

2. Unless otherwise noted, all data from this and other chapters, including quotations, come from the author's original fieldwork. The peanut incident is also reported in *Opportunities suspended* (Advancement Project and Harvard Civil Rights Project 2000).

3. See *We interrupt this crisis* (CADRE and Justice Matters 2004), *Lessons in racial justice movement building* (Padres & Jóvenes Unidos and Advancement Project 2014), and *Suspended education* (Lahoud 2000).

4. See "7 students charged in a brawl that divides Decatur, Ill.," Dirk Johnson, *New York Times*, November 10, 1999, retrieved from: https://partners.nytimes.com/library/national/race/111099race-ra.html.

5. See *Opportunities suspended* (Advancement Project and Harvard Civil Rights Project 2000).

6. See *Education on lockdown* (Advancement Project 2005).

7. *Beyond policy* (HoSang 2006); *Mapping the field of school reform organizing in California* (Chow et al. 2001).

8. "Handcuffed 5-year-old sparks suit," Brian Dakss, *CBS News*, April 25, 2005, retrieved from: https://www.cbsnews.com/news/handcuffed-5-year-old-sparks-suit/. For an

early statement by Noguera, see *Schools, prisons, and social implications of punishment* (Noguera 2003). Early reports by Skiba and Losen include *The color of discipline* (Skiba et al. 2002) and *Defining and redirecting a school-to-prison pipeline* (Wald and Losen 2003).

9. See, for example, "Holmes County, Indianola collaborate, hold public hearings on special education issues," in *Struggles: Newsletter of Southern Echo*, Winter 2001, p. 5. Jackson, MS: Southern Echo, Inc.

10. See *We interrupt this crisis* (CADRE and Justice Matters 2004).

11. The report was produced by the Center for Economic and Social Rights, where Sullivan-Yuknis worked just prior to forming NESRI, in partnership with the New York University Institute for Education and Social Policy where Kavitha Mediratta led a program of research and advocacy supporting education organizing; see *Civil society and school accountability* (Sullivan 2003).

12. See *More education, less suspension* (CADRE 2006).

13. While LAUSD and others used the term SWPBS, the more general term has become Positive Behavioral Interventions and Supports (PBIS). PBIS developed in part to meet the needs of students with disabilities and is mentioned in the IDEA reauthorization act passed in 1997.

14. *Bringing a human rights vision to public schools* (Sullivan and Sekaran 2007).

15. For the New Orleans report, see *Pushed out* (Sullivan and Morgan 2010).

16. See *The Education Subcommittee takes on zero tolerance* (Hirji 2005).

17. See *North High School report* (Padres & Jóvenes Unidos 2004: 25). On PJU's organizing, see also *Strategies for systemic change* (Fernández, Kirshner and Lewis 2016).

18. See *Are zero tolerance policies effective in the schools?* (Skiba et al. 2006).

19. Many foundations formed part of the collaborative early on, including the Open Society Foundations, W.K. Kellogg Foundation, Cricket Island Foundation, Nellie Mae Education Foundation, NoVo Foundation, Robert Wood Johnson Foundation, Ford Foundation, and others.

20. The collaborative produced a number of publications and policy recommendations, for example, *Inequality in school discipline* (Skiba, Mediratta, and Rausch 2016) and *You can't fix what you don't look at* (Carter et al. 2017).

21. For the foundation's evaluation of its funding initiative, see *Tilling the field* (Fiester 2015). See also *A powerful partner* (Mediratta 2015).

22. DSC's full membership and decision-making policy is available at: www.dignityinschools.org.

23. DSC revised the model code in 2019; see *A model code on education and dignity* (Dignity in Schools Campaign 2019).

24. The joint issue brief was updated and re-released in 2018: https://dignityinschools.org/resources/police-in-schools-are-not-the-answer-to-school-shootings/. "You can't build peace with a piece," available at: https:// dignityinschools.org/ resources/ statement- by- youth- of- color- on- school- safety- and- gun- violence/.

25. See the joint reports *Two wrongs don't make a right* (Advancement Project, Alliance for Educational Justice, and GSA Network 2012) and *Power in partnership* (Advancement Project, Equality Federation Institute, and GSA Network 2015). See also *Organizing intersectionally* (Winder 2018).

26. For an early report on disproportionality in school discipline by race and gender, see *Black girls matter* (Crenshaw, Ocen, and Nanda 2015).
27. "School Discipline Data Reports-Suspensions, 2016–2017 School Year," *LAUSD*, http://schoolinfosheet.lausd.net.
28. See *Lessons in racial justice movement building* (Padres & Jóvenes Unidos and Advancement Project 2014).
29. See *Speaking up and walking out* (Rojas and Wornum 2018).
30. See "Student suspensions fall sharply in New York City," Alex Zimmerman, *Chalkbeat*, November 1, 2019, retrieved from: https://ny.chalkbeat.org/2019/11/1/21109129/student-suspensions-fall-sharply-in-new-york-city-reversing-an-unusual-bump-the-year-before.
31. See Chapter 6 for a discussion of the SB100 campaign.
32. See, for example, the "Cradle to Prison" state fact sheets published by the Children's Defense Fund in 2009, available at: www.childrensdefense.org/reports. For scholarly examples, see *The trouble with Black boys* (Noguera 2009), *Inequality in school discipline* (Skiba, Mediratta, and Rausch 2016), and *Closing the school discipline gap* (Losen 2015).
33. For more details on Atlantic Philanthropies strategies, see *Tilling the field* (Fiester 2015).
34. *Moving past punishment toward support* (Weingarten 2015).
35. *Tilling the field* (Fiester 2015).
36. For details, see *The evolution of public awareness* (Warren, Krupscznk, and Morgia 2015).
37. "Seeing the toll, schools revise zero tolerance," Lizette Alvarez, *New York Times*, December 2, 2013, retrieved from: http://www.nytimes.com/2013/12/03/education/seeing-the-toll-schools-revisit-zero-tolerance.html?pagewanted=all.
38. *Breaking schools' rules* (Fabelo et al. 2011).
39. *Guiding principles* (U.S. Department of Education 2014).
40. For another analysis of the movement's campaign to influence the federal government, see *Grassroots organizing* (Mediratta 2012).

Chapter 4

1. *Lynching in America* (Equal Justice Initiative 2015).
2. *Local people* (Dittmer 1994: 424). See also *I've got the light of freedom* (Payne 1995) and *A movement's legacy* (Tieken and Warren 2016).
3. See *Advancing community organizing skills* (Southern Echo 2000: 22–23). On the history and organizing approach of Southern Echo, see chapter 6 of *A Match on Dry Grass* (Warren, Mapp, and Community Organizing and School Reform Project 2011).
4. On the struggle for school desegregation, see *The hardest deal of all* (Bolton 2005).
5. Johnson refers loosely to notorious Mississippi Governor James Vardaman (1904–1908) who believed that education ruined former slaves for work on the plantation; these views were widely shared by whites even in the post-WWII era; see *Dark journey* (McMillen 1990: 93). Standardized test score rankings by state from the National Assessment of Educational Progress, available from the National

Center for Educational Statistics: for Mathematics in 1996 at https://nces.ed.gov/ nationsreportcard//pdf/main1996/97488.pdf and for Reading in 1992 at https://nces. ed.gov/nationsreportcard//pdf/main1994/96045.pdf. Mississippi moved into 49th place in reading in 1994 above Georgia; Holmes County spending data available from the National Center for Educational Statistics at: http://www.nces.ed.gov/ccd.

6. On the civil rights movement in Holmes County, see *Thunder of freedom* (Sojourner 2013), *Minds stayed on freedom* (Youth of the Rural Organizing and Cultural Center 1991) and *Everyday heroes* (Delaney 2012).

7. See also *The fight for equality in Mississippi's Delta schools continues* (Null 2004).

8. Mary and Alice Canton are pseudonyms.

9. See the film *Corrections* by Ashley Hunt. Release date: January 25, 2001. The Tougaloo institute was discussed in *Education Struggles*, newsletter of the Mississippi Education Working Group, May 2000, p. 8.

10. Neely documented many of these early examples of the Prevention of Schoolhouse to Jailhouse in her 2003 Master's Thesis; see *School bells to jail cells* (Neely-White 2003). The Indianola incident is reported in *Education Struggles*, newsletter of the Mississippi Education Working Group, May 2000, p. 6.

11. "Care of juvenile offenders in Mississippi is faulted," David M. Halbfinger, *New York Times*, September 1, 2003, retrieved from: https://www.nytimes.com/2003/09/01/us/ care-of-juvenile-offenders-in-mississippi-is-faulted.html?searchResultPosition=1.

12. "Lawsuit filed over treatment of girls at state reform school in Mississippi," Adam Nossiter, *New York Times*, July 12, 2007, retrieved from: https://www.nytimes.com/ 2007/07/12/us/12prison.html?searchResultPosition=2.

13. *Opportunities suspended* (Advancement Project and Harvard Civil Rights Project 2000).

14. See the "Prevention of School House to Jail House Timeline," Southern Echo, p. 2 (un-published document).

15. "Imprisoned youth get legal access under court settlement," Southern Poverty Law Center *Features and Stories,* January 21, 2005, available at: https://www.splcenter.org/ news/2005/01/21/imprisoned-youth-get-legal-access-under-court-settlement.

16. According to a December 18, 2006 letter from the Coalition to "Youth, Parents, Family and Friends of Mississippi's incarcerated children" (unpublished document).

17. Flagg quoted in "New bill funds juvenile justice reforms," Southern Poverty Law Center *Features and Stories*, March 29, 2006, available at: https://www.splcenter. org/news/2006/03/29/new-bill-funds-juvenile-justice-reforms. The 2007 gains are documented in "Mississippi Coalition for the Prevention of Schoolhouse to Jailhouse," SPLC, 2008 (internal report).

18. "Jackson rally urges closure of Columbia," Nicklaus Lovelady, *The Clarion-Ledger*, July 1, 2007, p. 1B.

19. "SPLC settlement protects neglected students in Mississippi County," Southern Poverty Law Center *News*, August 22, 2007, available at: https://www.splcenter.org/ news/2007/08/22/splc-settlement-protects-neglected-students-mississippi-county. "Shackling of teenage girls prompts SPLC action," Southern Poverty Law Center *News*, June 13, 2007, available at: https://www.splcenter.org/news/2007/06/13/ shackling-teenage-girls-prompts-splc-action.

20. "Rally for juvenile justice reform kicks off center's lobbying work," *Southern Poverty Law Center News*, January 16, 2007, available at: https://www.splcenter.org/news/2007/01/16/rally-juvenile-justice-reform-kicks-centers-lobbying-work.

21. See *Are we closing the school discipline gap?* (Losen et al. 2015: 30).

22. See "Tunica students protest principal's firing," *WMC5 Action News*, August 28, 2014, retrieved from: https://www.wmcactionnews5.com/story/26393194/several-people-hold-protest-at-mississippi-high-school/.

23. See "Tunica schools turn around after takeover," Kate Royals, *Mississippi Today*, January 9, 2017, retrieved from: https://mississippitoday.org/2017/01/09/tunica-schools-takeover-reaps-a-turnaround/.

Chapter 5

1. On the background to the uprisings, see *Reading Rodney King* (Gooding-Williams 2013).

2. For details of social, economic, and political changes in South LA, see *Black Los Angeles* (Hunt and Ramon 2010).

3. For an overview, see the essays in *Latino Los Angeles* (Ochoa and Ochoa 2005).

4. On the police raid, see *State of resistance* (Pastor 2018: 3) and "The raid that still haunts L.A.," John L. Mitchell, *Los Angeles Times*, March 14, 2001, retrieved from: https://www.latimes.com/archives/la-xpm-2001-mar-14-mn-37553-story.html. On policing, see *Policing Los Angeles* (Felker-Kantor 2018). On the history of incarceration in LA, see *City of inmates* (Hernandez 2017). On prison building, see *Golden gulag* (Gilmore 2007).

5. See *Confronting the graduation rate crisis in California* (Wald and Losen 2005) and *California's support for K–12 education is improving* (Kaplan 2017). On inequities in public education in California, see the special double issue of *Teachers College Record* on *Williams v. State of California* (Oakes 2004).

6. See *Black, Brown, and over-policed in L.A. schools* (Community Rights Campaign 2013).

7. Quotation in *We interrupt this crisis with our side of the story* (CADRE and Justice Matters 2004: 19).

8. For NESRI's early human rights framework, see *Civil society and school accountability* (Sullivan 2003).

9. See *More education, less suspension* (CADRE 2006).

10. See *Bringing a human rights vision to public schools* (Sullivan and Sekaran 2007) and *Deprived of dignity* (Sullivan 2007).

11. For details on the new policy, see "Discipline foundation policy—schoolwide positive behavior supports," Donnalyn Jacques-Anton, Los Angeles Unified School District Policy Bulletin, February 27, 2007. On CADRE's campaign, see *A parent-led victory* (CADRE 2007). On the People's Hearing, see *2006 People's hearing fact sheet*. Los Angeles: CADRE, June 14, 2006 (unpublished document). The story featuring

CADRE was "A new policy to keep students in line," Charles Proctor, Los Angeles *Times*, February 12, 2007: B.1.

12. *Redefining dignity in our schools* (Chin et al. 2010).

13. See *Black, Brown, and over-policed in L.A. schools* (Community Rights Campaign 2013).

14. All data as reported in *Black, Brown, and over-policed in L.A. schools* (Community Rights Campaign 2013). For further details, see *Counterproductive and wasteful* (Sapp and Blasi 2012).

15. The two examples come from *Counterproductive and wasteful* (Sapp and Blasi 2012: 3 and 6).

16. For an early report, see *End the tickets* (Community Rights Campaign 2009).

17. See "L.A. City Council scales back truancy law," Angel Jennings, *Los Angeles Times*, February 23, 2012, retrieved from: https://www.latimes.com/local/la-xpm-2012-feb-23-la-me-0223-truancy-law-20120223-story.html.

18. See *Police in LAUSD schools* (Community Rights Campaign and DSC-LA 2010). On the public records data, see *Los Angeles School Police citations draw federal scrutiny*, Susan Ferriss, Center for Public Integrity, available at: https://publicintegrity.org/education/los-angeles-school-police-citations-draw-federal-scrutiny/. For an expose of abuse by LA School Police during this time, see "LAUSD's finest: LA school police," Max Taves, *LA Weekly*, September 2, 2009, retrieved from: https://www.laweekly.com/lausds-finest-los-angeles-school-police/. On the policy change, see "LA schools to end zero-tolerance policies and criminalization of students," Renee Lewis, *Aljazeera America*, August 19, 2014, retrieved from: http://america.aljazeera.com/articles/2014/8/19/zero-tolerance-school.html.

19. "LAUSD Police arsenal includes armored vehicle, grenade launchers, Chief confirms," Melissa Paymer and Lynette Romero, *KTLA5*, September 14, 2014, retrieved from: https://ktla.com/news/local-news/lausd-police-arsenal-includes-armored-vehicle-grenade-launchers-chief-confirms/.

20. Aguilar is quoted in "What Obama's new military-equipment rules mean for K–12 school police," Molly Knefel, *Rolling Stone*, May 29, 2015, retrieved from: https://www.rollingstone.com/politics/politics-news/what-obamas-new-military-equipment-rules-mean-for-k-12-school-police-60065/.

21. "How we got the tanks and M-16s out of LA Schools," Eric Mann, *Counterpunch*, May 20, 2016, retrieved from: https://www.counterpunch.org/2016/05/20/how-we-got-the-tanks-and-m-16s-out-of-la-schools/.

22. FREE LA stands for Fight for the Revolution that Will Educate and Empower Los Angeles.

23. "Fare evasion to no longer be a crime for minors in California," Bob Egelko, *SFGate*, August 22, 2016, retrieved from: https://www.sfgate.com/news/article/Fare-evasion-to-no-longer-be-a-crime-for-minors-9178363.php. "L.A. County severely restricts solitary confinement for juveniles," Abby Sewell and Garrett Therolf, *Los Angeles Times*, May 3, 2016, retrieved from: https://www.latimes.com/local/lanow/la-me-ln-juvenile-solitary-20160503-story.html.

24. See *The CalGang criminal intelligence system* (California State Auditor 2016). See also "LAPD scandal opens window into California's secret gang database as reforms debated," Anita Chabria, Leila Miller and Nicole Santa Cruz, *Los Angeles Times*, February 3, 2020, retrieved from: https://www.latimes.com/california/story/2020-02-03/california-attorney-general-xavier-becerra-changes-course-on-revamping-the-states-gang-database.

25. "You can't build peace with a piece," available at: https://dignityinschools.org/resources/statement-by-youth-of-color-on-school-safety-and-gun-violence/.

26. See "LAUSD votes to shift school discipline and limit suspensions," May 14, 2013, *Brothers, Sons, Selves Coalition*, available at: https://www.libertyhill.org/brothers-sons-selves.

27. The ban was extended through eighth grade in 2019; see "California expands ban on 'willful defiance' suspensions in schools," Nina Agrawal, *Los Angeles Times*, September 10, 2019, retrieved from: https://www.latimes.com/california/story/2019-09-10/school-suspension-willful-defiance-california. On the 2014 measure, see *Fix school discipline bills AB420 fact sheet*, Fixschooldiscipline.org, available at: http://www.fixschooldiscipline.org/wp-content/uploads/2014/11/AB-420-Fact-Sheet-Implementation.pdf.

28. See "School district moves to part ways with San Francisco Police Department," Annika Hom, *Mission Local*, June 20, 2020, retrieved from: https://missionlocal.org/2020/06/school-district-moves-to-part-ways-with-san-francisco-police-department; "School board votes to defund, disband Oakland school police," Ashley McBride, *Oaklandside*, June 25, 2020, retrieved from: https://oaklandside.org/2020/06/25/school-board-vote-defund-disband-oakland-school-police; and "L.A. Unified police chief resigns after district slashes department budget," Howard Blume and Sonali Kohli, *Los Angeles Times*, June 30, 2020, retrieved from: https://www.latimes.com/california/story/2020-06-30/lausd-unified-budget-school-police-reopening.

29. "School discipline data reports-suspensions, 2016–2017 School Year," LAUSD, available at: http://schoolinfosheet.lausd.net.

30. On LA school police arrests, see *Policing our students* (Allen et al. 2018). On arrests in Watts, see *Diverting Los Angeles youth from the criminal justice system* (Neighborhood Data for Social Change 2020).

31. *How can you love the kids but hate the parents?* (CADRE and Public Counsel 2017). Statewide, African-Americans comprised 5.8% of total student enrollments, but 15.5% of all students suspended in 2016–2017; see "Suspension, expulsion rates fall sharply in California, but racial and ethnic disparities remain," Carolyn Jones, Oakland: EdSource, November 1, 2017, available at: https://edsource.org/2017/suspension-expulsion-rates-fall-sharply-in-california-public-schools-but-racial-disparities-remain/589722. A UCLA study found that from 2014–2017, Black youth comprised 25% of the total police arrests, citations, and diversions in LA, despite representing less than 9% of the student population; four of the five zip codes with the highest student interaction with police were in South LA; see *Policing our students* (Allen et al. 2018); the diversion program is a pre-arrest program designed to divert students away from the criminal justice system.

Chapter 6

1. See *Suspended education* (Lahoud 2000).
2. See *The new Jim Crow* (Alexander 2010); on Burge, see *The Chicago police torture scandal* (Taylor 2014).
3. See "Illinois high schools are 'dropout factories,'" Jacquelyn Martin, *The Dispatch-Argus*, October 29, 2007, retrieved from: https://qconline.com/news/illinois/illinois-high-schools-are-dropout-factories/article_e0238b6d-73ff-5c03-a206-c247d3a27347.html.
4. On the state of Chicago schools and school closings, see *The new political economy of urban education* (Lipman 2011), *Ghosts in the schoolyard* (Ewing 2018), *School closings in Chicago* (De la Torre et al. 2015), and *Death by a thousand cuts* (Journey for Justice Alliance 2014).
5. See *Let them call me rebel* (Horwitt 1989) and *The assassination of Fred Hampton* (Haas 2011).
6. Later funding for VOYCE came from Communities for Public Education Reform, the Just and Fair Schools Fund and Communities for Just Schools Fund, among others.
7. See *Student-led solutions to the nation's dropout crisis* (VOYCE 2008).
8. Some groups worked directly in middle schools too; for example, SWOP had sustained organizing work with middle school students at Morrill Elementary School.
9. From 2007–2014 VOYCE leveraged about $750,000 annually in funding for its member groups, almost $5 million in all.
10. See "Discipline: From zero tolerance to restorative justice," Maureen Kelleher, *Catalyst Chicago*, September 4, 2015, retrieved from: https://www.chicagoreporter.com/discipline-from-zero-tolerance-to-restorative-justice/; and "Restoring classroom justice," Lewis Wallace, *In These Times*, September 4, 2007, retrieved from: http://inthesetimes.com/article/3304/restoring_classroom_justice. See also COFI's *Parent to parent guide* (Power-PAC 2015).
11. *Failed policies, broken futures* (VOYCE 2011); *Discipline practices in Chicago schools* (Stevens 2015).
12. See *Failed policies, broken futures* (VOYCE 2011). According to Project NIA, the Chicago Police Department reported 6,430 school-based arrests in 2010, with Black students accounting for 74% and Latinx students for 22%; see *Policing Chicago Public Schools* (Kaba and Edwards 2012: 8). See also *Handcuffs in hallways* (Mbekeani-Wiley 2017).
13. Juan is a pseudonym. See *Failed policies, broken futures* (VOYCE 2011: 7).
14. See "Parent, student groups criticize charter schools' student fines," Noreen S. Ahmed-Ullah, *Chicago Tribune*, February 14, 201, retrieved from: https://www.chicagotribune.com/news/ct-xpm-2012-02-14-ct-met-charter-fines-20120214-story.html and "State bill would limit suspensions, end fines for students," Noreen S. Ahmed-Ullah, *Chicago Tribune*, April 16, 2014, retrieved from: https://www.chicagotribune.com/news/ct-xpm-2014-04-16-chi-school-discipline-illinois-20140416-story.html.
15. See "More tolerance in CPS code of conduct," Noreen S. Ahmed-Ullah, *Chicago Tribune*, July 28, 2011, retrieved from: https://www.chicagotribune.com/news/ct-xpm-2011-07-28-ct-met-cps-code-of-conduct-20110728-story.html. The district

made more substantial changes in the code of conduct in 2014 after VOYCE launched the SB100 campaign. In interviews for this project, district officials report appreciating the role of VOYCE as both providing a push from the outside and working on code revision committees, but they also believe that internal processes were moving the district toward reform as well.

16. See *Interventions* (Contractor and Staats 2014).
17. The opposition of Chicago Public Schools is reported in "State bill would limit suspensions, end fines for students," Noreen S. Ahmed-Ullah, *Chicago Tribune*, April 16, 2014, retrieved from: https://www.chicagotribune.com/news/ct-xpm-2014-04-16-chi-school-discipline-illinois-20140416-story.html. Participants interviewed for this project, however, reported differing views on the role of the district. VOYCE and other advocates reported that, although the district did not support the bill, they did not aggressively oppose it either. District officials said that the district supported some clauses of the bill and not others.
18. See "Campaign for Common Sense Discipline fact sheet," available at: https://voyceproject.org/wp-content/uploads/2014/04/Fact-Sheet-1.pdf.
19. See "Campaign for Common Sense Discipline fact sheet," available at: https://voyceproject.org/wp-content/uploads/2014/04/Fact-Sheet-1.pdf; *Opportunities suspended* (Losen and Gillespie 2012).
20. Scholars of cognitive science recognize that people often offer explanations of their actions, like listening to the stories of students in this case, when possibly unconscious factors like the changes in political context, also matter; see *The righteous mind* (Haidt 2012). On changing dynamics in the Democratic Party, see *Brown is the new white* (Phillips 2016). On conservatives and criminal justice reform, see *Prison break* (Dagan and Teles 2016).
21. Data compiled by the Illinois State Board of Education and reported in "Data reporting and collections: Expulsions, suspensions and truants by district" and "Policy: School discipline," available at: www.isbe.net.
22. The campaign to save Dyett is described in *#FightForDyett* (Brown 2018).
23. A different version of the material in this chapter appears in *Our stories are powerful* (Moyer, Warren, and King 2020), which includes an extended discussion of the role of storytelling.

Chapter 7

1. See *Why study the US South?* (Morris and Monroe 2009) and *A new majority research bulletin* (Suitts 2015). See also *Social justice organizing in the U.S. South* (Institute for Southern Studies 2009).
2. On student demographics, see "FY2019 District Profile Report," Ohio Department of Education, available at: http://education.ohio.gov/Topics/Finance-and-Funding/School-Payment-Reports/District-Profile-Reports/FY2019-District-Profile-Report.
3. See *Know the gap* (Learn to Earn Dayton 2017: 25–27).

4. See "Dayton Public to limit suspensions," Jeremy P. Kelley, *Dayton Daily News*, June 18, 2014, retrieved from: https://www.daytondailynews.com/news/dayton-public-limit-suspensions/uM7yB628rYnS1OBX1uQNnL/; and "Law will change Ohio school safety, behavior, suspensions," Jeremy P. Kelley and Laura A. Bischoff, *Dayton Daily News*, July 8, 2018, retrieved from: https://www.daytondailynews.com/news/laws-will-change-ohio-school-safety-behavior-suspensions/Z4zV9fc5dNu0Lrbx0oitrJ/. Further treatment of RJN can be found in *"I can't make a teacher love my son"* (Sankara-Jabar 2018).

5. On the conditions at Tallulah, see "Profits at a juvenile prison come with a chilling cost," Fox Butterfield, *New York Times*, July 15, 1998, retrieved from: https://www.nytimes.com/1998/07/15/us/hard-time-special-report-profits-juvenile-prison-come-with-chilling-cost.html. For the quotation from FFLIC, see "Act 1225 mapping project," FFLIC website, available at: https://www.fflic.org/act-1225-mapping-project. On the impact of the 2003 reform, see the resources available on the Louisiana Center for Children's Rights website at: www.laccr.org.

6. See *Pushed out* (Sullivan and Morgan 2010). On the connection between schools and prisons in New Orleans, see *The prison school* (Simmons 2017).

7. See "Now an all-charter district, New Orleans schools experiment still faces questions," Della Hasselle, *The Times-Picayune*, August 12, 2019, retrieved from: https://www.nola.com/news/education/article_30fbef6e-b476-11e9-a3b5-57480c7a30f7.html. For further discussion of charter schools in New Orleans, see *Charter schools* (Buras 2014) and *Twenty-first-century Jim Crow Schools* (Sanders, Stovall, and White 2018).

8. There is a robust scholarly debate about the effectiveness of charter schools in raising test scores in New Orleans, but it largely takes place out of historical context that matters for community perspectives; see *"Drenched in the past"* (Jabbar 2015).

9. Louisiana allows suspensions for willful disobedience, disturbing school, and treating authority with disrespect. DSC's Accountability Guidelines available at: www.dignityinschools.org.

10. "Gwinnett group accuses school police officers of assaulting student," Eric Stirgus, *Atlanta Journal Constitution*, April 20, 2017, retrieved from: https://www.ajc.com/news/local-education/gwinnett-group-accuses-school-police-officers-assaulting-student/OrlEsDALCIZkZQjTrA0w9K/.

11. See "Stopping the cycle: Parent group ruffles feathers with hard-line approach," Josh Green, *Gwinnett Daily Post*, January 10, 2009, retrieved from: https://www.gwinnettdailypost.com/archive/stopping-the-cycle-parent-group-ruffles-feathers-with-hard-line-approach/article_07189b3e-7614-5010-b4e2-af00a4d32cae.html.

12. A Black man was elected to the school board in 2018, the first person of color elected. On the racial composition of the school board, see "Diverse field in Gwinnett school board race could bring a first," Arlinda Smith Broady, *Atlanta Journal-Constitution*, May 17, 2018, retrieved from: https://www.ajc.com/news/local-education/diverse-field-gwinnett-school-board-race-could-bring-first/nL3WVdYZ1TVltYerJgcQ9K/.

13. 2017–2018 data reported in *From lockers to lockdown* (The Georgia Coalition Working to End the School-to-Prison Pipeline 2019: 8). See also "Complaints of disciplinary inequity prompt Gwinnett schools' review," Arlinda Smith Brody, *Atlanta*

Journal Constitution, November 24, 2019, retrieved from: https://www.ajc.com/news/local/complaints-disciplinary-inequity-prompt-gwinnett-schools-review/9u3HscyB2nB95AJfJUmu5K/.

14. See "Stopping the cycle: Parent group ruffles feathers with hard-line approach," Josh Green, *Gwinnett Daily Post*, January 10, 2009, retrieved from: https://www.gwinnettdailypost.com/archive/stopping-the-cycle-parent-group-ruffles-feathers-with-hard-line-approach/article_07189b3e-7614-5010-b4e2-af00a4d32cae.html.

15. See "Chesterfield parent advocate arrested at Meadowbrook High," NBC12, April 30, 2015, retrieved from: https://www.nbc12.com/story/28936299/chesterfield-parent-advocate-arrested-at-meadowbrook-high/. "Advocate prevails in dispute with Chesterfield school division," Markus Schmidt, *Richmond Times-Dispatch*, August 19, 2016, retrieved from: https://www.richmond.com/news/local/advocate-prevails-in-dispute-with-chesterfield-school-division/article_023649b0-e596-5803-ac2d-5d4508d650ff.html.

16. "Henrico mom uses billboard to slam school's treatment of students with special needs," NBC12, September 30, 2016, retrieved from: https://www.nbc12.com/story/33284280/henrico-mom-uses-billboard-to-slam-schools-treatment-of-students-with-special-needs/.

17. "Henrico court upholds advocate's trespassing conviction on eve of Anne Holton report on special education in the county," C. Suarez Rojas, *Richmond Times-Dispatch*, September 27, 2018, retrieved from: https://www.richmond.com/news/local/henrico-court-upholds-advocate-s-trespassing-conviction-on-eve-of/article_c9c1d7de-a483-5298-862a-17122b9f762d.html.

18. See *Race, reason and massive resistance* (Mays 2008). Demographic data from Henrico County Schools website, available at: https://henricoschools.us/.

19. See *Suspended progress* (Langberg and Ciolfi 2016) and *Opportunities suspended* (Losen and Gillespie 2012).

20. See *A review of equity and parent engagement in special education in Henrico County Public Schools* (Holton et al. 2018).

21. See "Advocate escalated Henrico's legal fees to shine light on racial inequality and shortcomings in special education services," C. Suarez Rojas, *Richmond Times-Dispatch*, September 30, 2018, retrieved from: https://www.richmond.com/news/local/advocate-escalated-henrico-s-legal-fees-to-shine-light-on/article_68c02467-5ec6-5b85-ac4f-f523b27278fc.html. For the report, see *A review of equity and parent engagement in special education in Henrico County Public Schools* (Holton et al. 2018).

Chapter 8

1. Shakara's last name has been withheld. News account of the assault and quotation in "A classroom conflict between an officer and a student in South Carolina," Krishnadev Calamur, *The Atlantic,* October 27, 2015, retrieved from: https://www.theatlantic.com/national/archive/2015/10/south-carolina-spring-valley-officer-student/412588/.

2. "150,000 sign petition calling for prosecution of officer fired for flipping student," Polly Mosendz, *Newsweek*, December 18, 2015, retrieved from: https://www. newsweek.com/petition-calling-prosecution-officer-fire-flipping-student-reaches-150000-407025. "United Nations panel recommends changes to U.S. school discipline," Evie Blad, *Education Week's blogs*, February 1, 2016, retrieved from: http:// blogs.edweek.org/edweek/rulesforengagement/2016/02/united_nations_panel_ recommends_changes_to_us_school_discipline.html?qs=%22disturbing+sch ools%22. "No charges for 2 girls, officer in viral Spring Valley video incident," Clif LeBlanc, *The State*, September 2, 2016, retrieved from: https://www.thestate.com/ news/local/article99603512.html.

3. Niya quoted in *We came to learn* (Advancement Project and Alliance for Educational Justice 2018b: 57).

4. On the movement's education platform, see "How Black Lives Matter activists plan to fix schools," Emily Deruy, *The Atlantic*, August 5, 2016, retrieved from: https://www. theatlantic.com/education/archive/2016/08/the-ambitious-education-plan-of-the-black-lives-matter-movement/494711/.

5. See *We came to learn* (Advancement Project and Alliance for Educational Justice 2018b: 41–43) and "Video captures violent encounter between school cop and Benjamin Franklin senior," Victor Fiorillo, *Philadelphia*, May 10, 2016, retrieved from: https://www.phillymag.com/news/2016/05/10/video-ben-franklin-high-school-cop/.

6. *Derailed: The schoolhouse to jailhouse track* (Browne 2003). On Denver, see "Role of police redefined in Denver schools," Julie Poppen, *Chalkbeat*, February 19, 2013, retrieved from: https://chalkbeat.org/posts/co/2013/02/19/role-of-police-redefined-in-denver-schools/.

7. See *We came to learn* (Advancement Project and Alliance for Educational Justice 2018b: 34–37). See also *The people's plan for police-free schools* (Black Organizing Project 2019).

8. Quoted in *We came to learn* (Advancement Project and Alliance for Educational Justice 2018b: 37).

9. See *Counselors not cops* (Dignity in Schools Campaign 2016a) and *A resource guide on counselors not cops* (Dignity in Schools Campaign 2016b); see also "Responding to tragedy in our schools: Learning from Columbine in the aftermath of Sandy Hook," Dignity in Schools Campaign letter to Vice President Joseph Biden, January 5, 2013 (unpublished).

10. *We came to learn* (Advancement Project and Alliance for Educational Justice 2018b) and *We came to learn action kit* (Advancement Project and Alliance for Educational Justice 2018a). Text of the 2019 resolution supplied by Jonathan Stith.

11. *Cops and no counselors* (Whitaker et al. n.d.). On the research on causes of arrest, and a discussion of LGBTQ and immigrant students, see *We came to learn* (Advancement Project and Alliance for Educational Justice 2018b). On the policing of Black girls, see *Black girls matter* (Crenshaw, Ocen, and Nanda 2015).

12. For a review of the research, see *Cops and no counselors* (Whitaker et al. n.d.: 6–7). For a broader discussion of police in schools, see *The real school safety problem* (Kupchik 2016).

13. *The $3.4 trillion mistake* (Communities United et al. n.d.) and *The $746 million a year school-to-prison pipeline* (Terenzi, Foster, and Urban Youth Collaborative youth leaders 2017).

14. "TDSB votes down police presence in high schools," Andrea Gordon, *Toronto Star*, November 22, 2017, retrieved from: https://www.thestar.com/yourtoronto/education/2017/11/22/tdsb-votes-down-police-presence-in-high-schools.html.

15. *How Black Oaklanders finally expelled the school police* (Rios 2020). See also "The end of police in schools," Lauren Camera, *US News & World Report*, June 12, 2020, retrieved from: https://www.usnews.com/news/the-report/articles/2020-06-12/schools-districts-end-contracts-with-police-amid-ongoing-protests.

16. Quoted in *Black girls matter* (Daniel and White 2018: 130). See also *Telling our stories* (Daniel and Valladares 2016).

17. See *Black girls MIA: A herstory*, Miami Black Girls Matter Coalition, available at: https://www.blackgirlsmia.org/.

18. *The hidden truth* (Power U Center for Social Change and Advancement Project 2017).

19. See *The school girls deserve* (Hudson and Brathwaite n.d.).

20. See *Black girls matter* (Crenshaw, Ocen, and Nanda 2015) and *Pushout* (Morris 2016).

21. Quoted in "The school-to-prison pipeline affects girls of color, but reform efforts pass them by," Ruth Jeannoel, *The Guardian* (U.S. edition), June 11, 2015, retrieved from: https://www.theguardian.com/commentisfree/2015/jun/11/school-prison-pipeline-girls-of-color-reform.

22. For changes in the Chicago Teacher Union as well as a broader discussion of the impact of attacks on teachers unions, see *A fight for the soul of public education* (Ashby and Bruno 2016).

23. See *Restorative practices* (Advancement Project et al. 2014).

24. See *Taking restorative practices school-wide* (Anyon 2016).

25. Quotations from Sally Lee and Elana "E.M." Eisen-Markowitz in this section are taken from the essay "Teachers Unite!" (Lee and Eisen-Markowitz 2018).

26. See *Teachers talk* (Sullivan and Keeney 2008).

27. The Growing Fairness documentary and toolkit are available at: www.teachersunite.org.

28. See, for example, *Strategies for parent engagement* (Community Organizing and Family Issues 2016) and *Parent-to-parent guide* (Power-PAC 2015). COFI's organizing is practiced through its sister organization called Power-PAC.

29. See "Teacher's guide to building a restorative classroom," Safe Schools Consortium, available at: https://communitiesunited.org/sites/apncorganizing.org/files/RJ_handbook.pdf.

Conclusion

1. On policy changes across districts and states, see "Suspensions are down in U.S. schools but large racial gaps remain," Anya Kamenetz, National Public Radio, December 17, 2018, retrieved from: https://www.npr.org/2018/12/17/677508707/

suspensions-are-down-in-u-s-schools-but-large-racial-gaps-remain; see also *Interventions* (Contractor and Staats 2014).

2. On national trends, see "Suspensions are down in U.S. schools but large racial gaps remain," Anya Kamenetz, National Public Radio, December 17, 2018, retrieved from: https://www.npr.org/2018/12/17/677508707/suspensions-are-down-in-u-s-schools-but-large-racial-gaps-remain. A more recent study found that rates of suspension fell at secondary schools but not at elementary schools; see *Lost opportunities* (Losen and Martinez 2020). As of this writing, the 2015–2016 year was the last year in which trend data have been analyzed; the Department of Education had just released the 2017–2018 data.

3. On California trends, see "Suspension, expulsion rates fall sharply in California, but racial and ethnic disparities remain," Carolyn Jones, EdSource, Oakland: EdSource, November 1, 2017, retrieved from: https://edsource.org/2017/suspension-expulsion-rates-fall-sharply-in-california-public-schools-but-racial-disparities-remain/589722; see also *Years of reform efforts* (Jones 2020) and *The unequal impact* (Losen and Martin 2018). For Los Angeles, see "School discipline data reports-suspensions, 2016–2017 School Year," *LAUSD*, http://schoolinfosheet.lausd.net.

4. See "Student suspensions fall sharply in New York City," Alex Zimmerman, *Chalkbeat*, November 1, 2019, retrieved from https://ny.chalkbeat.org/2019/11/1/21109129/student-suspensions-fall-sharply-in-new-york-city-reversing-an-unusual-bump-the-year-before. On Chicago, see "Data reporting and collections: Expulsions, suspensions and truants by district" and "Policy: School discipline," available at: www.isbe.net.

5. Trend data from the Civil Rights Data Collection as reported by the ACLU in *Cops and no counselors* (Whitaker et al. n.d.: 35). Although reporting arrests and referrals has been required of districts since 2009–2010, there appears to be a considerable amount of missing data that affects the reliability of estimates and trends; see *Lost opportunities* (Losen and Martinez 2020).

6. See, for example, the *Culturally relevant and culturally responsive schools toolkit* developed by the West Dayton Youth Task Force and promoted by the Dignity in Schools Campaign for its 2017 Week of Action, available at: http://dignityinschools.org/wp-content/uploads/2017/10/CRC_Toolkit_Booklet_ToPrint.pdf; See also the endorsement of the #WeChoose campaign by the Dignity in Schools Campaign, listed at: https://j4jalliance.com/campaigns.

7. See, for example, CADRE's latest in a series of shadow reports, *How can you love the kids but hate the parents?* (CADRE and Public Counsel 2017) and *The 5th annual Denver community accountability report* (Padres & Jóvenes Unidos 2016).

8. See the *Handbook of critical race theory in education* (Lynn and Dixson 2013), *Leading change* (Ganz 2010), and *"Our stories are powerful"* (Moyer, Warren, and King 2020). For a review of theories that explain how advocacy groups influence policy decisions, see *Testing theories* (Burstein 2020).

9. For a discussion of how the Industrial Areas Foundation framed its work, which included the pioneering Alliance Schools, see *Dry bones rattling* (Warren 2001). For a

critique of universalistic approaches that do not target racism, see *Universalism and deconcentration* (Thompson 1998).

10. For further discussion of the promise and obstacles to intersectional organizing and cross-movement solidarity, see *Intersectional organizing and educational justice movements* (Warren et al. 2021).

11. See *From boarding schools to suspension boards* (Community College Equity Assessment Lab 2019).

12. For further discussion of storytelling as a force for legislative action, see "Our stories are powerful" (Moyer, Warren, and King 2020).

13. For a discussion of the role of alliances as well as policy windows in the effort to win new federal guidance on school discipline, see also *Grassroots organizing* (Mediratta 2012).

14. For the classic discussion of the influence of political opportunities in social movements, see *Political process and the development of Black insurgency* (McAdam 1982).

15. See "Trump picks billionaire Betsy DeVos, school voucher advocate, as education secretary," Emma Brown, *Washington Post*, November 23, 2016, retrieved from: https://www.washingtonpost.com/local/education/trump-picks-billionaire-betsy-devos-school-voucher-advocate-as-education-secretary/2016/11/23/c3d66b94-af96-11e6-840f-e3ebab6bcdd3_story.html and "Great news: Administration rescinds Obama school-discipline guidance," Roger Clegg, *National Review*, December 21, 2018, retrieved from: https://www.nationalreview.com/corner/great-news-administration-rescinds-obama-school-discipline-guidance/. For a broader analysis of the rise of white Nationalism and the Trump administration, see *Alt-America* (Neiwert 2018).

16. See, for example, the Marjory Stoneman Douglas High School Public Safety Act passed in Florida, available at: http://www.fldoe.org/safe-schools/.

17. See the text of the Counseling not Criminalization Act, for example, at: https://www.murphy.senate.gov/imo/media/doc/Counseling%20Not%20Criminalization%20in%20Schools%20Act_FINAL.pdf.

18. See DSC's "Membership and decision-making policy," revised 2013, available at www.dignityinschools.org.

19. See the report by the co-founder of the Advancement Project that helped provide a foundation for the formation of the new organization, *Louder than words* (Hair 2001); for a more recent treatment of movement lawyering co-written by the lawyer who directed the Advancement Project's Ending the Schoolhouse-to-Jailhouse Track project, see *It's about power, not policy* (Freeman and Freeman 2016).

20. For a comprehensive treatment of how professional advocates came to dominate the immigrant rights movement, which considers many of these factors, see *The immigrant rights movement* (Nicholls 2019).

21. For a discussion of how the strategic capacity and effectiveness of movements increase when they include diverse leadership as well as transparency and democratic processes, see *Resources and resourcefulness* (Ganz 2000) and *Why David sometimes wins* (Ganz 2009).

22. For a discussion of some of these tensions in the civil rights movement, see Chapter 2; see also *The origins of the civil rights movement* (Morris 1984) and *Parting the waters* (Branch 1988).

23. See *Local citizenship in a global age* (Stahl 2020).

24. For a thoughtful analysis of the limits of localism, see *Contesting community* (DeFilippis, Fisher, and Shragge 2010).

25. See *#FightForDyett* (Brown 2018).

26. On the IAF, see *Dry bones rattling* (Warren 2001); for other treatments that stress the importance of deep as well as broad organizing, see *Faith in action* (Wood 2002), *Why David sometimes wins* (Ganz 2009), and *How organizations develop activists* (Han 2014). For the classic treatment of the power of protest movements, see *Poor people's movements* (Piven and Cloward 1977). On contemporary global protest, see *The age of mass protest* (Brannen, Haig, and Schmidt 2020).

27. The Brothers, Sons, Selves Coalition mobilized large numbers to win the School Climate Bill of Rights in Los Angeles, but that has not been the norm in the school-to-prison pipeline movement.

28. For further discussion of this tradition, see *How long? How long?* (Robnett 1997) and *Community organizing or organizing community?* (Stall and Stoecker 1998).

29. On healing justice, see *Hope and healing in urban education* (Ginwright 2016) and *Justice as healing* (McCaslin 2005).

30. See *Short-changed* (Pittz and Sen 2006). A recent study found that only 0.8% of education philanthropy, or $108 million out of $14 billion, went to fund efforts to address the root causes of racial inequities in education by empowering communities through organizing and its associated advocacy work; see *#JusticeIsTheFoundation* (Schott Foundation for Public Education 2021).

31. See *Lost opportunities* (Losen and Martinez 2020), *11 million days lost* (Losen and Whitaker 2018), *The unequal impact* (Losen and Martin 2018), *Schools report fewer out-of-school suspensions* (Harper, Ryberg, and Temkin 2018), and *School climate and safety* (U.S. Department of Education 2018).

32. See *Schools report fewer out-of-school suspensions* (Harper, Ryberg, and Temkin 2018).

33. See *An analysis of school funding equity* (Morgan and Amerikaner 2018), *Inequitable opportunity to learn* (Cardichon et al. 2020), *The testing charade* (Koretz 2017), *For white folks who teach in the hood* (Emdin 2016), *Death by a thousand cuts* (Journey for Justice Alliance 2014), and *The new political economy of urban education* (Lipman 2011).

34. See the National Equity Atlas produced by PolicyLink and the USC Program for Environmental and Regional Equity, available at: https://nationalequityatlas.org. See also *Whither opportunity?* (Duncan and Murnane 2011).

35. For a discussion of intersectionality and promising examples in the educational justice movement, see *Lift us up! Don't push us out!* (Warren 2018a) and *Intersectional organizing* (Warren et al. 2021). For a pioneering discussion of connecting education movements to broader policy change, see *Radical possibilities* (Anyon 2005).

36. For a discussion of obstacles to intersectional organizing, see *Intersectional organizing* (Warren et al. 2021).

Appendix

1. On the purposes of qualitative research, see *Report of the Workshop on Scientific Foundations of Qualitative Research* (Ragin, Nagel, and White 2004). I generally follow the approach to qualitative research and design discussed in *Qualitative research design* (Maxwell 2013) and *Causal explanation* (Maxwell 2004). On case study research, I find the following useful: *Case study research* (Yin 2003) and *Case studies and theory development* (George and Bennett 2005). On qualitative data collection and analysis, I draw from *Analyzing social settings* (Lofland et al. 2006) and *Qualitative interviewing* (Rubin and Rubin 2005), among others.
2. To help guide and inform data analysis, I draw from *The coding manual* (Saldana 2015) and *Qualitative data analysis* (Miles, Huberman, and Saldana 2014).
3. Although scholars need to be cautious in the causal claims they make, process tracing allows for linking processes to outcomes, which is an important type of causal explanation; see *Causal explanation* (Maxwell 2004) and *Process tracing* (Bennett and Checkel 2015).
4. I generally follow the advice in *Qualitative research design* (Maxwell 2013) on identifying bias and addressing validity threats.
5. On rigor in community engaged scholarship, see *Is collaborative, community-engaged scholarship more rigorous?* (Warren et al. 2018). On relationships in and processes of community engaged scholarship more broadly, see, for example, *Just research* (Fine 2018) and *Decolonizing educational research* (Patel 2015).
6. On researcher positionality, I have been influenced by *Black feminist thought* (Collins 2000) and *Race, culture, and researcher positionality* (Milner 2007), among others.

References

Advancement Project. 2005. *Education on lockdown: The schoolhouse to jailhouse track.* Washington, DC: Advancement Project.

Advancement Project, AFT, NEA, and National Opportunity to Learn Campaign. 2014. *Restorative practices: Fostering healthy relationships & promoting positive discipline in schools: A guide for educators.* Washington, DC: Advancement Project, AFT, NEA, and National Opportunity to Learn Campaign. http://schottfoundation.org/resources/restorative-practices-toolkit.

Advancement Project, and Alliance for Educational Justice. 2018a. *We came to learn action kit.* Washington, DC: Advancement Project & Alliance for Educational Justice. https://advancementproject.org/wp-content/uploads/ActionKitView/index.html#page=28.

Advancement Project, and Alliance for Educational Justice. 2018b. *We came to learn: A call to action for police-free schools.* Washington, DC: Advancement Project. https://advancementproject.org/wecametolearn/.

Advancement Project, Alliance for Educational Justice, and GSA Network. 2012. *Two wrongs don't make a right: Why zero tolerance is not the solution to bullying.* Washington, DC: Advancement Project. www.advancementproject.org.

Advancement Project, Equality Federation Institute, and GSA Network. 2015. *Power in partnership: Building connections at the intersections of racial justice and LGBTQ movements to end the school-to-prison pipeline.* Washington, DC: Advancement Project. www.advancementproject.org.

Advancement Project and Harvard Civil Rights Project. 2000. *Opportunities suspended: The devastating consequences of zero tolerance and school discipline.* Cambridge, MA: Advancement Project and Harvard Civil Rights Project.

Alexander, Michelle. 2010. *The new Jim Crow: Mass incarceration in the age of colorblindness.* New York: New Press.

Allen, Terry, Isaac Bryan, Andrew Guerero, Alvin Teng, and Kelly Lytle-Hernandez. 2018. *Policing our students: An analysis of L.A. School Police Department data (2014–2017).* Los Angeles: The Million Dollar Hoods Project. http://milliondollarhoods.org/wp-content/uploads/2018/10/Policing-Our-Students-MDH-Report-Final.pdf.

Amenta, Edwin, Neal Caren, Elizabeth Chiarello, and Yang Su. 2010. "The political consequences of social movements," *Annual Review of Sociology,* 36: 287–307.

Amenta, Edwin, and Francesca Polletta. 2019. "The Cultural Impacts of Social Movements," *Annual Review of Sociology,* 45: 279–299.

American Bar Association. 2013. *National inventory of collateral consequences of conviction.* Washington, DC: American Bar Association. https://niccc.csgjusticecenter.org/.

Ammerman, Nancy Tatom. 1996. *Congregations and community.* New Brunswick, NJ: Rutgers University Press.

Andrews, Kenneth T. 2004. *Freedom is a constant struggle: The Mississippi civil rights movement and its legacy.* Chicago: University of Chicago Press.

Andrews, Kenneth T., and Bob Edwards. 2004. "Advocacy organizations in the US political process," *Annual Review of Sociology*, 30: 479–506.

Andrews, Kenneth T., and Sarah Gaby. 2015. "Local protest and federal policy: The impact of the civil rights movement on the 1964 Civil Rights Act," *Sociological Forum*, 30: 509–527.

Anyon, Jean. 2005. *Radical possibilities: Public policy, urban education, and a new social movement*. New York: Routledge.

Anyon, Yolanda. 2016. *Taking restorative practices school-wide: Insights from three schools in Denver*. Denver: Denver School-Based Restorative Practices Partnership.

Ashby, Steven, and Robert Bruno. 2016. *A fight for the soul of public education: The story of the Chicago teachers strike*. Ithaca, NY: Cornell University Press.

Atlas, John. 2010. *Seeds of change: The story of ACORN, America's most controversial antipoverty community organizing group*. Nashville, TN: Vanderbilt University Press.

Baggetta, Matthew, Hahrie Han, Chaeyoon Lim, Kenneth T. Andrews, and Marshall L. Ganz. 2010. "Leadership, membership, and voice: Civic associations that work," *American Journal of Sociology*, 115(4): 1191–1242.

Bahena, Sofia, North Cooc, Rachel Currie-Rubin, Paul Kuttner, and Monica Ng. 2012. *Disrupting the school-to-prison pipeline*. Cambridge, MA: Harvard Educational Review.

Baker, Bruce D. 2018. *Educational inequality and school finance: Why money matters for America's students*. Cambridge, MA: Harvard Education Press.

Balfanz, Robert, Vaughn Byrnes, and Joanna Fox. 2014. "Sent home and put off track: The antecedents, disproportionalities, and consequences of being suspended in the 9th grade." Pp. 151–165 in Daniel J. Losen (ed.), *Closing the discipline gap: Equitable remedies for excessive exclusion*. New York: Teachers College Press.

Bennett, Andrew, and Jeffrey T. Checkel. 2015. *Process tracing: From metaphor to analytic tool*. New York: Cambridge University Press.

Bennett, William J., John DiIulio, and John P. Walters. 1996. *Body count: Moral poverty—and how to win America's war against crime and drugs*. New York: Simon & Schuster.

Black, Derek W. 2016. *Ending zero tolerance: The crisis of absolute school discipline*. New York: NYU Press.

Black Organizing Project. 2019. *The people's plan for police-free schools*. Oakland, CA: Black Organizing Project.

Bolton, Charles C. 2005. *The hardest deal of all: The battle over school integration in Mississippi, 1870–1980*. Jackson: University Press of Mississippi.

Bosi, Lorenzo, Marco Giugno, and Katrin Uba. 2016. *The consequences of social movements*. New York: Cambridge University Press.

Boyte, Harry C. 2004. *Everyday politics: Reconnecting citizens and public life*. Philadelphia: University of Pennsylvania Press.

Branch, Taylor. 1988. *Parting the waters: America in the King years, 1954–63*. New York: Simon & Schuster.

Branch, Taylor. 1998. *Pillar of fire: America in the King years, 1963–65*. New York: Simon & Schuster.

Brannen, Samuel J., Christian S. Haig, and Katherine Schmidt. 2020. *The age of mass protests: Understanding an escalating global trend*. Washington, DC: Center for Strategic and International Studies.

Brown, Jitu. 2018. "#FightForDyett: Fighting back against school closings and the journey for Justice." Pp. 73–81 in Mark R. Warren and David Goodman (eds.), *Lift us up! Don't push us out! Voices from the front lines of the educational justice movement.* Boston: Beacon Press.

Browne, Judith A. 2003. *Derailed: The schoolhouse to jailhouse track.* Washington, DC: Advancement Project.

Buras, Kristen L. 2014. *Charter schools, race, and urban space: Where the market meets grassroots resistance.* New York: Routledge.

Burstein, Paul. 2020. "Testing theories about advocacy and public policy," *Perspectives on Politics* 19(1): 148–159.

CADRE. 2006. *More education, less suspension: A call to action to stop the pushout crisis in South Los Angeles.* Los Angeles: CADRE.

CADRE. 2007. *A parent-led victory in the fight to end pushout in Los Angeles schools.* Los Angeles: CADRE. http://www.cadre-la.org/core/wp-content/uploads/2011/03/CADRE_parent_led.pdf.

CADRE, and Justice Matters. 2004. *We interrupt this crisis—with our side of the story.* Los Angeles: CADRE and Justice Matters.

CADRE, and Public Counsel. 2017. *How can you love the kids but hate the parents? A shadow report on the unfulfilled promises of LAUSD school discipline reform in South LA.* Los Angeles: CADRE and Public Counsel.

California State Auditor. 2016. *The CalGang criminal intelligence system, California state auditor report 2015-130.* Sacramento: California State Auditor. http://www.auditor.ca.gov/pdfs/reports/2015-130.pdf.

Cardichon, Jessica, Linda Darling-Hammond, Man Yang, Caitlin Scott, Patrick M. Shields, and Dion Burns. 2020. *Inequitable opportunity to learn: Student access to certified and experienced teachers.* Palo Alto, CA: Learning Policy Institute.

Carson, Clayborne. 1981. *In struggle: SNCC and the Black awakening of the 1960s.* Cambridge, MA: Harvard University Press.

Carter, Prudence L., Russell Skiba, Mariella I. Arredondo, and Mica Pollock. 2017. "You can't fix what you don't look at: Acknowledging race in addressing racial discipline disparities," *Urban Education*, 52(2): 207–235.

Cerrone, Kathleen M. 1999. "The Gun-Free Schools Act of 1994: Zero tolerance takes aim at procedural due process," *Pace Law Review*, 20(1): 131–188.

Chakara, Mackenzie. 2017. *From preschool to prison: The criminalization of Black girls.* Washington, DC: Center for American Progress. https://www.americanprogress.org/issues/race/news/2017/12/08/443972/preschool-prison-criminalization-black-girls/.

Charron, Katherine Mellen. 2009. *Freedom's teacher: The life of Septima Clark.* Chapel Hill: University of North Carolina Press.

Chin, Maisie, Ruth Cusick, Laura Faer, Amy Lawrence Cornichon, Rob McGowan, Agustín Ruelas, and Bryan Ventura. 2010. *Redefining dignity in our schools: A shadow report on school-wide positive behavior support implementation in South Los Angeles, 2007–2010.* Los Angeles: CADRE, Mental Health Advocacy Services and Public Counsel Law Center.

Chow, Mamie, Laurie Olsen, Ruben Lizardo, and Carol Dowel. 2001. *Mapping the field of school reform organizing in California: Los Angeles and the San Francisco Bay Area.* Providence, RI: California Tomorrow and Annenberg Institute for School Reform at Brown University.

Collins, Patricia Hill. 2000. *Black feminist thought: Knowledge, consciousness, and the politics of empowerment.* New York: Routledge.

Communities United, Make the Road New York, Padres & Jóvenes Unidos, and Right on Justice Alliance. n.d. *The $3.4 trillion mistake: The cost of mass incarceration and criminalization, and how justice reinvestment can build a better future for all.* Chicago: Communities United, Make the Road New York, Padres & Jóvenes Unidos, and Right on Justice Alliance. www.reinvest4justice.org.

Community College Equity Assessment Lab. 2019. *From boarding schools to suspension boards: Suspensions and expulsions of Native American students in California public schools.* San Diego: Community College Equity Assessment Lab. https://cceal.org/wp-content/uploads/2019/09/Suspension-Boards-Final.pdf.

Community Organizing and Family Issues. 2016. *Strategies for parent engagement.* Chicago: Community Organizing and Family Issues.

Community Rights Campaign. 2009. *End the tickets: Alternatives for youth campaign.* Los Angeles: Labor Community Strategy Center.

Community Rights Campaign. 2013. *Black, Brown, and over-policed in L.A. schools: Structural proposals to end the school-to-prison pipeline in the Los Angeles Unified School District and to build a national movement to stop the mass incarceration of Black and Latino communities.* Los Angeles: Labor Community Strategy Center.

Community Rights Campaign, and DSC-LA. 2010. *Police in LAUSD schools: The need for accountability and alternatives.* Los Angeles: Community Rights Campaign.

Contractor, Danya, and Cheryl Staats. 2014. *Interventions to address racialized discipline disparities and school "push out."* Columbus, OH: Kirwan Institute for the Study of Race and Ethnicity.

Cookson, Peter W., Jr. 2020. *A world of hardship: Deep poverty and the struggle for educational equity.* Learning Policy Institute: Palo Alto, CA. https://learningpolicyinstitute.org/blog/covid-deep-poverty-struggle-education-equity.

Crenshaw, Kimberlé Williams, Priscilla Ocen, and Jyoti Nanda. 2015. *Black girls matter: Pushed out, over policed, and underprotected.* New York: African American Policy Forum & Center for Intersectionality and Social Policy Studies. www.aapf.org.

Dagan, David, and Steven Michael Teles. 2016. *Prison break: Why conservatives turned against mass incarceration.* New York: Oxford University Press.

Dahill-Brown, Sara E. 2019. *Education, equity, and the states: How variations in state governance make or break reform.* Cambridge, MA: Harvard Education Press.

Daniel, Julia, and Michelle Renee Valladares. 2016. "Telling our stories, claiming our space, and becoming change-makers: Lessons for the field from Black girls and women organizers." Pp. 203–221 in Jerusha O. Conner and Sonia M. Rosen (eds.), *Contemporary youth activism: Advancing social justice in the United States.* Santa Barbara, CA: Praeger.

Daniel, Julia, and Terrenda White. 2018. "Black girls matter: An intersectional analysis of young Black women's experiences and resistance to dominating forces in school." Pp. 44–56 in Norvella Carter and Michael Vavrus (eds.), *Intersectionality of race, ethnicity, class, and gender in teaching and teacher education: Movement toward equity in education.* Boston: Brill.

Darling-Hammond, Linda. 2007. "Race, inequality and educational accountability: The irony of 'No Child Left Behind,'" *Race Ethnicity and Education*, 10(3): 245–260.

Darling-Hammond, Linda. 2010. *The flat world and education: How America's commitment to equity will determine our future.* New York: Teachers College Press.

De la Torre, Marisa, Molly F. Gordon, Paul Moore, and Jennifer Cowhy. 2015. *School closings in Chicago.* Chicago: Consortium on Chicago School Research.

DeFilippis, James, Robert Fisher, and Eric Shragge. 2010. *Contesting community: The limits and potential of local organizing.* New Brunswick, NJ: Rutgers University Press.

Delaney, Ann. 2012. "Everyday heroes: The civil rights movement in Holmes County, Mississippi," Masters Thesis, SUNY Brookport.

Delgado, Gary. 1997. *Beyond the politics of place: New directions in community organizing in the 1990s.* Oakland, CA: Applied Research Center.

Dignity in Schools Campaign. 2016a. *Counselors not cops: Ending the regular presence of police in schools.* New York: Dignity in Schools Campaign. http://dignityinschools.org/wp-content/uploads/2017/10/DSC_Counselors_Not_Cops_Recommendations-1.pdf.

Dignity in Schools Campaign. 2016b. *A resource guide on counselors not cops.* New York: Dignity in Schools Campaign. http://www.dignityinschools.org/wp-content/uploads/2017/10/Resource_Guide-on-CNC-1.pdf.

Dignity in Schools Campaign. 2019. *A model code on education and dignity: Presenting a human rights framework for schools.* New York: Dignity in Schools Campaign. http://dignityinschools.org/toolkits/model-code/.

Dittmer, John. 1994. *Local people: The struggle for civil rights in Mississippi.* Urbana: University of Illinois Press.

Duncan, Greg J., and Richard J. Murnane. 2011. *Whither opportunity? Rising inequality, schools, and children's life chances.* New York: Russell Sage Foundation Press.

Edwards, Bob, and Michael W. Foley. 2003. "Social movement organizations beyond the beltway," *Mobilization,* 8: 85–105.

Emdin, Christopher. 2016. *For white folks who teach in the hood . . . and the rest of y'all too: Reality pedagogy and urban education.* Boston: Beacon Press.

Epstein, Rebecca, Erin Godfrey, Thalia Gonzalez, and Shabnam Javdani. 2020. *Data snapshot 2017–2018: National data on school discipline by race and gender.* Washington, DC: Georgetown Law Center on Poverty and Inequality and the RISE Research Team at New York University. https://genderjusticeandopportunity.georgetown.edu/wp-content/uploads/2020/12/National-Data-on-School-Discipline-by-Race-and-Gender.pdf.

Equal Justice Initiative. 2015. *Lynching in America: Confronting the legacy of racial terror.* Montgomery, AL: Equal Justice Initiative.

Ewing, Eve L. 2018. *Ghosts in the schoolyard: Racism and school closings on Chicago's South Side.* Chicago: University of Chicago Press.

Fabelo, Tony, Michael D. Thompson, Martha Plotkin, Dottie Carmichael, Miner P. Marchbanks III, and Eric A. Boot. 2011. *Breaking schools' rules: A statewide study on how school discipline relates to students' success and juvenile justice involvement.* New York: Council of State Governments Justice Center. https://knowledgecenter.csg.org.

Felker-Kantor, Max. 2018. *Policing Los Angeles: Race, resistance, and the rise of the LAPD.* Chapel Hill: UNC Press.

Fernández, Jesica S., Ben Kirshner, and Deana G. Lewis. "Strategies for systemic change: Youth community organizing to disrupt the school-to-prison nexus." Pp. 93–112 in Sofia Bahena, North Cooc, Rachel Currie-Rubin, Paul Kuttner, and Monica Ng (eds.), *Disrupting the school to prison pipeline.* Cambridge, MA: Harvard Educational Review.

Fiester, Leila. 2015. *Tilling the field: Lessons about philanthopy's role in school discipline reform.* New York: Atlantic Philanthropies and Atlas Learning Project.

Fine, Michelle. 2018. *Just research in contentious times: Widening the methodological imagination.* New York: Teachers College Press.

Fisher, Robert. 1994. *Let the people decide: Neighborhood organizing in America.* New York: Twayne Publishers.

Fisher, Robert. 2009. *The people shall rule: ACORN, community organizing, and the struggle for economic justice.* Nashville, TN: Vanderbilt University Press.

Foley, Michael W., and Bob Edwards. 2002. "How do members count: Membership, governance and advocacy in the nonprofit world." Pp. 19–32 in Elizabeth J. Reid and Maria D. Montilla (eds.), *Exploring organizations and advocacy: Governance and accountability.* Washington, DC: The Urban Institute Press.

Freeman, Alexi Nunn, and Jim Freeman. 2016. "It's about power, not policy: Movement lawyering for large-scale social change," *Clinical Law Review,* 23: 147–166.

Freire, Paulo. 2000 [1970]. *Pedagogy of the oppressed.* New York: Continuum.

French-Marcelin, Megan, and Sarah Hinger. 2017. *Bullies in blue: Origins and consequences of school policing.* New York: ACLU. www.aclu.org.

Ganz, Marshall. 2000. "Resources and resourcefulness: Strategic capacity in the unionization of California agriculture, 1959–1966," *American Journal of Sociology,* 105(4): 1003–1062.

Ganz, Marshall. 2009. *Why David sometimes wins: Leadership, organization, and strategy in the California farm worker movement.* New York: Oxford University Press.

Ganz, Marshall. 2010. "Leading change: Leadership, organization, and social movements." Pp. 527–568 in Nitin Nohria and Rakesh Khurana (eds.), *Handbook of leadership theory and practice.* Boston: Harvard Business School Press.

Garza, Alicia. 2014. "A herstory of the #BlackLivesMatter movement." Pp. 23–28 in Janelle Hobson (ed.), *Are all the women still white?* Albany: SUNY Press.

George, Alexander L., and Andrew Bennett. 2005. *Case studies and theory development in the social sciences.* Cambridge, MA: MIT Press.

Gilliam, Walter S., Angela N. Maupin, Chin R. Reyes, Maria Accavitti, and Frederick Shic. 2016. *Do early educators' implicit biases regarding sex and race relate to behavior expectations and recommendations of preschool expulsions and suspensions.:* New Haven, CT: Yale University Child Study Center. https://medicine.yale.edu/childstudy.

Gilmore, Ruth Wilson. 2007. *Golden gulag: Prisons, surplus, crisis, and opposition in globalizing California.* Berkeley: University of California Press.

Ginwright, Shawn. 2016. *Hope and healing in urban education: How urban activists and teachers are reclaiming matters of the heart.* New York: Routledge.

Gooding-Williams, Robert. 2013. *Reading Rodney King/reading urban uprising.* New York: Routledge.

GSA Network. n.d. *LGBTQ youth of color: Discipline disparities, school push-out, and the school-to-prison pipeline.* Oakland, CA: GSA Network. www.gsanetwork.org.

Haas, Jeffrey. 2011. *The assassination of Fred Hampton: How the FBI and the Chicago police murdered a Black Panther.* Chicago: Chicago Review Press.

Haidt, Jonathan. 2012. *The righteous mind: Why good people are divided by politics and religion.* New York: Vintage.

Hair, Penda D. 2001. *Louder than words: Lawyers, communities and the struggle for justice.* New York: Rockefeller Foundation.

Han, Hahrie. 2014. *How organizations develop activists: Civic associations and leadership in the 21st century.* New York: Oxford University Press.

Harper, Kristen, Renee Ryberg, and Deborah Temkin. 2018. Schools report fewer out-of-school suspensions, but gaps by race and disability persist. Bethesda, MD: Child TRENDS. https://www.childtrends.org/schools-report-fewer-out-of-school-suspensions-but-gaps-by-race-and-disability-persist.

Heitzeg, Nancy, A. 2016. *The school-to-prison pipeline: Education, discipline, and racialized double standards*. Santa Barbara, CA: ABC-CLIO.

Henig, Jeffrey R. 2013. *The end of exceptionalism in American education: The changing politics of school reform*. Cambridge, MA: Harvard Education Press.

Henig, Jeffrey R., Rebecca Jacobsen, and Sarah Reckhow. 2019. *Outside money in school board elections: The nationalization of education politics*. Cambridge, MA: Harvard Education Press.

Hernandez, Kelly Lytle. 2017. *City of inmates: Conquest, rebellion, and the rise of human caging in Los Angeles, 1771–1965*. Chapel Hill: University of North Carolina Press.

Hines-Datiri, Dorothy, and Dorinda J. Carter Andrews. 2020. "The effects of zero tolerance policies on Black girls: Using critical race feminism and figured worlds to examine school discipline," *Urban Education*, 55(10): 1419–1440.

Hinton, Elizabeth. 2016. *From the war on poverty to the war on crime: The making of mass incarceration in America*. Cambridge, MA: Harvard University Press.

Hirji, Rosa. 2005. "The Education Subcommittee takes on zero tolerance." In *Newlsetter of the Children's Rights Litigation Committee of the American Bar Association*, 7–9. Washington, DC: American Bar Association.

Hirschfield, Paul J., and Katarzyna Celinska. 2011. "Beyond fear: Sociological perspectives on the criminalization of school discipline," *Sociology Compass*, 5(1): 1–12.

Hlass, Laila. 2017. "The school to deportation pipeline," *Georgia State University Law Review*, 34(3): 697–763.

Holton, Ann, Adai Tefera, Melissa Cuba, and Ashlee Lester. 2018. *A review of equity and parent engagement in special education in Henrico County Public Schools*. Henrico, VA: Henrico County Manager, Henrico County Public Schools Superintendent, and the Henrico County Public School Board. https://henricoschools.us/pdf/FactsFiguresTesting/ReviewofEquityandParentEngagementinSpecialEducation.pdf.

Horwitt, Sanford D. 1989. *Let them call me rebel: Saul Alinsky, his life and legacy*. New York: Knopf.

HoSang, Daniel. 2006. "Beyond policy: Ideology, race and the reimagining of youth." Pp. 3–19 in Shawn Ginwright, Pedro A. Noguera and Julio Cammarota (eds.), *Beyond resistance! Youth activism and community change*. New York: Routledge.

Huang, Francis L. 2018. "Do Black students misbehave more? Investigating the differential involvement hypothesis and out-of-school suspensions," *The Journal of Educational Research*, 111(3): 284–294.

Hudson, Khadija, and Brittany Brathwaite. n.d. *The school girls deserve: Youth-driven solutions for creating safe, holistic and affirming New York City public schools*. New York: Girls for Gender Equity. https://www.ggenyc.org/the-schools-girls-deserve/.

Hunt, Darnell, and Ana-Christina Ramon. 2010. *Black Los Angeles: American dreams and racial realities*. New York: NYU Press.

Incite! Women of Color Against Violence. 2007. *The revolution will not be funded: Beyond the non-profit industrial complex*. Cambridge, MA: South End Press.

Institute for Southern Studies. 2009. *Social justice organizing in the U.S. South*. Durham, NC: Institute for Southern Studies. www.southernstudies.org.

Irby, Decoteau J. 2014. "Trouble at school: Understanding school discipline systems as nets of social control," *Equity & Excellence in Education*, 47(4): 513–530.

Irving, Angela. 2010. "We've had three of them: Addressing the invisibility of lesbian, gay, bisexual, and gender nonconforming youths in the juvenile justice system," *Columbia Journal of Gender and Law*, 19: 675–701.

Jabbar, Huriya. 2015. "'Drenched in the past': The evolution of market-oriented reforms in New Orleans," *Journal of Education Policy*, 30(6): 751–772.

Johnson, Ollie A., and Karin L. Stanford. 2002. *Black political organizations in the post-civil rights era*. New Brunswick, NJ: Rutgers University Press.

Jones, Carolyn. 2020. *Years of reform efforts contribute to declining African-American suspension rates in California*. Oakland, CA: EdSource. https://edsource.org/2020/african-american-suspension-rate-drops-in-california-after-years-of-reform-efforts/621970.

Journey for Justice Alliance. 2014. *Death by a thousand cuts: Racism, school closures and public school sabotage*. Chicago: Journey for Justice Alliance.

Kaba, Mariame, and Frank Edwards. 2012. *Policing Chicago Public Schools: A gateway to the school-to-prison pipeline*. Chicago: Project NIA.

Kafka, Judith. 2011. *The history of "zero tolerance" in American public schooling*. New York: Palgrave Macmillan.

Kaplan, Jonathan. 2017. *California's support for K–12 education is improving, but still lags the nation*. Sacramento: California Budget & Policy Center. https://calbudgetcenter.org/resources/californias-support-k-12-education-improving-still-lags-nation/.

Kim, Catherine Y., Daniel J. Losen, and Damon T. Hewitt. 2010. *The school-to-prison pipeline: Structuring legal reform*. New York: New York University Press.

Kirshner, Ben. 2015. *Youth activism in an era of educational inequality*. New York: NYU Press.

Kleidman, Robert. 2004. "Community organizing and regionalism," *City and Community*, 3(4): 403–421.

Koretz, Daniel. 2017. *The testing charade: Pretending to make schools better*. Chicago: University of Chicago Press.

Kupchik, Aaron. 2016. *The real school safety problem: The long-term consequences of harsh school punishment*. Berkeley: University of Califiornia Press.

Lahoud, Jeremy. 2000. *Suspended education: A preliminary report on the impact of zero tolerance on Chicago Public Schools students*. Chicago: Generation Y, a project of the Southwest Youth Collaborative.

Langberg, Jason, and Angela Ciolfi. 2016. *Suspended progress*. Charlottesville, VA: Legal Aid Justice Center. https://www.justice4all.org/wp-content/uploads/2016/05/Suspended-Progress-Report.pdf.

Larson, Jennifer M., Jonathan Nagler, Jonathan Ronen, and Joshua A. Tucker. 2019. "Social networks and protest participation: Evidence from 130 million Twitter users," *American Journal of Political Science*, 63(3): 690–705.

Laura, Crystal T. 2014. *Being bad: My baby brother and the school-to-prison pipeline*. New York: Teachers College Press.

Lawrence, Steven. 2005. *Social justice grantmaking: A report on foundation trends*. New York: Foundation Center.

Learn to Earn Dayton. 2017. *Know the gap, close the gap*. Dayton, OH: Learn to Earn Dayton.

Lee, Chana Kai. 1999. *For freedom's sake: The life of Fannie Lou Hamer*. Champaign: University of Illinois Press.

Lee, Sally, and Elena Eisen-Markowitz. 2018. "Teachers Unite! Organizing school communities for transformative justice." Pp. 92–100 in Mark R. Warren and David Goodman (eds.), *Lift us up Don't push us out! Voices from the front lines of the educational justice movement*. Boston: Beacon Press.

Lipman, Pauline. 2011. *The new political economy of urban education: Neoliberalism, race and the right to the city*. New York: Routledge.

Lofland, John, David A. Snow, Leon Anderson, and Lyn H. Lofland. 2006. *Analyzing social settings: A guide to qualitative observation and analysis*. Belmont, CA: Wadsworth.

Longo, Nicholas V. 2007. *Why community matters: Connecting education with civic life*. Albany: State University of New York Press.

Losen, Daniel, and Jonathan Gillespie. 2012. *Opportunities suspended: The disparate impact of disciplinary exclusion from school*. Los Angeles: UCLA Civil Rights Project.

Losen, Daniel J. 2011. *Discipline policies, successful schools, and racial justice*. Boulder, CO: National Education Policy Center. http://nepc.colorado.edu.

Losen, Daniel J. 2015. *Closing the school discipline gap: Equitable remedies for excessive exclusion*. New York: Teachers College Press.

Losen, Daniel J., Cheri Hodson, Michael A. Keith II, Katrina Morrison, and Shakti Belway. 2015. *Are we closing the school discipline gap?* Los Angeles: The Center for Civil Rights Remedies, UCLA. https://civilrightsproject.ucla.edu.

Losen, Daniel J., and Kacy Martin. 2018. *The unequal impact of suspension on the opportunity to learn in CA*. Los Angeles: The Civil Rights Project / Proyecto Derechos Civiles, UCLA. https://escholarship.org/uc/item/50b4g9h1.

Losen, Daniel J., and Paul Martinez. 2020. *Lost opportunities: How disparate school discipline continues to drive differences in the opportunity to learn*. Palo Alto, CA & Los Angeles, CA: Learning Policy Institute & Center for Civil Rights Remedies at the Civil Rights Project, UCLA.

Losen, Daniel J., and Amir Whitaker. 2018. *11 million days lost: Race, discipline and safety at U.S. public schools*. Los Angeles: Center for Civil Rights Remedies, UCLA Civil Rights Project, and the ACLU of Southern California. https://www.aclu.org/sites/default/files/field_document/final_11-million-days_ucla_aclu.pdf.

Luttrell, Wendy. 2010. *Qualitative educational research: Readings in reflexive methodology and transformative practice*. New York: Routledge.

Lynn, Marvin, and Adrienne D. Dixson. 2013. *Handbook of critical race theory in education*. New York: Routledge.

Mallett, Christopher A. 2016. *The school-to-prison pipeline: A comprehensive assessment*. New York: Springer.

Manna, Paul. 2010. *Collision course: Federal education policy meets state and local realities*. Washington, DC: CQ Press.

Maxwell, Joseph A. 2004. "Causal explanation, qualitative research, and scientific inquiry in education," *Educational Researcher*, 33: 3–11.

Maxwell, Joseph A. 2013. *Qualitative research design: An interactive approach*. Thousand Oaks, CA: Sage.

Mays, David John. 2008. *Race, reason, and massive resistance: The diary of David J. Mays, 1954–1959*. Athens: University of Georgia Press.

Mbekeani-Wiley, Michelle. 2017. *Handcuffs in hallways: The state of policing in Chicago Public Schools*. Chicago: Sargent Shriver National Center on Poverty Law.

McAdam, Doug. 1982. *Political process and the development of Black insurgency, 1930–1970*. Chicago: University of Chicago Press.

McCaslin, Wanda D. 2005. *Justice as healing: Indigenous ways*. St. Paul, MN: Living Justice Press.

McLaughlin, Milbrey W., Merita A. Irby, and Juliet Langman. 1994. *Urban sanctuaries: Neighborhood organizations in the lives and futures of inner-city youth.* New York: Jossey-Bass.

McMillen, Neil R. 1990. *Dark journey: Black Mississippians in the age of Jim Crow.* Champaign: University of Illinois Press.

McRoberts, Omar M. 2005. *Streets of glory: Church and community in a Black urban neighborhood.* Chicago: University of Chicago Press.

Mediratta, Kavitha. 2012. "Grassroots organizing and the school-to-prison pipeline: The emerging national movement to roll back zero tolerance discipline policies in U.S. public schools." Pp. 211–236 in Sofia Bahena, North Cooc, Rachel Currie-Rubin, Paul Kuttner, and Monica Ng (eds.), *Disrupting the school to prison pipeline.* Cambridge, MA: Harvard Educational Review.

Mediratta, Kavitha. 2015. "A powerful partner: Philanthropy's role in promoting positive approaches to school discipline" *American Educator* (Winter). https://www.aft.org/ae/winter2015-2016/mediratta.

Mediratta, Kavitha, and Norm Fruchter. 2001. *Mapping the field of organizing for school improvement.* New York: Institute for Education and Social Policy, New York University.

Mediratta, Kavitha, Seema Shah, and Sara McAlister. 2009. *Community organizing for stronger schools: Strategies and successes.* Cambridge, MA: Harvard Education Press.

Meiners, Erica R. 2007. *The right to be hostile: Schools, prisons and the making of public enemies.* New York: Routledge.

Miles, Matthew B., A. Michael Huberman, and Johnny Saldana. 2014. *Qualitative data analysis: A methods sourcebook.* Los Angeles: Sage.

Milkman, Ruth. 2017. "A new political generation: Millennials and the post-2008 wave of protest," *American Sociological Review,* 82(1): 1–31.

Miller, Byron A. 2000. *Geography and social movements: Comparing antinuclear activism in the Boston area.* Minneapolis: University of Minnesota Press.

Milner, H. Richard, IV. 2007. "Race, culture, and researcher positionality: Working through dangers seen, unseen, and unforeseen," *Educational Researcher,* 36(7): 388–400.

Monarrez, Tomas, Brian Kisida, and Matthew Chingos. 2019. *Charter school effects on school segregation.* Washington, DC: Urban Institute.

Morgan, Ivy, and Ary Amerikaner. 2018. An analysis of school funding equity across the U.S. and within each state. The Education Trust: Washington, DC: https://edtrust.org/resource/funding-gaps-2018/.

Morris, Aldon D. 1984. *The origins of the Civil Rights Movement: Black communities organizing for change.* New York: Free Press.

Morris, Jerome E., and Carla R. Monroe. 2009. "Why study the US South? The nexus of race and place in investigating Black student achievement," *Educational Researcher,* 38(1): 21–36.

Morris, Monique. 2016. *Pushout: The criminalization of Black girls in school.* New York: The New Press.

Morsy, Leila, and Richard Rothstein. 2016. *Mass incarceration and children's outcomes: Criminal justice policy is education policy.* Washington, DC: Economic Policy Institute. https://www.epi.org/publication/mass-incarceration-and-childrens-outcomes/.

Moyer, Jeffrey S., Mark R. Warren, and Andrew R. King. 2020. "'Our stories are powerful': The use of youth storytelling in policy advocacy to combat the school-to-prison pipeline," *Harvard Educational Review,* 90(2): 172–194.

Muhammad, Khalil Gibran. 2019. *The condemnation of Blackness: Race, crime, and the making of modern urban America*. Cambridge, MA: Harvard University Press.

Mundt, Marcia, Karen Ross, and Charla M. Burnett. 2018. "Scaling social movements through social media: The case of Black Lives Matter," *Social Media + Society*, 4(4).

Munoz, Carlos, Jr. 2007. *Youth, identity, power: The Chicano movement*. New York: Verso.

Murakawa, Naomi. 2014. *The first civil right: How liberals built prison America*. New York: Oxford University Press.

Neal, La Vonne I., Audrey Davis McCray, Gwendolyn Webb-Johnson, and Scott T. Bridgest. 2003. "The Effects of African American movement styles on teachers' perceptions and reactions," *The Journal of Special Education*, 37(1): 49–57.

Neely-White, Drustella. 2003. "School bells to jail cells: A comprehensive analysis of the high rate of prison incarceration associated with African Americans in Mississippi," MA Thesis. Jackson State University.

Neighborhood Data for Social Change. 2020. *Diverting Los Angeles youth from the criminal justice system*. Los Angeles: USC Price Center for Social Innovation. https://usc.data.socrata.com/stories/s/Diverting-Los-Angeles-Youth-from-the-Criminal-Just/yhp8-ztif.

Neiwert, David. 2018. *Alt-America: The rise of the radical right in the age of Trump*. London: Verso.

Nicholls, Walter J. 2013. *The DREAMers: How the undocumented youth movement transformed the immigrant rights debate*. Stanford, CA: Stanford University Press.

Nicholls, Walter J. 2019. *The immigrant rights movement: The battle over national citizenship*. Stanford, CA: Stanford University Press.

Nicholls, Walter J., Justus Uitermark, and Sander van Haperen. 2020. "Going national: How the fight for immigrant rights became a national social movement," *Journal of Ethnic and Migration Studies*, 46(4): 705–727.

Noguera, Pedro A. 2003. "Schools, prisons, and social implications of punishment: Rethinking disciplinary practices," *Theory into Practice*, 42(4): 341–350.

Noguera, Pedro A. 2009. *The trouble with Black boys: Race, equity and the future of public education*. San Francisco: Jossey-Bass.

Null, Elizabeth Higgins. 2004. "The fight for equality in Mississippi's delta schools continues." *Shelterforce*. https://shelterforce.org/2004/07/01/the-fight-for-equality-in-mississippis-delta-schools-continues/.

Oakes, Jeannie. 2004. "Williams v. State of California," *Teachers College Record*, 106(10 and 11).

Oakes, Jeannie, and John Rogers. 2005. *Learning power: Organizing for education and justice*. New York: Teachers College Press.

Ochoa, Enrique, and Gilda L. Ochoa. 2005. *Latino Los Angeles: Transformations, communities, and activism*. Tucson: University of Arizona Press.

Office for Civil Rights. 2016. *A first look: 2013–2014 civil rights data collection*. Washington, DC: U.S. Department of Education. www.crdc.ed.gov.

Orfield, Gary, and Susan E. Eaton. 1997. *Dismantling desegregation: The quiet reversal of Brown v. Board of Education*. Boston: New Press.

Orr, Marion. 1999. *Black social capital: The politics of school reform in Baltimore, 1986–1998*. Lawrence: University Press of Kansas.

Padres & Jóvenes Unidos. 2004. *North High School report: The voice of over 700 students*. Denver: Padres & Jóvenes Unidos.

Padres & Jóvenes Unidos. 2016. *The 5th annual Denver community accountability report.* Denver: Padres & Jóvenes Unidos. https://padresunidos.org.

Padres & Jóvenes Unidos, and Advancement Project. 2014. *Lessons in racial justice movement building: Dismantling the school-to-prison pipeline in Colorado and nationally.* Denver: Padres & Jóvenes Unidos.

Page, Joshua, and Joe Soss. 2020. "Who's looting whom? Criminal justice as revenue racket," *ASA Footnotes,* 48(4).

Pardo, Mary S. 1998. *Mexican American women activists: Identity and resistance in two Los Angeles communities.* Philadelphia: Temple University Press.

Pastor, Manuel. 2018. *State of resistance: What California's dizzying descent and remarkable resurgence mean for America's future.* New York: New Press.

Patel, Leigh. 2015. *Decolonizing educational research: From ownership to answerability.* New York: Routledge.

Patterson, Kelly L., and Robert Mark Silverman. 2013. *Schools and urban revitalization: Rethinking institutions and community development.* New York: Routledge.

Payne, Charles M. 1995. *I've got the light of freedom: The organizing tradition and the Mississippi freedom struggle.* Berkeley: University of California Press.

Payne, Charles M. 2008. *So much reform, so little change: The persistence of failure in urban schools.* Cambridge, MA: Harvard Education Press.

Payne, Charles M., and Carol Sills Strickland. 2008. *Teach freedom: Education for liberation in the African-American tradition.* New York: Teachers College Press.

Phillips, Steve. 2016. *Brown is the new white: How the demographic revolution has created a new American majority.* New York: The New Press.

Pittz, Will, and Rinku Sen. 2006. *Short changed: Foundation giving and communities of color.* Oakland, CA: Applied Research Center.

Piven, Frances Fox, and Richard A. Cloward. 1977. *Poor people's movements: Why they succeed, how they fail.* New York: Pantheon Books.

Polletta, Francesca, and James M. Jasper. 2001. "Collective identity and social movements," *Annual Review of Sociology,* 27: 283–305.

Post, Margaret. 2011. *Grassroots coalitions and state policy change: Organizing for immigrant healthcare.* El Paso, TX: LFB Scholarly Publishers.

Power U Center for Social Change, and Advancement Project. 2017. *Miami-Dade County Public Schools: The hidden truth.* Miami and Washington, DC: Power U Center for Social Change and Advancement Project.

Power-PAC. 2015. *Parent-to-parent guide: Restorative justice in Chicago Public Schools.* Chicago: Community Organizing and Family Issues.

Putnam, Robert D. 2000. *Bowling alone: The collapse and revival of American community.* New York: Simon & Schuster.

Ragin, Charles C., Joane Nagel, and Patricia White. 2004. *Report of the Workshop on Scientific Foundations of Qualitative Research.* Washington, DC: National Science Foundation.

Ransby, Barbara. 2003. *Ella Baker and the Black freedom movement: A radical democratic vision.* Chapel Hill: University of North Carolina Press.

Ransby, Barbara. 2018. *Making all Black lives matter: Reimagining freedom in the twenty-first century.* Berkeley: University of California Press.

Ravitch, Diane. 2020. *Slaying Goliath: The passionate resistance to privatization and the fight to save America's public schools.* New York: Alfred A. Knopf.

Rios, Edwin. 2020. "How Black Oaklanders finally expelled the school police," *Mother Jones* (November/December). https://www.motherjones.com/crime-justice/2020/10/how-black-oaklanders-finally-expelled-the-school-police/.

Ripley, Amanda. 2016. "How America outlawed adolescence," *The Atlantic*. https://www.theatlantic.com/magazine/archive/2016/11/how-america-outlawed-adolescence/501149/.

Ritchie, Andrea. 2017. *Invisible no more: Police violence against Black women and women of color*. Boston: Beacon Press.

Robinson, Cedric J. 2000. *Black Marxism: The making of the Black radical tradition*, 2nd ed. Chapel Hill: UNC Press.

Robnett, Belinda. 1997. *How long? How long? African-American women in the struggle for civil rights*. New York: Oxford University Press.

Rojas, Carlos, and Glorya Wornum. 2018. "Speaking up and walking out: Boston students fight for educational justice." Pp. 20–28 in Mark R. Warren and David Goodman (eds.), *Lift us up Don't push us out! Voices from the front lines of the educational justice movement*. Boston: Beacon Press.

Rotberg, Iris C., and Joshua L. Glazer (eds.). 2018. *Choosing charters: Better schools or more segregation?* New York: Teachers College Press.

Rothstein, Richard. 2017. *The color of law: A forgotten history of how our government segregated America*. New York: W.W. Norton.

Rubin, Herbert J., and Irene S. Rubin. 2005. *Qualitative interviewing: The art of hearing data*. Thousand Oaks, CA: Sage.

Rusch, Lara. 2012. "Going regional: The evolution of an organizing strategy in Detroit," *City & Community*, 11(1): 51–73.

Saldana, Johnny. 2015. *The coding manual for qualitative researchers*. Thousand Oaks, CA: Sage.

Sampson, Robert J., Doug McAdam, Heather MacIndoe, and Simon Weffer-Elizondo. 2005. "Civil society reconsidered: The durable nature and community structure of collective civic action," *American Journal of Sociology*, 111(3): 673–714.

Sanders, Raynard, David Stovall, and Terrenda White. 2018. *Twenty-first-century Jim Crow schools: The impact of charters on public education*. Boston: Beacon Press.

Sankara-Jabar, Zakiya. 2018. "'I can't make a teacher love my son': A Black parent's journey to racial justice organizing." Pp. 2–10 in Mark R. Warren and David Goodman (eds.), *Lift us up Don't push us out! Voices from the front lines of the educational justice movement*. Boston: Beacon Press.

Sapp, David, and Jeremy Blasi. 2012. *Counterproductive and wasteful: Los Angeles' daytime curfew pushes students away from school and diverts resources away from real community safety*. Los Angeles: ACLU of Southern California, Public Counsel Law Center and Community Rights Campaign.

Schlosberg, David. 1999. "Networks and mobile arrangements: Organisational innovation in the US environmental justice movement," *Environmental Politics*, 8(1): 122–148.

Schlozman, Kay Lehman, Sidney Verba, and Henry E. Brady. 2012. *The unheavenly chorus: Unequal political voice and the broken promise of American democracy*. Princeton, NJ: Princeton University Press.

School Justice Partnership North Carolina. 2019. *Toolkit: A step-by-step guide to implementing a school justice partnership*. Raleigh: School Justice Partnership North Carolina. https://www.nccourts.gov/assets/documents/publications/SJP-Toolkit-08092019.pdf?y9uEHWI7.GujdUyYpWPRf8P8LZKux6BY.

Schott Foundation for Public Education. 2021. *#JusticeIsTheFoundation: New data on racial equity and racial justice funding in education philanthropy*. Quincy, MA: Schott Foundation for Public Education. http://schottfoundation.org/justiceisthefoundation.

Schutz, Aaron, and Marie Sandy. 2011. *Collective action for social change: An introduction to community organizing*. New York: Palgrave MacMillan.

Sentencing Project. 2018. *Report to the United Nations on racial disparities in the U.S. criminal justice system.* Washington, DC: The Sentencing Project. www.sentencingproject. org.

Sharkey, Patrick. 2013. *Stuck in place: Urban neighborhoods and the end of progress toward racial equality.* Chicago: University of Chicago Press.

Shedd, Carla. 2015. *Unequal city: Race, schools and perceptions of inustice.* New York: Russell Sage Foundation Press.

Simmons, Lizbet. 2017. *The prison school: Educational inequality and school discipline in the age of mass incarceration.* Berkeley: University of California Press.

Skiba, Russell J., Kavitha Mediratta, and M. Karega Rausch. 2016. *Inequality in school discipline: Research and practice to reduce disparities.* New York: Springer.

Skiba, Russell J., Robert S. Michael, Abra Carroll Nardo, and Reese L. Peterson. 2002. "The color of discipline: Sources of racial and gender disproportionality in school punishment.," *The Urban Review,* 34(4): 317–342.

Skiba, Russell J., and Reece Peterson. 1999. "The dark side of zero tolerance: Can punishment lead to safe schools?," *The Phi Delta Kappan,* 80(5): 372–382.

Skiba, Russell J., Cecil R. Reynolds, Sandra Graham, Peter Sheras, Jane Close Conoley, and Enedina Garcia-Vazquez. 2006. *Are zero tolerance policies effective in the schools? An evidentiary review and recommendations* Washington, DC: American Psychological Association. https://www.apa.org/pubs/info/reports/zero-tolerance.pdf.

Skocpol, Theda. 2003. *Diminished democracy: From membership to management in American civic life.* Norman: University of Oklahoma Press.

Skocpol, Theda, Marshall Ganz, and Ziad Munson. 2000. "A nation of organizers: The institutional origins of civic voluntarism in the United States," *American Political Science Review,* 94(3): 527–546.

Skocpol, Theda, Ariane Liazos, and Marshall Ganz. 2006. *What a mighty power we can be: African American fraternal groups and the struggle for racial equality.* Princeton, NJ: Princeton University Press.

Snyder, Howard N. 2005. *Juvenile arrests 2003.* Washington, DC: Office of Juvenile Justice and Delinquency Prevention. www.ncjrs.gov.

Sojourner, Sue. 2013. *The thunder of freedom: Black leadership and the transformation of 1960s Mississippi.* Louisville: University Press of Kentucky.

Sojoyner, Damien M. 2016. *First strike: Educational enclosures in Black Los Angeles.* Minneapolis: University of Minnesota Press.

Soule, Sarah A. 2013. "Diffusion and scale shift." Pp. in David A. Snow, Donatella Della Porta, Bert Klandermans, and Doug McAdam (eds.), *The Wiley-Blackwell encyclopedia of social and political movements.* Oxford, UK: Wiley Publishing.

Southern Echo. 2000. *Advancing community organizing skills, part 5: Public education as a policy battleground.* Jackson, MS: Southern Echo.

Speer, Paul W., and Hahrie Han. 2018. "Re-engaging social relationships and collective dimensions of organizing to revive democratic practice," *Journal of Social and Political Psychology,* 6(2): 745–758.

Speer, Paul W., and Joseph Hughey. 1995. "Community organizing: An ecological route to empowerment," *American Journal of Community Psychology,* 23(5): 729–749.

Squires, Gregory D. 2011. *Organizing access to capital: Advocacy and the democratization of financial institutions.* Philadelphia: Temple University Press.

Stahl, Kenneth A. 2020. *Local citizenship in a global age.* New York: Cambridge University Press.

Stall, Susan, and Randy Stoecker. 1998. "Community organizing or organizing community? Gender and the crafts of empowerment," *Gender and Society*, 12: 729–756.

Stevens, W. David et al. 2015. *Discipline practices in Chicago schools: Trends in the use of suspensions and arrests.* Chicago: University of Chicago Consortium on Chicago School Research. https://consortium.uchicago.edu/sites/default/files/2018-10/Discipline%20Report.pdf.

Su, Celina. 2009. *Streetwise for book smarts: Grassroots organizing and education reform in the Bronx.* Ithaca, NY: Cornell University Press.

Sughrue, Jennifer A. 2003. " Zero tolerance for children: Two wrongs do not make a right," *Educational Administration Quarterly*, 39(2): 238–258.

Sugrue, Thomas J. 2008. *Sweet land of liberty: The forgotten struggle for civil rights in the north.* New York: Random House.

Suitts, Steve. 2015. *A new majority research bulletin: Low income students now a majority in the nation's public schools.* Atlanta: Southern Education Foundation.

Sullivan, Elizabeth. 2003. *Civil society and school accountability: A human rights approach to parent and community participation in NYC schools.* New York: Center for Economic and Social Rights and New York University Institute for Education and Social Policy.

Sullivan, Elizabeth. 2007. *Deprived of dignity: Degrading treatment and abusive discipline in New York City & Los Angeles public schools.* New York: National Economic and Social Rights Initiative.

Sullivan, Elizabeth, and Elizabeth Keeney. 2008. *Teachers talk: School culture, safety and human rights.* New York: NESRI and Teachers Unite.

Sullivan, Elizabeth, and Damekia Morgan. 2010. *Pushed out: Harsh discipline in Louisiana schools denies the right to education.* New York: NESRI and FFLIC.

Sullivan, Elizabeth, and Sharda Sekaran. 2007. *Bringing a human rights vision to public schools: A training manual for organizers.* New York: NESRI and CADRE.

Swarts, Heidi J. 2008. *Organizing urban America: Secular and faith-based progressive movements.* Minneapolis: University of Minnesota Press.

Taylor, Gerald. 2014. "The Chicago police torture scandal: Legal and political history," *CUNY Law Review*, 17(2): 329–382.

Taylor, Keeanga-Yamahtta. 2016. *From #BlackLivesMatter to Black liberation.* Boston: Haymarket Books.

Terenzi, Katherine, Kesi Foster, and Urban Youth Collaborative youth leaders. 2017. *The $746 million a year school-to-prison pipeline: The ineffective, discriminatory, and costly process of criminalizing New York City students.* New York: The Center for Popular Democracy and the Urban Youth Collaborative.

The Georgia Coalition Working to End the School-to-Prison Pipeline. 2019. *From lockers to lockdown.* Atlanta: The Georgia Coalition Working to End the School-to-Prison Pipeline. https://gcdd.org/images/Initiatives/GCDD_Final_Grant_Report-School_to_Prison.pdf.

Thompson, Heather Ann. 2010. "Why mass incarceration matters: Rethinking crisis, decline, and transformation in postwar American history," *The Journal of American History*, 97(3): 703–734.

Thompson, J. Phillip. 1998. "Universalism and deconcentration: Why race still matters in poverty and economic development," *Politics and Society*, 26(2): 181–219.

Tieken, Mara, and Mark R. Warren. 2016. "A movement's legacy: Southern Echo and the continued struggle for racial justice in the Delta," *Sociological Focus*, 49(1): 84–101.

Tilly, Charles, and Sidney Tarrow. 2015. *Contentious politics*. New York: Oxford Universtiy Press.

Torres, A. Chris, and Joanne W. Golann. 2018. *NEPC review: Charter schools and the achievement gap*. Boulder, CO: National Education Policy Center. https://nepc.colorado.edu/sites/default/files/reviews/TTR%20Torres-Golann%20No%20Excuses_1.pdf.

Travis, Jeremy, Bruce Western, and Steve Redburn (eds.). 2014. *The growth of incarceration in the United States: Exploring causes and consequences*. Washington, DC: The National Academies Press.

Turney, Kristin, and Rebecca Goodsell. 2018. "Parental incarceration and children's well-being," *The Future of Children*, 28(1): 147–164.

U.S. Commission on Civil Rights. 2019. *Beyond suspensions: Examining school discipline policies and connections to the school-to-prison pipeline for students of color with disabilities*. Washington, DC: U.S. Commission on Civil Rights. https://www.usccr.gov/pubs/2019/07-23-Beyond-Suspensions.pdf.

U.S. Department of Education. 2014. *Guiding principles: A resource guide for improving school climate and discipline*. Washington, DC: U.S. Department of Education.

U.S. Department of Education. 2018. *School climate and safety: 2015–16 civil rights data collection*. Washington, DC: Office for Civil Rights, U.S. Department of Education. https://www2.ed.gov/about/offices/list/ocr/docs/school-climate-and-safety.pdf.

Van Dyke, Nella, and Holly J. McCammon (eds.). 2010. *Strategic alliances: Coalition building and social movements*. Minneapolis: University of Minnesota Press.

Van Meter, Kevin. 2010. *Uses of a whirlwind: Movement, movements, and contemporary radical currents in the United States*. Oakland, CA: AK Press.

Verba, Sidney, Kay Lehman Schlozman, and Henry E. Brady. 1995. *Voice and equality: Civic voluntarism in American politics*. Cambridge, MA: Harvard University Press.

Villanueva, Edgar. 2018. *Decolonizing wealth: Indigenous wisdom to heal divides and restore balance*. Oakland, CA: Berrett-Koehler Publishers.

Voss, Kim, and Irene Bloemraad. 2011. *Rallying for immigrant rights: The fight for inclusion in 21st century America*. Berkeley: University of California Press.

VOYCE. 2008. *Student-led solutions to the nation's dropout crisis*. Chicago: VOYCE.

VOYCE. 2011. *Failed policies, broken futures: The true cost of zero tolerance in Chicago*. Chicago: VOYCE. http://voyceproject.org/.

Wacquant, Loïc. 2009a. *Prisons of poverty*. Minneapolis: University of Minnesota Press.

Wacquant, Loïc. 2009b. *Punishing the poor: The neoliberal government of social insecurity*. Durham, NC: Duke University Press.

Waitoller, Federico R., Nicole Nguyen, and Gia Super. 2019. "The irony of rigor: 'No-Excuses' charter schools at the intersections of race and disability," *International Journal of Qualitative Studies in Education*, 32(3): 282–298.

Wald, Johanna, and Daniel J. Losen. 2003. "Defining and redirecting a school-to-prison pipeline," *New Directions for Youth Development*, 99: 9–15.

Wald, Johanna, and Daniel Losen. 2005. *Confronting the graduation rate crisis in California*. Cambridge, MA: The Civil Rights Project at Harvard University. https://civilrightsproject.ucla.edu/research/k-12-education/school-dropouts/confronting-the-graduation-rate-crisis-in-california/crp-confronting-dropouts-ca-2005.pdf.

Walker, Edward T. 2014. *Grassroots for hire: Public affairs consultants in American democracy*. New York: Cambridge University Press.

Walker, Edward T., and John D. McCarthy. 2007. "The influence of organizational structure, membership composition and resources on the survival of poor people's social movement organizations." Pp. 43–62 in Martha Chen, Renana Jhabvala, Ravi Kanbur, and Carol Richards (eds.), *Membership-based organizations of the poor*. New York: Routledge.

Walker, Edward T., John D. McCarthy, and Frank Baumgartner. 2011. "Replacing members with managers? Mutualism among membership and nonmembership advocacy organizations in the United States," *American Journal of Sociology*, 116(4): 1284–1337.

Walker, Jack L. 1991. *Mobilizing interest groups in America: Patrons, professions, and social movements*. Ann Arbor: University of Michigan Press.

Warren, Mark R. 2001. *Dry bones rattling: Community building to revitalize American democracy*. Princeton, NJ: Princeton University Press.

Warren, Mark R. 2014. "Transforming public education: The need for an educational justice movement," *New England Journal of Public Policy*, 26(1): Article 11. http://scholarworks.umb.edu/nejpp/vol26/iss1/11.

Warren, Mark R. 2018a. *Lift us up Don't push us out! Voices from the front lines of the educational justice movement*. Boston: Beacon Press.

Warren, Mark R. 2018b. "Research confronts equity and social justice: Building the emerging field of collaborative, community engaged education research," *Urban Education*, 53(4): 439–444.

Warren, Mark R., Patricio Belloy, Andrew R. King, Bianca Ortiz-Wythe, José Calderon, and Pam Martinez. 2021. "Intersectional organizing and educational justice movements: Strategies for cross-movement solidarities," *The Assembly*, 3. https://journals.colorado.edu/index.php/assembly/issue/view/99.

Warren, Mark R., José Calderón, Luke Aubry Kupscznk, Gregory Squires, and Celina Su. 2018. "Is collaborative, community-engaged scholarship more rigorous than traditional scholarship? On advocacy, bias, and social science research," *Urban Education*, 53(4): 445–472.

Warren, Mark R, Luke Krupscznk, and Lindsay Morgia. 2015. "The evolution of public awareness of racial disparities in school discipline: Media treatments of zero tolerance and the school-to-prison pipeline." Unpublished paper presented to the annual meeting of the *American Educational Research Association*. Chicago.

Warren, Mark R., Karen L. Mapp, and Community Organizing and School Reform Project. 2011. *A match on dry grass: Community organizing as a catalyst for school reform*. New York: Oxford University Press.

Warren, Mark R., Soojin Susan Oh, and Mara Tieken. 2016. "The formation of community-engaged scholars: A collaborative approach to doctoral training in education research," *Harvard Educational Review*, 86(2): 233–260.

Weingarten, Randi. 2015. "Moving past punishment toward support," *American Educator*, 39(2): 1.

Weissman, Marsha. 2015. *Prelude to prison: Student perspectives on school suspension*. Syracuse, NY: Syracuse University Press.

Welsh, Richard O., and Shafiqua Little. 2018. "The school discipline dilemma: A comprehensive review of disparities and alternative approaches," *Review of Educational Research*, 88(5): 752–794.

Western, Bruce. 2006. *Punishment and inequality in America*. New York: Russell Sage Foundation Press.

Western, Bruce. 2018. *Homeward: Life in the year after prison*. New York: Russell Sage Foundation Press.

Western, Bruce, and Becky Pettit. 2010a. *Collateral Costs: Incarceration's effect on economic mobility*. Washington, DC: Pew Charitable Trusts.

Western, Bruce, and Becky Pettit. 2010b. "Incarceration and social inequality," *Daedalus*, 139(3): 8–19.

Whitaker, Amir, Torres-Guillen Sylvia, Michelle Morton, Harold Jordan, Stephanie Coyle, Angela Mann, and Wei-Ling Sun. n.d. *Cops and no counselors*. Washington, DC: ACLU. https://www.aclu.org/report/cops-and-no-counselors.

Wildeman, Christopher. 2009. "Parental imprisonment, the prison boom, and the concentration of childhood disadvantage," *Demography*, 46(2): 265–280.

Wilson, William Julius. 1996. *When work disappears: The world of the new urban poor*. New York: Knopf.

Winder, Geoffrey. 2018. "Organizing intersectionally: Trans and queer youth fighting for racial and gender justice." Pp. 156–164 in Mark R. Warren and David Goodman (eds.), *Lift us up Don't push us out! Voices from the front lines of the educational justice movement*. Boston: Beacon Press.

Wood, J. Luke, Frank Harris III, and Tyrone C. Howard. 2018. *Get out! Black male suspensions in California public schools*. San Diego, CA: Community College Equity Assessment Lab and the UCLA Black Male Institute.

Wood, Richard L. 2002. *Faith in action: Religion, race and democratic organizing in America*. Chicago: University of Chicago Press.

Wood, Richard L. 2007. "Higher power: Strategic capacity for state and national organizing." Pp. 162–192 in Marion Orr (ed.), *Transforming the city: Community organizing and the challenge of political change*. Lawrence: University Press of Kansas.

Wood, Richard L., and Brad R. Fulton. 2015. *A shared future: Faith-based organizing for racial equity and ethical democracy*. Chicago: University of Chicago Press.

Wood, Richard L., Kathy Partridge, and Brad R. Fulton. 2012. *Building bridges, building power: Developments in institution based community organizing*. Jericho, NY: Interfaith Funders.

Yin, Robert K. 2003. *Case study research: Design and methods*. Thousand Oaks, CA: Sage Publications.

Yoshikawa, Hirokazu, J. Lawrence Aber, and William R. Beardslee. 2012. "The effects of poverty on the mental, emotional, and behavioral health of children and youth," *American Psychologist*, 67(4): 272–284.

Youth of the Rural Organizing and Cultural Center. 1991. *Minds stayed on freedom: The civil rights struggle in the rural south—An oral history*. New York: Westview.

Index

For the benefit of digital users, indexed terms that span two pages (e.g., 52–53) may, on occasion, appear on only one of those pages.

328   INDEX

"You Can't Build Peace with a Piece (gun),"
74, 144, 216–17, 256
Young, Marilyn, 107, 111
Young People's Social Justice
Agenda, 220
Young Women's Initiative, 226
Youth Governance Initiative, 95–96
Youth Justice Coalition, 18, 69, 74, 117–18,
132–33, 139–44, 145, 149–50, 220,
256, 263, 264–65
Youth on Board/Boston Student Advisory
Council, 78
Youth Organizing Project, 78
Youth United for Change, 75

zero tolerance policies. See also school-to-
prison pipeline
adoption of, 26
anti-bullying campaigns, 30, 75–77
bans on, 175
disciplinary beatings, 96
exclusionary discipline (see
exclusionary discipline)
expulsion bans, 146
expulsion rates, 29, 126, 293n.31

Federal guidance ending, 84–87, 175–
76, 250
felony assault, 54, 97
impacts of, 11–12, 27, 30–31, 34,
56, 76, 80
law enforcement referrals, 57
mob action, 55
narrative change, 80–84
no weapons, 96–97
public perceptions of, 57–58, 83–
84, 249–50
racial bias in, 27, 28–29, 32–33, 54,
55–56, 57, 81–82, 148, 162, 173–74,
190–91, 199–201, 240–41, 293n.31
reform of, 17–18, 50, 61–62, 63–
65, 77–80
resistance to, 153–55
school pushout, 62, 63–65, 105, 160
in school-to-prison pipeline, xi, 2, 4,
9–10, 11
status offenses, 94
suspensions (see suspensions)

Zimmerman, George, 214
Zipperman, Steve, 137